W9-BYY-359

All About Food

Its History and Traditions

Hilde Gabriel Lee

Hildesigns Press
Keswick, Virginia

Published by Hildesigns Press
1918 Piper Way
Keswick, Virginia 22947
(434) 296-0885
e mail: hildelee@adelphia.net

Copyright © 2002 by Hilde Gabriel Lee

Book Design by Hilde G. Lee, Hildesigns
Cover painting © 2002 by Hilde G, Lee

This book, or any portions thereof, may not be reproduced or transmitted in any form or by any means, electronic or mechanical, including photocopying, recording, or by any information storage and retrieval system, without permission in writing from the publisher.

Library of Congress Cataloging in Publication Data
ISBN 0-9639605-4-7

CONTENTS

Introduction

My interest both in food and history go back a number of years. My grandmother was a well-known cateress in Germany. Early in my life she instilled in me a love of good food and a curiosity about how to prepare it. Food became more than a way of sustaining life for my family, who had escaped the wrath of Nazi Germany. In this new country with strange foods, cooking became a challenge for my mother, who often consulted me as to the English definitions of various foods. With my mother's and grandmother's encouragement, I developed a special interest in food and cooking.

All through my school years in America, I also acquired a fascination with history as a way to learn about my new country. When I entered college I decided to major in International Relations and minor in History.

In the last fifteen years both of my interests culminated in one of my first books on food, "Taste of the States," published in 1992. It was a food history of each state of the Union, focusing on the peoples and their foods accompanied by appropriate fine art created by American artists.

A little more than a decade ago, I started writing a weekly food column for the Charlottesville Daily Progress in Charlottesville, Virginia. Although many of my columns focused on local events and personalities, I found myself drawn to researching the history of the foods that I wrote about. I developed a special fascination for items I saw in the grocery store, such everyday things as carrots, lettuce, oranges, etc. I wondered where they originated and how they got to America. In my research I was surprised that many native American food ingredients had first traveled to Europe and then been brought back to America with the early immigrants.

The further I delved into the subject the more fascinated I became and decided that food history might be of interest to the general public. My friends started encouraging me to put my research into book form. Thus this book.

However, it is impossible to write about every food item, thus I have tried to pick those of general interest.

My research made me realize how fortunate we are with the wide selection of food and spices we have today in relation to the those available to our ancestors. Our neighborhood supermarket is stocked with items that were unheard of a few generations ago.. It has also emphasized for me that the search for food over many millenniums has been an important factor in stimulating world trade, improving national economies, helping advance technology, and, not unimportantly, enhancing our well-being.

I hope this book adds to your enjoyment of food and gives you subjects for dinner-table conversations. I also hope it will be a reference book that you will enjoy reading. The recipes in this book are many of my favorites. They range from simple pasta dishes to more formal meat entrees.

I particularly want to thank my husband, Allan, for his help and encouragement in writing this book.

Bon Appetite,

Hilde G. Lee

Vegetables

Vegetables

There are three types of vegetables — root, vine, and stalk. They share several characteristics: vegetables are savory rather than sweet; salt is added to the majority of them to make them more palatable, and they are often served with poultry, meat, or fish.

Food historians have told us that many of our present-day vegetables were cultivated in prehistoric times. The nomadic tribes learned the value of agriculture and settled into permanent living quarters, raising the same food crops year-after-year.

There seems to have been a spontaneous beginning of primitive vegetable farming in widely separate parts of the world — in China, the Middle East, and South America. By 3000 B.C. the peoples of the Middle East were growing turnips, onions, peas, lentils, leeks, garlic, and radishes. The Chinese grew cucumbers, turnips, and radishes. The Chinese laborers building the Great Wall in the third century B.C. were given a regular ration of fermented vegetables, including cabbage, beets, turnips, and radishes. Meat was always in short supply. The Egyptians who built the pyramids also subsisted on a vegetable diet.

From their early cultivation in the Middle East and Asia, vegetables began to spread to Europe. Farmers in lands conquered by the Romans began to grow the crops the Romans introduced — carrots, leeks, artichokes, cauliflower, garlic, onions, and lettuces. The Muslim invaders of Spain introduced spinach, eggplants, carrots, and citrus fruits to that area. By the Middle Ages, there was extensive vegetable farming throughout Europe.

Archaeological sites have revealed that squash, beans, and corn were grown in Mexico before 5000 BC. Tomatoes and potatoes originated further south in Peru. The early Peruvians preserved potatoes using a sun-dried technique. By 1000 B.C. the Incas developed freeze-drying. They froze potatoes in the snows of the Andes, then allowed them to thaw and squeezed out the juice until they were dry.

Following the Spanish conquest of parts of the New World in the late fifteenth century, there was an exchange of crops between the Old World and the New. For the next two centuries many of the vegetables we know today were gradually established on both continents. From the Americas came corn, potatoes, sweet potatoes, tomatoes, peppers, kidney beans, green (French) beans, pumpkins, and Jerusalem artichokes. Settlers from Europe introduced to America, broad (Fava) beans, chick-peas, radishes, carrots, and cabbages. Black-eyed peas, okra, and yams came with the slaves from Africa.

Over the centuries different vegetables have found their place in the human diet. Europeans were skeptical in accepting some of the American vegetables. Tomatoes were thought to be poisonous, but what would Italian cuisine be without them today? It was not until the mid-eighteenth century that the potato was considered edible in England. There it gave a new dimension to the diet of the poor which had consisted of onion broth, bread and root vegetables.

The invention of the canning process at the end of the eighteenth century and the invention of the freezing process by Clarence Birdseye in 1929 made vegetables readily accessible.

Artichokes

Edible Thistle

Artichokes are one of those vegetables most people either strongly like or dislike. The artichoke is an unique vegetable as it is the only edible thistle we know of. It is a delicate and flavorful vegetable that lends itself to a variety of culinary applications. Those who do not want to prepare a fresh artichoke for a recipe will find frozen or canned artichoke hearts in most supermarkets.

The artichoke has been around for ages, dating back as far as ancient Roman times. There is also a reference to it in Greek literature. Food historians believe that the first artichokes grew wild in Northern Africa. Several ancient recipes from that region call for artichokes. Korchef, for example, is a favorite traditional couscous from Morocco that includes artichokes.

From their African origin, artichokes found their way to Sicily and quickly took root as a commonly-found vegetable throughout Southern Europe. In Italy the artichoke or carciofi, as it is called there, is an integral part of that country's cuisine. Sea bass with artichokes, cold marinated artichokes, and pasta dishes with artichokes can be found in many regions of Italy. It is also made into a liqueur, called Cynar and is often made from artichokes growing in local gardens.

Catherine de Medici introduced artichokes to France, although, according to some food historians, earlier Charlemagne, the first emperor of France, had ordered his gardeners to cultivate them. During the Middle Ages artichokes were only cultivated in Sicily and around Granada where they were grown by the Moors. By the late 1400s artichokes had made their way north in Italy to Tuscany where Catherine de Medici was born in 1519.

It was Catherine de Medici, the fourteen-year old bride of Henry II of France, who gave notoriety to the artichoke by her scandalous fondness of the vegetable. At that time it was unheard of for a maiden or young woman to eat a vegetable reputed to be an aphrodisiac.

Catherine ate them nevertheless. On one occasion she ate so many artichokes that according to a contemporary chronicler she "liked to burst." A shocked elderly woman of the period wrote, "If one of us had eaten artichokes at her age, we would have been pointed out in the street. Today young women are more forward than pages at court."

Over the years each Italian growing region has created its own hybrid and unique artichokes with a diversity of colors and textures. Eleven botanical varieties of artichokes have been chronicled.

As in Italy many varieties have also been developed in France. Small violet-colored artichokes are grown in Provence for their delicacy. Large green Laon artichokes are prized for their long and pointed, meaty leaves. The Camus artichoke of Brittany is perhaps the most common and consistent variety. It bears a strong resembles to the only variety commercially cultivated in the United States, the Glove artichoke.

Artichokes did not come to this country until the turn of this century when French immigrants settled in Louisiana and brought artichoke plants with them. For a time New Orleans was the hub of artichoke cultivation and distribution in the United States.

A short time later, Italian immigrants who settled in San Francisco brought artichoke seeds with them from Europe. About a hundred miles south of San Francisco, the climate and soil were found to be ideal for Globe artichoke cultivation. It was there around the small town of Castroville in Monterey County, that Globe artichoke agriculture began to take off in the 1920s.

California now produces one hundred percent of all artichokes commercially grown in the United States, and of that, seventy-five percent of them are produced in Monterey County, spanning about eighty-two hundred acres. The total value of the annual artichoke crop exceeds $50 million.

Globe artichokes grow on long stalks and are the bud of a flowering thistle. The plants grow in perfect rows, like soldiers standing at attention. Each plant resembles a giant fern with long, arching frond-like leaves. The leaves of the upper portion of the plant protect the buds, which grow into edible artichokes.

Each stalk of the artichoke plant will yield about a dozen artichokes. The first to ripen are called the primaries. These are the largest buds that appear at the tip of the stalk, and they are packed 16 to a case. A week or so later, the secondaries ripen just below the first harvest and they are packed twenty-four to forty-eight to the case. Finally, the "babies," as they are known commercially, ripen at the lowest point of the stalk and they are marketed at sixty to the case.

Workers carrying big open backpacks hand harvest the artichokes every seven days during the peak season, which is March through May. During this time the three-tiered ripening and harvesting takes place. Once all of the stalks have been exhausted, they are cut back by hand to about one foot above ground. The trimmed material is turned back into the soil and acts as fertilizer. A second harvest from new growth takes place in August and peaks in October.

Artichokes are sorted by size and boxed in the field. The boxes are then transported to the shipping plant where the artichokes are quickly cooled to preserve their freshness. The entire process is done by hand — from planting, to harvesting, to packing, to stumping.

This recipe using artichokes is from the chef of a small restaurant in Grenada, Spain. He served this potato-artichoke dish with roasted lamb. It is also good with roasted chicken.

Artichoke and Potato Casserole

1 package (9 ounces) frozen artichoke hearts
3 tablespoons butter
2 tablespoons olive oil
1 medium onion, thinly sliced
4 medium potatoes, peeled, thinly sliced
1 garlic clove, bruised
1/2 cup sliced black olives
Salt and freshly ground pepper
1/2 cup freshly grated Parmesan cheese

Cook the artichoke hearts in boiling water for 5 minutes. Drain and cut into thin slices.

Heat 1 tablespoon of the butter with the olive oil in a large skillet over medium heat. Sauté the onion slices until golden. Then reduce the heat. Add the potatoes to the skillet and toss to coat them well. Add the artichoke hearts and remove the skillet from the heat.

Rub a 2-inch-deep ovenproof baking dish with the bruised garlic; then discard the garlic. Spread the vegetable mixture over the bottom of the dish. Sprinkle the olive slices over the mixture, and sprinkle with salt and pepper. Dot the top with the remaining 2 tablespoons of butter. Bake in a preheated 400° F. oven for 15 minutes. Remove from the oven, stir well, and continue baking about 15 minutes longer or until the potatoes are tender. Sprinkle the top with the cheese and bake until golden, an additional 5 to 10 minutes. Serves 4 to 6.

Asparagus

Green and White

Even though asparagus is now available throughout much of the year, we still regard it as a spring vegetable. One sure sign of spring is the abundance of asparagus in the produce section of our markets. The long green stalks, whether thick or thin, lend themselves to a variety of preparations — from simple stir-frys to sauced dishes.

Asparagus is an ancient vegetable and is believed to be native to the Eastern Mediterranean. Tomb art shows that the Egyptians ate wild asparagus no larger than a child's forefinger. Apparently it grew wild along the Nile, because it was not domesticated until the Romans found out how to cultivate it several centuries later. They cooked it al dente, so that the stalks remained crisp.

Most of the ancient civilizations preferred wild asparagus because they believed it had a superior taste. The Greeks, for example, cherished the wild asparagus plant, which grew larger in that area of the Mediterranean. The Greeks named it "aspharagos" meaning " as long as one's throat." The name was conferred on these slender spears because overeager Greek diners often swallowed the whole spear.

Some wild asparagus can still be found in Italy and occasionally in the United States. Since birds are great transmitters of asparagus seeds, wild asparagus can frequently be found near the cultivated variety.

The history of asparagus between the ancient civilizations and the seventeenth century is obscure. It was grown in France at that time and is mentioned in English botanical writings of the sixteenth century. Historians agree that asparagus is an Old World plant and was brought to the New World, but by whom or when, nobody knows.

One of the first mentions of asparagus in America was in a gardening book published in 1775. Thomas Jefferson's farm records show that he grew asparagus at Monticello in the early 1800s. As the pioneers traveled west they took asparagus cutting with them, developing colloquial names for the vegetable like "sparrow grass" and "grass." Even today the wholesale vegetable trade calls asparagus "grass."

There are different regional tastes in asparagus. Americans like green asparagus and tend to prefer the thicker stalks. The French, Belgians, Germans, and central Europeans prefer large snow-white stalks, which are milder in flavor. European tastes are apparently changing and green asparagus has gained popularity. The purple-tipped green variety of asparagus is favored in Italy.

Green and white asparagus are both from the same plant. The difference is achieved by different cultivation methods. Green asparagus is cut after the shoots have risen above ground to the height the grower desires. White asparagus, on the other hand, is kept from sunlight by repeatedly mounding soil over the stalk as it grows. (Belgian endive is also grown beneath the ground to keep them white.)

Most asparagus stalks are white at the bottom. This results from the fact that most asparagus is harvested with a special knife that cuts the stalks below ground level.

In Europe, asparagus is usually peeled before cooking to remove the tough outer fibers. It is often eaten with the fingers down to its last morsel. To avoid the use of the finger-eating, Europeans started using asparagus tongs which were invented in 1815 and were produced in silver. They are still available in some tabletop stores in Europe, but are rather awkward to handle. Americans tend to peel only the larger stalks, and most of the time we cut our asparagus and eat it with a fork.

The oriental influence on American cuisine has made stir-fried asparagus popular. We also use asparagus in soups, quiches, frittatas and salads. As a main vegetable it is frequently just steamed and then topped with a sauce or melted butter.

My Asparagus Soup may be served either warm or chilled. The use of rice in the soup tends to cut the harshness of the asparagus and also acts as a thickening agent. Italians are fond of asparagus and often serve it dressed with Parmesan cheese and melted butter.

Asparagus Soup

2 pounds asparagus
1 tablespoon butter
1 small onion, chopped
1/2 cup rice
5 cups chicken broth
Salt and white pepper, to taste
1/4 cup cream

Trim the asparagus and cut it into 1-inch pieces. Set aside 12 tips and blanch them in boiling water for 2 minutes. Refresh the tips under cold water and reserve them for garnish.

Melt the butter in a medium saucepan over medium heat. Add the onion and sauté for 3 minutes, or until the onion is translucent. Add the rice, the asparagus pieces, and the chicken broth. Bring to a boil, reduce the heat, and simmer, covered, for 25 minutes.

Purée the soup in batches in a food processor or blender. Then strain the soup through a sieve over a large bowl. Add salt and pepper, to taste, and blend in the cream. Refrigerate the soup, if serving it cold, or heat it to warm, but do not boil. (The soup may be prepared a day ahead and refrigerated.) Ladle soup into soup bowls and garnish with the asparagus tips. Serves 6

Asparagus Parma Style

3 pounds fresh asparagus
1 teaspoon salt
3/4 cup freshly grated Parmesan cheese
1/2 teaspoon freshly ground black pepper
4 tablespoons unsalted butter

Cut off the tough asparagus ends. Peel the asparagus, if desired. Rinse the asparagus under cold water and tie them, not too tight, in several bunches with kitchen string or rubber bands

Place 3 inches of water in a tall stock pot. Bring the water to a boil over medium-high heat, add the salt and asparagus, and cook, covered, until tender, about 5 to 8 minutes, depending on the size of the asparagus,. Remove the asparagus from the pot, cut off the strings or rubber bands, and pat them dry with paper towels. Transfer the asparagus to 6 individual plates.

Sprinkle the green tips with Parmesan cheese and season with black pepper. Melt the butter in a small saucepan, over medium heat until light brown and pour it over the asparagus and serve immediately. Serves 6.

Beans, green

The Versatile String Bean

Christopher Columbus was the first to encounter the American green bean in Cuba in the late 1400s. He sent some back to Spain, but they made no impression. The Spanish thought of this bean plant as ornamental and relished it blossoms. Bean plants glorified Spanish gardens for more than half a century.

In 1519 the Spanish conquistadors found this American bean in Mexico and were told that is was called haricot, derived from the Aztec ayacotl. American green beans were also found in Florida ten years later and shortly thereafter by Jacques Cartier at the mouth of the St. Lawrence River.

Beans are part of a very complex legume (pod) family. These legumes include beans, lentils, peanuts, and peas. Beans are then further categorized by green (fresh and in the pod) and dried beans.

Most beans are dried and preserved out of the pod. Green beans, commonly called string beans, are one of the very few varieties of bean that we eat green and in the pod.

Green beans (in France they are known as haricot vert) are one of the three categories of the world's beans. The other two are soybeans and broad beans, also known as fava beans.

According to archeologists the American green bean dates back to 7000 B.C. and was already being cultivated at that time. When the first settlers came to America the bean plant had developed a number of varieties that were capable of flourishing in different climates. For example, beans were an important food of the American Indians in the cold, damp Northeast, and also of the Pueblo Indians in the dry, hot Southwest.

American bean plants range in size from tall climbing vines to low bushes. They vary in shape: oval, fat, round, flat, and kidney-shape. Their color ranges from yellow to black. Green or string bean refers to the fresh bean still in its pod. Dried beans (out of the pod) are typically referred to by their variety, such as pinto, black, navy, great northern, soldier, and numerous others. Each region of the country has its own variety of dried beans, many dating back to Indian times.

Although the American Indians used some of the beans fresh they removed most of the beans from the pod and dried them. They taught the first settlers how to cook dried beans. Over the years dried beans became one of the mainstays of the cooking of the Americas. Black beans are the basis of Cuba's bean soup and also are often combined with rice in a dish called "Moors and Christians" because of the two contrasting colors. Red pinto beans were the backbone of cowboy cooking in the nineteenth century and were known as "Mexican strawberries." Today many varieties of string beans have been hybridized to become stringless.

Even though it took several centuries, the American green bean eventually became more popular in Europe than the fava bean. The first reported use of the American green bean was in Spain when a cook accidentally put a bunch of green beans into a soup pot. It was too late to throw the soup out and start over, so she served it anyway to great acclaim.

Some New World green beans were sent to Pope Clement VII in 1528. His gardener grew them and after the Pope tasted the new beans he approved. Some of the bean plants were sent to Alesandro di Medici who also liked them. He gave some bean plants to his daughter Catherine to take to France when she left to marry Henry II in 1533. However, it took two centuries before green beans (haricot vert) were accepted in French cuisine. Today small, slender green beans are an intricate part of French cooking. Italians have also accepted the American green bean as part of their cooking and favor it over the fava bean.

The following recipe for Green Beans with Tomatoes is Italian in origin. No water is added to the cooking as there is enough moisture in the beans and tomatoes.

Pickled beans have been popular since Colonial Days and was a way of preserving this green summer vegetable.

Green Beans with Tomatoes

2 pounds green beans
3 tablespoons extra virgin olive oil
1 small onion, chopped
1 small carrot, chopped
2 garlic cloves, left whole
1 pound fresh ripe tomatoes, chopped
6 fresh basil leaves, julienned
Salt and pepper, to taste

Remove the ends and any strings from the beans. Then soak them in a large bowl of ice-cold water for 30 minutes.

Heat the oil in a 3-quart saucepan over medium heat. Add the onion, carrot, and garlic cloves. Sauté until lightly golden, about 7 minutes, then remove the garlic.

Add the chopped tomatoes, basil and beans. Season with salt and pepper and mix well. Do not add any liquid. Cover the saucepan and simmer the beans slowly for 30 minutes. The beans should be cooked, but still firm. Cook the beans for a few more minutes, uncovered, and then transfer them to a serving dish. Serves 6.

Green Bean Pickles

2 pounds green beans, trimmed
2 cups cider vinegar
1/3 cup sugar
2 tablespoons mixed pickling spices, tied in
    a cheesecloth bag
1 tablespoon whole black peppercorns
1 bay leaf
1 garlic clove
1 large onion, chopped
1 small red bell pepper, seeded and chopped
3 large sprigs dill
3 pint jars. sterilized

Cook the beans in boiling salted water for 1 minute. Rinse under cold running water and drain.

Place the vinegar, sugar, pickling spices, peppercorns, bay leaf, and garlic in a medium saucepan. Bring to a boil. Reduce heat and simmer, uncovered, for 10 minutes. Discard the spice bag. Add the onion and bell pepper, simmer 10 minutes longer. Discard the bay leaf and garlic.

Pack the beans upright in the sterilized jars, up to 1 inch from the top. With a slotted spoon, divide the onions and red peppers evenly among the 3 jars. Place a dill sprig in each jar and pour in the hot syrup up to 1/2 inch from the top. Seal the jars. Process in a hot water bath for 15 minutes. Makes 3 pints.

Beets

Two Vegetables in One

Beets are a two-part vegetable — edible leaves and dark ruby red roots. Both have a distinctive taste and texture and may be served at the same meal or at different times. The young leaves are often added to salads. The leaves of the beet plant are known as chard and have been developed instead of the root.

Food historians have had difficulty establishing where the beet originated as it was being cultivated in prehistoric times. The early Romans ate only the leaves of the beet plant. It was not until the second century A.D. that both the leaves and root were being consumed.

Charlemagne did not include beets in his plans for his vegetable garden, but his gardeners planted beets without his knowledge. Beets, however, were not popular in France until the Renaissance, and it was never one of the favorite French vegetables. Chard (the leaves) was popular in France and Germany where the stalks were cooked like asparagus and the leaves like spinach.

Beets have a high tolerance for salt and were often planted on lands reclaimed from the sea, such as the lowlands of Holland. They were also planted in filled-in eel ponds in Italy.

The beet is a biennial plant, producing the edible root the first year and seed the second. It grows best in cool climates as high temperatures will cause the root to be pale in color. With hybridization different colored beets, as well as miniature beets, are being cultivated primarily in California.

The other well-known beet is the sugar beet. It is not edible but is the source of some of the world's sugar. It is a long tapered beet with white flesh and an almost white skin. Until it was discovered as a source of sugar this beet was used primarily as animal feed.

The sugar beet became popular when the English blockaded France at the time of Napoleon, cutting off France's supply of cane sugar. Napoleon heard that sugar could be obtained from beets and ordered that 70,000 acres be planted. A French financier, Benjamin Delessert, opened a refinery to process the beets and was very successful. By 1880 sugar beets were being widely used as a source of sugar and continue to be grown.

Borscht is a favorite of Russia. This meatless version can be served as an appetizer or as a main course. Although regular cabbage can be used in this recipe, savoy cabbage is more flavorful. If fresh beets are unavailable, canned ones may be substituted.

Borscht

8 cups beef broth
5 cups chopped savoy cabbage
1¹/₂ stalks celery, chopped
1 carrot, chopped
1¹/₂ cups diced beets (about 4 beets)
1 large onion, chopped
1 bay leaf
4 tablespoons red wine vinegar
2 teaspoons Worcestershire sauce
3 tablespoons light brown sugar
Salt and pepper, to taste
Sour cream, for garnish

Place the beef broth, cabbage, beets, celery, carrot, onion, bay leaf, vinegar, Worcestershire sauce, and sugar in a large stock pot. Bring to a slow boil and simmer the soup for 1 hour. Long, slow cooking improves the flavor. Add salt and pepper, to taste. Ladle into soup bowls and serve with a dollop of sour cream. Serves 6 to 8.

Broccoli

Tiny Unopened Flowers

Broccoli, a biennial plant, is a member of the cabbage family. It is harvested before its flowers have opened. It is served more frequently in restaurants than any other vegetable. Chinese restaurants feature broccoli in many of their dishes.

Although broccoli became popular in the United States in the 1920s, it was grown by John Randolph in Williamsburg in the 1770s. He described the taste of the stems as that of asparagus and the heads like cauliflower.

According to one story, broccoli was rediscovered in Boston when the new Suffolk Downs racetrack opened. The surrounding lawn had not been seeded by opening day and the track grounds keeper, an Italian, was told to plant something quickly that would look good and grow fast. He choose the plant that looked good to him — Broccoli. While it was beautifully green, it was rather difficult to walk on. Shortly after the racetrack opened, the local vegetable markets were flooded with this new, unknown vegetable called broccoli.

Broccoli was originally an Italian plant and was in great favor during Roman times. Where it came from is still a mystery. Some sources indicate that the Romans may have created broccoli from cabbage.

Caesar and his entourage loved broccoli with such a passion that it was served three times during a banquet. Its method of preparation never varied. It was simply boiled with a mixture of cumin and coriander seeds, chopped onion, and a few drops of olive oil.

One of the greatest "foodies" of the world, Catherine de Medici, brought broccoli with her to France when she married Henry II in 1533. From France broccoli migrated to England in the 1720s, and then to China.

Broccoli with Orange Sauce is a tangy accompaniment to roasted or grilled meats.

Broccoli with Orange Sauce

1 1/2 pounds broccoli
1/4 cup butter, melted
1/4 cup freshly grated Parmesan cheese

Wash and peel the broccoli and cut into lengthwise strips with flowerets attached. Cook in boiling water for 4 to 5 minutes, or until barely tender. Drain and rinse in cold water and drain again. Dip each broccoli stalk in melted butter and place it in a 9x13-inch baking dish. Sprinkle with Parmesan cheese.

Sauce

3 tablespoons butter
3 tablespoons all-purpose flour
1 cup milk
1/4 cup whipping cream
3 tablespoon fresh orange juice
1 tablespoon fresh lemon juice
1 tablespoon grated orange peel
1 tablespoon grated lemon peel
1/4 cup sliced almonds, for garnish

In a small saucepan, melt the butter over low heat. Remove from heat and stir in the flour. Return the saucepan to the heat and slowly add the milk, stirring constantly, until a thick sauce forms. Add the cream, orange and lemon juices, and peels, stir until creamy. Pour the sauce over the broccoli and sprinkle with almonds. Bake in a preheated 425° F. oven for 10 minutes, until the sauce is bubbling and the almonds are slightly toasted. Serves 6.

Brussels Sprouts

Little Cabbages on a Stalk

Brussels sprouts were given their name by the French because they were introduced into French cooking from Belgium, where they grew. No one knows when Brussels sprouts were first cultivated in the region surrounding Brussels. Some records say that they were grown there as early as the thirteenth century. They also grew wild in northern Germany and the Germans call them "Rosenkohl," meaning rose cabbages, as they resemble rose buds.

Historians are uncertain as to when Brussels sprouts were first eaten. Some say they were eaten in Roman times because the Romans believed that the consumption of Brussels sprouts enhanced ones mental agility. Mark Anthony is said to have chewed Brussels sprouts for days before the battle of Actium, but apparently to no avail as he lost the battle.

Roman chefs prized these mini-cabbages and imported them from the coastal regions of western Europe, where they grew wild. Because these cabbages grew in the form of a head, Roman doctors assumed that Brussels sprouts were a cure for drunkenness and perscribed them for the headaches resulting from that condition.

Belgian Botanists first described the Brussels sprout in 1587 and identified it as a member of the cabbage family. The plant did not attract much attention as a food until a century later. By 1793 the Belgians was exporting their sprouts. Brussels sprouts have been a source of Flemish national pride ever since. In 1820 Belgium designated the Brussels sprout as the country's official green vegetable. They have graced ornate palace dining tables and roughly hewn farmhouse peasant tables alike. In Belgian cookery Brussels sprouts are frequently paired with smoked sausages or ham.

In the middle of the nineteenth century Brussels sprouts crossed the English Channel and became popular in England. Today the English are the largest consumers of Brussels sprouts in the world. The British devote about seven times the amount of acreage to this crop as we do in the United States, where it is grown primarily in California and New York. Brussels sprouts are among the few Western vegetables that have been adopted by the Chinese.

Brussels sprouts are typically grown as a fall crop. Connoisseurs claim that they are at their best after the first snow falls. A touch of frost seems to sweeten their flavor.

These miniature cabbages, one and a half inches across at maximum, grow on a stalk. The top of the stem is graced with large leaves which loosely form a cabbage head. As the top sprouts, which generally ripened first, are picked, others develop below them. Harvesting is a continuous process for a month or two. One plant can yield as many as one hundred sprouts.

The smallest and tightest Brussels sprouts are the best tasting. In Belgium it is considered a delicacy to serve Brussels sprouts no larger than a fingernail. They should be crisp to the touch and bright green. The sprouts tend to open over time, even when stored in the refrigerator.

The classic way to prepare Brussels sprouts is to parboil or blanch them. Before doing so, pull off any loose leaves and make a tiny X cut in the base of the sprout to hasten cooking. The English like to combine their cooked sprouts with cooked chestnuts and serve them with melted butter. In this country we frequently cook them with equal amounts of small mushrooms and some chopped red pepper.

Cabbage

Has Many Relatives

Although cabbage was first heard of in the Mediterranean area, it did not originate there as it is not a plant of that warm region. Cabbage grows best in cool, moist climates. It is thought to have originated in the cool climate of northern and central Eueope, particularly along the coast where it benefited from the damp air. Cabbage is one of the few vegetables that spread from north to south, instead of initially being brought north by the Romans.

Besides being one of the oldest cultivated vegetables, botantists tell us that cabbage is related to several other vegetables — broccoli, brussels sprouts, cauliflower, collards, kale, Chinese cabbage, and kohlrabi.

The Greeks accepted cabbage with great reluctance, but the Romans were more favorable to it. The Greeks, however, ate great amounts of cabbage because it was filling and easy to grow.

In Roman times cabbage was in such great demand that it became too expensive except for the most affluent. Farmers paid great attention to the growing of cabbage and heads weighing more than twenty pounds were not unusual. The Romans developed many of the variations of cabbage we know today.

During the Middle Ages people did not consume many vegetables. One variety of cabbage, Senlis (no longer available), was served at royal banquets as a first course because when cut open it gave off the pleasant odor of musk. Catherine de Medici brought several varieties of Italian cabbage with her when she married the future king Henry II.

Botantists say that the color of red cabbage comes from its chemical composition. The French, however, have a more charming story. It seems that in the days when unmarried mothers were considered to have disgraced themselves, a young pregnant woman returned from the fields balancing a huge cabbage on her swollen stomach. Upon coming into town she was ridiculed and assualted. The bishop who came by at the right moment took the cabbage from her and put it under his mantel. When he handed the cabbage back to her it had taken on the deep red color of his robes.

Until the beginning of the twentieth century, most agronomists assumed that cabbage was native to western Europe. However, during the Boxer Rebellion in China, scrolls from 1000 B.C. were uncovered thatdetailed the perscription of white cabbage as the only cure for barrenness in males of advanced age.

Sauerkraut was first made in China more than two thousand years ago, during the building of the Great Wall. The coolies who built the wall subsisted on rice and cabbage pickled in rice wine. When Genghis Khan plundered China around 1200 A.D. he brought the recipe for pickled cabbage back to Eastern Europe. In time the recipe spread to most of the northern and eastern European countries and became known as sauerkraut. Pickled cabbage is still enjoyed in China.

The following recipe for Pork Loin in Savoy Cabbage is of German origin. Cooking the pork loin it the cabbage keeps the meat moist and adds additional flavor. Serve with boiled or mashed potatoes.

Pork Loin in Savoy Cabbage

1 medium head Savoy cabbage
6 ounces crimini mushrooms
4 ounces shiitake mushrooms
4 tablespoons olive oil
4 slices lean bacon, trimmed of large fat
  areas and cut into 1-inch pieces
1 large onion, chopped
Salt and pepper, to taste
1 1/2 pounds pork loin, trimmed of all fat
1/2 cup white wine
1/2 tablespoon Dijon mustard
2/3 cup whipping cream

Remove 6 outer leaves from the cabbage and cut out the center core. Blanch the cabbage leaves in boiling water for 3 minutes. Then remove them from the water, rinse them in cold water, and dry them with paper towels.

Chop the mushrooms. Heat 1 tablespoon of the olive oil in a skillet over medium heat. Add the mushrooms and sauté until all liquid has evaporated. Then remove the mushrooms from the skillet and place them in a bowl. Add 1 tablespoon olive oil to the skillet, and then add the bacon and onions. Sauté until the onions are transparent. Add the bacon-onion mixture to the mushrooms.

Sprinkle the pork loin lightly with salt and pepper. Using the same skillet heat another 2 tablespoons olive oil over medium heat. Add the pork and lightly brown it on all sides. Remove the meat to a plate and let it cool.

Use a cutting board to assemble the dish. Lay two pieces of butcher's twine larger than twice the long circumference of the roast on the board as if to make a package. Then place the cabbage leaves on top of the twine, making sure that they overlap (about a 10x10-inch square). Reserving 4 tablespoons of the mushroom mixture, spread half of the mixture onto the center of the cabbage leaves. Lay the pork loin on top of the mushrooms and top the meat with the remaining mushrooms. Fold the cabbage leaves around the roast and secure with the butcher's twine. Tie several more pieces of twine around the cabbage leaves to hold them in place.

Put the pork-cabbage roulade in a shallow baking dish and bake in a preheated 350° F. oven for 50 minutes or until a meat thermometer registers 160° F. when inserted into the center of the pork.

Place the pork roulade on a plate and keep it warm while making the gravy. Add the wine to the baking dish and heat over medium heat, scraping up any loose particles. Add the mustard, the remaining 2 tablespoons of mushrooms, and the cream. Bring to a boil and reduce until the sauce coats the back of a spoon.

To serve, remove the twine, slice the pork roulade and top with some of the sauce.

Serves 4.

Carrots

Many Colors

Carrots are the subject of cartoons, health food articles, and cookbooks. Bugs Bunny loves them and children are told to eat them because it will make them have good eyesight. Carrots are also used in making Cheddar cheese to give it that rich orange color.

Carrots have not always been the orange variety we know today, as early varieties were red, purple, black, and white. In Egypt, purple carrots are still being cultivated and used for food, while in Europe the various other colored carrots are raised primarily as animal fodder. Gourmet food stores often feature purple and yellow carrots in their produce sections.

Carrots were first grown in Afghanistan some three thousand years ago. From there the carrot was transported to the Mediterranean area and also eastward to India, China, and eventually Japan. The carrot did not endear itself to the Greeks and Romans, as they preferred turnips. Some Greeks and Romans, however, regarded carrots as an aphrodisiac. The Roman emperor, Caligula, reportedly had carrots force-fed to the entire Roman Senate in an effort to turn wise men into love-sick ones. The Romans are also believed to have been the first to eat carrots to prevent night blindness.

In the Middle ages, physicians prescribed carrots as a cure for everything from dizziness to snake bite. Until about the fifteenth century, only the Asian population ate carrots because they enjoyed their flavor. When carrots were first introduced in France and England, in the fifteenth century, only the feathery leaves were used, not as food but to decorate hairdos, hats, dresses, and coats of the well-to-do. Carrots in Europe had returned to a wild state by that time and developed a poison.

In the sixteenth century French and German horticulturists were successful in ridding the carrot plant of its poison, and making it a successful food plant. The pale yellow strain of carrots that they developed became popular as a flavoring for soups and stews, since it did not distroy the color of the dish. A century later the bright orange carrot was hybridized in Holland and, because of its color, it surpassed all other cultivated varieties of carrots in popularity.

The French helped popularize the consumption of carrots in Europe. They became so fond of them that almost an entire region, Crecy, was devoted to their cultivation. Today any dish listed on a French menu that contains the word "Crecy" means that one of its main ingredients is carrots.

When the first settlers came to America they brought carrot seeds with them. The first carrots were planted in Virginia in 1609, and then later in New England in 1629. The early English settlers made jam with carrots and also used them to produced wine. Both of these uses of carrots are no longer being practiced and, as one food historian expressed his sentiment, "Thank God."

Botanists believe that in the early 1700s some of the carrots planted in North America reverted back to their wild state . Today we can still find these inedible wild carrots along the roadsides. We know them as Queen Anne's lace, the name referring to Queen Anne of England who ruled from 1702 to 1714.

Carrots contain more sugar than any other vegetable, except beets. They are seldom the main attraction of any dish except soups. Carrots are used along with other vegetables for hors d'oeuvre dips, in salads, and are one of the main ingredients of a cake. The Irish prepare a pudding with carrots and refer to the vegetable as "underground honey." In Jewish cuisine, tzimmes is a popular carrot pudding which is further sweetened with honey.

The orange carrot is rich in beta-carotene. Scientists tell us that the deeper the orange color the greater the beta-carotene content. Because of that, the older the carrots, the better they are for you.

Carrots can be purchased in the supermarkets either loose, packaged by the pound, or by the bunch. Miniature carrots, which are peeled, have become popular, and are available in one or two pound packages. These miniature carrots were developed in California and require a little less cooking time.

The flavor of the Velvet Carrot Soup is enhanced with ginger and sesame oil. It may be prepared several days in advance and simply reheated at serving time. The Glazed Carrots are slowly simmered in a combination of beer, beef broth, and sugar, which gives a nice glaze and an interesting taste to the carrots.

Carrot Velvet Soup

3 tablespoons butter or margarine
1 medium onion, chopped
1 leek, white part only, chopped
3 tablespoon chopped fresh ginger
1 teaspoon Oriental (toasted) sesame oil
4 cups chicken broth
3/4 cup dry white wine
1 1/4 pound carrots, peeled and cut in
*   chunks*
Curry powder, to taste
Salt and pepper, to taste
Chopped fresh parsley, for garnish

Melt the butter in a large saucepan. Add the chopped onion, leek, ginger and sesame oil and cook over low heat until onion and leeks are limp and transparent, about 15 minutes. Stir the mixture often. Add the chicken broth, wine, and carrots and continue to cook, covered, until the carrots are very soft, about 25 to 30 minutes. Puree the soup in batches in a food processor until very smooth and velvety. Return the soup to the saucepan and heat; then season with curry powder and salt and pepper, to taste. Ladle into individual soup bowls and garnish with parsley. Serves 6.

Glazed Carrots

2 pounds carrots, halved and cut
*   into 2- to 3-inch piece*
1 teaspoon grated lemon peel
1/4 teaspoon freshly ground black pepper
1 tablespoon sugar
3 tablespoons butter, cut in pieces
1 cup beef broth
1 cup beer

Place the carrots in a large skillet and sprinkle them with lemon peel, pepper, and sugar. Dot with butter. Gently add the beef broth and beer. Bring to a boil, reduce heat, and simmer over low heat, uncovered, for about 30 to 40 minutes or until the carrots are done. Stir occasionally. When done remove the carrots with a slotted spoon and reduce the remaining liquid over medium-high heat until it is syrupy. Return the carrots to the skillet and coat with the syrup. Serves 6.

Cauliflower

Cabbage Relative

Mark Twain once said that cauliflower is a cabbage with a college education. He was not far from wrong as cauliflower is a species of cabbage, just as is broccoli. Over the years different parts of the cabbage plant have been developed until they became another vegetable. In cauliflower the flowers were developed for eating. When picked the flowers of the cauliflower have formed into a hard mass, while broccoli is harvested before the flowers have opened.

There have been many varieties of cauliflower developed over the years. The most familiar is the white cauliflower. In Italy you can purchase white, purple, or green cauliflower. France, Holland and Algeria each grow their own type. There is also another type of European cauliflower with long stalks that are eaten instead of the flower. A recent innovation has been broccoflower which is green and is shaped like a cauliflower, but tastes similar to broccoli.

Cauliflower was a food of the ancient Romans who got it from Asia Minor. However, it lost favor during the Dark Ages and since it was not cultivated it returned to its original cabbage form.

When the Moors invaded Spain in the ninth century they brought cauliflower with them. The Spanish promptly regarded it as a homely plant — a cabbage that blooms like a flower. Cauliflower was regarded as an ornamental plant, except that it had one use. Small, perfect cauliflowers were often pressed into the décolletage of an unmarried Spanish maiden to call attention to her "natural endowments."

Re-developed in the seventeenth century, cauliflower enjoyed a period of high fashion cuisine, particularly at the French court. During the reign of Louis XV a cauliflower dish was named for the king's mistress, Madame du Barry.

In central and northern Europe cauliflower was popular during the Lenten season because it is a filling food. It has remained in favor in northern European countries and is widely consumed in India where it is spiced with curry powder.

Cauliflower has been grown on Long Island since the 1620s. Today the growers use the same cultivation method as was developed in the Middle East two thousand years ago. The growth of the cauliflower plant is watched scrupulously. When a small round rosette of green forms in the center of the plant, the outer leaves are gathered and drawn together in a loose pouch. The leaves continue to grow as does the bud in the center. By harvest a large, pure white head has formed because it has grown without sunlight, sheltered by the pouch of leaves.

This simple cauliflower dish pairs well with grilled meats.

Cauliflower with Almond Butter

1 small cauliflower
1/4 cup butter
1/4 cup slivered almonds

Cook the cauliflower in boiling salted water until tender. Drain and keep hot. Heat the butter in a small skillet, add the almonds and sauté until golden brown. Place cauliflower in a hot serving dish. Top with almond butter.
Serves 4.

Celery and Celery Root

A Popular Stalk

The Greeks and Romans regarded celery as a funeral plant since it was used to decorate tombs. The Greeks had high regard for celery. They awarded great green bunches of it to victorious athletes. It was a very welcome gift as celery contains ninety-five percent water. However, the Greeks who generally were not fond of vegetables used celery only for seasoning.

The Romans made wreaths of celery which they wore on their heads to protect them from hangovers. They had higher regard for celery and cultivated it in their gardens, although they preferred the stronger taste of the wild plant. The Romans cooked celery as a vegetable. They even made a dessert with celery cooked with honey and pepper.

Food historians claim that both celery and celery root were developed by the gardeners of the king of Persia around 2000 B.C. Cyrus the First was a vegetarian and a finicky eater. To vary his dull diet, he ordered the royal gardeners to come up with something different for him to eat. Celery was the result, according to ancient lore.

A bunch of leafy green celery was sent as a wedding gift to the Empress of China during the T'ang dynasty by the Persians. This confirms the high regard they had for celery.

With the collapse of the Roman Empire, celery was no longer cultivated and only the wild variety was used sparingly in the Middle Ages. It was reintroduced in 1641 in Paris when it was grown in the royal gardens. In France celery was used primarily as a seasoning. Before that time the leaf of wild celery had become a decorative motif in Gothic cathedrals as well as adorning the crowns of the nobility.

The rest of Europe acquired celery from Italy. The English took to celery not only as a vegetable, but munched it raw with salt at tea time. They also cooked it beets, pomegranates, and lemon. The Italians cooked celery in a tomato sauce.

By the early 1900s the quality and taste of celery had been greatly improved. More than thirty kinds were listed in seed catalogs.

Celery root (celeriac) enjoys enormous popularity in Europe, but not in this country. Although it has a distinctive flavor, its gnarled appearance leaves a lot to be desired. It is also difficult to peel and slice. This variety is cultivated for its roots, not its stalks.

The following light, tasty Celery Root Salad combines the mildness of endive and sharpness of watercress with celery root.

Celery Root Salad

Dressing

1 large shallot, minced
1/2 cup olive oil
2 tablespoon white wine vinegar
3 tablespoons mayonnaise
1 tablespoon Dijon-style mustard
1/4 teaspoon salt
1/4 teaspoon freshly ground black pepper

1 celery root (about 1 pound) peeled and cut julienne
1 pound endive, cut into 1-inch pieces
2 bunches watercress, coarse stems removed

Combine dressing ingredients and set aside until ready to serve. Place celery root, endive and bite-size pieces of watercress in a bowl and refrigerate. To serve, toss the mixed vegetables with the dressing. Serves 8.

Corn

Staff of Life for Many

Corn is truly an American vegetable and has a number of very unique qualities. It is a very diverse plant. Some types are only two feet tall, while others grow as high as twenty feet. The size of the ears also varies from the length of a thumbnail to two feet. The giant size grows in Mexico's Jala Valley.

The number of kernels on an ear of corn differ according to size of the ear. There are anywhere from sixteen to five hundred kernels, but they are always arranged in an even number of rows. The kernels are usually white or yellow, but may also be red, purple, blue, brown, or nearly black. In recent years, variegated yellow and white corn has been developed and become very popular.

Corn, which originated in South and Central America is grown all over the world — from 58 degrees north latitude in Canada and Russia to 40 degrees south latitude in South America and Africa. Corn likes a lot of hot sun and a moderate amount of rainfall.

Corn is one of the few food plants that cannot reproduce itself without the aid of man. Its seeds or kernels are prevented from making contact with the soil by the tough and impermeable shuck wrapped tightly around the ear. If man did not open the ear and sow the dried seeds, corn would become extinct within a few years.

The Encyclopedia Britannica describes corn as "the grain that built the hemisphere." Its domestication brought about change from a nomadic life to a settled one for the Aztec, Mayan, and Incas, all of whom built great empires thousands of years ago.

Leif Ericson, upon returning to Europe after he and his crew briefly touched the northern coast of North America around 1000 A.D., described a type of flour and some strange seeds the Indians were using. It was not until some five hundred years later that Columbus took corn seeds back to Europe. Food historians have described corn as the most valuable food plant contributed by the New World to the Old.

When Cortez reached the interior of Mexico in 1520, he found the Mexicans eating corn tortillas and tamales, both of which are still staple foods in Mexico. He also found corn was so plentiful that Mexicans planted it along the roadsides to provide food for the hungry traveler. No one in Mexico at that time died of hunger, while in Europe many thousands perished for lack of food.

In Peru the Spanish explorers and conquerors found that the Inca Empire's prosperity was built on corn. Everyone between the ages of twenty-five and sixty had to work the corn fields, which were fertilized with guano brought from off-shore islands where the birds nested.

The Spaniards reversed the Inca priorities which had put corn first and gold second. Eventually the Incas revolted. In their attempt to impress the Spanish with the importance of food, they captured a conquistador, Don Antino Arriaga, and poured molten gold down his throat. Although the rebels were put to death, corn cultivation again became the first priority.

The cultivation of corn slowly worked its way north from Central America and Mexico. Even though corn kernels dating from 4500 B.C. have been found in caves in New Mexico, it was not until two thousand years later that corn was first cultivated by eastern Indians. Historians say the first such recorded planting was in Ohio.

Corn eventually became the staple food of most native American Indians. It has the ability to adapt itself to the local growing conditions over a period of years. That is why the traditional corn grown in the northern part of the country is quite different from that grown in the Southwest. Although today there is only one species of corn, there are many varieties and sub-varieties.

Corn saved the first white Virginians from starvation in the winter of 1607-08. The Indians gave Captain John Smith five hundred bushels of corn to tide the settlers over until spring. Corn also provided sustenance to the Pilgrims during their first winter. Over the next two centuries Americans became dependent primarily on corn as wheat proved difficult to grow, both in the Northeast and the South.

The Europeans, except for the Italians, resisted this strange grain which did not resemble any plant they knew. Most Europeans used corn for animal food, but the Italians found that the dried kernels could be ground into meal for one of their favorite dishes — polenta. This dish dated back to Roman times, and had, over the years, successively been made of millet, barely, wheat, and finally corn.

Today the favorite corn for human consumption is sweet corn. Historians report that in 1799 white settlers found the Iroquois growing sweet corn along the banks of the upper Susquehanna River in central New York. The settlers brought sweet corn seeds back to the Atlantic coastal areas, but no particular interest was generated. Americans did not develop a liking for sweet corn until large farms in the Midwest started cultivating it after the Civil War. Today it is one of America's favorite vegetables.

This Hopi Corn Tart originated in New Mexico. It may be served with maple syrup for brunch.

Hopi Corn Tart

8 tablespoons (1 stick) plus 1 teaspoon
*   butter or margarine, softened*
1/4 cup ground pumpkin seeds
6 medium ears corn
1/2 cup whipping cream
1/3 cup sugar
3 eggs, separated
1 teaspoon baking powder
1/8 teaspoon cinnamon
1/8 teaspoon salt
3 tablespoons dark rum
Maple syrup, optional

Rub the bottom and sides of a round 10-inch, 2-inch-deep, baking dish with the teaspoon of butter. Sprinkle the bottom with 2 teaspoons of the ground pumpkin seeds.

Cut the kernels from the ears of corn and place them in a bowl. With the back of a knife scrape the cobs over the bowl to extract the juices. Place half of the kernels in the bowl of a food processor. Add the cream and process until fairly smooth. Then combine the mixture with the corn in the bowl.

In a large bowl, beat the remaining butter with the sugar until light and fluffy. Beat in the egg yolks, one at a time, beating well after each addition. Then beat in the baking powder, cinnamon, salt, and rum. Stir in the corn mixture and the remaining pumpkin seeds.

Beat the egg whites until stiff and then gently fold them into the corn mixture. Pour the mixture into the baking dish and bake in a preheated 350° F. oven for 35 minutes until golden brown and slightly puffed. Let stand 5 minutes before serving. May be served with maple syrup. Serves 6 to 8.

Cucumbers

Cool and Green

According to the Old Testament Moses' one regret, after the Red Sea had parted and his people were safely out of Egypt, was that he had not brought a peck of cucumber seeds into the desert. Israelites and Egyptians ate this cylindrical green vegetable at almost every meal. They usually dipped it (raw) into bowls of salted water before eating it. At the time it was believed that eating three raw cucumbers daily would protect the body from bites of deadly insects and vipers.

The cucumber is a member of the gourd family and its relatives include squash and melon. It is thought to be a native of what is now Pakistan, where the overflowing Indus River makes the land muddy and fertile for the growing of cucumbers.

The original sub-continent Indian species of cucumber, still found in parts of India, had a brownish skin and an extremely bitter flesh. Time and hybridization has provided a green skin and a sweeter flavor.

Ancient Greeks considered the cucumber so ambrosial that they mixed the pulp with honey and snow and only served it on very special occasions, such as a victory celebration or a royal wedding.

The Romans served cucumbers every day when they were in season. They flavored them with fish sauces, vinegar, and herbs, which completely masked the cucumber flavor. Roman addiction to the cucumber was so great that the Emperor Tiberius consumed at least ten every day of the year.

The Romans stole the cucumber from the Greeks after a defeat in the wars with King Pyrrhus of Epirus. Previously the Macedonians and Persians, in turn, had gotten cucumber seeds from the Medes, who probably got them from Babylonian gardens. After the fall of the Roman Empire cucumbers fell out of favor and disappeared from the culinary scene.

The first record of cucumbers in Europe occurred in France during the reign of Pepin the Wise at the end of the eight century. According to his gardener's records Pepin ordered cucumbers to be planted in triple rows around his vineyards to protect them from borers and cutworms. Fifty years later his son decided to eat a cucumber. It must have been good.

Shortly thereafter Charlemagne said that cucumbers were a favorite "fruit." He ate them only as dessert, in sweet tarts and custards. Later French chefs, who had good sense, turned the cucumber custard from sweet to savory.

This popular soup is so refreshing and cool as a cucumber with a subtle hint of mint.

Cool as Cucumber Soup

2 large cucumbers
1 1/2 cups plain yogurt
1/3 cup buttermilk
2 tablespoons finely chopped fresh mint
Salt and pepper, to taste
Fresh lemon juice
Mint leaves, for garnish

Cut 12 very thin slices from one of the cucumbers and reserve for garnishing. Peel the cucumbers, halve them lengthwise and scoop out the seeds.

Finely chop the cucumbers in a food processor and then transfer to a large bowl. Stir in the yogurt, buttermilk, and mint. Season to taste with salt, pepper, and lemon juice.

Refrigerate until cold. Ladle into chilled bowls and garnish with cucumber slices and mint leaves. Serves 6.

Eggplant

Not Everyone's Favorite

Eggplant is not everyone's favorite vegetable. Traditionally eggplant is a deep brownish purple and elongated in shape with one end being considerably chubbier than the other. Now there is Japanese eggplant which is a small elongated, bright purple vegetable. There is also a baby Italian eggplant that is a miniature of the big ones.

Then there is a new white eggplant shaped like a large plum or egg. It has a much milder, sweeter taste without the bitter tinge that the small Italian eggplants tend to have. The white eggplants are firmer, contain less moisture, and in cooking or sautéing hold their shape better. Since the skin of white eggplant is thicker than any of the other eggplant, it is wise to peel them before cooking.

Eggplant has been a staple food in the Middle East and around the Mediterranean. It adds bulk and fleshy texture to meals that contain little or no meat.

The bulbous eggplant is a native of Southeastern Asia, although some historians believe it originated in India while others claim it came from China. The first eggplants grown in China were small, pendant-shaped with a pearly-hued appearance similar to a birds' egg.

In the third century the Chinese speculates on the possibility that this large bulb could be used as table fare. It took another three hundred years for an adventuresome Chinese diner to taste a piece of egg plant on the end of a chopstick. It was not a huge success. The first Westener to taste eggplant was an Indian traveler so smitten with the eggplant's appearance that he ate it raw and promptly had a fit, or just a bad stomach ache.

How the eggplant traveled west to Europe is unknown. The Greeks and Romans were not familiar with it. Moors brought the eggplant to Spain from where it spread to Italy and the rest of Europe.

Italy incorporated eggplant in its cuisine in the fifteenth century. The plant reached England in the late sixteenth century, and France about a century later. It really did not turn-over-any-worlds, so to speak, in any of the European countries. It did, however, become popular in Italy after it appeared on the menu of Pope Pius V in 1570. Eggplant has remained a favorite vegetable in the Middle East and in Italy.

Louis XIV liked to see exotic and unknown foods grace his table and was pleased when his chef who was also in charge of the royal kitchen gardens grew this unknown plant and prepared it for the French king.

Thomas Jefferson is responsible for bringing the first planting of eggplant to this country. Always in search of new foods, Jefferson had seeds and cuttings of unknown foods sent to him regularly from abroad. The first eggplant in the United States was grown at Monticello.

In France eggplant lost favor because it was thought to cause epilepsy. However, under the new government of 1795 after the revolution, the hippies and beautiful people of the time made eggplant their crusade. They gobbled down slices upon slices of it not only in the restaurants put also in the gardens of Paris. Eggplant became a fad food.

Eggplant has never gained great popularity in the United States except among those of Italian or Middle Eastern origin. When it was first grown in America it had the same connotations as tomatoes — it was considered to be poisonous.

One of the most famous eggplant dishes is the Italian Eggplant Parmigiana in which fried slices of eggplant are baked in a tomato sauce and cover with a layer of Mozzarella cheese. The southern Italians and Sicilians also include eggplant in a number of their pasta dishes.

Eggplant and tomatoes seem to have an affinity for each other. They are used in the French Ratatouille.

The following is my version of a Ratatouille, with an American addition — corn. Mushrooms are also added for extra flavor and moisture. The dish may be prepared early in the morning, refrigerated and baked just in time for dinner to be served. It is excellent with grilled lamb or chicken.

American Ratatouille

3 small Italian eggplants,
  sliced 1/4-inch thick
5 tablespoons olive oil
2 onions sliced
1 cup sliced mushrooms
1 medium red pepper, chopped
1 medium green pepper, chopped
1 clove garlic, chopped
Kernels from 4 ears of fresh corn
Salt and pepper, to taste
4 medium zucchini, sliced
4 to 5 medium tomatoes, sliced
1/2 teaspoon dried thyme
1/4 cup freshly ground Parmesan cheese

Sprinkle the eggplant slices with salt and let them sit in a colander for 30 minutes. Then rinse and pat dry with paper towels. This process removes the bitterness from the egg plant.

Heat 3 tablespoons of the olive oil in a large skillet over medium heat. Add the onions and sauté them until wilted. Add the mushrooms, peppers, eggplants, and garlic and continue sautéing until the eggplants begin to soften. Place the mixture into a large round or oblong casserole. Add the corn, salt, and pepper, to taste.

Arrange the zucchini slices and tomato slices in alternating, overlapping rows on top of the eggplant mixture. (May be prepared ahead to this point and refrigerated.) Just before baking, sprinkle the casserole with 1 tablespoon of the olive oil and the thyme. Bake in a preheated 350° F. oven for 35 minutes. Then drizzle the remaining tablespoon of olive oil over the vegetables and sprinkle the Parmesan cheese on top. Continue baking for another 15 minutes. Serves 8.

Fennel

Taste Similar to Anise

There are three basic varieties of fennel, all being members of the carrot family. One is the bulbous vegetable we see at the supermarket. It is called sweet, finocchio, or Florence fennel. Another is the plant that grows the fennel seeds used as a spice. It is called common fennel and does not have any edible root. The third type is known as Italian or Sicilian fennel, also called carosella. It does not have a bulb and the Italians eat only the young shoots, usually raw. Italian fennel can seldom be found in American markets.

Which part of the fennel is used depends of the type of fennel. Since common fennel has no bulb, it is not suitable as a vegetable. However, its shoots are eaten either raw or cooked. Common fennel frequently grows four-to-five feet high and looks like dill.

The broad bulbous base of sweet fennel is used either as a cooked vegetable or raw in salads. The feathery leaves of sweet fennel also resemble dill and can be used in sauces or added to the liquid when poaching fish.

While the fennel family may be new to many, it is one of the oldest vegetables under cultivation, traditionally in Mediterranean countries. Fennel has also been used in China for centuries, being one of the ingredients of Chinese five-spice powder. The other four are anise, Szechwan pepper, cloves, and cinnamon.

Fennel was reported as being one of the "four hot seeds" and one of the "five appetite stimulants" used in Medieval Europe. According to Chaucer's writings, it was one of the nine holy herbs of the Anglo-Saxons during the Middle Ages.

The other medieval hot seeds were anise, caraway, and coriander, while the other appetite stimulants were celery, asparagus, parsley, and knee holly. As for the other two holy herbs, we will never know as Chaucer chose not to record them.

Sweet fennel originated in Italy where it is still eaten as a vegetable, raw in salad and also raw as part of the antipasti course. France, on the other hand, uses common fennel as an herb, primarily in fish cookery and salads.

In Provence common fennel leaves and seeds are used to refine the taste of pickled olives, cucumbers, and capers. Fennel stalks are fed to rabbits in that region to add additional taste to an otherwise bland meat.

Originally fennel seeds were grown by the ancient Egyptians who used them primarily for medicinal purposes. Fennel seeds were also used by the Romans to season pork, lamb, seafood, and beans. They also used them to flavor many of their breads. The Greeks used fennel seeds to flavor their favorite drink, ouzo. Fennel seeds, with their flavor of anise, became a popular ingredient in cakes and pastries throughout central Europe. The seeds found their way to the Far East where they became an ingredient in curries.

Today Italians use large quantities of both fennel seeds and the vegetable. Fennel-pork sausages made both in a mild and hot version and used in many pasta sauces.

In the last decade, sweet fennel has become more popular in the United States, although it is rarely on restaurant menus. It is grown commercially in California and is often found in the produce section of our markets.

Fennel's taste is similar to licorice and anise, but much lighter and less persistent. It becomes even more delicate when cooked. Americans seem to find the taste strange, while Europeans regard it as ordinary as vanilla.

Chopped raw sweet fennel bulbs can be combined with chopped apples or other fruit in a refreshing salad. As a vegetable it can be steamed in chicken broth similar to celery, or it can be combined with lamb or pork in a stew to impart additional flavor to the meat and then be eaten as a side vegetable.

For an Italian treat try one of my favorite soup recipes, Sardinian Minestrone with Fennel. This recipe uses mild Italian sausages, fennel seeds, and chopped fennel bulbs. Fennel gives a sharpness in contrast to the orange and olives in the following salad.

Sardinian Minestrone with Fennel

3 tablespoons extra virgin olive oil
1 medium onion, chopped
1 teaspoon fennel seeds
4 ounces mild Italian sausage,
  casings removed
1/2 cup chopped parsley leaves
1 medium carrot, finely chopped
1 stalk celery, finely chopped
2 garlic cloves, finely chopped
1 pound fennel bulbs, quartered and cut
  into 1/2-inch slices
1 (14 ounce) can diced tomatoes with juice
1/2 teaspoon salt
7 cups chicken broth, or half water and half
  chicken broth
1 (14 ounce) can kidney beans, rinsed and
  drained
1 (14 ounce) can chickpeas, rinsed and
  drained
3 ounces short pasta
Freshly grated Parmesan cheese

Heat the olive oil in a soup pot. Add the onion, fennel seeds, and sausage. Sauté over low heat, breaking up the sausage meat and stirring occasionally until the onion is soft, about 5 to 7 minutes. Add the parsley, carrot, celery, and garlic and sauté for another 5 minutes.

Add the fennel, tomatoes, salt, and chicken broth. Bring to a boil, then lower heat and cook on very low heat for 45 minutes or until the fennel is tender. Add the beans and chick peas and continue cooking for 10 minutes. Then bring to a boil, add the pasta and cook over medium-low heat for 12 to 15 minutes until the pasta is done. Serve in soup bowls, sprinkled with the Parmesan cheese.

Serves 6 to 8.

Fennel, Orange and Olive Salad

3 medium-sized fennel heads
2 oranges
1/2 cup sliced black olives
5 tablespoons olive oil
Juice of 1/2 lemon
Salt and pepper, to taste
1/4 teaspoon cumin seeds
Lettuce leaves

Wash the fennel, dry and cut in half lengthwise. Then slice the halves thinly and place them in a large salad bowl.

Peel the oranges and slice them thinly crosswise, removing pith and seeds from each slice. Cut each slice into quarters. Add oranges and olives to the bowl.

Combine the olive oil and lemon juice in a small bowl and season with a little salt and a generous dash of pepper. Pour the dressing over the salad and sprinkle with cumin seeds. Allow the salad to marinate in a cool place (not the refrigerator) for 1 hour. Line four plates with lettuce leaves and divide the salad among the plates. Serves 4.

Kale

Curlier, the Better

Kale is a member of the cabbage family and is sometimes called cow cabbage. More of it is fed to livestock than to people.

Kale, like its relative head-cabbage, is an ancient vegetable. Scientists say that the curlier the kale the better it is for human consumption. Although kale is a healthy food many people avoid it because its flavor is too strong.

The Egyptians believed that they were being punished by the Gods and deprived of kale because at the time it had a short growing season — from November to March. In Akhenaton's tomb, the sarcophagus was filled with kale leaves carved of jade so that there would always be fresh-looking kale.

Kale is usually regarded as a winter vegetable, although it is available year around in our markets. It grows best in cool climates with lost of moisture.

The Scots are the world champion kale eaters, followed by the English and other northern Europeans. In England kale is considered to be a plant with mystical powers. The Irish say that fairies ride kale stalks in the light of the moon. When an Irish farmer finds the curly kale leaves in disarray at sunup, it means his crops will flourish and grow tall.

Danish cooks serve kale with roasted loin of pork or ham. The Germans served it chopped and boiled. Italy and France kale received little attention, although it was cultivated in the kitchen gardens at Versailles in 1620.

Even though kale was a northern European vegetable, it became the basis of a national dish in Portugal. Caldo Verde (green broth) consisted of a special Portuguese variety of kale which is more strongly flavored and is closely related to wild kale.

In America kale is a vegetable of the South and is part of the general category of greens. Kale and collard greens are often cooked together in the same pot. Other greens, such as mustard greens or turnip tops may also be added. Greens are traditionally cooked with salt pork or a ham hock.

The following Kale Soup is Danish in origin. With the addition of a poached egg in each bowl, the soup becomes a meal.

Danish Kale Soup

2 tablespoons butter or margarine
1 onion, chopped
1 clove garlic, chopped
1/8 teaspoon ground cinnamon
1 pound kale, stems removed and finely
*   chopped*
4 cups beef broth
4 eggs
1 teaspoon vinegar
Salt and pepper, to taste
Chopped chives or green onions

Melt the butter in a large saucepan over medium-low heat. Add the onion and sauté until the onion is soft, but not brown. Add the garlic and cook 2 minutes longer. Stir the cinnamon into the onion mixture. Add the kale and stir. Then add the broth and heat to boiling. Reduce heat and simmer, covered, for 20 minutes.

While the soup is cooking poach the 4 eggs in simmering water to which the vinegar has been added. Remove the eggs with a slotted spoon and place them in serving bowls. Spoon the hot soup over the eggs. Sprinkle with salt and pepper and the chopped chives. Serves 4.

Lettuce

Lettuce Is Big Business

Because American dollar bills are green, "A wad of lettuce" is slang for a roll of dollar bills. The idea of lettuce and money is quite old. The Italians used to call a gift of money "one of Sixtus V's salads," because the sixteenth-century pontiff, is said to have helped old friends by sending them a head of lettuce full of paper money.

Today the cultivation of lettuce is big business. Five billion heads of commercial lettuce, principally Iceberg, are harvested annually in the United States, with seventy percent of the production in California and fifteen percent in Arizona. That amounts to a consumption of thirty pounds of lettuce per person per year — more lettuce than quarts of milk or loaves of bread.

In this country the great lettuce business conglomerates are called "grower-shippers" because they handle both aspects of the industry. These companies are endowed with a spirit of gambling as their product is very delicate and economically risky. As the lettuce trains head east individual cars must be rerouted in real time as regional markets dictate.

Cultivated lettuces are annuals, not perennials, and lettuce fields require constant re-seeding and clearing. The bills for water, fertilizers, insecticides, and herbicides are enormous. Harvesting is costly. Heads of lettuces, even when sown on the same day, are not ready for cutting at the same time. Since each head of lettuce must be cut by hand, lettuce producing is a very labor-intensive business.

Lettuce has been on the human menu since about 800 B.C. No one knows where it originated, although food historians say that it was probably around the Caucuses where there is not extreme heat.

Lettuce was among the 250 plants grown in the Gardens of Babylon. It was popular with the Persian kings around 550 B.C., as well as with the Egyptians. Lettuce seeds have been found in some of the Egyptian tombs.

The lettuce of those times did not form heads, but had leaves on a tall central stalk. At the time, the ancient Greeks called lettuce "asparagus," a word applied generally to all spike-like plants. In addition to green lettuce, there was also a variety of white lettuce (probably very light green) which was very sweet and tender. It was the first to reach Italy where it became one of the three favorite Roman vegetables along with cabbage and artichokes.

The Romans were the first to cultivate lettuce so that it would form heads, although there are no historical writings as to how it was done. Being grown in the form of a head, like cabbage, Roman lettuce was prepared like a vegetable. It was cooked with onions and then pureed. By the first century, however, the Romans served lettuce cold with a dressing.

Depending on who was emperor and what fads were fashionable at the time, lettuce was served either at the end or the beginning of a meal. The latter remained popular for a long time as the Romans had come to realize that lettuce stimulates the appetite.

By the third century lettuce had spread north and west from the Mediterranean area. The Anglo-Saxons gathered wild lettuce but did not cultivate it. Charlemagne introduced lettuce into his garden, which caused it to become a common home-garden vegetable. However, it was not readily available in French markets, as watercress was preferred.

In the late 1500s lettuce became a status symbol for the French nobility. Three or four varieties of lettuce were served at the great banquets. At the time there were only four varieties being cultivated in France — the small, the common, the curled, and the Roman (today's Romaine).

There are two explanations for the name Romaine lettuce, which was first used in France. One credits Rabelais, a French humorist and satirist, with bringing back lettuce seeds given him by the Pope in Rome in 1534 and planting them in his garden. This explanation has been discredited as Romaine lettuce was grown by the Popes in Avignon two centuries earlier.

The other name for Romaine is Cos, which is a clue to where the Romans first got this lettuce. It is still an important crop on the Greek island of Cos, which receives an unusual amount of sun. Romaine is the only lettuce able to resist the resulting heat.

In the seventeenth century the popularity of lettuce skyrocketed in France because it was a favorite of Louis XIV. He preferred it seasoned with tarragon, sweet basil, or if possible violets. At the time of the French Revolution it was fashionable to eat "sharpened" salads in both France and England. They consisted of lettuce with anchovies, herring, or other dried or marinated fishes, and seasoned with capers and mustard.

Columbus is supposed to have introduced lettuce to the New World. In the following centuries it was eaten mostly by people who grew it in their gardens. America, a nation of basically meat-eaters, resisted salads until about World War I. Today Americans are so devoted to salads that few meals are served without some form of uncooked greens.

Today the general term lettuce encompasses a great variety of greens. Red radicchio, white Belgian endive, red and green leaf lettuce, curly endive, escarole, arugula, spinach, sorrel, bibb lettuce, Romaine, and Chinese cabbage are some of the varieties of greens available for the salad bowl.

One of the well-known uses of Romaine lettuce is in a Caesar Salad. It is not a product of Rome or even Italy, but was created more than seventy-five years ago by an Italian, Caesar Cardini in the hot and grimy-looking town of Tijuana, Mexico. He owned a number of restaurants in this frontier town seventeen miles south of San Diego.

At that time for many American thrill seekers and gourmets, a trip to Tijuana meant a chance to gamble, drink, and enjoy the food at Caesar's Place. Such Hollywood notables of the time as Jean Harlow, Clark Gable, and W.C. Fields frequented the restaurant.

It was at Caesar's Place on July 4, 1924 that Caesar Cardini created his now world famous Caesar Salad. As with many inventions, the first Caesar Salad was created purely to deal with an emergency. That particular 4th of July patrons descended on Caesar's in such great numbers that found Mr. Cardini unprepared to feed them all. When he realized that his supply of fresh vegetables would not serve his big crowd he began to improvise. He loaded a service cart with some of the staples available in his Italian kitchen, rolled up the sleeves of his white shirt, and rolled the service cart into the middle of the dining room.

Cardini was ready to go to work with a large salad bowl, romaine lettuce, garlic-flavored olive oil, lemons, coddled eggs, Worcestershire sauce, croutons, and salt and pepper. He combined the ingredients with such a flourish that it left his spectators in awe. The Caesar Salad was born. The original Caesar salad did not use anchovies.

Mushrooms

Edible Fungi

Mushrooms are fungi, but not all fungi are mushrooms — as fungi include yeasts and lichens. Mushrooms are the "fruiting bodies" of the main body of the fungi which remains underground.

Not all mushrooms are edible, but a great many are. About eighty species of mushrooms are found in France, but only twenty are edible. Great Britain and the United States have been sadly lacking in mushroom cultivation. For years only one mushroom, the white button, was widely available. Today we have many more — crimini, portobello, shiitake, oyster, enoki, and less commonchantrelle and morel.

The first cultivators of mushrooms were probably the Japanese, who have been raising shiitake mushrooms for at least two thousand years. The ancient Greeks and Romans did not cultivate mushrooms, but simply encouraged wild ones to grow.

In Europe mushroom cultivation started accidentally in France in the early 1700s. It was fashionable at that time to grow one's own melons and pineapple in hotbeds of composted manure in greenhouses. Many gardeners found their hotbeds producing an "unplanned weed" in the form of a mushroom. This gave the gardeners the idea of cultivating wild mushrooms, which had never been domesticated.

Commercial gardeners soon found that the caves outside Paris were ideal for growing mushrooms and have been doing so ever since. These mushrooms became known as "champignons de Paris."

The practice of mushroom cultivation spread slowly at first, because of secrecy surrounded it. Much of the early work on mushrooms involved fighting diseases and developing methods of propagation. Slowly mushroom cultivation spread to Sweden and England during the eighteenth century.

It was not until the early 1900s that mushrooms cultivation began in this country. Today the United States is one of the world's leading growers of cultivated mushrooms.

In the past twenty years shiitake cultivation has become a commercial entity as well as a hobby for home gardeners.

Shiitake mushrooms have increased in popularity in recent years. They only used to be available in dried form, imported from Japan. Now, however, fresh shiitakes are readily available in bulk or in plastic containers.

The woodsy tasting, chestnut brown, parasol-shaped shiitake mushroom is named after the Japanese shiia trees, whose hardwood logs spawned the mushrooms in the woods of Japan. Shiitake mushrooms have been used in Japanese and Chinese cooking for centuries.

Most shiitake mushrooms are log-grown. Hardwood logs are cut into manageable sections, holes are drilled into each log, and the holes are then filled with sawdust that has been inoculated with shiitake spawn. A styrofoam plug is then inserted in each hole. Finally the logs are stacked in a square, Lincoln-log style.

After the inoculation the logs remain dormant for four to six months, usually over the winter, to allow the spawn to grow throughout the logs. Then they are sprinkled with water daily. It takes three to seven days for a crop of mushrooms to sprout and mature. After a crop is harvested the logs are re-stacked, sprinkled, and the spawn grows anew. This same method is also used in commercial operations, where the logs are placed either indoors or outside.

The morel mushroom is not cultivated and is rarely found in the markets. It is found in the wild among dead leaves underneath the trees in the early spring. That is when morels start poking their dark brown-black, spongy honeycomb-like caps through the ground.

Morels have a distinctive cap and stem. They are different from most other wild or cultivated mushrooms in that the stem and cap are both hollow. Most cooks discard the stem as it is quite tough, while the cap is tender and has a smoky, earthy, nutty flavor. The darker the mushroom the stronger the flavor.

The chanterelle mushroom has gained popularity in recent years. It is grown primarily in Oregon. Although it is rarely available fresh in eastern markets, it is available dried. Chanterelles are flower-shaped and range from egg-yellow to light orange in color. They have a fruity, peppery, nut-like flavor that adds a distinctive taste to many dishes.

Two mushrooms that are becoming readily available are the oyster and enoki mushrooms. Until about fifteen years ago, oyster mushrooms were only found in the wild. The entire mushroom can be used since its stem is as delicate as its smoky-gray cap. The subtle oyster flavor of these mushrooms is best brought out when they are sautéed in butter.

Enoki mushrooms were first imported from Japan, but are now cultivated, primarily in California. They are very small with long stems and tiny caps. Enoki mushrooms have a very mild flavor, slightly reminiscent of apples. They are best used raw in salads where their appearance is more important than the flavor. It is wise to buy them only if there is no brown spots on them, as that indicates oxidation.

Unfortunately porcini mushrooms are primarily available dried. They are the most important mushrooms of Europe. These mushrooms are found in the birch and Aspen forests of the western part of the United States and Canada and are rarely marketed fresh.

There are several varieties of dried mushrooms generally available — porcini, shiitake, morels. They come in packages of either one variety or a mix of several varieties. I have found that the smoky, woodsy flavor of porcini mushrooms is enhanced by drying.

It takes about a quarter of the amount of dried mushrooms to produce the same flavor as fresh ones as most fresh mushrooms contain approximately seventy-five percent water. That is why many recipes recommend sautéing or cooking the mushrooms until all liquid has evaporated. This produces the most intense flavor.

Mushrooms in Cream Sauce with fresh tarragon are served in puff pastry shells for an interesting first course. Puff pastry shells are available in the frozen food section of the supermarket. This mushroom sauce is also excellent on any thin spaghetti.

Mushrooms in Cream Sauce

4 tablespoons butter of margarine
1/2 pound shiitake mushrooms, sliced
1/2 pound cremini mushrooms, sliced
1/2 cup dry white wine
1/2 cup whipping cream
2 tablespoons finely chopped fresh tarragon
Salt and pepper, to taste
4 puff pastry shells

Melt the butter in a large sauté pan. Add the mushrooms and cook until all of the liquid has evaporated and the mushrooms begin to brown lightly. Add the wine and cream and cook over medium heat until the sauce coats a spoon, about 3 to 4 minutes. Add the tarragon and salt and pepper, to taste. Simmer a few more minutes to blend the flavors and serve hot in warm puff pastry shells. Serves 4.

Okra

The Gumbo Vegetable

Okra was brought to the Western Hemisphere by black slaves from Africa. Its origin is tied to Africa by its name which comes from a language spoken on the Gold Coast. Slaves from Angola also brought okra to America but called it "ngombo." This name quickly was changed to gumbo, which eventually came to mean a stew in which okra was an ingredient.

This stew was adopted from the Indians who made it with any type of meat including owl. To thicken the stew the Indians used filé powder made from dried sassafras leaves. They soon found that the okra brought by the slaves would also thicken the stew and consequently gave it the name gumbo.

In 1627 in Carolina, a twelve pound sack of okra sold for twelve shillings, a bargain no settler could resist as okra grew profusely.

Okra is the edible pod of a bush of the Hibiscus family. The blossoms are very showy — pale yellow at dawn, deep gold by noon, and crimson when the sun sets.

The Moors called okra pods "sun vessels." They believed that the ripened seeds contained therapeutic properties, which once consumed would remain in a man's body forever. This notion was shared by many Arabs and Africans and caused okra to be highly prized. The Arabs deemed okra a rare delicacy and prepared it only for special occasions such as weddings.

Okra is always harvested unripe, about ten weeks after planting when the okra pods are about nine inches in length. If allowed to ripen, okra becomes very fibrous and is not digestible. It is primarily used in stews and is usually cut into slices which look like little wheels with seeds in between the spokes.

The clean, pleasing taste of okra is overshadowed by it being mucilaginous, a good thickener for stews. Most people do not like the slight sliminess of okra. It is seldom cooked as a separate vegetable except in India. In Texas okra is combined with tomatoes and in South Carolina it is combined with rice in a dish called "Limping Susan."

Europeans have had little interest in okra, except in Spain where it was introduced by the Moors in the ninth century. There is also some interest in okra in the Middle East.

Today okra is regarded as a Third World vegetable. In India, where a slightly different variety of okra is grown, it is eaten fresh, prepared like asparagus, or pickled. In the Middle East okra is combined with chopped meat and cooked. Okra has become a part of various stews in the Caribbean.

Limping Susan is a dish of the coastal region of Georgia and the Carolinas okra and rice flourished at one time.

Limping Susan

4 strips bacon, diced
1/2 pound okra, cut into 1/2-inch rounds
1 cup long-grain rice
1 tablespoon chopped fresh basil
2 cups beef broth
1/8 teaspoon hot pepper sauce
Salt and pepper, to taste

Sauté the bacon in a medium saucepan over medium heat until crisp. Add the okra; stir and cook 1 minute. Stir in the remaining ingredients. Bring to a boil. Then cook, covered, over low heat until the rice is tender, about 25 minutes. Remove the cover and continue cooking until the mixture is fairly dry. Serves 4 to 6.

<u>Onions</u>

All Powerful in Ancient Times

Several sections of ourcountry have their own unique varieties of onions. These include the Walla Walla in Washington, the Maui in Hawaii, the Texas Sweet in Texas, and the Vidalia in Georgia. All of these onions are sweet and are suitable to eat raw. They are ideal in salads with tomatoes and fresh basil.

Onions have a long history. Primitive man reportedly used onion juice as a deodorant, rubbing it over his entire body. It is estimated that onions have been grown for food for more than five thousand years and are the most common of all of our seasonings. Only salt is more universally used for flavoring.

Although the onion is thought to be a native of Asia, hundreds of species have been found growing wild in Europe and North America. Anthropologist place the site of the first onion cultivation in Central Asia where the plant was thought to have divine power. Where an onion bloomed a temple was erected. Where an onion withered, the land was considered to be fallow and not even beasts of the field were allowed to graze. Although onions were cultivated no one ate them. The golden fruit with its many layers was regarded as a symbol of eternity and was held close to the heart whenever an oath was spoken.

The Sanskrit language of the ancient Sumerians in the Middle East first recorded the use of onions as a staple in the diet. The laws at that time stipulated that the needy receive a monthly ration of bread and onions. Onions were apparently regarded primarily as food for the poor, who ate them raw on bread — a combination which formed their staple diet.

The ancient Egyptians also considered the onion to be sacred. The priests wore entwining ropes of onions around their naked bodies as they said their daily prayers. Onions caused the first sit-down strike in history. Slaves building the Pyramid at Cheops in the fifth century B.C. refused to work until they were given their daily ration of onions and garlic. Several vegetables were sculptured in precious metals by Egyptian artisans, but only onions were crafted in gold.

Onions also symbolized the universe for a small sect of ancient Egyptians living along the Nile. For them the nine layers of the petal-like onion represented eternity. When the layers were peeled away, a bud-like stem remained which symbolized new growth — the beginnings of new life. The name onion is derived from the Latin "unio" meaning unity as related to something composed of many layers.

The onion is the plant most often shown in Egyptian art, as it was part of the staple diet of the poor who subsisted on bread, onions, and beer. Onions were also depicted on altars. Baskets of them were offered to the Gods at funerals. This was a second choice because bread was considered to be a better offering.

Alexander the Great fed his armies onions to give them courage. The Greeks fed their athletes onions in order to "lighten the balance of the blood." The athletes started the day with an onion the size of a fist and ended the day with one the size of a thumb. The Romans went even further and provided their gladiators with a complete breakfast of onions.

Excavations at Pompeii found a basket of cooked onions in one of the city's better equipped brothels. The onion was held in low esteem in Pompeii, where the guild of fruit and vegetable vendors refused to admit onion mongers. They were forced to form a separate association, considered to be the lowliest of all.

The Romans introduced onions to Britain, considering them a health food as well as a food flavoring. When the Romans left, the British continued to cultivate onions for food and for use in folk medicine. An English book entitled "The Great Herbal," published in 1596, claimed that onion juice rubbed on a bald head would make hair grow. Onions were used to clear up acne and relieve the pain of arthritis.

During the Middle Ages, the ancient Germans used onions to season roasts and stews. Although still considered to be food of the common people, onions became a favorite of Charlemagne, who ordered them planted in his gardens. Onions became so popular in France that they were often listed as one of the crops acceptable for rent payment to the feudal lord. Onions became so dear that frequently a string of tressed onions was the sole annual payment for land use.

Although wild onions, particularly ramps (more like a wild leek, but much stronger in flavor) were growing in North America, it was the Europeans who introduced yellow onions to the New World. Historians believe that Columbus brought yellow onions to the Dominican Republic on his second voyage in 1494. Other Spanish explorers brought onions to South and North America. The Indians of Mexico took an immediate liking to yellow onions as they were similar in flavor of their own wild onion, the ramp.

Both Spanish and French explorers partook of the native onions. Pere Marquette, who explored the region of the Great Lakes, told of being saved from starvation by eating "nodding onions and tree onions," both native wild varieties.

The Pilgrims brought onion seeds with them and planted them as soon as land was cleared. Some of the early New England settlers believed that hanging a string of onions over their front door would catch germs on their way into the house and prevent disease.

President Washington's favorite vegetable was the onion. He particularly enjoyed them cored, stuffed with mincemeat, and baked. General Grant firmly believed that onions would cure dysentery and other hot weather ills. In the summer of 1864 he sent a telegram to the War department declaring that he would not move his army without onions. Shortly thereafter three wagon loads of onions arrived at the front.

Over the years many different varieties of the Eurasian onions have been developed and many have become a part of our food heritage. The most popular onion in the United States is the globe onion, either yellow or white. It accounts for at least seventy-five percent of our onion production. The globes are usually of moderate size, are crisp in texture, and have a strong taste and aroma.

Spanish or Bermuda onions are milder and contain more sugar. The French use them in soups and stews because they caramelize during slow sautéing.

The following is one of my favorite onion recipes. This Tomato-Cheese and Onion Pie may be served for lunch or a light supper. Use sweet onions and either yellow or red tomatoes for this pie.

Tomato, Cheese, and Onion Pie

Pastry

1 1/4 cups flour
5 tablespoons butter
2 tablespoons vegetable shortening
4 to 5 tablespoons ice water
1 egg yolk
1 teaspoon Worcestershire sauce

Place the flour into the bowl of a food processor. Add the butter and shortening and process until the mixture resembles coarse meal. With the motor running add the ice water 1 tablespoon at a time. Process just until the dough forms a ball. (If necessary add 1 or 2 tablespoons more ice water.)

Place the dough on a floured surface and roll it out to fit a 10-inch deep dish pie plate. Line the pie plate with the dough and refrigerate for 30 minutes. Then line the pan with aluminum foil, shiny side down, weight it with beans or pie weights and bake the pie shell in a preheated 425° F. oven for 10 minutes. Carefully remove the pie weights and the aluminum foil. Beat together the egg yolk and Worcestershire sauce and light brush the mixture over the bottom of the pie crust. Bake for another 5 minutes. Cool the crust slightly while preparing the filling. Reduce the oven heat to 350° F.

Filling

3 tablespoons butter
2 large Vidalia onions, sliced
1/2 pound Gruyère cheese
2 tablespoons flour
2 large tomatoes
3 eggs
3/4 cup whipping cream

Melt the butter in a large frying pan; add the onions and sauté over medium heat until they turn golden, stirring frequently. This will take about 10 minutes.

Grate the cheese and toss it with the flour.

To assemble the pie, sprinkle a large handful of the cheese mixture over the pie crust. Spread the onions on top. Slice the tomatoes and arrange the slices over the onions. Sprinkle with the remaining cheese. Beat the eggs with the cream and pour the mixture over the pie. Bake in a preheated 350° F, oven for 40 minutes, or until the top is golden brown and the pie is firm in the middle. Serves 6.

Parsnips

Sadly Neglected

Parsnips are usually right next to the carrots in the produce display. They look lovely together — the contrast of the orange of the carrots and the cream color of the parsnips. Some people cook them together, but not many of us bother to cook them at all. Parsnips have a sweet taste and lend themselves to a number of preparations, including soups and side dishes.

The parsnip has long been a neglected vegetable. It lost prominence in the vegetable world to the potato when it was brought to Europe from South and Central America. Although parsnips do not resemble potatoes, they are both root vegetables and contain a considerable amount of starch. Through the years cooks have decided that there is not a place for both vegetables on the same menu.

In the 1500s Europeans primarily ate dried or smoked fish unless they lived near the sea and had access to fresh fish. To be palatable dried fish required a vegetable accompaniment. Parsnips and salt cod became a popular combination, although turnips and carrots were also used. However, parsnips were considered to be more nourishing. The heyday of the parsnip was in the Middle Ages, when abstinence from meat during religious observances, such as Lent, was strictly observed. Fish and vegetables, particularly heavy, starchy ones were preferred during these periods.

By the second half of the sixteenth century, parsnips were a highly regarded vegetable much honored in prose and poetry. The supremacy of the parsnip lasted well into the eighteenth century, at which time Europeans started eating potatoes as part of their regular diet. They found that the neutral taste of the potato was a suitable accompaniment to almost any food. Consequently, the pungent parsnip was doomed to become less-favored.

The origin of the parsnip is rather vague. Some food historians say it originated in northern Europe and others claim northern Eurasia was its original home. Both theories could hold water since in the eastern part of the United States the parsnip was brought from Europe while along the Pacific coast parsnips grew wild. Some historians believe that they were brought from Asia across the land bridge thatis now the Bering Strait.

During Roman times and into the Middle Ages wild parsnips were preferred over cultivated ones because they were readily available and sweeter. Winter weather was good for parsnips because it turned their starch to sugar.

Parsnips were first brought to Latin America in 1564 by the Spanish and then to Virginia in 1608 and to Massachusetts in 1629. Although parsnips were not new to the settlers, they were a new vegetable to the Indians. They became so fond of parsnips that in a retaliatory raid by General John Sullivan on the Iroquois in western New York in 1779, Sullivan purposely destroyed their entire crop of parsnips as a sort of coup-de-gras.

Most of us are familiar with the long funnel-shaped parsnip, but there was a round variety introduced into the United States in 1834. Although the round parsnip is preferred in some European countries because it ripens sooner and has a more intense flavor, it never caught on here.

There can be a wide variation in quality of parsnips. Those pulled during hot weather tend to be tasteless. Soft parsnips are pithy and large ones can be woody. Look for firm, medium-sized ones with well-shaped roots.

The following two recipes -- Parsnip and Orange Soup and Sweet and Sour Parsnips -- will hopefully inspire you to cook this negelected vegetable. The soup has an English origin. The parsnip and orange combination produces a nice melding of flavors.

The Sweet and Sour parsnips are of Pennsylvania Dutch extraction. One of the rules of a Pennsylvania Dutch dinner is that seven sweets and seven sours must be served. Although the exact number is not followed anymore, the sweets and sours are still popular with Pennsylvania Germans who feel that they give balance to the meal.

Parsnip and Orange Soup

2 tablespoons butter or margarine
1 medium onion, chopped
1 medium potato, peeled and diced
2 pounds parsnips, peeled and diced
4 cups chicken broth
1/2 cup orange juice
Rind of 1/2 orange, cut in wide strips
1/4 teaspoon pepper
1/2 cup whipping cream

Melt the butter in a large saucepan, and add the onion, potato, and parsnips. Cook, covered, over low heat until the vegetables are softened, about 10 minutes. Add the chicken broth, orange juice, orange rind., and pepper. Simmer, covered, for 20 to 25 minutes or until the vegetables are done. Transfer the solids to the bowl of a food processor and purée. If a finer texture is desired push the mixture through a fine sieve. Return the purée to the saucepan and incorporate it with the liquid. Stir in the cream, heat through, and serve. Serves 6.

Sweet and Sour Parsnips

4 medium parsnips
4 strips bacon, cut into 1-inch pieces
1 small onion, chopped
1 tablespoon all-purpose flour
2 tablespoons white wine vinegar
1 teaspoon honey
1/4 teaspoon nutmeg
Salt and pepper, to taste

Peel the parsnips and cut them into julienne strips, about 1/4 by 2 and 1/2-inches. Cook the parsnips in a medium saucepan in boiling water until tender. Drain and reserve 1 cup of the cooking liquid.

Cook the bacon in a large skillet over medium heat, stirring often, until browned. Remove bacon pieces to paper towels to drain. Leave 1 and 1/2 tablespoons of the fat in the skillet. Add the onion and sauté until softened. Add the flour and cook over low heat until combined. The add the cup of parsnip water and stir with a wire whisk until smooth. Bring to a boil and simmer for 5 minutes. Stir in the vinegar, honey, and nutmeg. Taste for tartness and sweetness and add a little more vinegar or honey, if desired. Add the parsnips and heat through. Stir in the bacon and season with salt and pepper to taste. Serves 4.

Peas

Favorite of Nobility

There is only one species of edible peas, but there are several hundred varieties. The field pea is no longer considered to be for human consumption and is grown only for livestock fodder. Many botanists believe that this field pea is not really a wild pea but one that was formerly cultivated in vegetable gardens.

A truly wild pea is almost impossible to find these days, although peas have been part of man's diet since the Bronze Age. Early traces of peas have been carbon-dated in the prehistoric lake dwellings at Herzogenbuchsee, Switzerland in about 9,750 years before the birth of Christ. Food historians tell us that this is the oldest record for any vegetable that is still consumed.

The peas favored by cavemen were far from the kind we have now. The earliest peas were as large as marbles and probably as tasty. Archeologists believe that they were always roasted and peeled (like chestnuts) before they were eaten.

Uncultivated peas grew in bogs and rambled rather than climbed, which made picking them a considerable chore. But they must have been worth the trouble for in time they were planted and tended as crops.

From Switzerland to India is no short distance, but pea seeds somehow migrated there and flourished in the cool climate of India's Himachal Pradesh. However, the cultivated peas that were eaten in India and later in Greece and Rome were dried and involved lengthy cooking.

For centuries a tender pea, straight from its green pod, was regarded to be a near-lethal pellet and was dried to cure it of its "noxious and stomach-destroying canker." Farmers in Rome often left green peas on the vine in their fields to supposedly kill foraging rabbits. The rabbits had better sense than the farmers and flourished instead.

Dried peas in Roman times were a household staple that was cooked for hours until it became a thick gruel. It was splashed with olive oil and vinegar and eaten for breakfast. This brings to mind "Pease porridge," which according to the old English nursery rhyme, stayed in the pot until nine days old. That recipe was a staple of western Europe in one form or another for more than five hundred years.

It was a French gardener named Michaux, who convinced the world that green peas were not only edible, but were delectable. In the sixteenth century he developed a hybrid pod that climbed on trellises and grew sweeter and more tender with each foot of elevation.

These legumes, at first known as "miches" (small lumps) in honor of their developer, eventually received a more generic name, "vert pois" (green or garden peas), and became the rage in France, especially with the nobility.

In one of her letters, dated 1696, Madame de Maintenon warmed to the subject of the pea at the court of Louis XIV. "The impatience to eat them, the pleasure of having eaten them, the joy of eating them again, are the three questions that have occupied our princes for the last four days!" Peas were an important matter of state.

A keen observer of the pea's effect on court life, the Madame also wrote" There are ladies here, who having supped with the King and supped well, retire to the privacy of their chambers; there to feast in secret on dishes of petits pois." She concluded that this was both a fashion and a madness. Pea-preoccupation did not abate until the French Revolution when this vegetable became part of the diet of the common man.

It is not clear when peas were first grown and eaten in England. Most food historians say that some pea varieties were imported during the reign of Henry VIII in the early 1500s. During the reign of Elizabeth I peas were brought to England from Holland. They were regarded as great treats by women because they came from so far away and cost so much.

According to Pierre Martyr, a French historian, the first peas in the New World were planted by Christopher Columbus in 1493. The new vegetable was enthusiastically accepted by the Indians and they were growing them in Florida by1602. The Spaniards found peas growing in New Mexico in 1540, attesting to the fact that peas must have traveled from Florida or Mexico with migrating Indians.

Jacpues Cartier's report that Indians were growing peas in 1535 where Montreal now stands seems unlikely. Cartier's description better fits beans, which were unknown in Europe at the time. However, by the early 1600s peas were being grown in Virginia and New England. "A store of green peas . . . as good as ever I eat in England," reported the Reverend Francis Higginson of the Plymouth Colony in 1629.

Thomas Jefferson and James Monroe annually had a friendly contest to determine whose garden peas were the first to ripen. At that time "a mess" of tender young peas was a sure sign that summer had arrived. Living in close proximity the two statesmen not only discussed politics, but also the state of their gardens. At one time Thomas Jefferson had thirty varieties of peas in his garden as it was his favorite vegetable.

The fresh mint and sour cream mixture in this Green Pea Salad provide an interesting flavor combination that is an excellent complement to grilled salmon or other grilled fish. If jicama is unavailable, canned sliced water chestnuts may be substituted.

Green Pea Salad

2 pounds fresh green peas, shelled
1 medium jicama, peeled and chopped
  (about 3/4 cup)
1/4 cup chopped red pepper
2/3 cup toasted pine nuts
1 garlic clove, finely chopped
1/4 cup fresh mint leaves
Pinch of Cayenne pepper
1/4 teaspoon salt
3/4 cup sour cream
1/3 cup mayonnaise

Blanch the peas in boiling water for 4 to 5 minutes. Rinse under cold water and drain. Place in a bowl with the chopped jicama, red pepper, and the toasted pine nuts.

In the bowl of a food processor place the garlic, mint leaves, cayenne pepper, salt, sour cream, and mayonnaise. Pulse on and off until the ingredients are well blended. Add the dressing to the vegetables and toss. Serve on lettuce leaves. Serves 6.

Peppers

Red, Green, Orange Yellow, Purple

All vegetable peppers, sweet and hot alike, are members of the Capsicum family. Sweet peppers are often referred to as "bells" by virtue of their shape. The hot peppers are known as chili peppers, or chilies, and grow in a multitude of sizes and shapes, from long and skinny to conical and round. They have varying degrees of hotness. (see, chilies in Spice Section)

Red bell peppers are not hotter than green ones, merely riper. Bell peppers turn a little sweeter as they ripen. They require more care as they are growing, thus they are more expensive than green peppers. Sweet yellow, orange, and purple peppers are also available.

Christopher Columbus sighted green and red peppers growing on the vine almost immediately after landing in the West Indies in 1492. Once Columbus had sampled cooked peppers in dishes that the local Indians offered him, his eyes and tongue confirmed that he had found what he thought were the berries of Piper Nigrum, the seasoning we know as black pepper. Unfortunately this was not true.

On the return voyage to Spain, Columbus loaded the hold of his ship with peppers for he felt that the Europeans would love this new vegetable — hot or sweet. Although new for Europeans, peppers had been cultivated in Central and South America by the Incas for more than three thousand years.

Upon reaching Europe the red and green vegetables were named "Spanish Peppers" and their popularity spread along the Mediterranean coast. In Spain and Italy sweet peppers became an integral part of the cuisine.

Polenta Stuffed Peppers add an Italian touch to roasted or grilled meats. Use green, red, orange, and yellow peppers for this dish.

Polenta Stuffed Peppers

5 bell peppers, mixed colors
1 medium onion, chopped
1/2 cup chopped mushrooms
2 tablespoons olive oil
1/2 cup basil leaves, chopped
1/2 cup parsley leaves, chopped
2 1/3 cups milk
2 1/3 cups water
1 1/3 cups cornmeal
2 large eggs
8 tablespoons grated Parmesan cheese
Salt and pepper, to taste
1 cup chicken broth

Cut the peppers in half lengthwise and remove seeds and membranes. Chop 2 of the halves and combine with the onions and mushrooms. Heat the olive oil in a skillet over medium heat; add chopped pepper mixture and sauté for 3 minutes. Combine the basil and parsley and set aside.

In a saucepan heat the milk and water to barely boiling. Lower heat to medium and add the cornmeal in a slow stream, stirring constantly. Continue to cook over low heat until the mixture is thick and begins to pull away from the sides of the pan. Remove from the heat and blend in the eggs, one at a time. Then add the pepper mixture, half of the basil mixture, 5 tablespoons of the Parmesan cheese, and salt and pepper, to taste.

Stuff the pepper halves with the polenta mixture and place them in a flat oven proof dish. Pour the chicken broth around the peppers. Sprinkle the remaining 3 tablespoons of Parmesan cheese and remaining herbs over the pepper halves. Bake in a preheated 375° F. oven for 45 minutes. Serves 6 to 8.

Potatoes

Staple of the Incas

The potato, originated in South America, goes back many, many centuries. Before 6000 B.C. nomadic Indians collected wild potatoes high on the central Andean plateau, that centers around the ancient city of Cuzco in Peru. During the next millennia the Indians were no longer nomadic and settled on the plateau. They developed a potato agriculture, making the tuber a staple of the great Inca civilization that in the sixteenth century covered 2,600 miles of western South America.

Today potatoes are still being cultivated on this 12,000 feet high, plateau in the Andes. Andean farmers raise as many as three thousand of the five thousand potato varieties, embracing all eight species. Each of the species has its own name and characteristics. For example, Quechua, a long flat potato is called mishipasinghan, meaning cat's nose. A knobby, hard-to-prepare potato is called lumchipamundana, meaning a potato that makes a bride weep. Not only do potatoes have numerous shapes but also a variety of colors in addition to the familiar yellow and gold — red, purple, black, and brown.

After conquering the Incas, the Spaniards took the potato to Europe at the beginning of the sixteenth century. They adopted the Inca name for the potato -"papa" - and historians say that this name was later combined with the Caribbean name for sweet potato - "batata" - hence the name potato. Columbus only encountered sweet potatoes on his various journeys to the Caribbean.

When the potato first arrived in Europe it was considered to be unfit for human consumption. Potatoes were fed to the hogs. During times of famine in Europe, particularly in England and Ireland, people decided that if potatoes made the hogs fat, they, too, could eat them. Potatoes became a mainstay of the Irish diet.

The white potato took a century and a half and two ocean crossings to get from its native South America to North America. In 1719 Irish immigrants settled in Londonderry, New Hampshire, bringing the potato with them from Ireland. That is why it is called the Irish potato, even though it originally came from South America. In the middle of the 1800s thousands of Irish immigrated to the United States because of the potato famine in Ireland.

The first commercial growing of potatoes in North America occurred in 1762 in a field crop in Salem, Massachusetts. The following year potatoes grown in the Connecticut Valley were exported to West Indian planters, who wanted the cheapest possible food for their slaves.

The first potato grower in Idaho was Henry Harmon Spalding, a Presbyterian missionary. He planted potatoes in 1836 to teach the Nez Percé Indians how to provide food for themselves other than by hunting. Homesteaders grew potatoes to sell to the miners who came through the state.

The Mormons, however, were the first to grow potatoes commercially in the West. They had been sent by the church to colonize a location north of the Salt Lake Valley, which turned out to be just across the state line in what is now Idaho. In the summer of 1860, these farmers had raised thirty-three bushels of potatoes. By the time Idaho was admitted to the Union in 1890, its main crop was potatoes which had become famous for their superior quality.

In 1872 Luther Burbank, the great horticulturist, developed and perfected a long white potato with a rough russet skin known today as the Idaho potato. Adapted to the Northwest, the Russet Burbank has made Idaho the leading potato producer in the nation. The Idaho Potato Board calls the Russet Burbank potato the "Tiffany of Tubers." Because of its low moisture content, this potato can easily be stored for long periods of time.

Two people who contributed greatly to the commercialization of the Idaho potato are Joe Marshall and J. R. Simplot. Marshall was successful in convincing the Union Pacific Railroad to provide suitable rail cars, enabling the Idaho potato to be marketed in the Midwest and the East.

Simplot developed dehydrated potatoes and sold them to the government for the troops in World War II. An employee of Simplot's, Ray Dunlap, invented the frozen French Fry. Today Simplot's companies supply McDonald's with more than fifty percent of their frozen French fries. Simplot's companies use more than a billion pounds of potatoes annually.

I am very fond of the Yukon Gold potato, a fairly recent addition to the produce section of our markets. It has more flavor and is excellent for mashed potatoes and in any sautéed or fried potato dish, such as the following Rosemary Potato Pie. The dish resembles a pie in shape but is actually fried potatoes with a wonderful rosemary flavor.

Rosemary Potato Pie

2 pounds Yukon Gold potatoes
6 tablespoons butter
1 1/2 teaspoons chopped fresh rosemary
* leaves*
3/4 teaspoon dried thyme
Salt and freshly ground black pepper,
* to taste*

Peel the potatoes and slice them very thin. Drop the slices into cold water as they are being peeled to prevent them from discoloring. When all are sliced, drain and pat the potatoes dry.

Melt 2 tablespoons of the butter in a 10-inch non stick skillet. Swirl the butter to coat the surface. then remove the skillet from the heat. Arrange one third of the potato slices in the skillet so that the bottom is covered.

Cut the remaining butter into three sections and cut each into small pieces. Sprinkle the butter over the potatoes. Then sprinkle the potatoes with 1/2 teaspoon of the rosemary and 1/4 teaspoon of the thyme, and salt and pepper. Repeat, making 2 more layers of potatoes, butter, and seasonings. Press each layer down with a spatula.

Place the skillet over medium-low heat and cook until the bottom is crisp and golden brown, about 35 to 40 minutes. Then invert the potatoes onto a flat plate and slip them back into the skillet. Continue cooking until the other side is golden, about 10 minutes. Place the potatoes on a serving plate, cut into wedges and serve immediately. Serves 6.

Pumpkins

Not Just for Halloween

For centuries before the Europeans came to the Americas, pumpkins were one of the staple foods of the native Indians. Food historians believe that this vegetable, a member of the squash family, probably originated in Central America. By the 1500s pumpkins and other squashes were cultivated by the Indians from South America to North America. However, the earliest Indians (1000 - 300 B.C.,) who were nomads, dried the pumpkin seeds and used them for food since they were easy to carry.

As the Indians settled into villages they cultivated pumpkins and other squashes. Food historians say that squashes were the first of the Indian triad — corn, beans, and squash — to be cultivated. The Indians boiled or baked their pumpkins. They baked a whole pumpkin by placing it in the ashes or embers of a dying fire. The flesh of the pumpkin was then moistened with animal fat, maple syrup, or honey before eating.

The Indians also dried pumpkins by cutting them into rings and hanging the rings up to dry. This gave them a vegetable to use in the winter months. Dried pumpkin was also ground into meal and used the same as cornmeal to make breads and puddings.

The first pumpkins known to Europeans were discovered in about 1540 when some of the scouts of Spanish explorer, Francisco Vasquez de Coronado, reported that melons(probably pumpkins) were growing in what is today the Southwest. In 1584 Jacques Cartier, the French explorer, reported that he had found big melons (squashes) in the St. Lawrence region (upper New York state). The French word "gros melons," however, was translated as pompions (pumpkins).

In seventeenth century New England, ripe pumpkins were sliced, then diced and put into a two or three gallon iron pot to be stewed in the fireplace for most of the day. Periodically more pieces of pumpkin were added to the pot as its contents boiled down. After cooking all day the mixture had the consistency of applesauce. A little butter, vinegar, and ginger, if available, were added to the mix. This pumpkin puree was served as an accompaniment to fish or meat.

Some of this pumpkin puree was also used by the settlers for pumpkin pies — strictly an American invention. While the English had long been making pastry for meat and fruit pies and the Indians had been stewing pumpkins, it was the New England colonists who combined the pastry and pumpkin for an entirely different dish. The first pumpkin pie is reported to have been served at the third Thanksgiving meal celebrated by the Pilgrims.

To the mashed stewed pumpkin, the settlers added milk, eggs, spices, and molasses. The mixture was them poured into a pastry shell and baked until the filling was firm but creamy, and the pie crust crisp and golden. In preparing the pumpkin pie filling the New Englanders were following a basic English custard pie recipe of milk, eggs, and sugar. Lacking sugar, however, they used molasses. Molasses became such an important ingredient in pumpkin pies that on several occasions, New England towns put off their Thanksgiving celebration for a week or more while awaiting a shipment of molasses from the West Indies.

In the first genuine American cookbook entitled "American Cookery" by Amelia Simmons published in 1796 there was a recipe for "pompkin pie." Although the book was very small, only 46 pages, it did contain recipes for most of the American culinary inventions to that date.

In the mountainous regions of the East dried pumpkin was used as a substitute for molasses since pumpkin meat is naturally sweet. As the settlers moved westward they took with them seeds for potatoes, beans, cabbage, squash and pumpkins.

Today pumpkins are associated with fall, Halloween and pumpkin growing contests. Recently a pumpkin weighing just over five hundred pounds, which was grown in Nova Scotia, won the contest.

My pumpkin pie recipe includes some sour cream in the filling to cut the richness of the pumpkin flavor and some walnuts to provide some contrast.

Pumpkin Pie

Filling

1 3/4 cups canned pumpkin
3 eggs
1 1/2 teaspoon ground ginger
1 teaspoon nutmeg
1 teaspoon cinnamon
1/3 cup molasses
1 tablespoon light brown sugar
1/2 cup whipping cream
1 cup sour cream
3/4 cup small walnut pieces
Pastry for single crust pie (recipe follows)

Mix the pumpkin, eggs, ginger, nutmeg, and cinnamon into a smooth texture in a medium-size bowl. Add the molasses, sugar, whipping cream, and sour cream and blend well.

Roll out the pastry dough to fit a 9-inch pie pan. Fit the dough into the pan and flute the edges. Pour the pumpkin filling into the pie shell and bake in a preheated 350° F. oven for 50 to 55 minutes or until the filling is set and a knife inserted toward the center comes out clean. Cool before serving. Serves 8.

Pastry

1 cup all-purpose flour
3 tablespoons butter or margarine
2 tablespoons solid vegetable shortening
3 to 4 tablespoons ice water

Place the flour in a bowl and cut in the butter until the mixture resembles coarse crumbs. Add the water, a tablespoon at a time, and stir with a fork until the dough can be formed into a ball. Wrap the dough in plastic wrap and chill for at least 1 hour.

Radishes

With or Without Pod

Radishes are members of the mustard family. They have to be harvested young. An old radish is worthless as its pulp is woody and frequently develops a hollow center. Also after a radish has passed its peak, it grows a pod to cover the bulb.

In the mid-1800s many cookbooks contained recipes for cooking these pods, and for cooking the green tops of the radishes. Now there is a special variety of radish that is grown primarily in India for its pod. The pod is cooked and the slender root of this particular radish is discarded. In India and Spain the green radish leaves are either cooked like greens or eaten raw in a salad.

Radishes are one of the world's oldest vegetables having been cultivated in Europe as early as Neolithic times. The origin of the radish is uncertain, because its wild ancestor has long disappeared. Some botanists say that the radish was a troublesome weed in the Mediterranean area, others say that the ancestor of today's radishes are Spanish in origin.

Most scientists, however, agree that the radish probably originated in the Far East, most likely in China. The oldest reference to radishes comes from a Chinese writing in 1100 B. C. Chinese art often depicted the radish, particularly in paintings on porcelain. Today radishes are still used extensively in Chinese and Japanese cooking.

Although the ancient Egyptians cultivated radishes mainly for its oil, they also ate them. This was before the Egyptians cultivated olives. Early Egyptians paintings depict radishes, onions, and leeks as the foods that supplied energy to the workers building the pyramids. It must have been the leeks and onions that provided the energy as radishes are touted today by weight-conscious people as a vegetable containing little nourishment.

The Roman nobility complained that farmers were growing less grain in order to raise radishes in great quantities for their highly profitable and flavorful oil. In China a special variety of radish is still cultivated today for its seeds and oil.

In most countries radishes are raised for their roots. In this country the red or red and white variety, which may be a sphere, an oblong, or a cone are the most popular. Radish eating is usually confined to pre-meal munching, or they are sliced to add spiciness to salads. Today they are regarded as an appetite stimulant. Earlier in this century radishes were served in a salad of their own, or in France they were cooked in the same manner as turnips. The very pungent seeds of the wild radish can be used as a substitute for mustard seeds.

It is strange that the red root radish variety has remained the only type used in most Western civilizations today. Most of the other varieties have remained popular primarily in the Far East and Eastern European countries.

Until recently daikon, the Oriental radish, was only available in Oriental markets, but now is often found in supermarkets. Daikon is a white radish. It is relatively mild and juicy-crisp, ranging in weight from one to two pounds. In the Far East it is served raw or cooked with the main meal.

Grated daikon, formed into a pretty heap, is the traditional accompaniment to Japanese raw fish dishes, such as sashimi. It is also served with broiled fish. Mixed with lemon juice or vinegar, grated daikon is a traditional Japanese dressing for vegetables, poultry, and seafood. Very large daikon are also carved by Japanese chefs into flowers and ornamental fantasies to accompany special meals.

In many Far Eastern countries the daikon is pickled . Stir-fried daikon slices or strips are turnip-like in sweetness, but milder. In the Orient chunks of daikon are added to stews to season and add some sweetness. Daikon cooks very quickly and thus should be added to a stew near the end of the cooking time.

Shredded, salted, drained, and rinsed daikon is the filling for breads and pastries in India and China. Shredded daikon combined with rice flour, fish, pork, mushrooms and sausage are the ingredients of the famous Chinese savory steamed pudding, called Lo Baak Go.

Black radishes, along with pickled mushrooms, sausage, beet salad, herring and onions, sturgeon, caviar, black bread, and vodka, are essentials of the Russian Zakuski. The Zakuski is similar to our appetizers and was originally served in the homes of the Russian nobility at the time of the Czars as a welcome to guests. For the Zakuski black radishes were often grated and mixed with thick sour cream and chives or scallions. Today the finer restaurants in Moscow and St. Petersburg feature Zakuski as one of the courses on their menus.

In most countries black radishes are served as an appetizer, as in the Russian Zakuski. A traditional Jewish preparation of black radish is as a condiment (like a chutney) eaten with meat. The black radish is shredded and cooked with sugar and honey until transparent, then mixed with ground ginger and almonds.

Black radishes are the shape and size of turnips, with a black skin and white interior. They are not to be confused with the thick elongated, black-skinned horseradish, which is also a member of the mustard family, as is the Japanese green horseradish, wasabi.

Black radishes are a cold climate favorite, originally grown for winter storage. They keep almost indefinitely when stored in a cool place and they do not become pithy or sprout.

This salad of daikon, zucchini, and red peppers is a colorful, sweet salad with a radish-like bite that can be served as a first course or to accompany meats.

Oriental Salad

2 small zucchini, scrubbed
1/2 pound slender daikon, scrubbed
1 small red pepper, cut into tiny dice
1/4 teaspoon salt
1/2 teaspoon sugar
2 tablespoon rice vinegar
2 tablespoons peanut oil
2 tablespoons Oriental sesame oil
Lettuce leaves, optional

Drop the zucchini into a large pot of boiling, salted water. Boil for about 4 minutes or until the pressure of your fingers leaves an indentation. Immediately drop the zucchini in ice water, cool. Drain and slice into thin slices.

Cut the daikon into thin rounds (halve lengthwise, if wide). Combine the daikon with the zucchini and red pepper in a serving dish.

Combine the salt, sugar, and vinegar. Add the peanut and sesame oils. Toss the dressing with the vegetables and chill until ready to serve. Serve on lettuce, if desired. Serves 4.

Rutabagas

Swedish Turnip

Rutabaga does not really have a long history and traditionally was considered peasant food in Europe . It is a crossbreed of cabbage and turnip. The first written mention of it was by a Swiss botanist named Jean Bauhin in 1620. He had experiment with the cabbage-turnip combinations and a giant sort of turnip with a large globular root was the result.

Nothing was heard from the rutabaga until a French botanist mentioned it in his writings in 1700. Whether the vegetable was grown in France for public consumption is not known. English records do show that rutabagas were planted in the royal garden in 1699.

Somewhere in this period rutabagas were planted in Sweden because the vegetable was also called "swedes." They were known as swedes in England because they had been brought from Sweden to the British Isles. Rutabagas are a cold weather vegetable and have become one of the staple crops of northern Europe, where they have helped nourish populations through wars and famine. The English, Scots, and Scotch-Irish were the first to bring them to this country.

Rutabagas were the subject of a bitter dispute that was aired in the New York newspapers in 1818. William Cobbett, the proprietor of a seed store in New York, claimed that he sold the best dollar-a-pound seeds in the city. Intended as a put-down of his competitor, Grant Thorburn, Cobbett claimed that he had introduced rutabaga to this country. Thorburn retaliated in the press by claiming he sold the best seeds for a dollar-a-pound and then proceeded to devastate his opponent with facts about rutabagas. Thorburn pointed out that in 1796 William Prout was already growing rutabagas commercially on a large piece of ground in Washington, D.C. (now occupied by the Navy Yard).

Although rutabaga may have declined in popularity over the years, it is usually available in the produce section of our markets. Most of our rutabagas come from Canada, with California taking up the slack during winter months.

Unless you get rutabagas directly from a farm, you will find that they have a wax coating. This is to prevent dehydration and shriveling. The wax coating is harmless and preserves the freshness even when stored in the refrigerator. It is peeled away with the skin.

There are several ways to prepare rutabaga. After peeling, it can be cut into chunks and placed around a roast instead of potatoes, or in combination with them. It can also be steamed and mashed with either potatoes or carrots, which gives the dish an additional flavor. Rutabaga adds a special flavor to vegetable soups.

Colcannon represents a spoonful of history because it relates to the origin of America's Scotch-Irish heritage. The recipe combines rutabaga, a vegetable known to the Scots, with potatoes which was a staple of the Irish. When the Scots immigrated to Ireland in the mid-1600s they combined the two vegetables in one dish and then brought the recipe to this country a century later.

Try rutabaga in the old-fashioned Scotch-Irish recipe, Colcannon, which I adapted for modern use. If you like you may sprinkle the top of the Colcannon just before baking with some paprika for color or with some grated Parmesan cheese for an added flavor.

The Rutabaga Casserole is a favorite of those of Scandinavian heritage and is often served at Christmas.

Colcannon

1 large baking potato, peeled and cut into
   large cubes
1 large rutabaga, peeled and cut into
   large cubes
1 1/2 cups finely shredded Savoy cabbage
4 tablespoons butter
2 tablespoons whipping cream
3 to 4 tablespoons milk
Salt and pepper, to taste
1/4 cup chopped red onion

Cook the potatoes and rutabagas in lightly salted water in a saucepan until tender, about 25 to 30 minutes. In the meantime blanch the cabbage in boiling water for about 4 minutes until crisp-tender. Drain the cabbage. When the potatoes and rutabagas are done, drain them thoroughly.

Mash the hot potatoes and rutabagas with 2 tablespoons of the butter and the cream and milk. Add more liquid, if necessary, to make a thick, smooth purée. Season with salt and pepper, to taste.

Melt 1 tablespoon of the remaining butter in a skillet over medium heat, add the onions and sauté until translucent. Then add the cabbage, and cook, stirring constantly, for a minute or two. Gently stir the cabbage mixture into the mashed potatoes and place in a 1 and 1/2 quart casserole. Dot the top with the remaining tablespoon of butter and bake in a preheated 350° F. oven for 15 minutes. Serve immediately. Serves 4.

Rutabaga Casserole

2 rutabagas, about 2 pounds
1/4 cup (1/2 stick) butter
2 tablespoons brown sugar
1/2 teaspoon salt
1/4 teaspoon pepper
1/2 teaspoon ground allspice
2 eggs, separated
2 slices brown bread, crumbled
   into fine crumbs

Peel the rutabagas. Cut them into 2x3-inch cubes and place in a saucepan with water to cover. Bring to a boil, reduce heat, and simmer, covered, for 35 to 40 minutes or until tender.

Drain the rutabaga and place in a bowl with 2 tablespoons of the butter. Mash the rutabaga, blending it with the butter until smooth. Add the brown sugar, salt, pepper, and allspice.

Beat the egg whites until stiff; set aside. Beat the egg yolks until light. Stir the egg yolks into the rutabaga mixture, then gently fold in the egg whites. Transfer to a greased 11x9-inch oval gratin dish. Melt the remaining 2 tablespoons of butter and combine it with the bread crumbs. Sprinkle this over the rutabaga mixture. Bake in a preheated 350° F. oven for 1 hour. Serves 8.

Spinach

Popeye's Favorite

Thanks to the comic strip, Popeye, American children grew up believing that eating spinach would build up muscles of iron.

The first known reference to spinach was in an ancient legend of the Medes who inhabited Persia centuries ago. The Medes prescribed twelve washings for every leaf of spinach that went into a cooking pot. Eleven of these washings were in water and were meant to free the vegetable of its dark, earthly associations. The twelfth washing was in human tears. This was to season the spinach with God's wisdom.

Spinach originally grew wild near the desert lands of Dasht-e-Kavir and was transplanted to Persian gardens. There it was cultivated mainly to satisfy the appetites of the much-prized Persian cats. The absence of a proper Sanskrit name for spinach indicates that the first seeds were planted well after the death of Christ. In Persia (Turkey) it is still known as isfänäkh, meaning green hand.

According to food historians, the ancient Greeks and Romans were not familiar with spinach. However, in the sixth century spinach traveled east from Persia into China. The Chinese population liked it in soups. Spinach became known as "Persian herbs."

The Chinese raised spinach extensively along the outer fringes of their rice fields, where the soil is sandiest. In time this green vegetable was transported to India and Nepal, where it became known as "China flower."

The invading Moors introduced spinach to Spain in the twelfth century, along with beheadings, circumcisions, and several other so-called cultural events. Only spinach took root. Within a hundred years this green leaf was known all over Europe as "spanacha," or Spanish greens. It is not known whether the Cru-saders brought spinach to Europe from the Muslim world or whether it spread northward from Spain. Probably a little of both.

In 1351, spinach was on a list of vegetables recommended for monks on fast days. In England a book complied at the court of Richard II in 1390 titled, "The Forme of Cury," mentions spinach. Another English manuscript of 1440 relating to cookery states that the chief vegetables eaten in England at the time were cabbage, leeks, radishes, and spinach. In France spinach became popular a century later.

By the sixteenth century spinach had become a favorite Lenten food, because winter-sown seeds produced plants just right for eating by the time of Lent. Catherine de Medici, who was from Florence and married the French king Henry II, was so fond of spinach that to this day the description 'á la Florentine" identifies a French dish containing spinach.

It was not until the sixteenth century that smooth-leafed spinach came into existence. Olivier de Serres, a noted botanist, described this smooth-leaf spinach as being more delicate in taste and lighter in color.

Some food historians tell us that Columbus brought spinach to the New World. Others claim it was part of the Mayflower cargo. It really does not matter how spinach got here for it was unpopular with settlers and natives alike. A child's prayer of the Pilgrims asked for the Good Lord's protection from fire, famine, flood, and unclean foreign leaves — meaning mainly sandy spinach.

By the early 1800s three varieties of spinach were growing in American gardens, one of which was the smooth leaf variety. Thomas Jefferson grew several varieties of spinach at Monticello.

Today California grows fifty percent of all American spinach, although Zavala County in

Texas claims to be the "Spinach Capital of the World. Much of the packaged spinach in our stores comes from New Zealand, where a hybrid of the original spinach is grown. Its smooth leaves are very tender and flavorful.

In the following recipe for Pasta with Spinach-Gorgonzola Sauce the spinach compliments the sharp taste of the cheese. I often add toasted walnuts to the sauce.

Pithiviers, originally a dessert tart of puff pastry filled with almond cream, is a specialty of the town of Pithiviers, south of Paris. Filled with ham, spinach, and cheese, this version makes a delectable brunch entree that may be made ahead and served warm or cold.

Pasta with Spinach-Gorgonzola Sauce

2 tablespoons butter
4 ounces Gorgonzola cheese, crumbled
1 bunch fresh spinach (10 ounces), cooked, drained, and chopped into small pieces
1 beef bouillon cube, crumbled
1/4 cup dry white wine
1 garlic clove, minced
Freshly ground black pepper
1/2 to 3/4 cup whipping cream
Freshly grated Parmesan cheese, for garnish
8 ounces fettuccine or fusilli

In a 2-quart saucepan, melt the butter and cheese over low heat. Stir to blend. Add spinach, bouillon cube, and wine. Simmer about 5 minutes. Add the garlic and pepper. Gradually stir in the cream to form a soft, but not runny, sauce. Simmer 3 to 4 minutes.

Cook pasta in boiling water until just tender. Drain and place in a warm dish. Pour the sauce over the pasta and garnish with freshly grated Parmesan cheese. Serves 4 as a first course or 2 as a main course.

Pithiviers With Ham And Spinach

1 bunch spinach, cleaned and de-ribbed
1 1/2 cups cooked diced ham
4 ounces tangy goat cheese, crumbled
3 whole green onions, finely sliced
1/4 teaspoon freshly ground pepper
3 large eggs
1 package (17 ounces) frozen puff pastry sheets (2)

Steam spinach until tender. Cool and squeeze dry. There should be about 1 cup. Chop the spinach finely and combine it with the ham, cheese, onions, pepper, and 2 beaten eggs. Mix well.

Cut each pastry sheet into a circle (about 9 inches in diameter). Place 1 circle on a cookie sheet and spread the spinach filling evenly in the center, leaving an inch uncovered all around the edge. Beat the remaining egg and brush the uncovered part with some of the egg wash. Top with the second pastry circle and seal it all the way around. Using the blunt-sided tip of a knife, pull the pastry edge in about 1/2 inch at 1-inch intervals to create a scalloped edge all around. Brush the tart with beaten egg. Cut a 1/2-inch-round vent hole in the center and, using the point of a knife, make a pattern of spiral lines from the edges toward the center, cutting into the dough about 1/16 of an inch.

Refrigerate the tart for at least 2 hours. Bake in a preheated 375° F. oven for about 30 minutes, or until puffed and golden brown. Serves 6

Squash

One of the "Three Sisters"

The squash family of plants, including pumpkins and gourds, are thought to be native to America. However, records show that squashes were grown in the hanging gardens of Babylon and in Roman times. Among the first Roman recipes on record is one for squash soup. Some Roman dinners consisted entirely of different kinds of squash, with each having a different flavor.

The Indians of Peru grew squash more than two thousand years ago. It was a part of the Indian food triad, known as the "three sisters" — beans, corn and squash. These were the basis of their diet. As soon as European explorers reached the New World they began writing about the importance of squash in the native diet. Although there were similar vegetables to the squash in Europe, the American varieties were far superior. Several of these varieties — the yellow summer squashes, the butternut and the acorn squash — are native to America. The very name squash is Indian; a shortening of the Narragansett askutasquash.

Squash is an old native American food. Stems, rinds, and seeds found in the mountain caves of Mexico date squash to about 3000 B.C. Ancient Indian people called squash "the apple of God," as the seeds were believed to increase fertility when planted close together. Braves with large squash crops inevitably produced large families, which in turn led to larger crops.

The Indians usually baked squash whole in the embers of a fire while the colonists used the fireplace, flavoring the squash with honey, maple syrup, or animal fats.

Winter squashes grow slowly and are harvested late. They have tough skins which protect the flesh from the cold. Thus, unlike their summer cousins, they can be stored in a cool place for several months. This was an especially desirable feature in colonial times.

The majority of the winter squashes have deep yellow or orange flesh with a slightly sweet, nutty taste. Winter squashes must always be fully ripe when picked and, unlike summer squash, needs to be cooked to be enjoyed. The seeds may be toasted and used as snack food.

Yellow crookneck, patty pan, and zucchini are some of the summer varieties of squash, although they are available all year. Although summer squashes have different names they are very similar in flavor and are interchangeable in recipes.

The brown rice adds an interesting flavor to the mild squash in this Squash Quiche.

Squash Quiche

2 cups winter squash, peeled and cubed
1 cup cottage cheese
2 eggs
1/2 cup milk
1/4 teaspoon ground nutmeg
2 cups cooked brown rice
1/4 cup chopped walnuts

Place the squash with a small amount of water in a saucepan. Bring to a boil and cook over medium heat for about 10 minutes or until the squash is very tender. Drain it. In a food processor combine the cottage cheese and eggs, and process until smooth. Add the squash, milk and nutmeg and process until smooth.

Pat the cooked rice into the bottom of a greased 10x6x2-inch casserole. Pour squash mixture on top; bake in a preheated 350° F. oven for 40 to 45 minutes or until set. Let stand for 5 minutes, sprinkle with nuts. Then cut into squares and serve. Serves 8.

Sweet Potatoes

A Sweet Morning Glory

The sweet potato has absolutely no relation to the white potato. It belongs to the morning glory family. The only kinship the white and sweet potatoes have is the derivation of the word "potato," which is the European version of the Indian word for sweet potato, "batata."

Contrary to the belief of many that sweet potatoes and yams are not of the same species, they are related botanically. The word "yam" was first applied to sweet potatoes by the African slaves in the South. It was a corruption of their word "to eat." Southern whites, however, continued to call them sweet potatoes. In the 1930's a moist, orange-fleshed sweet potato from Puerto Rico was introduced into the South. It was marketed as a Louisiana yam in an effort to distinguish it from the somewhat mealier and drier commonplace sweet potato. True yams grow primarily in tropical climates.

Sweet potatoes are native to the Western Hemisphere and were extensively eaten long before the white man came. Archaeologists trace them back to Peru where their digs attest to the fact that these tubers were cultivated at least as early as 750 B.C. The Incas and Mayas of Central and South America grew several types of sweet potatoes. They even used them for dyes.

Christopher Columbus carefully documented the existence of a strange root vegetable that he was served three times a day. He reported that the Caribbean Indians used the pulp of this vegetable to make bread.

At the time the Indians subsisted on a diet of fish, coconut, and sweet potatoes. They boiled the sweet potatoes in a communal pot. Columbus's Spanish crewmen learned to enjoy this meal. Upon returning to Spain they praised the quality of the sweet potato, comparing its taste to a mingling of ripe oranges and roasted chestnuts.

Columbus brought sweet potato plants back to Spain, where the plants thrived in the mild climate. The Spaniards liked them much better than the white potato. In the following century cultivation of the sweet potato spread to Portugal and Italy. Until the middle of the last century sweet potato vines were popular house plants in Spain.

Henry VIII, who ruled England in the early 1500s, learned of the sweet potato from his first wife, Catherine of Aragon, who was Spanish. He liked the flavor of the tuber so much that he insisted that Spain export sweet potatoes to England, which they did with great reluctance.

Henry VIII adored the sweet potato and was noted for his ability to eat two dozen at one sitting. He also instructed his chefs to turn them into sweetened and very spicy pies. Henry's palate was so devoted to what he called "the Spanish potato" that after his divorce from Catherine of Aragon, he gave a prize of land and gold to the gardener who could grow them in Britain. The incentive proved worthwhile and by the mid-1500s sweet potatoes were blooming all over England. Even with their perfuse blooming, however, the vines did not produce any tubers due to the cool and often rainy British summers.

Eventually the sweet potato was carried to the Far East by explorers. The Spanish explorer, Balboa took sweet potatoes to the Philippines and later Portuguese voyagers, such as Magellan, transported the vines to India, China, and Malaysia. In the southern parts of Japan sweet potatoes are known as "Chinese potatoes," and in the north they are simply Japanese potatoes. Sweet potatoes have become an integral part of Japanese tempura. Slices of sweet potato are dipped in a very light batter and then deep fried.

In North America, DeSoto found sweet potatoes growing along the Mississippi in what is now Louisiana. Records show that sweet potatoes were cultivated in Jamestown in 1648, where their Indian name "batatas" was converted to "bastards." This name remained until the righteous members of the community had it purged and the plant became legitimate as the "Virginia potato," or simply as potato. It was not until almost a century later when the Irish introduced the white potato to New England that the word "sweet" was added to differentiate between the two potatoes. Sweet potatoes were a dietary staple during the Revolutionary War when other foods were in very short supply.

In the 1800s, sweet potatoes were baked or used in making puddings and pones. They were also fried, mashed, candied, boiled, or made into soufflés. "Possum and Sweets" was a popular dish. They were often paired with pork, particularly ham, creating a balance of salty and sweet flavors. In the South cooked sweet potatoes were traditionally mashed, mixed with sugar and some orange juice, then topped with marshmallows and baked in the oven.

Sweet Potatoes and corn are combined in this soup with a Southwestern flavor. The jalapeno pepper and oregano add just a touch of spice.

Sweet Potato Soup

2 tablespoons butter or margarine
1 medium onion, chopped
*1 1/2 pounds sweet potatoes peeled
    and cut into large cubes*
1/4 teaspoon pepper
*5 cups chicken broth (or half canned
    chicken broth and half water)*
1 3/4 cups fresh or canned corn kernels
1/3 cup chopped red bell pepper
*1 Jalapeno pepper, seeded and finely
    chopped*
*1 teaspoon chopped fresh oregano,
    or 1/2 teaspoon dried oregano*
Fresh cilantro leaves, for garnish

Melt the butter in a medium-size saucepan, add the onion and sauté the onion until limp, but not brown. Add the sweet potatoes, pepper, and chicken broth. Bring to a boil and cook, covered, over low heat for 25 to 30 minutes, or until the potatoes are tender.

Strain the soup and puree the solids in a food processor. (A hand-held blender may also be used to puree the solids in the saucepan.) Return the liquid and puree to the saucepan and add the corn, red pepper, Jalapeno pepper, and oregano. Bring to a slow boil and simmer 5 to 7 minutes until the corn is tender. Ladle into soup bowls and garnish with cilantro leaves. Serves 4

Tomatoes

Once the Size of Cherries

A little more than two hundred years ago the tomato was considered to be poisonous by Europeans and Americans. The tomato plant was used as an ornamental in the garden for its bright ball-like fruit. At that time some may have eaten the leaves and stems, which are toxic, and thus the fruit of the tomato plant got the reputation of being harmful. Today tomatoes are used in most of the world's cuisines.

The tomato originated in the lower Andes in what is today Peru. However, the Peruvian Indians (Incas), who were so apt at developing other foods, ignored cultivating the tomato. Archeology has provided no information on the tomato's early history, and food historians have speculated the Incas simply gathered and ate the wild fruit when it was in season.

The Incas probably did not cultivate the tomato because at the time it was very small, about the size of a large cherry. It was also very perishable, unlike most of the food plants they did cultivate, such as potatoes, corn, peppers, and squash. Over the years the tomato spread to Mexico, arriving there at about 2000 B. C.

The Spanish conquistadors brought tomato seeds from Mexico and Peru back to Spain. Tomato seeds were then taken to Naples from Spain, as Naples had come under Spanish rule in 1522.

From the Mediterranean region, the tomato plant traveled north into France, then Germany, and eventually England. The French called it "The Apple of Love," and the Germans "The Apple of Paradise. The English, however, while admiring the brilliant red color of the tomato, disclaimed it as a food because they continued to believe it was poisonous.

The first to use tomatoes in Europe where the Italians. They were tomato pioneers both in the kitchen and in the garden. The first cook to use tomatoes much as they are used today was Francesco Leonardi, who experimented with numerous tomato dishes between 1750 and 1780. He was also the chef of Catherine II of Russia. During this period Italian agronomists began experimenting with enlarging the size of tomatoes.

The French were not as enthusiastic as the Italians about tomatoes, although cooks in the south of the country used them. The northern French enthusiasm centered around the use of the tomato as an ornamental plant, primarily to cover outhouses and arbors. French seed catalogs of the mid-1700s listed it as an ornamental plant.

It was not until 1778 that the tomato plant was advertised in French seed catalogs as a food. It was the Empress Eugenie, the Spanish wife of Napoleon III, who introduced tomato dishes into France in the 1850s. However, the general public was not aware of the food qualities of the tomato until the 1900s.

The English also approached the tomato with depredation, using it at first only in ketchup and other sauces. The mixture of vinegar and spices with the tomato was regarded as a safety device against possible toxic effects. By 1836 the tomato sauce had become well known in England as Charles Dickens had one of his characters, Pickwick, mentioning "Chops and tomato sauce," in a letter.

The same English fear of tomatoes being poisonous carried over into the American colonies until the early nineteenth century. The War of 1812 brought the cooking of New Orleans to the attention of the rest of America. The Creoles in New Orleans were using tomatoes in their gumbos and jambalayas.

Thomas Jefferson was one of the first Americans to grow tomatoes. Records show that tomatoes were used in the White House during his presidency. They could be purchased at various Washington markets and had a surprisingly long season, from mid-July to mid November.

In the United States, as elsewhere, the tomato, because of its perishability, was grown in home gardens long before it was cultivated commercially. Louisiana was the first region to develop this vegetable for stews and sauces, but it was still not eaten raw. By 1835, due to improved transportation, the northern markets were selling tomatoes during the summer months. Within thirty years they were offered all year around.

More than a half a century later, during World War I, farm clubs for boys and girls encouraged growing more healthy foods. They concentrated on the tomato. In 1929 the Bureau of Home Economics promoted an ideal diet which included eating fifty-five pounds of tomatoes annually per person. Consciousness of the importance of vitamins and minerals had raised this tomato recommended consumption from thirty-six pounds annually.

The Supreme Court even became involved in the tomato. Botanically it is a fruit, but legally it is a vegetable. The Court ruled in 1893 that it was used like a vegetable, thus it must be considered one.

When we think of the tomato today, a large red round fruit comes to mind. Until 1830, however, the tomato was deeply ribbed and ready to be separated into triangular segments, like an orange. At the time this was the best tomatoes that the Italians had bred from the small yellow fruit of Peruvian origin. This type of tomato is rarely grown now.

Now most tomatoes are variations of one species, with the only true tomato being the yellow cherry tomato which is still grown from seeds. Since World War II American botanist have experimented with producing larger more hardy tomatoes that would be less perishable in shipping.

Spaghetti á la Naples has been a favorite in that city for centuries. The mashed anchovies and crushed hot pepper flakes give this sauce a piquant taste, typical of southern Italy.

Spaghetti á la Naples

1/3 cup olive oil
2 tablespoons butter
2 cloves garlic, crushed
1 (28-ounce) can diced tomatoes
1 tablespoon capers, rinsed
3/4 cup pitted, sliced black olives
1/4 teaspoon dried hot pepper flakes
1/2 teaspoon dried oregano
1/2 (small) can anchovies, rinsed, mashed
2 tablespoons chopped parsley
Salt, to taste
10 ounces spaghetti
Freshly grated Parmesan cheese

In a saucepan, heat the olive oil and butter. Add the garlic and sauté for 1 minute. Then add the tomatoes, capers, olives, hot pepper flakes, and oregano. Cook over medium heat 20 to 25 minutes. Add the mashed anchovies. Reduce heat to low and continue cooking for 10 more minutes. Add the parsley and salt to taste, if necessary.

While the sauce finishes cooking, cook the spaghetti in boiling, salted water until al dente. Drain and place in a warm bowl. Mix the pasta with 2/3 of the sauce. Spoon remaining sauce over the top. Serve with freshly grated Parmesan cheese. Serves 4.

Turnips and Kohlrabi

Purple-White and Green Bulbs

With skins of purple and white, the turnip as an attractive vegetable. While there are also yellow turnips, the white-purple combination is more prevalent. Unlike their cousins, the ugly rutabaga, turnips are easy to peel and slice. The two vegetables have a similar taste. Kohlrabi is much milder and sweeter. Unlike the turnip, which is a root, kohlrabi is a light green bulb that grows above the ground.

The turnip is probably the oldest vegetable known to mankind. Near Beijing in China there are some cave paintings that show prehistoric man eating raw turnips. Later cave paintings, after fire was discovered, show turnips being roasted with meat on flat stones. More recent cave paintings in France show turnips being boiled in clay pots.

As far back as the ancient Greeks and Romans the turnip has been primarily a food for the poor and for country folk. Apparently, however, the upper-class Romans did on occasion serve a type of mush made with turnips. The taste of the vegetable was probably not recognizable since the mush was liberally seasoned with cumin, rue (a woody herb), benzoin (a fragrant resin from trees), honey, and boiled grapes. All of this was blended with a little oil. The Romans also used turnips to throw at unpopular persons, indicating the low esteem they had for vegetable and target.

The turnip grows best in cooler climates and in the Middle Ages the turnip was one of the most common vegetables in Europe. Here, too, it was eaten mainly by the peasantry and the poor who seldom had access to meat. Lords and ladies ate game and would not think of partaking of such a lowly vegetable.

The Germans and Eastern Europeans ate turnips in considerable quantities. The French were not as enthusiastic about the turnip and preferred to mask their taste with leeks, when they were forced to eat them at all. The British acquired the turnip in the fifteenth century and learned to enjoy it baked or roasted They used the green tops raw in salads or cooked like spinach. In northern Italy in the sixteenth and seventeenth centuries, turnips were the third most important product after wine and wheat. In Europe, at that time, turnips were grown considerably larger than they are now, weighing as much as forty pounds each.

By the time the first settlers landed at Jamestown in 1607, turnips had been growing in North America for more than sixty years. Jacques Cartier, the French explorer had planted turnip seeds in Canada in 1540, during his third voyage to this continent. Later French Jesuit missionaries started raising turnips along the banks of the St. Lawrence River.

The Virginia colonists brought turnip seeds with them and the first crop was grown in 1609; the Massachusetts colony began growing them twenty years later. By the time of the Revolutionary War turnips were being grown in most of the thirteen colonies.

The Indians took to them almost immediately because turnips were far superior to the wild roots that had been an important part of their diet. They grew to depend on them to the point that when General John Sullivan wanted to punish the Indians, he destroyed a large field of turnips the Indians were growing near Geneva, New York. As the settlers moved west, they took turnips with them as fas as the Pacific Northwest. Along the way, local Indians adopted turnips. The Indian women on the Plains baked or roasted them whole in their skins, as they had done with other roots.

Turnips even found their way into the famous novel, "Gone with the Wind." When Sherman's troops burned Tara, Scarlett O'Hara went into the vegetable garden and exclaimed, "As long as we have turnips, we will never go hungry."

Kolhrabi originated in Asia and was brought to Europe by Attila the Hun in the fourth century. It flavored the stew pots of the Roman Empire, but fell out of favor after the collapse of the Empire. Kolhrabi grew in Charlemagne's garden, but was fed only to the cows, because it was said to cause fighting men to become docile. Today it is more prevalent in Europe than North America.

The Turnip Gratin combines the pungent taste of turnips with the aromatic taste of rosemary. The Turnips Paprika is my adaptation of Czechoslovakian dish. Kohlrabi may also be used.

Turnip Gratin

1 pound turnips, peeled, halved and very
  thinly sliced
2 tablespoons all-purpose flour
1/2 teaspoon crumbled, dried rosemary
1 cup freshly grated Parmesan cheese
Salt and pepper, to taste
3/4 cup whipping cream
2/3 cup chicken broth

Place the turnips in a saucepan, cover with water, bring to a boil and blanch for 1 minute. Drain the turnip slices thoroughly, then place them on a paper towel and blot dry.

In a buttered 11-inch oval gratin dish (or a 1 and 1/2-quart shallow baking dish) arrange one-third of the turnip slices in an even layer and sprinkle them with 1 tablespoon of the flour, 1/4 teaspoon of the rosemary, 1/3 cup

of the Parmesan cheese, salt and pepper, to taste. Arrange half of the remaining turnip slices over the Parmesan, sprinkle with the remaining tablespoon of flour, 1/4 teaspoon rosemary, 1/3 cup Parmesan cheese, and some salt and pepper. Then arrange the remaining turnip slices on top and sprinkle with salt and pepper.

Combine the whipping cream and the broth in a small saucepan, bring it barely to a boil, and pour the mixture over the turnips. Sprinkle the top with the remaining 1/3 cup Parmesan cheese. Cover the gratin with aluminum foil and bake in a preheated 375° F. oven for 15 minutes. Remove the foil and bake uncovered for another 10 minutes or until the gratin is golden brown and the turnips are tender. Serves 4.

Turnips Paprika

2 tablespoons butter or margarine
2 green onions, finely chopped
1 pound turnips, peeled and diced
6 tablespoons dry white wine or vermouth
1 1/2 teaspoons sugar
1 1/2 tablespoons sweet Hungarian paprika
1/3 cup whipping cream
Salt and pepper, to taste
Chopped fresh parsley

Melt the butter in a medium saucepan; add the turnips and onions; toss to combine. Mix together the wine, sugar, and paprika in a small bowl and pour the mixture over the turnips. Cook, covered, until the turnips are tender, about 15 minutes. Stir in the cream and cook, uncovered, until slightly thickened, about 5 minutes. Add salt and pepper, to taste and sprinkle with some chopped parsley. Serves 4.

Zucchini

Green Squash

At the end of summer many garden vegetables have stopped producing. Not so the zucchini. It will keep growing the slender green vegetable as long as the weather is favorable.

Zucchini is a member of the summer squash family and is called green squash in some areas. It, like all other squash, is American in origin, but was not the most popular of the varieties in the New World. The green squash, brought back to Europe by early explorers, first made a name for itself in Italy. Thus the rest of the world has come to regard Italian squash as zucchini.

The Italians christened the long, tender, green gourd "zucchini," which is a derivative of the word "sweetness." No one knows when zucchini went to Italy. Most historians credit an early Italian explorer of the Americas with bringing back seeds for the green squash and planting them in the Po Valley, where it has grown for more than three hundred years.

According to Italian legend, however, zucchini seeds were given by the gods to the inhabitants of Abruzzi (a region in eastern Italy). They were told to protect the zucchini seeds from non-Italians, which they did until Columbus brought the seeds back to America. Charming story, but not true.

When the Spanish explorers first came to the New World they wrote about the various types of squash they found here, and they also took seeds home. In most of Europe, however, squash did not become popular until the nineteenth century. In England squash became known as "vegetable marrow," and zucchini is still known by that name.

The Zucchini Frittata, a typically Italian dish, makes a tasty luncheon dish. It may also be cut into 2-inch squares and served as an hors d'oeuvres at room temperature. The Roasted Zucchini pairs well with grilled meats.

Zucchini Frittata

5 eggs
1/4 cup olive oil
1/4 cup all-purpose flour
1 teaspoon baking soda
1 teaspoon baking powder
1 cup grated Cheddar cheese
1/2 cup grated Parmesan cheese
1 medium onion, chopped
6 cups sliced zucchini

Grease and lightly flour a 9x13-inch baking dish. Mix all of the ingredients except the zucchini together in a bowl. Add the zucchini and pour the mixture into the prepared pan, spreading it evenly. Bake in preheated 350° F. oven for 25 minutes or until golden brown. Serve warm or at room temperature. Serves 6 to 8 for lunch or 12 to 16 as hors d'oeuvres.

Roasted Zucchini

3 medium zucchini
1/2 red pepper
1/2 yellow pepper
1 tablespoon soy sauce
1 tablespoon olive oil

Cut the zucchini and peppers into thin julienne strips. Spread the vegetables on a cookie sheet and bake in a preheated 400° F. oven for 7 to 8 minutes until crisp tender. Immediately place the zucchini mixture in a bowl, add the soy sauce and olive oil and very lightly toss. Serves 4.

Fruits

Fruits

Fruit has always sustained and delighted mankind, whether found in the wild or cultivated. Aside from the health-giving properties and its culinary versatility, fruit is the most ravishing product of nature. It delights the eye as well as our sense of smell and taste. Through the ages fruit has been an inspiration to painters and poets alike.

Fruits are the edible parts of flowering plants. The wide varieties of fruit are divided into four categories — berries, fruits of the orchard, fruits of the tropics, and fruits of the vine. Berries go back to ancient times when they were wild woodland fruits. No berry has a more dramatic history than the strawberry which, in ancient times, became associated with the goddess of love. Unsweetened fruits, such as tomatoes, beans, avocados, etc. are classified as vegetables.

Fruits of the orchard were first mentioned four thousand years ago when apple and pear trees grew in the orchards of the Hittites. Plums were first reported as being grown in the Middle East between the Tigris and Euphrates rivers. The damson plum has changed little since the height of Greek and Roman civilizations. Many of the orchard fruits, such as oranges, peaches and apricots, originated in the Far East.

Early Western explorers in the Pacific thought they had found Paradise when they encountered their first palm-fringed tropical island with its abundance of luscious fruit. A luxury to Western civilization these fruits were a necessity of life to tropical cultures. The coconut, for example, one of the most versatile of tropical fruits provides food and drink, as well as oil for cooking. The banana is one of the most important food crops of the world and provides an inexpensive staple food for millions.

Fruits of the vine include all types of melons and grapes. Melons have long been a favorite fruit of the French and Italians, who often serve slices of melon with ham as an appetizer. Grapes have also been a much-loved fruit since the dawn of history. Although wine has become the destiny of many grape varieties, there are many varieties that are prized as eating fruit. Many grapes are dried to preserve them and then used to flavor a wide variety of tasty dishes. We know them as raisins.

Apples

As Old as History

There are more than seventy-five hundred varieties of apples throughout the world, of which twenty-five hundred are available in the United States. The most common apple in American markets is the Red Delicious. Stately, beautiful, and dark red, it is the apple most people visualize when thinking of eating apples. The success of the Red Delicious is not based on its flavor, but on its ability to be shiped and stored well.

No one knows how long apples have been in existence. The Bible tells us it was in the Garden of Eden. Food historians do not know when or where the cultivated apple first made its appearance, whether it was in southern Europe or in Asia.

Food historians also say that man's great interest and love of apples began with the Romans, who discovered the art of grafting and budding fruit trees. They cultivated many varieties that originally came from the eastern half of the vast Roman Empire. The results of these "fruitful" experiments were spread throughout Europe as the Roman forces increased the boundaries of the Empire, moving northward until it reached its furthest outpost — England. With the fall of the Roman Empire people lost interest in fruit and vegetable cultivation during the Dark Ages.

In medieval times fruit cultivation again became firmly established and by the thirteenth century several varieties of apples had come into existence. The English were the most avid apple fans and propagated many new varieties.

The first English settlers in America brought apple seedlings with them. Every farm had at least one or two apple trees. These trees reminded them of the old country. By the beginning of the 1700s there were nearly a hundred varieties of apples growing in the colonies — from Georgia to New England.

No fruit was more important to pioneer life than the apple. A valuable addition to the pioneers' limited diet of pork and corn, apples could be used in many different ways—eaten fresh, cooked, dried, or fermented for cider, applejack, and vinegar.

One of the most devoted apple lovers became one of our most beloved folk heroes. He was John Chapman, better known as Johnny Appleseed, who left a trail of apple orchards throughout Ohio, Indiana, and Illinois. Born in Massachusetts in 1774, he was a vegetarian and a religious disciple of Emmanuel Swendenborg, a Swedish mystic and philosopher. Chapman spent forty years in the wilderness planting apple trees and preaching the Gospel. He is said to have gone barefoot most of the time, clad only in a rude coffee sack.

Chapman, carrying a spade and a burlap bag of apple seeds, began planting and pruning apple trees throughout the Ohio Valley at the age of twenty-seven. This strangely clothed visionary was seen wandering through the countryside planting apple orchards in whatever fertile areas he could find. On return trips to these areas, he tended and transplanted the young trees so that even the most primitive cabin had an orchard surrounding it.

He traveled alone, carrying his kitchen, an inverted saucepan, on his head. Chapman never married, hoping that for his life of celibacy he would be granted two wives in heaven. He preached that "fruit is next to religion."

Although apple trees are usually propagated by grafting, Johnny Appleseed denounced this method as sinful. He grew his trees only from seed, most of which he obtained from the waste of the cider presses in western Pennsylvania.

Two by-products of apples, apple cider and

apple butter, have been made since colonial times. Apple cider, including the fermented type known as hard cider, is still produced today — both for home use and commercially. Until the development of commercial canning, apple butter was only made and consumed locally on the farms.

In the late 1860s, Jesse Hiatt, a farmer in Madison County, Iowa, discovered an unknown apple seedling in his orchard and cut it down. The next year it came up again stronger than before, and Hiatt decided that if the tree was so determined to live, he would nurture it. When the tree began to bear, however, the apples did not resemble any other variety. They were strawberry-colored, streaked with dark red, and very sweet and flavorful.

For years Hiatt took samples of his mysterious apples, which he called Hawkeyes, to various horticultural shows. In 1893 Hiatt entered four Hawkeyes in a competition in Missouri, sponsored by Stark Nurseries. The apples won first prize, and Stark Nurseries negotiated the propagating rights for the trees. They renamed the apple Red Delicious.

The Golden delicious did not originate in France as many had thought, but was produced from a stray seedling found by A. H. Mullins in Clay County, West Virginia in 1890. It was introduced by Stark Nurseries in 1914.

Ground almonds are used in this tart dough which is the base for thinly sliced tart apples. Serve the tart with whipped cream.

Upside-Down Apple Tart

8 tablespoons (1 stick) butter or margarine
1 1/4 cups all-purpose flour
2 teaspoons sugar
1/2 cup ground almonds

1 egg yolk
3 tablespoons ice water

Cut the butter into the flour in a bowl until the mixture resembles fine crumbs. Stir in the almonds and sugar. Combine the egg yolk and water and slowly stir into the flour mixture with a fork. Stir well to combine. Shape the dough into a ball and place between 2 large sheets of plastic wrap. With a rolling pin, roll the dough 1 inch larger than a 9-inch round cake pan. Place the dough in the refrigerator to chill for 20 minutes, while preparing the apples.

Apple Topping

3 tablespoons butter or margarine
1/4 cup sugar
5 large tart apples, peeled, cored and sliced
  very thin
1/2 teaspoon cinnamon
1/2 teaspoon nutmeg

Place the butter and sugar in a 9-inch round cake pan and melt the mixture over low heat. Continue cooking, stirring constantly with a wooden spoon, until the mixture is a light golden brown. Remove from heat, cool slightly, and add the apple slices, making sure that the top is reasonably flat. Sprinkle the apples with the cinnamon and nutmeg.

Unwrap the pastry and fit it over the apples, tucking the edges under the crust. Bake in a preheated 400° F. oven for 30 to 35 minutes, or until the crust is lightly browned.

After removing the tart from the oven, immediately turn it upside down on a serving plate. Leave the pan on the tart for a few minutes to let all of the juice permeate the crust. Serve warm or cool. Serves 8.

Apricots

A Mulit-Cultural Fruit

The Chinese are reported to have first cultivated apricots before 2000 B.C. From there the fruit was transported westward by silk dealers, reaching Persia by the first century B.C. and Greece and Rome soon after. With the fall of the Roman Empire the cultivation of apricots ceased, until the Crusaders re-imported them from the Middle East. In the ninth century, however, the Moors brought apricot seedlings to Spain.

The apricot is a member of the rose family and is mainly grown in warm temperate parts of the world. It needs a fairly cold winter and moderate high temperatures in spring and early summer to survive.

Although the apricot was known in France in the fifteenth century, it did not arrive in England until King Henry VIII's gardener brought it from Italy in 1542. Two hundred years later an English apricot species called Moor Park became famous in other European countries and is still grown today.

The Chinese, and later the Japanese, cultivated a species of apricot known in the West as Japanese flowering apricot, which is often mistaken for a plum. Small and sour, the Orientals salted and pickled it as a relish. Many Japanese believe that one should be eaten first thing in the morning to cleanse the system.

In China from the seventh century onward, apricots were preserved not only by drying, but also by salting and even smoking. The black smoked apricots were very famous.

In the Middle East apricots were pitted and stuffed with almonds as a confection. They also added a sweet flavor to cooked lamb.

The Mission Fathers brought apricots to California when they established the missions. Today the species brought by the Mission Fathers is regarded as the best eating variety. Only a small percentage is sold fresh as most of the fruit is dried.

My Frozen Apricot Soufflé, can be made several days ahead and frozen. The freezing process is similar to cooking in the elimination of any bacteria in uncooked eggs.

Frozen Apricot Pistachio Soufflé

1 1/2 cups finely chopped dried apricots
1/3 cup apricot brandy
1/4 cup brandy
2/3 cup water
1/2 teaspoon cinnamon
1 3/4 cups whipping cream
3 eggs separated
1/3 cup sugar
1/2 teaspoon vanilla extract
1 cup unsalted, shelled pisatchios, chopped

In a saucepan combine the apricots, brandies, water, and cinnamon. Cook over very low heat until the apricots are soft and most of the liquid has evaporated. Set aside and cool.

Whip the cream until stiff and place in refrigerator. Add half of the sugar to the egg yolks and beat until thick and lemon colored. Whip the egg whites until stiff, then add the remaining sugar and vanilla, beating until stiff.

Fold the egg yolk mixture into the whites, then gently fold the eggs and apricots into the whipped cream. Pile 1/3 of the mixture into a 4-cup soufflé dish. Sprinkle with 1/3 of the nuts. Repeat twice more, making 3 layers. Freeze, uncovered for 6 hours. Then wrap with plastic wrap and continue freezing until ready to serve. Remove the soufflé from the freezer and put in the refrigerator for 2 hours before serving, to soften. Serves 8.

Avocados

Ancient Fruit

Until the mid-1900s few people outside of the tropics and subtropics had seen, let alone tasted, an avocado.

Avocados have been cultivated for food for centuries. Their large seeds have been found in Mexican excavations dating back to the seventh century B.C. Some historians claim that avocados are native to Peru, others say Mexico.

There are two main types of avocados grown in the United States. The West Indian type or Fuerte, only grows in Florida. It is also known as the alligator pear. This avocado has a smooth , bright green skin. Mexican avocados, also known as Haas avocados are a specialty of California. The skin of this avocado is pebbly and ranges in color from dark green to almost black. The flesh of a ripe avocado is always a pale golden green with a buttery texture and a rich, slightly nutty flavor.

Depending on the variety, an avocado can weigh as little as three ounces and as much as four pounds. Like many fruits, avocados ripen best off the tree and are shipped unripe.

Avocados were brought to California by the Spanish. It was slow to become accepted as a food because it was rumored that the fruit was an aphrodisiac. Sales increased when the Avocado Association hired a public-relations firm to tout the avocado's nutritional properties and promoted it as a chic new addition to salads and other dishes.

For years avocado groves blanketed much of the coastal area of Southern California where the sandy soil and temperature moderated by the ocean favored their growth. Over-planting and flooding of the market, however, forced many growers to tear out their groves and turn to other agricultural crops.

Traditionally, the yellow-green flesh of the avocado is mashed and combined with spices for Guacamole. Avocados are also used in soups, salads, and many light entrees.

Mexican seasonings, cool crunchy lettuce, and avocado abound in this hearty salad.

Taco Salad

1 pound lean ground beef
1 medium onion, chopped
1 (8 ounce) can tomato sauce
3/4 cup water
1 teaspoon chili powder
1 1/2 teaspoons Mexican seasonings
1 (16 ounce) can kidney beans
1/2 head lettuce, torn into bite-size pieces
2 medium tomatoes, cut into chunks
1/2 medium green pepper, chopped
1/2 medium red pepper, chopped
1 (2.2 ounce) can sliced black olives
1 Haas avocado, cut into chunks
3/4 cup shredded sharp Cheddar cheese
3/4 cup shredded Monterey Jack cheese
1 cup broken chorn chips
Additioanl corn chips

Cook the beef and onions in a large skillet over medium-high heat until the meat is no longer pink. Drain any fat. Add the tomato sauce, water, chili powder, Mexican seasonings, and kidney beans. Stir well to combine and cook over low heat for 10 to 15 minutes until the sauce is smooth, stirring occasionally.

Gently combine the lettuce, green and red peppers, olives, and avocado in a large bowl. Spoon the sauce over the lettuce and toss. Top with the cheeses and then corn chips. Serve immediately and pass additional corn chips, if desired. Serves 4 to 6.

Bananas

Picked Green but Turn Yellow

What is morning cereal without a banana? According to the food experts more bananas are consumed daily than any other fruit.

Although we basically have one type of banana from which to choose, in the tropical regions there are countless varieties, similar to the varieties of apples and pears in this country. We occasionally see plantains in our markets, which are edible only when cooked.

The banana plant looks like a palm tree, but is not a tree at all. It is a perennial that grows a complete new "trunk" every year and dies back almost to its roots after it has flowered and fruited. Banana plants often grow to the height of 40 feet every year.

The "trunk" of the banana plant is composed of overlapping bases of leaves wrapped tightly to make a fairly rigid column. New leaves constantly emerge at the top.

Eventually the large flowering stem forms at the top. Bananas develop a short way back from the flowering tip of the stem causing the stem to bend over. The fruit is arranged in a double row of ten to twenty, which forms a half spiral around the stem. It is picked green and ripens on the way to market.

Bananas originated in Southeast Asia, the area that is today Malaysia and Indonesia. Grown in the wild this plant was known as the monkey banana and was used for food from the beginning of recorded human history.

At some time in the prehistoric era cultivation of the banana began and early man tried to grow bananas with the least amount of seeds. At some time the monkey banana plant was crossed with an inedible wild species, and the resulting hybrid was of superior edible quality without seeds.

The earliest record of banana cultivation occurred in India in the sixth century B.C. The banana became known to the Greeks in the fourth century when Alexander the Great encountered it in India.

The banana reportedly reached China about 200 A.D. By the T'ang dynasty (618 to 907) it was well established in southern China, but was considered a rare and exotic fruit in the north of China. The banana was still relatively unknown in northern China into the twentieth century as exemplified by the following incident which occurred during the nationalist wars of the 1930s:

The northern Manchurian warlord, Wu Chûnsheng, had been invited to attend a banquet in Peking. At the end of the meal, a bowl of fresh fruit was set in front of him. He selected a banana and ate it, peel and all. His host, wishing to offer a tactful hint, also took a banana and conspicuously peeled it before eating it. Wu, now well aware of his error but not wanting to lose face, took a second banana and said, "I always eat these things with the peel on," and proceeded to do it again.

By 1000 A.D. the banana had reached Africa, probably directly from the Malay region to Madagascar. By the end of the fourteenth century bananas were being cultivated throughout the continent of Africa. During this same period bananas were taken eastward from Southeast Asia to the Pacific Islands.

The Arabs spread banana cultivation throughout lands bordering the southern Mediterranean, but no further north than Egypt.

Because the climate in southern Europe is too cool for the banana plant, the fruit remained unknown to most Europeans. The first European contact with bananas came at the beginning of the 1400s when Portuguese sailors found them in West Africa and brought them to the Canary Islands. The Canaries have remained an important banana growing area.

In 1516 the Spanish missionary Friar Tomas de Berlanga took banana roots from the Canaries to the West Indies. Later he brought the banana to the American mainland. Other missionaries followed his example and banana plants quickly spread throughout Central America and northern parts of South America.

During the nineteenth century occasional small consignments of bananas were sent by fast ships from the Canaries to Europe and from Cuba to the United States. Early varieties of bananas did not keep well and had to arrive in less than two weeks, making them a luxury.

The international banana trade was started by two American entrepreneurs, Captain Lorenzo D. Baker and Minor C. Keith, who independently in 1870 and 1872 began to ship bananas from the Caribbean to New Orleans, Boston, and New York. They established plantations throughout Central America.

In 1899 Baker and Keith merged their interests to form the United Fruit Company. This organization had, and still has, great influence in Central America and the Caribbean Islands, for most of the trade of these lands depends on it. Thus the producing countries acquired the derogatory name "banana republics," while liberal politicians castigated the company for its allegedly repressive influence.

However, the United Fruit Company must be given credit for making the banana a familiar and inexpensive fruit in temperate lands. Other companies followed its lead. West Indian bananas began to appear in Europe. Once the Europeans had seen the handsome, big, yellow Caribbean bananas they lost interest in the small, brown ones from the Canaries.

One of my favorite entrees using bananas is this Sweet and Spicy Chicken Curry.

Sweet and Spicy Chicken

1 tablespoon butter or margarine
1 tablespoon vegetable oil
6 large chicken legs, skinned and cut into
    2 pieces each
3 onions peeled and diced
1 tablespoon all-purpose flour
2 tablespoons curry powder
1 teaspoon cumin powder
1/4 teaspoon cayenne pepper
1/2 teaspoon black pepper
1/2 teaspoon salt
2 garlic cloves, minced
1 cup chicken broth
1 Granny Smith apple, unpeeled and diced
1 banana, peeled and sliced
1 large tomato, cut into cubes
2 tablespoons shredded fresh mint
1/4 cup chopped peanuts

Heat the butter and oil in a large skillet over medium-high heat. Add the chicken and sauté until it is brown on all sides. Transfer the chicken to a another large skillet and discard all but 2 tablespoons of the accumulated fat.

Add the onions to the hot fat in the skillet and sauté for 2 to 3 minutes over medium heat. Then add the flour, curry powder, cumin powder, cayenne pepper, black pepper, salt, and garlic and mix well with the onions. Add the chicken broth, stir, and bring to a boil. Pour this mixture over the chicken.

Add the apple, banana, and tomato and bring to a boil over medium-high heat. Cover and reduce the heat, and simmer gently for 30 to 35 minutes or until the chicken is done. Sprinkle the mint and peanuts on top and serve immediately with steamed rice. Serves 6.

Berries

Delightful Morsels

Berries are not a recent addition to our cooking. Botanists' records show that in 5,000 B.C. Mesolithic peoples living in what now are Poland, Germany, Scandinavia, and England enjoyed a variety of berries. By 3,000 B.C. people had learned to supplement their diets, which consisted mostly of meat and grains, with wild raspberries, blackberries, strawberries, and elderberries. In Siberia, prehistoric peoples were storing berries in icy pits to ensure a fruit supply during the winter months.

Even after civilizations formed themselves into nations and were cultivating fruits and vegetables, they still relied only on wild berries. The only exception was the cultivation of black mulberries by the early Romans. Later the Romans brought mulberry seedlings with them when they conquered what is today England. Asians cultivated the white mulberry tree, the leaves of which became an important source of food for silk worms.

For centuries berries were regarded as a food supplement and as a medicine. Only the elite enjoyed them for the taste alone. While Henry III of England (reigned 1216-72) enjoyed drinks made with berries, the majority of berries were commonly used as coloring agents for meat stews, pigments for paints, or medicine to cure various ills including constipation.

Edward I who succeeded Henry (reigned 1272-1307) was the first to transplant strawberries and raspberries from the wild to the royal gardens. As a result the strawberry was one of the first berries to graduate from medicinal status to that of a food. Shortly thereafter gooseberries, blackberries, raspberries, and elderberries became part of the kitchen gardens of the nobility. The berries were usually planted along the garden walls where the vines could be espaliered.

Berries soon became fashionable and even the smallest English cottage had some berries growing in its garden. English cooks developed recipes for delicate berry puddings and tarts, and even used strawberry leaves to brighten salads.

Late in the seventeenth century strawberries became an important commercial product in England. The berries were sold in London markets by women who had migrated to the strawberry growing area just for the season. Many of these women came from the Shropshire region of England and came to be known as "Shropshire girls." They would leave the strawberry farms on the outskirts of London at dawn with baskets weighing as much as forty pounds on their heads and walk to London at a brisk pace in groups of twenty or more, arriving in London in time for morning sales. Along the way they shouted "Strawberries, scarlet strawberries," to advertise their wares.

By the eighteenth century berries were grown in local gardens all over Europe. In the next century many botanists worked on hybridization to develop better berries.

Although many of the colonial pioneers who settled America were city folk were unfamiliar with agriculture, they did recognize some of the wild berries growing in their new homeland. They found wild strawberries and raspberries, with which they were familiar. They also found wild blueberries, which were similar to the European bilberry (a smaller berry with a purple center). Even though the settlers may have been familiar with some of the native wild berries, it was the Native Americans who showed the settlers how to use them.

The Indians used the berries in many ways. They ate them both fresh and cooked. The

Iroquois so prized the wild blueberries that they ventured into poisonous-snake-infested areas to pick them. However, they would first smear their moccasins with hog fat to frighten away the vipers. The Indians also mixed various berries, particularly strawberries, with cornmeal to make a strawberry bread.

The most useful trick the Indians taught the colonists was how to dry berries for later use. The Native Americans commonly dried berries either over a fire or in the sun. They then added the dried berries, especially blueberries, to their breads, soups, and puddings. They also used dried berries to make pemmicans, a dried mixture of meat and fat. Berries were also used by the Indians for dyes.

Once the settlers knew how to use the berry plants, they harvested the woodlands and marshes and also began planting their gardens with berry plots. Both George Washington and Thomas Jefferson had extensive plantings of berries in their gardens.

From the beginning of the nineteenth century, hybridizing efforts improved the quality and size of American berries. The advent of commercial canning led to large farm cultivation of berries as they could now be preserved in large quantities. Railroad transportation also enabled farmers to ship their berries from the farm to distant cities. Commercial strawberry growing, in particular, became widespread during the 1840s and 1850s.

After the Gold Rush of 1849, people began pouring into California. They soon found rich agricultural land on the north and central coasts. Central California soon became the primary strawberry growing region of the United States, while the Pacific Northwest became known for its raspberries, blackberries, currants, and gooseberries. Blueberries are now grown commercially in Maine, Michigan, New Jersey, and North Carolina.

One of my favorite berry desserts is my Berries and Cream. A variety of fresh berries are served over a molded creamy dessert made with sour cream and either whipping cream or a thawed whipped topping, such as Cool Whip.

Berries and Cream

2/3 cup sugar
1 envelope unflavored gelatin
1 1/2 cups water
1 1/4 cups sour cream
1 1/2 teaspoons vanilla extract
1 cup whipping cream, or thawed
    dessert topping (such as Cool Whip)
1 cup blueberries
1 cup raspberries or blackberries
1 cup sliced strawberries

Mix the sugar and gelatin in a small saucepan. Add the water and stir over low heat to dissolve the sugar and gelatin. Remove from heat, pour into a bowl, and blend in the sour cream and vanilla. Chill until slightly thickened. Whip the cream until thick (or used thawed dessert topping) and fold it into the sour cream mixture. Pour into a 1-quart mold and chill until firm, about 3 hours. Unmold the cream onto a plate and pour the fresh fruit over it. Serves 4 to 6.

Blueberries

True Blue

Blueberries are a native North American fruit. The Indians used them long before the white settlers came. They pounded blueberries into the flesh of venison before smoke-drying the meat, thereby helping to cure the meat. The Indians also made blueberry tea from the roots, used blueberry syrup for coughs, and for dying clothing.

By the middle of the nineteenth century, blueberries were under cultivation in the woody swamp lands of Maine and New Hampshire, and in the cooler areas of other states where the soil is particularly acidic.

There are two varieties of blueberries — low bush and high bush. The commercial varieties of blueberries are called high-bush and are grown in Florida, North Carolina, New Jersey, and Michigan

The fresh low-bush variety do not travel well and are retailed only in local markets in Maine and New Hampshire. They are very tiny, have an intense flavor and are purple on the inside. Low-bush blueberries are primarily sold commercially to large bakeries and food processors for muffin and pancake mixes.

The harvesting of low-bush blueberries is very labor intensive since they must be picked by hand. During harvest in Maine, Micmac Indians are bused in from Nova Scotia to assist local people with the harvest of over 20 million pounds of "wild" blueberries every year.

Through hybridization, cultivated high-bush blueberries have become very large and grow on bushes four to five feet tall. It takes eight years for a hybrid blueberry bush to produce a substantial crop. It is then mechanically harvested several times during the growing season.

To preserve blueberries after purchase, store them in the refrigerator as soon as possible. Blueberries may be frozen in sealed plastic bags. Do not wash them until ready to use.

The following two recipe for Blueberry Tart is best when made with the larger cultivated variety. Fresh and baked blueberries are combined in this moist tart. Serve with whipped cream of vanilla ice cream, if desired.

Blueberry Tart

6 cups blueberries
1 cup plus 1 tablespoon all-purpose flour
5 tablespoons sugar
1/2 cup (1 stick) butter or margarine
1 tablespoon white wine vinegar
3 tablespoons ice water
1/8 teaspoon cinnamon

Rinse the blueberries and drain them.

Combine the 1 cup of flour and 2 of the tablespoons of sugar in a bowl. Cut in the butter or margarine until crumbly. Sprinkle the mixture with the vinegar and mix with a fork. Add 1 tablespoon of ice water at a time until a dough is formed and can be shaped into a ball. (1 or 2 more tablespoons of ice water may be needed.) Press the dough into the bottom and 1 inch up the sides of a 9-inch, ungreased springform pan.

Add 4 cups of blueberries to the dough-lined pan. Combine the 1 tablespoon of flour, the remaining 3 tablespoons of sugar, and the cinnamon and sprinkle evenly over the top of the blueberries. Bake in a preheated 400° F. oven for 45 to 50 minutes. Remove from the oven and immediately cover the filling with the remaining 2 cups of fresh blueberries. Cool the tart on a wire rack. Remove the rim and serve. Serves 8.

Cherries

Sweet and Sour

Food historians for centuries have claimed that cherries originated in Asia Minor, but today most writers believe that cherries got their start in northeastern Asia, then traveled West to Greece and Italy. They believe cherries arrived in North America via the Bering Strait from Asia.

Both sweet and sour cherries were cultivated in the Mediterranean area at the time of the ancient Romans and Greeks. By the first century A.D., the Roman historian, Pliny the Elder, recorded that eight varieties of cherries were under cultivation in Italy and that the fruit was grown as far away as Britain.

After the fall of the Roman Empire, the cultivation of cherries declined. The fruit was reintroduced into England in the early seventeenth century, at about the same time the colonists were taking this new fruit to New England. By 1640 two dozen varieties of cherries were being grown in England. Parallel developments had taken place in France and Italy, the two principal European countries cultivating cherries.

Distinct species of cherries were growing in America when the first settlers arrived. The first colonists found wild cherries and developed American cultivated varieties from them. They also brought European cultivated cherries with them.

Cherries can be designated sweet or sour. Sour in this case means more acid in the cherry. The sweet cherries, which include Bing and Royal Anne, are eating cherries. They are grown primarily along the Washington, Oregon, and California.

The United States is the leading cherry-producing country in the world. We grow more than one-third as much as all the western European countries combined. Traverse City, Michigan claims to be the cherry capital of the world, but so does Vignola, Italy. Cherries have grown in Vignola for at least 2000 years. Food experts tell us that the quality of cherries from Vignola is better, but Traverse City is ahead in quantity.

The cultivation of cherries in Michigan began when early French colonists brought cherry pits from Normandy and planted them along the St. Lawrence River and throughout the Great Lakes area. Today, Michigan grows more than seventy-five percent of all red tart cherries in the United States. Almost all of the cherry trees grow within a few miles of Lake Michigan. The cool spring air off the lake prevents the budding of the cherry trees until the danger of frost is past. The densest concentration of cherry trees in the world, 22,600 in every square mile, is found on the lake's eastern shore in the area near Traverse City.

Some of the cherry crop is naturally processed into dried cherries. A special drying process preserves the flavor of fresh, tart Montmorency cherries, originally a French variety, for use year-round. Eight pounds of fresh cherries produce one pound of dried cherries. Due to the low natural sugar content of this tart cherry, a small amount of sugar is added prior to dehydration to make preserving possible.

One of the special cherries is the black Morello. It is used for black cherry jam and in Germany for their Black Forest cake. Its pits are used to make the famous liqueur, Kirschwasser.

Maraschino cherries in syrup are prepared by pitting and bleaching the cherries, then adding syrup, bitter almond oil, and red or green coloring.

Cranberries

Thanksgiving Berry

The cranberry is one of the few native American fruits, along with the blueberry and some grape varieties. Long before the Pilgrims arrived, the Massachuset Indians combined crushed cranberries with dried deer meat and melted fat to make pemmican. When they cooked the berries they sweetened them with maple sugar or honey. Indian women used cranberry juice to dye their rugs and blankets.

The Indians believed that the cranberry had medicinal properties; cranberry tea was used to draw poison from arrow wounds. Later, American sailors ate cranberries to prevent scurvy while at sea.

The Cape Cod Nauset Indians called the little red berry ibimi or bitter berry. The Pilgrims called it cranberry, a contraction of "crane berry," since the little blossom resembled the head of a crane.

Cranberries will keep almost indefinitely because of their high acid content. They were the first American fruit shipped to Europe commercially. In 1677 Massachusetts sent King Charles II a handsome gift of ten barrels of cranberries, two barrels of cornmeal mush, and three thousand dried codfish. Along with this gift was sent the request that His Majesty's Massachusetts subjects be represented in Parliament and that there be relief from the restrictive trade laws. The gift was well received but there was no tax relief.

Early in the eighteenth century "Cape Cod bell cranberries" were being hawked in jars by vendors on the Strand in London. From England, the cranberry spread to the Continent. The French did not care for cranberries, but the Germans took to them, using them in a relish with apples and pears to accompany roasted meats and poultry.

Cranberry cultivation began in Massachusetts on Cape Cod in 1816, when Henry Hall, an early resident, found that the berries grew larger where the soil was covered with a layer of sand. He found that acidic peat soil, sand, and a fresh water supply were necessary requirements for cranberry growing. Most of the cranberry bogs in Massachusetts, therefore, are built on former peat swamps.

Retired sea captains took a special interest in the cranberry bogs, and some of them financed their acreage as they had financed their ships—by selling 64th interests in them. To this day there are cranberry bogs on Cape Cod that belong to many different owners, some of them heirs of the seafaring men who bought one or more "64ths" at the time the bogs were cleared and planted.

The growing of cranberries became commercialized on Cape Cod in about 1840, when granulated sugar became affordable so that the New England housewife could liberally use it to sweeten her tart cranberries. Although there are approximately one hundred different varieties of cranberries, only four—Early Black, Howes, Searles, and McFarlins—are now grown commercially.

Harvesting cranberries is a colorful process. Cranberry bogs are wet-harvested by mechanical water reels, also called "egg beaters." They stir up the water with sufficient force to dislodge the ripe berries from their vines. The berries float to the surface, forming a brilliant red mass. They are then guided to the shore, where conveyer belts transport the berries to waiting trucks.

In former days the cranberries were hand harvested with a shovel-like box that had prongs similar to a rake. In those days cranberries were mostly harvested by women. After mechanical harvesting of cranberries became the norm, the shovel-like box became popular as a tourist item on Cape Cod. Metal inserts were added to the box to make it an attractive planter.

Massachusetts currently is number one in the nation in cranberry production. About eightypercent of the state's four hundred cranberry growers belong to the Ocean Spray Cooperative. Most cranberry farms are relatively small, producing about a thousand barrels, each weighing a hundred pounds. The average yield is about 105 barrels per acre, so that the typical farm is less than ten acres.

When Ocean Spray was first formed in 1930 under the name of Cranberry Canners, the product line was simple—canned whole and jellied cranberry sauce and cranberry-juice cocktail. In 1939 Ocean Spray Cran was introduced, which is a concentrated cranberry juice designed to be mixed with alcoholic beverages. This was followed by dehydrated cranberries and cranberry-orange marmalade in the early 1940s.

Now other fruit juices have been blended with cranberry juice to make a variety of drinks. Today, cranberries are also grown in Wisconsin, Oregon, and Washington and sold under the Ocean Spray label.

This jellied cranberry salad includes pieces of pear which cut some of the tartness of the cranberries. Serve it with turkey for Thanksgiving.

Cranberry Salad

1 package (3 ounces) strawberry gelatin
1 cup boiling water
1 can (16 ounces) whole berry cranberry
*   sauce*
1 cup fresh or frozen cranberries
2 tablespoons sugar
3/4 cup finely sliced celery
1 large Bartlett pear, peeled, cored, and
*   coarsely chopped*
1/2 cup chopped walnuts

Place the strawberry gelatin in a medium-size bowl and add the boiling water. Stir to dissolve the gelatin. Add the cranberry sauce and stir until well blended. Place the cranberries, sugar, and 1/4 cup water in a 1-quart microwavable bowl, cover with vented plastic wrap, and microwave on high for 5 minutes or until the berries start to pop. Add the cooked berries to the gelatin mixture and cool to room temperature.

Then add the celery, chopped pear, and walnuts. Pour the mixture into a 6-cup, oiled ring mold and refrigerate for at least 4 hours.

To serve, unmold the salad on lettuce leaves and fill the center with additional pieces of pear, if desired. Serves 8.

Note: To cook cranberries on top of the stove, place them with the sugar and 1/3 cup of water in a small saucepan. Cook over medium heat until they start to pop.

Dates

Popular Since Biblical Times

One of the first foods eaten by man was the date, a staple of early Middle Eastern civilizations. Dates are still an important ingredient in many Middle Eastern cuisines and are used in cookies, cakes, steamed puddings, and some vegetable dishes in American cooking.

The date palm is probably of African origin and grows mainly in tropical and subtropical climates around the world — the Middle East, the Mediterranean regions, India, a small region of Spain, and southern California.

Marco Polo encountered dates in several places on his travels. The fruit was also well known in medieval Europe. By Elizabethan times, the English used dates in their sweet puddings. In the 1300s, dates were being served for dessert by the French aristocracy. When France conquered Algeria in 1830 dates became affordable for the average Frenchman.

Date palms were introduced into California by the Spanish in the second half of the eighteenth century. However, it was not until the early part of the twentieth century that a commercial date industry was established. By 1960 there were more than five thousand acres planted in dates in the Coachella Valley of California. Since then date plantation acreage has declined due to the high cost of the intensive manual labor involved in cultivating dates.

Two of the pioneers in American date production are Mr. and Mrs. Floyd Shields, who planted their first date orchards in 1924. Today the Shields orchards contain more than twelve hundred date palms and seven hundredcitrus tress — which grow beneath the palms. Many of the original date palms still produce fruit.

The Shields started their date orchard with twenty-five trees imported from Algeria and over the years have propagated the trees. There are now 119 different kinds of dates in their orchards with Black Beauty being the newest -- which has a more intense flavor than other varieties.

It takes five to ten years for an offshoot of the date palm to develop a root system of its own. After replanting, an additional eight to fifteen years are required before the palm will bear fruit.

The date palm has often been described as living with its feet in the water and its head in the sun, which makes it an ideal dessert plant. The roots have been known to go from twenty to forty feet deep seeking water.

Dates were never really gathered wild as some other early fruits and vegetables, but have always been cultivated because of their unique method of pollination. Date palms are either male or female. Nature did not make the male blossoms attractive to pollen-carrying insects and there was no natural pollination of the date trees. In ancient times, the date growers relied on the wind to distribute the pollen.

Now the male flowers are cut, the pollen is shaken out and placed on small cotton powder puffs. These puffs are then attached to long sticks and used to pollinate the female blossoms twice a week during February, March, and April. Each tree yields from fifty to one hundred and fifty pounds of dates.

The dates begin to ripen about the first of September and from then until Christmas dates are hand picked once a week. Since the dates in the clusters do not all ripen at the same time the fruit must be picked individually. Each picking requires the pickers to climb the palm tree, sometimes to the height of a hundred feet to reach the date palm clusters. After the dates are picked they are cleaned, graded, and packed.

Figs

Sweet and Delicious Fresh

Figs have been popular in the warmer climates of the world since Biblical times. Although fresh figs are difficult to find and are only available for a short time in the summer, they make delightful eating. The most popular fresh fig is the dark purplish brown variety known as the Mission Fig. Dried figs are available all year, but we tend to associate them with holiday baking.

There are numerous references to figs in the Bible. Figs are believed to have originated in Asia and were in great demand in the Near East as early as 3000 B.C. In Assyria figs were used to make a syrup that was used as a sweetener. They were grown in the hanging gardens of Babylon and were dried for preservation by being buried in the hot desert sands. They were also cultivated in Egypt and were an important part of the Phoenician economy, as well.

Figs were a favorite fruit of the ancient Greeks, whose poor soil was not conducive to growing very many grains, fruits, or vegetables. The Greeks thought that figs were a special gift of the gods and consequently planted large groves of fig trees in and near Athens. These figs were so superior in quality that they were in demand throughout Asia Minor, so much so that the Greeks passed laws to restrict their exportation.

Food historians tell us that the Greeks first brought figs to Italy, as the Romans rated foreign figs superior to their own domestic varieties. At one time the Romans imported as many as twenty-nine different varieties of figs from the Greek islands. The affluent Romans fed expensive Syrian figs to their hogs to improve the flavor of the meat.

Other Romans fed their pigs dried domestic figs and honey to give these animals extra large livers, from which they made pork foie gras. Many centuries later geese were force-fed figs for foie gras.

Figs spread from the eastern Mediterranean to other regions having warm climates along the European trade routes. In the third century B.C. an Indian ruler is supposed to have asked the Greeks to send him figs, grape syrup, and a philosopher. Reportedly they obliged with the first two items, but said the philosophers were not an article of commerce.

The Romans are credited with introducing the fig to what is today southern France. In the eight and ninth centuries the Arabs extended the cultivation of figs westward into Egypt and Spain .

In the fourteenth century dried figs were the rage in Paris where they were served as hors d'oeuvres or as desserts. Fig trees was introduced into England in the sixteenth century, but because of the cold climate were not very productive. Consequently, England and the other northern European nations used dried figs grown in the Mediterranean area. By the time of Elizabeth I every important English family stored dried figs which they used to make sweet puddings.

Figs were introduced into the New World by the Spanish explorers. In 1769 the Franciscan mission at San Diego was founded and began growing a Spanish black common fig, which became known as the Mission fig. Today California produces ninety-nine percent of all the commercially-grown figs in the United States. The Mission fig is only one of a number of varieties cultivated.

According to the Encyclopedia Britannica there are more than six hundred species of figs. There are figs which ripen underground, while others grow high in the air on plants dangling from trees. Some figs grow on low shrubs in the desert and others on tall trees in tropical forests. Their shape, size, and color also varies considerably.

The strangest fig, the sea fig, is called the beach apple in English and the sea squirt in French. It is a wine-colored fruit that glues itself to rocks on the bottom of the Mediterranean. The only thing it has in common with land-based figs is that it is edible.

Botanists tell us that the fig is not a single fruit but almost fifteen hundred different fruits, many of which are so small that they are normally thought of as seeds. The fig belongs to the same family as the mulberry and the breadfruit.

Pollination of the fig takes place with the aid of a tiny gnat-sized insect, called a fig wasp, that lives inside the fruit. Historically, the pollinated female fig wasp flew to an unripened fig and pollinated the female seeds through a tiny opening at the bottom of the fruit. Over the years this tiny insect has become extinct and today pollination takes place inside of each individual fruit. Some fig trees produce three crops a year, with two being more common.

One of my favorite ways to serve fresh figs as a dessert is with a sabayon sauce. Sabayon is the French name for the dessert sauce or light dessert the Italians call Zabaglione. It usually consists of sugar, egg yolks, and wine. Sabayon makes an elegant and versatile dessert which can be whipped up quickly and served hot or cold. In this recipe it is used as a sauce over fresh figs, but it is equally delicious over any fresh fruit, especially berries.

Fresh Figs With Wine Sabayon

Wine Sabayon

6 egg yolks
1/3 cup sugar
1 cup white wine

In the top of a double boiler set over simmering water, whisk the egg yolks and sugar together until foamy. (The water must not touch the top pot.) Add the wine, a little at a time, whisking constantly until the mixture is thick and is the consistency of softly whipped cream, about 10 minutes. The sabayon should never get so hot that you cannot put your finger in it. Remove from heat.

Fruit

2 to 3 ripe, fresh figs per person
1 tablespoon chopped, candied ginger per
  serving (optional)

Cut the figs in quarters and arrange them on plates. Drizzle with the sabayon and sprinkle with the chopped candied ginger, if desired. Serves 6.

Grapes

For Eating and Wine

Both wine grapes and table grapes have been enjoyed by man for many centuries. Even though the exact birthplace of grapes is unknown, food historians believe that grapes first appeared in the Middle East around the Caspian Sea. From there they spread south and west to Asia and Egypt where hieroglyphics show grapes being carried to the feasting table. The tomb of Tutankhamun contained a jar which was marked "unfermented grape juice." The hanging gardens of Babylon contained grape vines. Grapes and wine are mentioned in both the Old and New Testaments.

Brillat-Savarin, the well-known French gourmet, related this grape incident in one of his writings. After offering a guest a plate of grapes for dessert, the guest said, "Thank you," as he pushed the plate away, "I am not accustomed to taking my wine in pills."

Although some wine grapes can be eaten as table grapes and same table grapes can be converted into wine, grape growers over the centuries have meticulously developed distinctly different wine grapes and dessert or table grapes. Wine grapes have thick skins, many have lots of seeds, and most are tart. The tartness, or acidity, is one of the factors that makes these grapes suitable for wine.

The Romans obtained their first grapes from Sicily, where the Greeks had planted them. Even as far back as early Roman times, Pliny, the Roman botanist, described ninety-one varieties of grapes growing at the time. Only fifty of them were used for wine making. The ancient Romans grew special grapes for eating and others, such as large white grapes, were reserved for raisins. They also imported grapes from Malaga, in what is today Spain.

While several of the grapes now growing in northern Europe are native to the area, many of the wine grapes of France were brought there by the Romans. Regardless of how they got there, grapes were highly prized in France. Richard the Lion Hearted, a French noble at the time, decreed that any man stealing a bunch of grapes was to be punished by a fine of five sous or the loss of an ear, whichever the thief could best afford to lose.

The oldest and most famous grape vine in England is the Great Vine at Hampton Court which was planted in 1768 by "Capability" Brown, the renowned landscape gardener to King George III. At one time the vine bore two thousand bunches of Black Hambro dessert grapes each year. In the early twentieth century it was decided to trim away all but 650 of the bunches every year in order to preserve the plant's vigor. The Great Vine is still alive and healthy today, and its trunk is eighty-one inches in circumference. Its longest branch is 114 feet long.

There are more than eight thousand varieties of grapes in the world today, both natural and cultivated. All of the European varieties have developed from a single species, named "Vitis Vinifera," which historians believe originated in the Middle East. Today these vitis vinifera grapes are considered to be the best wine grapes and some of the best table grapes.

When America was settled about forty varieties were added to the list of world grapes. These wild grapes, however, had a certain muskiness to their taste and were dubbed as "foxy." In the 1800s many were used to make wine and some are still being used for that purpose today. Through the years these wild grapes were crossed with vinifera and produced such hybrid varieties as the Catawba, Concord, and Delaware. The Concord grape, named after the town in Massachusetts, became the basis of the popular drink — grape juice.

Beverages — juice, wine, and brandy — and raw fruit has not been the only use of grapes. The most obvious other product of grapes is their dried version — raisins. They were first produced in the Middle East by burying fresh grapes in the hot desert sand. Drying grapes into raisins removes only the water content and leaves all other nutrients in tact, particularly the natural sugar.

In ancient times other by-products of grapes had already developed. One was grape sugar distilled from ripe grapes. It was used as a sweetener in Roman times and the Middle Ages. Grape juice was often used to lend tartness to sauces in areas where citrus was unavailable. The Greeks used the young and tender grape leaves as a casing for various fillings, which they still do today.. Small birds were also wrapped in grape leaves for cooking, giving them more flavor.

Today grapes are grown throughout the world in all but the coldest areas of the globe. A recent development has been the red seedless Flame grape which along with the seedless Thompson green grape abounds in our local markets.

Grapes are the basis for Grape and Amaretti Delight, an elegant dessert of Italian origin. It combines the flavors of almond, grapes, and the tartness of Crème Fraîche.

Grape and Amaretti Delight

3 ounces Amaretti cookies
2 tablespoons Amaretto liqueur
8 ounces seedless red and green grapes
4 ounces Crème Fraîche
4 ounces Mascarpone cheese
5 tablespoons milk
1 tablespoon sugar
Grated rind of 1/2 lemon
2 tablespoons lemon juice
3/4 cup whipping cream

Coarsely grind the cookie crumbs in a food processor to yield 3/4 cup crumbs. Sprinkle the crumbs with the Amaretto liqueur. Wash the grapes and cut them in half.

In a bowl combine the Crème Fraîche, Mascarpone, milk, sugar, grated lemon rind, and lemon juice. Mix until very smooth. Whip the cream until stiff and then fold it into the Crème Fraîche mixture.

Layer some of the Crème Fraîche mixture into each of 4 small custard cups or stemmed champagne coupé glasses. Top each layer with the amaretti crumbs. Then add another layer of the Crème Fraîche mixture and top with the grape halves. Refrigerate for at least 2 hours before serving. Serves 4.

Kiwi Fruit

Hairy, Brown Fruit

Another name for kiwi fruit is Chinese gooseberry. Although kiwi fruit (the word kiwi refers to flightless bird) were first grown commercially in New Zealand, food historians say that it originated in eastern Asia.

Seeds of the kiwi fruit were taken from the Yangtze valley to New Zealand in the early twentieth century. Commercial cultivation began there in the 1930s.

The fruit ripens slowly after being picked and keeps well so that it can be easily exported. The first shipment of kiwi fruits reached England in 1953.

When nouvelle cuisine blossomed in France and elsewhere, kiwi fruit quickly assumed a star role as an exotic, decorative ingredient in many dishes. Thin slices of kiwi fruit decorated many entree plates in the 1970s. Once kiwi fruit became popular in Europe and North America, growers in the south of France and California began to cultivate them in competition with New Zealand.

Kiwi fruit is the size of a large egg. It has a thin skin which is brown and hairy on the outside. Inside is a firm, green flesh containing tiny, black, edible seeds around a whitish center. The taste is sweet and slightly acid, reminiscent of strawberries.

The name Chinese gooseberry was given to the fruit because it grows like a berry on a shrub. The plant is not large and produces about three hundred pounds of fruit a year.

Kiwi fruit has been the traditional fruit filling of a light meringue dessert called Pavlova, which was named in honor of the famous ballerina. It is the favorite dessert of New Zealand. Any type of fruit, sliced or in small pieces, may be used in a Pavlova. For a stunning visual effect try blueberries and slices of kiwi.

Pavlova

4 egg whites
1/4 teaspoon cream of tartar
1 cup superfine sugar
2 teaspoons cornstarch
2 teaspoons vinegar
1/4 teaspoon vanilla extract

Line a baking sheet with parchment paper and draw a 7-inch circle on the paper.

In a stainless steel bowl beat the egg whites until soft peaks form. Beat in the cream of tartar when egg whites are foamy. Beat in half of the sugar, a tablespoon at a time, until the egg whites are thick, glossy and stands in firm peaks. Combine the cornstarch with the remaining sugar and beat in a little at a time. Combine the vinegar and vanilla extract and gently fold it into the meringue.

Gently spoon the meringue into the circle on the paper; cover the circle and pile meringue high around the sides. Bake in the center of a preheated 300° F. oven for 15 minutes; reduce temperature to 250° F. and continue baking for 1 more hour or until the meringue is firm. Open the oven door and let the meringue cool on the baking sheet in the oven. Then completely cool and remove the paper.

Filling

1 1/4 cups very cold whipping cream
6 to 8 kiwi fruit, peeled and thinly sliced

One hour before serving, whip the cream until it stands in soft peaks. Spread it over the center and up the sides of the meringue. Arrange the kiwi fruit over the whipped cream. Refrigerate 1 hour before serving. Serves 6.

Lemons

Sour Goodness

Nearly all of the lemons grown in North America grow in California. Florida tried to raise lemons commercially, but periodic frosts in the late 1800s proved to be disastrous and eliminated most of the lemon plantations. In recent years some commercial lemon growing has taken place in the southern part of Florida but the humidity has caused many of the Florida lemons to be puffy and tasteless.

Lemon trees, which are believed to have originated in India, were known in Roman times more as ornamental plants than for fruit. Wall murals and mosaics with lemon trees are to be found in the ruins in Pompeii

Long before the Christian era the Romans believed that lemons were an antidote for all poisons. This belief came from the fact that a lemon eater survived a stern punishment. At the time two criminals were thrown into a pit of venomous snakes, one of whom had eaten a lemon beforehand and thus survived, while the other succumbed to snakebite.

Lemons, however, were always a rare fruit and thus expensive. By the time the Roman Empire collapsed the sporadic cultivation of lemons was abandoned in the Mediterranean area. Eventually the Moors (Arabs) planted lemon orchards in Spain when they occupied parts of that country in the eighth century, as well as in Sicily.

The people of northern Europe had no knowledge of lemons until the Crusaders first tasted the fruit in the Holy Land at the end of the twelfth century. Not long after that ships arriving in England from Spain and Portugal had as part of their cargo a confection which was called succade. It was a lemon-based sweet similar to our jelly beans.

Lemons themselves, however, were not transported north until the early 1400s. Until that time the sourness in any cooking was supplied by tart fruits, such as crab apples, green gooseberries, and quinces. Vinegar made from sour grapes was also a source of tartness.

In France special merchants, marchands d'aigrun (merchants of sourness) monopolized the sale of all citrus — oranges, lemons, limes, and grapefruit. Even today these merchants have retained their title although most of the oranges sold are of the sweet variety.

One of the first uses of lemons in northern European cooking was as an accompaniment for meat and poultry. They were stewed and served whole. Until the eighteenth century the reliability of the tartness of the lemon could not be depended upon. Usually they were sweet and only slightly acidic.

With more research and hybridization lemons became the sour fruit we know today. When lemons became more acidic they were regularly served with fish — a common combination that was first introduced by Cristoforo de Messiburgo, a well-known Italian chef. He was the first to marinate fish in lemon juice, grill it, and then serve it with lemon slices.

Certain tropical fruits such as papaya, guava, and avocado are best sprinkled with some lemon juice to enhance the delicate flavors of these fruits.

The lemon is a very unique fruit in that it is never eaten by itself. In India, however, green or very young lemons are preserved in mustard oil with spices. This is a great delicacy. In Morocco lemon slices are served salted.

Lemons are a part of cooking only through the use of their juice. Lemon juice was the first flavoring of soda water in 1840. Lemon peel is often an ingredient in cooking.

The Mongols were the first people recorded (in 1299) as enjoying lemonade. It was actually sweetened lemon juice preserved with alcohol. Later the English learned to like lemon punch in India. The word punch comes from the Sanskrit for five because of the five ingredients in the punch — alcohol, tea, lemon juice, water, sugar, and honey.

Lemonade, a combination of sugared lemon juice and water started in France in the mid-1600s. Limonadiers, who carried this drink in metal containers on their backs to sell on the street, became familiar sights in Paris.

In 1676 the French government granted a patent or monopoly to the lemonade men, creating a whole new guild, the Compagnie des Limonadiers. Many set up permanent shops on the streets of Paris and together with the sellers of coffee and chocolate, they gradually evolved into the cafe owners.

The familiar object we know as a lemon-juicer was the stroke of genius of an unknown inventor. A picture of the juicer first appeared in the 1897 Sears Roebuck Catalog. It showed a ribbed dome with an attached tray for catching the juice. The inventor realized that the human hand, which can twist the fruit, is far more efficient than any mechanical device. That was true until the electric juicer arrived.

Whichever juicer you prefer to use make some lemon juice and try my Lemon Chiffon Pie for a light dessert. It can be made early in the day and refrigerated until serving time.

Lemon Chiffon Pie

1 tablespoon unflavored gelatin
1/4 cup cold water
4 eggs, separated
2/3 cup lemon juice
1 cup sugar
1 teaspoon grated lemon rind
1/2 cup heavy cream
1 baked 9-inch pie crust or crumb crust

Sprinkle the gelatin over the water in a small bowl and let stand 10 minutes to soften.

Place the egg yolks, lemon juice, and half of the sugar in the top of a double boiler. Stir well to combine. Cook and stir over boiling water until the mixture thickens. (Do not let the water touch the bottom of the double boiler.) Remove from heat and add the softened gelatin and the lemon rind. Transfer the mixture to a bowl and cool to room temperature.

Beat the egg whites until they start to get stiff. Gradually beat in the remaining 1/2 cup of sugar and continue beating until the mixture holds stiff peaks. Fold the egg whites into the lemon mixture. Beat the heavy cream until stiff and fold it into the lemon mixture. Place filling into the pie crust, heaping it up in the center. Chill 4 to 5 hours before serving.

Serves 6.

Mangoes

A Very Aromatic Fruit

The flesh of the mango clings tightly to a single large stone, so cutting it becomes a little unwieldy. The best way to cut a mango after peeling it is to slice off the large flat surfaces and then cut off the remaining smaller sides.

Mangos has been cultivated since the start of recorded history. They are believed to be natives of eastern and southern India and Burma. Mangoes were slow to spread to other regions of the tropics and semi-tropics because the fruit is extremely perishable and does not travel well. That is the reason most of the mangoes in the store are under-ripe and have to be ripened at home.

Ancient travelers from China brought mangoes from India to North Africa in about 1000 A.D. The first planting of mangoes in the Western Hemisphere took place in Brazil in about 1700 and by the mid-1700s, they had been transplanted to the West Indies.

The only area in the United States where mangoes grow successfully is southern Florida. They have thrived there since the late 1800s. The fruit was a strange one to the local population and it was not readily accepted, except by commercial producers of chutney. Today mangoes are also grown in Mexico.

There are many colors to the skin of the mango — red, yellow, or a dull green. All of the flesh, however, is light yellow or orange. Mangos vary in length from two inches to more than ten inches and weigh anywhere from four ounces to more than four and a half pounds.

The orange-fleshed mango has become the basic ingredient for the Indian-inspired chutneys. However, chutneys can be made with other fruits such as peaches, pears, apples, pineapple, and also tomatoes. They can be either sweet or sour but are always enhanced by spices.

One of the most famous chutneys is the English product — Major Grey's Chutney. The Major, an English army officer stationed in India, created his famous recipe about 1860. He used whatever was at hand — mangoes, hot peppers, and spices. His purpose was to camouflage the indifferent taste and texture of the meat then being served to his troops. Major Grey continued to prepare this relish when he returned home and it soon became famous all over Europe.

Chutneys are not difficult to make. After the mixture has been put into jars, they should be boiled in a water bath for 5 to 10 minutes, time depending on the size of the jar. This chutney pairs well with roast meats and also curry dishes.

Mango Chutney

4 mangoes, chopped
2 cups cider vinegar
4 cups brown sugar
1/2 teaspoon ground ginger
1/2 teaspoon ground cloves
1 teaspoon allspice
1 large onion, chopped
2 garlic cloves, chopped
1/4 cup shopped fresh ginger
1 large red bell pepper, chopped
1 teaspoon red pepper flakes

Combine all of the ingredients in a large saucepan or Dutch oven. Bring the mixture to a boil and then cook over low heat until thickened to the desired consistency, about 1 and 1/2 to 2 hours. Spoon the chutney into 3 pint or 6 half pint jars, seal and process in a boiling water bath for 5 to 10 minutes.

Melons

Originally Small, Now Large

All species of melon originated somewhere in the Middle East, mainly Persia. Early paintings in ancient Assyrian depict festive tables with slices of melons. Historians say that King Merodach-Baladan of Assyria grew melons in his garden in 2100 B.C. At the time melons were also used for medicinal purposes.

Egyptian paintings dating back to 2400 B.C. included melons. Some food historians claim that the paintings depict cucumbers, not melons. However, a passage from the Bible (Numbers 11:5) mentions both foods, when the Hebrews wandering in the desert lamented, "the fish, which we did eat in Egypt freely, the cucumbers, and the melons."

By the third century B.C. the Greeks were raising melons. In the first century A.D. the Roman scholar, Pliny (A.D. 23-79), described a plant called "melopepo" grown in Campania (the region of Naples). He told of the plant's fruit not being suspended from the vine, as are cucumbers, but resting on the ground. Pliny further described this fruit as being round and yellow and when ripe detaching itself from the stem — a characteristic of melons.

Wall paintings in Herculaneum and Pompeii show melons cut in half and portraying their interiors. In general, the Romans preferred to import melons from Armenia. Melons at that time were only about the size of oranges today.

Archeological digs in China have found melon seeds dating to about 200 B. C. In 1973, the body of a Chinese noblewoman was exhumed in Hunan province. She was perfectly preserved having been buried sixty feet deep in a nested series of six airtight coffins. As she was so perfectly preserved, it was possible to do an autopsy. Melon seeds were found in her stomach and intestines.

Marco Polo on his journey to China reported on encountering melons in Afghanistan. There the melons were cut into slices and dried in the sun. The dried melons became very sweet and were chewed similar to jerky. Melons are still grown in Afghanistan, as well as in northern Pakistan and Kashmir.

With the collapse of the Roman Empire, the flow of melons from the middle East to Italy ceased and the fruit disappeared from Europe. Historians report that it returned to Italy in the fourteenth century, still in the orange-sized version. It was not long before cultivators developed more generous sizes.

Historical records show that Charlemagne ordered melons grown on his domain about 800 A.D., although they did not fare well in Charlemagne's garden, due to adverse climate. Historians speculate that he must have encountered melons in Spain where his armies campaigned. The Spanish province of Andalusia was the first European area to grow melons, probably planted there by the Moors when they conquered the area in the early 700s.

The successful introduction of melons to France is attributed to the Popes, when they abandoned Rome for Avignon early in the fourteenth century. It is also noted that French soldiers returning from Italy probably brought back melon seeds. Today some of the world's best melons are grown in southern France.

In northern France melons were grown in hot houses for the nobility. Seven varieties of melons were grown under glass for Louis XIV at Versailles. The gardeners watered the melons with honeyed or sweetened water to sweeten the fruit, or so they thought.

In the sixteenth century, Popes and melons were associated for another reason. Melon seeds brought from Armenia were planted in the papal domain of Cantalupo, near Tivoli — hence the origin of the name cantaloupe.

In America, Coronado's men, when exploring the Southwest, informed him that the area was rich in corn, beans, and melons. The report was wrong as there were no melons in the New World until Europeans brought them. Probably what they thought were melons were really squashes.

The Navahos began growing melons in the middle 1800s from seeds brought by the Spanish. The first official record of an imported melon was the Netted Gem variety, imported from France in 1881. This started commercial melon cultivation in the United States. The Netted Gem was followed by the Casaba, and in 1900 by the French White Antibes winter melon which became known as the honeydew.

Melons should not be picked before they are completely ripe. Unfortunately, today many are picked to finish their ripening on the way to the stores. Some fruits will continue to manufacture sugar after picking, if placed in the sun, but not melons. Their sugar content begins to decrease as soon as they are picked. They may soften in a warm environment, but they will not ripen.

When the sugar content of a melon reaches its optimum, a separation layer develops in the stem at the point where it joins the fruit. This acts like a shield that prevents further nutrients from entering the melon. When ripe the melon can be picked from the vine with the slightest pressure or it will fall to the ground automatically. A melon thus harvested will show no scar where the stem breaks. However, one that does have damage is a sign that the melon was unripe when picked. I have also found that I can tell if a melon is ripe when the end of the melon away from the stem feels slightly soft.

A ripe melon is sometimes hard to find. As the French poet Claude Mermet wrote in 1600. "Melons are like friends. Fifty have to be tried to find a single good one." The English, not to be out-done, translated Mermet's saying: "Friends are like melons. Shall I tell you why? To find one good, you must a hundred try."

One of my favorite cold soups is based on melons. Either cantaloupe or honeydew may be used, or a mixture of both. Fresh ginger adds a spiciness to this soup.

Gingered Melon Soup

5 cups honeydew, cantaloupe or other melon, cut into chunks
1 cup water
1 cup dry white wine
1/3 cup sugar
2 tablespoons finely chopped fresh ginger root
1/4 teaspoon ground cardamom
1 cup heavy cream
6 thin slices of lime, for garnish

In a large saucepan, bring all of the ingredients except the cream and lime slices to a boil. Lower heat and simmer for 5 to 10 minutes until the melon is soft. Let cool and then puree in batches in a blender or food processor. Blend in the cream. Chill overnight. Serve in mugs or soup bowls garnished with the lime slices. Serves 6.

Olives

Ancient Fruit with Many Uses

No fruit tree has exerted so profound an influence on the growth of civilization as the olive tree. It has provided the sustenance and the means of survival in all the countries that fringe the Middle Eastern desert in which the olive grows. The rich, oily fruit of the olive tree has shaped the distinctive flavors of the foods that are traditional to the Mediterranean area. Praises have been rained on this fruit throughout the ages, including several by Plato, who considered the olive his favorite food even though he reportedly had a very delicate stomach and was a light eater. The olive branch has been a symbol of peace throughout the ages.

Why all of this praise for something that now is rather unimportant? Today we use olives merely as an embellishment, an appetizer or condiment, or as an ingredient in salad dressings, or merely plop it into the depths of a martini. In ancient times olive dishes were often the most important dish of the meal. They have shaped the cuisine of the Middle East, Greece, Italy, Spain, and southern France for more than five thousand years.

The versatility of the olive made it indispensable in the ancient world in other roles besides that of food. "There are two liquids especially agreeable to the human body, wine inside and oil outside," wrote Pliny, the Roman scholar. At the time his countrymen anointed their bodies with scented olive oil. To the Greeks, especially the women, olive oil was a balm for winter months and was as prized by them as a mink coat is today.

Olive oil served as a cleanser, for the ancient civilizations had no soap. It was also a medicine as it penetrated the skin and supposedly bestowed good health and longevity. (In modern times it has been found that the olive tree contains salicylic acid, an active element in aspirin.) Burned in earthenware lamps, olive oil provided the most convenient source of light in ancient times. In Egypt it was used as a lubricant to help move the great blocks of stones used to build the pyramids.

Even in ancient times tuna and anchovy fillets were preserved in olive oil. The pulp, which remained after the oil was extracted, was fed to animals or utilized as fertilizer. The liquid residue thatremained after the oil was siphoned off was used by the ancient Romans as a weed killer and was sprayed on cabbages to discourage insects.

The olive tree provided close-grained hardwood. According to the Bible the tabernacle of Solomon's temple was constructed with olive wood. In those days spear shafts were made with olive wood.

Most food historians believe that the island of Crete was the birthplace of the olive. It grew wild there and was later cultivated in Egypt, as evidenced by Egyptian art which depicts olive picking. However, recent historical records show that olives were first cultivated in Syria and Palestine in the fourth millennium B.C. Olives and olive oil had become an element of international commerce by 2500 B.C., when the products were shipped from Crete to Egypt and Asia Minor. Later Greece became the center of olive cultivation, but it lost most of its olive trees when various conquerors cut them down in order to subjugate the Greeks.

Olives did not make the usual east to west journey as did some of the other fruits and vegetables of the Middle East. It came first to Spain from the eastern Mediterranean in the fourth century B.C. Gradually olive trees were brought to southern France and then to Italy (or Latium) in 550 B.C.

The Romans became heavy consumers of

olives. They ate them at the beginning of the meal as appetizers and at the end as palate cleansers. Also a Roman meal might include dishes in which olives were the principal ingredient. Olives and bread were the staple food of the Roman peasants and workers. The Roman lords gave inferior olives deficient in oil to their laborers and slaves and kept the best for their tables. The second best was used to make oil.

Olive oil as a cooking oil was not popular outside of the olive growing areas surrounding the Mediterranean. In most countries of the world, including several in the Mediterranean region, the chief cooking fat was lard. Although olive oil was popular as a cooking oil in Italy, some lard was also used. Greece and the Middle East depended on mutton for their cooking fat. Spanish cooks used olive oil exclusively as Spain was ruled by the Moors, who prohibited use of any pork products. To this day Spain is the world's foremost producer of olives. Olive oil was virtually unknown in Paris until the Revolution, when it was introduced by a Provençal restaurant which had opened there.

Once of Thomas Jefferson's greatest disappointments as an agriculturist was that olives would not grow in the southeastern United States. He planted olive cuttings at Monticello in 1774, but none grew. In 1791, Jefferson ordered five hundred olive tree seedlings from Aix-en-Provence to be sent to South Carolina. They did not grow either.

What Jefferson did not know was that olives were being grown elsewhere in America. The Franciscans who had moved into California from Mexico planted the first olive tress there in the 1760s. Californians, however, were not as impressed with the olive trees as was Jefferson, for it was not until this century that they began to develop an olive industry.

Olives are believed to have been planted in China in the sixth century. Nevertheless, they are little used there , as Chinese cuisine is incompatible with a cooking oil that imparts its own distinctive flavor into a dish. On the other hand, Japanese cooks uses some olive oil in the oil mixture for tempura frying.

Black olives are a key ingredient in the following Stuffed Tomatoes recipe. They are served at room temperature and are a flavorful accompaniment to grilled or roasted meats.

Stuffed Tomatoes

2/3 cup long-grain rice
1 cup black olives
Freshly ground pepper
3 tablespoons extra-virgin olive oil
4 large tomatoes, preferably beefsteak
12 fresh basil leaves, julienned or
*   1/3 cup chopped fresh parsley*

Steam the rice in lightly salted water until al dente. Let it cool completely and eliminate any excess moisture.

Pit and chop the olives. Place them in a bowl and add the rice, pepper and olive oil. Mix well and let stand for about 4 hours at room temperature so that the rice absorbs the olive flavor. Do not refrigerate.

Wash the tomatoes and cut them in half. Remove and discard the seeds and squeeze out the juice and scoop out the pulp. Place the tomato halves upside down on a board to drain for 30 minutes. Dry the inside of the tomatoes with paper towels.

Add the basil or parsley to the rice mixture and fill each tomato half with some of the mixture. Serve at once. Serves 4.

Oranges

Once an Exotic Fruit

In days of old children were ecstatic when they received a single orange for Christmas. It was a symbol of the wonderful riches of distant lands.

Today oranges abound in our super markets, typically of three types -- Navel, Valencia, or Indian River. The Navel orange, in season from October through December, is thick skinned, fairly easy to peel, and seedless. It is used for eating out-of-hand and makes attractive sections or slices.

The Valencia orange, in season from January through July, is a large heavy golden-yellow variety that is excellent for juice and flavor. It is also easy to peel and section. Over half of the orange production in the United States is Valencias. The Indian River variety is available from December through April and is a thin-skinned orange that is rich in juicy pulp.

Oranges are at their peak during the winter months and can be stored in a cool place for several weeks or at a controlled temperature for several months. Oranges can also be frozen for up to a year.

Historians tell us that the orange is more than 20 million years old and they believe that it originated in China. As early as 2500 B.C. the orange was cultivated in Greece and Rome. Orange seeds came to the Mediterranean area from India.

There was no mention of oranges in the Bible nor apparently were they grown in the hanging gardens of Babylon. It appeared they did not travel the usual trade route from the East through Asia Minor, but came via Arab dhows through the Indian Ocean to the coast of Egypt, then by camel to the Nile, and finally by boat in the Mediterranean to European ports.

By the twelfth century, the Moors, who had conquered Spain in the eight century, converted the region from Granada to Seville into one vast citrus orchard. About the same time, Sicily and southern Italy started cultivating oranges. The Mediterranean region of France is also orange-growing country.

In central France the royal families and the nobility had orangeries (greenhouses) in which they grew orange trees. Henry IV of France had one of these built at the Tuileries Palace in Paris for his mother-in-law, Catherine de Medici. Use of greenhouses to grow oranges were necessary in more northern climates of Europe because of the colder weather.

The most famous orangerie in France is the one at Versailles built by Louis XIV. It held twelve hundred orange trees growing in silver tubs.

The first oranges were brought to America by Christopher Columbus who had picked up seeds and saplings in the Canary Islands on his second voyage west. He planted the orange trees on the island of Hispaniola in 1493. The climate of the West Indies made the oranges flourish and within twenty-five years many of the Caribbean islands had orange groves.

History shows that the first orange seeds planted in the territorial United States were by Hernando de Soto, who planted them in Florida in 1539. Orange trees were growing profusely around St. Augustine when Sir Francis Drake sacked the city in 1586 and ordered the trees cut down. However, orange trees are hard to destroy and shoots soon sprouted from the severed trunks. A few years later the inhabitants of St. Augustine were again enjoying home-grown oranges.

The first orange trees in the western part of the United States came from Mexico. They were planted in the missions established by the

Spanish in Arizona and California. However, the California orange industry did not get started until a pair of navel orange trees were imported from Brazil. All of the navel oranges in California are supposedly descendent from these trees.

Oranges are not full-fledged tropical fruit and have been classified as sub-tropical because they can resist some frost. They prefer an even, warm heat with a few cool winter months. Orange trees grow from seed. They bear fruit after about ten years and continue to produce for another fifty years. In the United States the average tree in an orchard will yield up to fifteen hundred oranges annually.

Unlike other fruit, oranges do not continue to ripen after picking and must be tree ripened. They are normally picked almost year-round, from October through July.

Oranges are most frequently used in salads and desserts. They also add flavor interest to sauces for grilled or roasted meats and can be used in certain vegetable soups. Although most of us tend to bake lemon chiffon pies, an orange chiffon pie is equally tasty.

The orange peel adds a piquant flavor to the poached nectarines which are served in a wine sauce over baked custards. Peaches may be substituted for the nectarines.

Little Custards
With Poached Nectarines

2 1/4 cups milk
1 teaspoon vanilla extract
4 slices (1/4 inch thick) fresh ginger
3 whole eggs
1 egg yolk
1/3 cup mild honey

Put the milk, vanilla, and ginger in a medium-sized saucepan, and scald the milk. Beat the eggs together to mix; stir in the honey. Slowly whisk the hot milk into the egg mixture. Strain the custard mixture through a sieve into a pitcher and fill 6 buttered custard cups. Place the cups in a baking pan and fill the pan with 1 inch of water. Bake in the preheated 325° F. oven for 45 minutes. The custard is set when a knife inserted into the center comes out clean. Cool on a rack. Cover custards and chill in the refrigerator until serving time.

Poached Nectarines

1 cup dry white wine
1 and 1/2 cups water
Juice of half a lemon
1/4 cup honey
6 nectarines, peeled and sliced
Zest of 1/2 orange, cut into julienne strips

Combine the wine, water, lemon juice and honey in a large skillet or sauté pan, and bring to a boil. Add the nectarine slices and poach gently until they are soft, about 3 to 4 minutes. With a slotted spoon remove the slices to a bowl. Add the orange zest to the poaching liquid and reduce the liquid over high heat until 1 cup remains. Set aside to cool. When cool the poaching liquid may be combined with the nectarines and placed in the refrigerator until served.

To assemble, cut around the edges of the custards and unmold on individual serving plates. Arrange the nectarine slices around the custards, and spoon the poaching syrup and zest over the top. Serves 6

Peaches and Nectarines

They Are Not the Same Fruit

Have you ever wondered what the difference is between a peach and a nectarine? The obvious difference is that the skin of the peach is fuzzy and the nectarine is smooth. Contrary to popular belief, the nectarine is not a product of modern cross-breeding technology between the peach and a plum. It has been known to man for at least 2000 years.

The peach is the older of the two and is said to have been cultivated in China 4000 years ago. Originally the white variety of peach grew wild in Southwestern China. Chinese wild peach trees are gnarled and short. The fruit is small, has a large pit, but exquisite tasting flesh. These trees are bred from the seed, which is not the case with the majority of peach trees elsewhere in the world.

The nectarine also originated in China and was a natural mutation from the peach family. Like its cousin, it came westward via Persia and the old spice route, but had a much slower journey, not arriving in Europe until the sixteenth century. Occasionally, as if to prove its heritage, a smooth-skinned nectarine appears on a peach tree and vice versa.

In China, peaches were the symbol of immortality used by poets, sculptors and painters despite the fact that it grows on a short-lived tree. (Most peach orchards are replanted every eight-to-ten years.) Peaches, either real or painted on porcelain, were presented to friends as symbols of affection and an expression of hope for a long life.

Very early in civilized history the peach was introduced into Europe by way of Persia. When the Romans first started using them they called peaches "Persian plums" or "Persian apples."

In medieval times, peaches grown locally in more northern climates seem to have been small and not very good. There were also a lot of regions in the Mediterranean where peaches did not flourish because the climate was too hot. It was discovered that peach trees like a two month period of winter cold in order to work up strength for the following spring's leaves and flowers.

Louis XIV was probably responsible for the popularizing the peach in France where it had been growing since the thirteenth century. It is reported that he liked the fruit so much and was so impatient to eat it that whenever a bowl of peaches were placed before him he ate the fruit without peeling them. Louis XIV granted a pension to a man who grew peaches for him in his orchard outside of Paris.

The peach came to England from France. However, English climate is not favorable to the peach and England continues to import most of their peaches, or grows them in hot houses.

Peaches were brought to North America, more particularly to Florida and Mexico, by Spanish conquerors in the sixteenth century. The Indians fell in love with the peach and it quickly passed from tribe-to-tribe. The Natchez named one of their thirteen calendar months after the peach. When the English settlers reached Jamestown they found some peach trees. Peach orchards were developed throughout the colonies along the eastern seaboard. They were eaten raw, baked into pies and cobblers, and some were dried for winter use. Another method of preservation was the making of peach brandy. Today the cultivation of peaches in the United States is second only to that of apples.

For a delicious nectarine dessert see, Little Custards with Poached Nectarines on previous page.

Pears

Four Varieties Are Most Popular

Fall brings on a harvest of pears to our markets. Although there are more than 5,000 varieties of pears grown throughout the world, our markets feature primarily Anjou, Bosc, red and yellow Bartletts, and Comice. Most pears are grown in Oregon, Washington, and California.

Although these four varieties may be similar in taste, they do have subtle differences. The Anjou is a broad, large pear with firm flesh and a yellowish-green skin. It is sweet and succulent, and is delicious both raw and cooked. Botanists say this pear was developed in either France or Belgium in the nineteenth century. Through hybridization a red Anjou pear has also been developed.

The Bosc pear, with its slender neck and russet skin, is considered to be a winter pear. It has a sweet-tart flavor and is tasty both raw and cooked. The Bosc holds its shape well when baked or poached.

The Bartlett pear, which is known as the Williams pear in England, is a large bell-shaped fruit with a smooth yellow-green or reddish skin. Its flesh is sweet and juicy and may be eaten raw or cooked.

The Comice pear, which is best eaten uncooked, is a large fruit with meltingly smooth, sweet flesh and a lovely aroma. The Comice is considered to be the "queen of pears." It is so soft that some eat it with a spoon. Grown primarily in Oregon's Hood River Valley, each Comice pear is hand-picked and then wrapped in tissue paper before shipping.

Pears are easily bruised and, therefore, are picked while still hard. Unlike most fruit, the pear improves in both texture and flavor after it is picked. If the pear is left on the tree too long, it becomes mushy and gritty, and often times brown on the inside.

No one knows exactly where pears originated, although many food historians say that pears were first cultivated in China, as evidenced by pear seeds found in a Chinese tomb dating to 2100 B.C. Pears were grown by the ancient Hebrews and by the Greeks in Homer's time. From Greece pears were transported to Rome and Egypt. The Chinese introduced pears to India in the first century.

One of the most fascinating phenomena of pears in historic times was the speed with which different varieties were developed. In the course of two hundred years more than thirty varieties were developed in ancient Rome. By the seventeenth century, Italian botanists cataloged 209 varieties of pears. Charlemagne grew 168 kinds on his lands.

Pears came to America with various explorers and settlers. French Jesuit missionaries, while exploring the St. Lawrence Valley, brought pears to the Iroquois, who adopted them enthusiastically. Historical records mention that in 1629 pear seeds were sent to the Massachusetts Bay Colony and in 1647 the New Amsterdam colony acquired a pear tree from Holland. Records show that at about the same time, pear cider was being made in the Virginia colony from thirty to forty pear trees. French settlers also planted pear trees on the shores of the Detroit River in 1705.

Thomas Jefferson grew various varieties of pear trees from seedlings he had obtained in France. He noted that while French apples and peaches were inferior to American, the pears were "infinitely beyond anything we possess."

In the West, Spanish friars planted pears on the grounds of the California missions. Pears grow much better on the Pacific coast where a uniform climate is more favorable to their cultivation.

By the time of the American Revolution, 115 varieties of pears were being grown in the United States. Eventually one thousand varieties were cataloged by American botanists. This was small compared to the five thousand varieties of pears recorded in Europe. Even with the development of all of the different mutations of pears, there are less than a dozen that have remained popular.

One of the most famous pears was developed in 1870 in Berkshire, England by John Stair, a young school teacher. When this species of pear reached London it was renamed Williams. The pear was later taken to Dorchester, Massachusetts, by Enoch Bartlett and took on his name. Today Bartlett pears are grown on more than three-quarters of America's pear-producing acreage. The United States developed the red Bartlett, which is hardier than the yellow. Its red pigmentation makes it relatively more resistant to disease.

Most pears in our supermarkets are not ripe and need to be held at room temperature in either a brown paper bag or in a plastic fruit ripener for several days before eating or cooking. Slightly firm pears are better for cooking as they will hold their shape better.

Try a pandowdy with pears instead of the traditional apples. A pandowdy is similar to a deep-dish fruit pie with the fruit on the bottom and the cake or pastry on top. When served the crust is pushed into the fruit and the old time New Englanders referred to this form of eating as dowdying. Bourbon and cinnamon enhance the pears in this easy-to-make dessert.

Pear Pandowdy with Bourbon

4 ripe Bartlett pears, peeled, halved, cored,
  and thickly sliced
1 tablespoon lemon juice
2 tablespoons bourbon
4 tablespoons sugar
1 teaspoon cinnamon
1/2 teaspoon vanilla extract

Butter a 10-inch glass tart or quiche pan (do not use a metal pan). Arrange the pears in the bottom of the pan and sprinkle them with the lemon juice, bourbon, 3 tablespoons of the sugar, cinnamon, and vanilla. Set aside while preparing the pastry.

Pastry

1 egg
12 tablespoon butter or margarine,
  melted and cooled
1/2 cups sugar
1 cup flour
Pinch of salt

In the bowl of a food processor process the egg with a few pulses, and then slowly add the melted butter through the feed tube with the processor running. Add the sugar, flour, and salt and process until just combined. Spoon the batter over the pears, smoothing the top with a spatula. Sprinkle the remaining sugar over the top. Bake the pandowdy in a preheated 350° F. oven degree oven for 40 to 45 minutes, or until the top is crusty and pale golden. Cool on a wire rack before serving. Serves 6.

Persimmons

One American, One Japanese

During persimmon season there are frequently two types of persimmons in the produce section of our supermarkets — the Fuyu and Hachiya. Although both are now in limited quantities, this orange fruit was once much more popular.

The name for this orange fruit comes from the Algonquin "putchamin," which was Anglicized to persimmon. The Fuyu persimmon, a native of Japan, is the smaller, rounder, and lighter-orange variety of the two and is gaining popularity. It is tannin-free and not nearly as astringent as the larger persimmons native to this country. The Fuyu persimmon is best eaten raw and has become a favorite salad ingredient of mine in the fall. They are at their prime when they are bright orange and slightly firm to the touch, like a peach.

The larger acorn-shaped Hachiya persimmon is native to this country. I use the Hachiya in steamed persimmon puddings and cookies. The riper the Hachiya, the mushier it is.

The Indians found that the acorn-shaped Hachiya was best after the first frost. The frost slows the ripening process of the fruit and causes it to lose much of its astringency. After cold weather the sugar content increases in the fruit as long as it continues to ripen in the sun.

The first Europeans to encounter the Hachiya persimmon were the Spanish conquistadors who learned to subsist on them during their long, grueling marches in the Southern States. In 1540 Hernandez de Soto wrote that he had found Indians along the Mississippi River eating loaves of bread made of an orange prune-like fruit, that was larger than a nut and had three to four seeds. The Indians had dried the persimmons, then ground them into meal and made bread.

The early Virginia colonists found persimmons growing wild along the James River. Captain John Smith noted that "if not ripe it will drawe a mans moth awrie with much torment; but when it is ripe, it is as delicious as an Apricock." The early settlers also found that the ripe sweet fruit "yields on distillation after fermentation, a quantity of pleasant spirits."

Interest in the Japanese variety of persimmons was first aroused in this country when it was introduced by Commodore Matthew C. Perry in 1855. He brought back some young trees from Japan, but they became regarded primarily as ornamental. Today the Japanese persimmons are cultivated in California and on a more limited scale in Georgia and the Gulf States. Although peeled and eaten like an apple in Japan, the Fuyu persimmon has not as yet found such a popular market in this country — although they should as they have a pleasing taste and texture.

The words "Japanese persimmon" is a misnomer since the tree is actually a native of China. The fruit was adopted by the Japanese as one of their traditional foods for the New Year. The Chinese had long considered the fresh persimmon as a New Year's delicacy, although they also dry their persimmons for use all winter long. The Chinese peel and cut the fruit into thick slices, which are then strung on ropes. As the slices dry they turn blackish and a thick coating of sugar develops on the surface.

The sugar coating is scraped off the dried fruit and compacted into decorative molds to produce thin ornamental pieces of candy. Newly-married couples traditionally present these pieces of persimmon candy to friends from whom they have received wedding gifts. Persimmon sugar candy is also one of the eight tidbits offered with tea during the first course of Chinese banquets.

When settlers first came to American they found the native persimmon (Hachiya) growing wild and it became a tradition to make persimmon puddings each fall. The persimmon pulp was rubbed through an enamel colander and then mixed with flour, milk, sugar, baking soda, and butter in a big wooden bowl. Finally this mixture was poured into a mold or pan, and then either steamed or baked.

I have found that fresh persimmon puree from the Hachiya persimmon can be frozen for later use in steamed or baked puddings or in cookies. The following Persimmon Pudding may be baked and frozen for later use.

Persimmon Pudding

1 cup brandy
2 cups raisins, all dark or half dark and
 half light
1 cup sugar, or more if persimmons are not
 extremely ripe
2 cups all-purpose flour
1/8 teaspoon ground cloves
1/8 teaspoon nutmeg
2 teaspoons cinnamon
2 teaspoons baking soda
1/2 teaspoon salt
2 teaspoons vegetable oil
1 teaspoon vanilla extract
2 cups very ripe persimmon purée
2 cups chopped walnuts
3/4 cup milk

The day before you plan to make the pudding, add the brandy to the raisins, cover, and macerate for 24 hours.

Butter and flour a 9-inch angel food cake pan. (Two 8 x 4-inch loaf pans or smaller loaf pans may also be used.) Line the bottom of the pans with wax paper.

Combine all of the dry ingredients in a bowl. Combine the raisins and brandy, oil, vanilla, persimmon purée, and walnuts in another bowl. Add the dry ingredients alternately with the milk in thirds, blending well after each addition.

Pour the pudding into the prepared pan. If using smaller pans, fill only 3/4 full. Level the surface and bake in a preheated 325° F. oven for 1 and 1/4 to 1 and 1/2 hours. The pudding will bake in smaller pans for 1 to 1 and 1/4 hours. When done, the pudding should pull away from the sides slightly. It will be moist, but a cake tester should come out without any batter adhering to it.

Remove the pudding from the oven and cool it in the pan. Do not turn angel food cake pan upside down. When cool, remove pudding from the pan and peel off the paper.

The persimmon pudding may be frozen after baking and removed from the freezer the night before serving. It can be served at room temperature or wrapped in foil and reheated in a preheated 300° F. oven for 15 minutes.

The pudding may be served with a vanilla sauce or the following topping. Serves 12.

Topping

1 cup whipping cream, softly whipped
1 tablespoon brandy
2 tablespoons sugar
Pinch of nutmeg

Combine the above ingredients and serve a spoonful on top of each slice of pudding.

Pineapple

Gained Instant Favor

Pineapple is indigenous to the Americas. The Spaniards who first reached the New World, specifically the islands of the Caribbean, found pineapple growing there and later discovered it in Central and South America.

The Carib Indians hung pineapples or pineapple crowns at the entrances to their huts as a promise of welcome and an offer to serve refreshments. (To this day the pineapple is a symbol of hospitality in Southern homes.) However, even with this offer of hospitality the Caribs planted thick hedges of pineapple plants around their villages to keep strangers out.

Pineapples had been cultivated in Central and South America since the first millennium of our era as evidenced by ancient Peruvian pottery. Botanists think it is longer than that because no remains of pineapple have been found in archeological digs. Pineapple does not grow from seeds.

When the Europeans first encountered the pineapple, it was love at first sight. Columbus's men who found their first pineapples on the island of Guadeloupe were astonished by its flavor and fragrance. They reported that it had a delicious taste of melons, strawberries, raspberries and tart apples.

One half a century after its discovery by the Europeans, it was being grown in many tropical areas of the world and enjoyed by the affluent of Europe. Pineapples were being imported into Europe, although on a small scale for those who could afford them.

The transfer of pineapple to other countries was partly accidental. Ships leaving Central and South America took pineapples with them to provide fresh food for their crews during the long voyages. Pineapple, which is rich in vitamin C, helped prevent scurvy aboard ship. The crowns of the fruit, which were cut off when the pineapple was eaten, were planted wherever the ship touched land.

Pineapple cultivation did not start on the Hawaiian Islands until about three hundred years after its discovery by Columbus on his first voyage to the Caribbean island of Guadeloupe in 1492. The exact date when the fruit came to Hawaii is unknown. Records show that in 1813 pineapples grew in the garden of Don Francisco de Paula y Marin, a friend and advisor to King Kamehameha I.

The mainstay of today's pineapple industry is the "Smooth Cayenne" variety. In 1886 one thousand of these plants were imported into Hawaii from Jamaica by Captain John Kidwell. Although having excellent taste, the fruit did not keep well when shipped to the mainland.

James Dole, a young Harvard graduate, came to Hawaii from Boston in 1899 and pioneered the modern pineapple industry. He found that pineapple will grow on slopes too cool for sugar, Hawaii's main crop.

Dole began with a 64-acre homestead and, as he said, with "two horses, a plow, a harrow, a wagon, and a sixteen-year-old Chinese, complete with pigtail." At that time pineapple was not commonly known in America. One of Dole's first ads read, "Pineapple—you eat it with a spoon, like a peach!"

In 1901 Dole organized the Hawaiian Pineapple Company at Wahiawa on Oahu and planted more fields of pineapple. He built a small cannery, which was the forerunner of a giant factory in Honolulu. In 1903 Dole's cannery produced sixteen hundred cases of canned pineapple per year. Today, the same amount takes less than ten minutes.

Employing mechanized cultivation and research, Dole's venture skyrocketed to success. In 1921 he purchased the whole island of Lanai and converted fifteen thousand acres of its pasture land to pineapple, establishing the world's largest pineapple plantation.

Labor problems and excessive shipping rates to the mainland forced Dole to sell his company to Castle and Cooke in 1932. He remained active in the company until his retirement in 1948. He died in Hawaii in 1958.

Today Dole operates one of the largest fruit canneries in the world. During canning season each year, about ten million pineapples are washed, graded, peeled, cored, sliced or crushed, and canned daily. The mass production of canned pineapple was made possible by an invention of Henry G. Ginaca, a Dole employee. The machine, which bears his name, mechanized the peeling and coring operation.

Oahu, where pineapple was first planted, remains the center of the industry, with large plantings around Wahiawa. Honolulu continues to be the canning center; however, pineapple companies operate on five of the six major islands. Almost 700,000 tons of pineapple are produced annually on approximately 34,000 acres. Although the majority of the crop is still canned, refrigerated ships and air transportation have made it possible to ship fresh pineapple from Hawaii to the mainland.

Since pineapples are virtually seedless, they grow from shoots taken from the mother plant. Before planting the fields are plowed, disked, and carpeted by machine with tar paper to raise soil temperature, save moisture, and check the growth of weeds. On each acre about 17,000 shoots are hand planted through holes punched in the paper.

When the plant is twelve to fourteen months old, a bud grows at the top, which eventually becomes the fruit. Pineapple plants bear fruit in about twenty months. Each two- to three-foot plant produces only one pineapple.

One of my favorite pineapple recipes is for a Pineapple Upside-Down Cake. Serve this cake with whipped cream or vanilla ice cream.

Pineapple Upside-Down Cake

1/4 cup butter or margarine
1/2 cup brown sugar
1 (8 ounce) can sliced pineapple, drained
7 maraschino cherries
6 pecan halves

Heat oven to 350° F. Heat the butter in a round 9-inch layer cake pan in the oven until melted. Sprinkle brown sugar over the butter. Place 1 pineapple slice in the center of the pan. Fit remaining pineapple slices around the slice in the center. Place cherries in center of pineapple slices; also arrange pecans around the pineapple.

Cake Batter

1 1/4 cups all-purpose flour
1 cup sugar
1 1/2 teaspoons baking powder
3/4 cup milk
1/3 cup butter or margarine
1 egg
1 teaspoon vanilla

Beat all ingredients in a bowl with an electric mixer at low speed for 30 seconds. Then beat on high speed for 3 minutes, scraping the bowl occasionally. Pour the batter over the fruit in the pan. Bake cake in preheated 350° F. oven for 45 minutes. Invert onto a heat proof plate and let sit for a few minutes. Remove the pan. Serve warm. Serves 8.

Plums

Many Different Colors

Green, purple, rose, deep blue, and black — all are the colors of the plums that abound in our markets. Plums are one of the worlds most luscious fruits. They are second only to the peach in commercial production and surpasses the peach in the diverse climates in which they grow. Plums grow on every continent except the two polar regions.

Plums have the greatest diversification among stone fruits due to their many species, subspecies, varieties and sub varieties. The proliferation of plums is a rather recent phenomenon, occurring only in the last century and a half. Food historians tell us that the ancients knew only three or four species of plums. By the mid-1500s there were seven kinds of plums grown in Europe.

Plums have been cultivated in Asia since ancient times. They were first mentioned in the writings and songs of Confucius in 479 B. C. The plum tree plays a significant part in Chinese mythology and is associated with wisdom and longevity. Blossoms of the plum tree are carved on Chinese jade pieces to signify life after death.

Plums eventually were taken across Asia to the shores of the Mediterranean. Pompey the Great introduced them to the orchards of Rome and Alexander the Great eventually brought plums to the Mediterranean regions from where they spread throughout Europe.

The early settlers brought cuttings of plum trees to America. However, upon arriving they were surprised to find wild plums growing throughout the eastern coastal regions. The Indians had been enjoying this fruit for many years. Later some of the wild plums were domesticated and hybridized with the European varieties.

The three most popular plum types are the European, Damson, and Japanese species. Of the three the European types are grown over a wider area because they adapt easily to climatic conditions. Included in the European type of plums are the Stanley, Reine Claude (Green Gage) and the French and German prune (Fellenburg) types. These European plums are best for eating out-of-hand and canning.

Damson plums also grow well in this country. The fruit can be rather tart so it is used primarily for cooking and making preserves. Shropshire and French Damson are the most popular types in this country.

The Japanese-type plums grow best in the milder climates of California, because they bloom early and are susceptible to frost. Satsuma, Shiro, Burbank and Elephant Heart are the most popular Japanese types of plums.

Plums are known as prunes in France, and in earlier times, it is believed that both plum and prune meant the fresh fruit. Of course, the prune is the dried version of a variety of plum called La Petite d'Agen. It was brought to the United States in 1856 by French horticulturist Louis Pellier. He had come to California to participate in gold mining. After an unsuccessful mining career, he established prune orchards in Santa Clara County, south of San Francisco, and became financially successful.

The Green Gage plum differs from other plums by having a round rather than an oval pit. It is deliciously scented and flavored and has been cross bred to produce more sweetness and a larger fruit. The English name for this plum comes from Sir Thomas Gage, who introduced it into England from France in 1725.

The French version of the story of the Green Gage plum, gives an insight into political history. In France this plum is known as the Reine-Claude (Queen Claude). The queen for whom the plum was named was the first wife of Francis I (who reigned from 1515 to 1547), one of the most glamorous kings of France. However, since marriages at that time were pre-arranged, Francis accepted a wife with a congenital limp inherited from her mother. She also very obese and became progressively more so to the end of her short life.

Francis married Claude because she was the duchess of Brittany. The kings of France had tried desperately for years to acquire Brittany through a royal marriage. King Francis did his duty, and so did Claude. In spite of her cumbersome physical condition, she gave birth in eight years to seven children, four daughters and three sons, before dying from a lack of energy at the age of twenty-five. One of her sons became Henry II of France and Brittany.

While Claude lived, she presented a problem to diplomats and courtiers. The queen of France, by virtue of her rank, had to be complimented and flattered, but her unfortunate physical appearance made the customary tributes to grace and beauty a farce. A solution to this problem was to name the most luscious plum of France in her honor.

The earliest European plums were of the P. spinosa species. These plums are also known as sloe. Their pits have been found in early settlements in Switzerland dating back to Neolithic times. The sloe is the black sheep among plums, usually associated with drinking and swindling, and has no value except for making wine and sloe gin. It is too sour and bitter to eat.

The sloe plum is considered to be fraudulent in three ways: its juice is one of the ingredients in cheap wines pawned off on the public as port. Since the fruits of the sloe plum tree are small, nearly round, and blue with red-dish pulp, the unripe sloe plums are sometimes sold in France as olives and the leaves of the plant are used to imitate tea.

This German Plum Cake is made with a yeast dough, which has the most heavenly scent as it is baking. Serve the cake warm with whipped cream or ice cream.

German Plum Cake

2 pounds fresh Italian plums
1 package dry yeast
1 cup milk, lukewarm
3 1/2 cups all purpose flour
1/2 teaspoon salt
1 cup sugar
1/4 cup butter or margarine, softened
1 egg, slightly beaten
2 tablespoon butter or margarine

Wash and gently cut plums in half, removing the pits.

Sprinkle the yeast into 1/4 cup of the lukewarm milk and let stand until dissolved.

Mix the flour salt, and 1/3 cup of the sugar in a large bowl. Stir the dissolved yeast, butter, egg and remaining milk into the flour. Knead into a soft dough. Let rise in a warm place for 30 to 40 minutes. Punch the dough down and roll on a lightly floured board into an oblong 9 x13-inches. Fit into a greased pan of that size. Pinch the edges to make a slight edge around all sides. Let rise for 20 minutes.

Place the plums on top of the dough, cut side up. Sprinkle with the remaining sugar and dot with the 2 tablespoons of butter. Bake in a 350° F. oven for 35 to 40 minutes. Cut in pieces and serve slightly warm. Serves 8 to 10.

Rhubarb

Tart Stalks

For years there was a controversy as to whether rhubarb is a fruit or a vegetable. Botanically it has been classified as a fruit, but since it has a considerable amount of stem and leaves many food experts consider it a vegetable. The U.S. Customs Court at Buffalo, New York, made a bureaucratic ruling in 1947 that rhubarb is a fruit, based on the simple observation that is how it is normally eaten.

Whatever its classification, rhubarb is an ancient plant. It was first grown in northern Asia —Siberia, Mongolia, or northern China.

Rhubarb does not grow from seed, but has to be propagated by cutting the root into pieces with a bud attached to each, and then planting them separately -- the same as planting potatoes.

Rhubarb reached the Western world at the beginning of the Christian era. Iit has been determined that rhubarb was brought to the area by the barbarians and hence its name.

The name rhubarb comes from the Latin "Rhabarbarum." Rha was the word for barbarians and also the name of the European river along whose banks rhubarb was cultivated by the barbarians. The name of the Rha River today is the Volga. The plant became known as "rha barbarum," which was the origin of the Anglicized word rhubarb.

About 200 B.C. the Chinese had found that rhubarb possessed medicinal properties. For centuries rhubarb continued to be known for its medicinal qualities, particularly as an appetite stimulant and in larger doses as a laxative. It later became important to the Chinese as an article of trade with western Asia and the Arab countries. In medieval Europe the rhubarb plant was prevalent in monastery gardens and its dried, powdered form was used in abbey pharmacies.

Rhubarb plants reached England in the sixteenth century and the English were the first to eat it. For centuries, Europeans who developed a taste for rhubarb cooked the leaves like spinach and disregarded the stalk. To most Europeans, however, even the leaves were too tart to make them a common food.

It was a long time before people thought of eating the stem. The first recorded recipe appeared in 1783. John Farley, in his book, The London Art of Cookery, advocated slicing the stalks and cooking them like gooseberries. In the early 1800s recipes for rhubarb pies and tarts, plus rhubarb wine became available and were widely used. Rhubarb also became the basis for meat and poultry sauces. During the Victorian period in England, rhubarb became so popular that it was grown out of season in greenhouses.

The French never had much use for rhubarb, although it is sold in the markets in Paris. For centuries rhubarb was grown in the royal ornamental gardens, because of its attractive foliage. Today rhubarb is primarily consumed in France only along the northern French border and in French Flanders.

Rhubarb was scarcely grown in the United States before 1820. The first recorded cultivation of the plant was in New England. Today, it is commercially grown in the Pacific Northwest, California, Michigan, and New York. The rhubarb in our local markets comes mainly from California and Oregon.

The Matanuska Valley in Alaska, which has become a highly-productive agricultural area, also grows rhubarb. Because of the long days of warm climate in the summer, rhubarb grows fast in Alaska. It must be planted in a separate plot or it will overpower anything growing near it. In the Matanuska Valley rhubarb grows to a height of four feet compared to that of two feet in the "lower Forty-eight."

Rhubarb benifits from being partnered with other flavors, especially strawberry, orange, and spices such as cinnamon and ginger. Cooking quickly reduces it to a pulp, thus cook rhubarb pieces very briefly until just done to retain their shape.

Even though the French are not fond of Rhubarb my Rhubarb-Strawberry Tart is of French origin. The custard topping mellows the tartness of the rhubarb.

Rhubarb-Strawberry Tart

Crust

1 1/4 cups all-purpose flour
1/4 cup sugar
1/2 cup butter, preferably unsalted
2 to 3 tablespoons ice water

Combine the flour and sugar. Cut the butter into small pieces and cut it into the flour until the mixture resembles fine crumbs. Sprinkle with the ice water, and with a fork form it into a ball. Depending on the humidity of the day, more water may be needed. Place the dough in the refrigerator for at least 1 hour.

Filling

1 1/2 pounds rhubarb, trimmed and cut
  into 1-inch pieces
8 large strawberries, sliced
2/3 cup sugar
3 eggs separated
1/4 cup whipping cream
Grated rind of 1/2 lemon

Place the rhubarb and strawberries in a bowl and sprinkle with half of the sugar. Let the mixture sit for 30 minutes to draw out the juice.

In the meantime, roll out the pastry and line a buttered 10-inch tart pan with it. Prick the pastry well and bake it for 10 minutes in a preheated 375° F. oven.

Drain the rhubarb, reserving the juice, and place it in the pastry shell. Sprinkle the filling with half of the remaining sugar and return the tart to the oven to bake for 20 minutes.

Beat the egg yolks with the remaining sugar and beat in the rhubarb juice and the cream. Add the lemon rind. Beat the egg whites until stiff, but not dry, and fold them into the egg yolk mixture. Pour this custard over the rhubarb. Return the tart to the oven and bake for another 20 minutes. Serve warm or cold.

Serves 8.

Strawberries

Once a Great Luxury

Strawberries were one of the first packaged foods sold in the sixteenth century in England. They were packaged in "pottles," which were cone-shaped straw baskets, hence probably the name strawberries. As they had to be harvested, packaged, and brought to market speedily, strawberries at the time were very expensive and gained the reputation of being a snobbish food of the upper class.

Another theory on the origin of the name strawberry is that it comes from the practice of laying straw under the plants to protect the berries from pests in the soil. Some food historians believe that the name came from the plant's straying runners, as "streaw" can be taken to mean strew rather than straw.

Historically strawberries grew wild in middle and northern Europe, but offered little food value in exchange for the effort needed to gather them. In addition, their period of ripeness was short, about six weeks. They did not lend themselves to preservation nor did they improve with cultivation.

Strawberry cultivation first took place in France in the late 1300s. According to historians, King Charles V had strawberries planted in his royal gardens. They were also planted in the gardens of the Duchess of Burgundy, and in a hospital garden in the north of France. However, there was no domestication of the strawberry plant at thattime. Wild strawberry plants were merely transplanted to these gardens and to the gardens of the nobility.

By the fifteenth century strawberries had become popular for eatong and were being sold by street vendors in London. A century later they were also being sold on the streets of Paris with a warning that the berries were fragile and should be eaten as soon as possible.

From then on the strawberry also became a part of herbal medicine. The strawberry leaves were boiled for a tea to relieve gastric distress. Ripe strawberries were eaten to relieve hot flashes and redness of the face.

Probably the most faithful user of strawberries in history was Madame Tallien who, during Napoleon's time, added strawberry juice to her bath water to keep her skin soft and satiny. Twenty-two pounds of crushed strawberries were used every time she took a bath.

The existence of wild strawberries in North America was first recorded by Jacques Cartier in 1534. He reported seeing large wild strawberries in Canada. Almost a hundred years later strawberry plants were taken to Europe from the American colonies. Strawberry cultivation and propagation became an avid hobby of the English nobility who vied for the honor of producing the largest and most aromatic berry. Strawberry Hill and Strawberry Plantation became popular estate names on both sides of the Atlantic at the time.

Today the strawberry is a commonly cultivated fruit — both commercially and in home-gardens. The strawberry's botanical history is as tumultuous as its social one. The contemporary cultivated strawberry is actual a combination of two species.

One of the species was discovered in the early 1700s when a Frenchman, Amedee Francois Frezier, was sent to South America on a spying mission. The purpose of the mission has long been forgotten, but Frezier became intrigued with the deep red, large strawberries he found in Chile. Frezier smuggled some plants out of the country and they were planted in the king's gardens in Paris.

Once on the continent, it was inevitable that the South American species of strawberries should meet its North American counterpart — the Virginiana species. The Virginiana species had been previously sent to England by the Virginia colonists. It was received with great acclaim for its large size and prolific fruiting.

In the United States in the late 1700s and early 1800s strawberries were being grown primarily in home gardens. If they were available in the markets it meant that they were grown nearby. For example, in Philadelphia in the early 1800s strawberries were being cultivated in the suburbs near the market. At the time it was also fashionable to frequent the city's many "strawberry gardens" to eat the delectable berries on the spot.

Elsewhere strawberries were a luxury. In the 1840 presidential campaign Martin Van Buren was accused of using public money to raise that rare commodity for his own table.

One night in June of 1847, the Erie Railroad used its milk train to bring eighty thousand baskets of strawberries to New York City, which quickly became the largest market in the world for this fruit. In 1851 James Wilson developed a heavy-yield strawberry which made growing the fruit more profitable. By 1880 there were a hundred thousand acres of strawberries under cultivation in the United States compared to only fourteen hundred at the beginning of the century.

Today no other fruit yields more food per acre in a short time than the strawberry. Seventy-five percent of all strawberries consumed in the United States are grown in California, with harvests of one and a half billion pounds each season. Florida, the next largest producing state, produces four to five million trays — only as much as California harvests in a week during peak season.

Strawberries have a peculiar and unique structure. Botanists refer to them as "false" or "accessory" fruits. The seeds, which unlike those of any other fruit are on the outside, and are the true fruits of the plant. The fleshy berry to which the seeds are attached is an enlarged, softened receptacle. It corresponds to the small white cone that remains on the stem of a raspberry when the fruit is picked. The seeds of a strawberry are small and not as bothersome as those of the raspberry or blackberry.

For years one of my favorite desserts has been a Strawberry Pie. It is very simple to prepare. The filling is made with jello, frozen whipped topping, such as Cool Whip, and poured into a ready-made graham cracker pie crust.

Strawberry Pie

1 (3 ounce) package strawberry gelatin
1/2 (8 ounce) container frozen dessert
   topping (such as Cool Whip), thawed
2 cups strawberries, hulled and cut into
   thick slices
1 (6 ounce) graham cracker crust
   (ready-made)

Place the gelatin in a bowl and pour 1and 2/3 cup boiling water over it. Stir to dissolve the gelatin. Let cool until it starts to congeal. (To speed up the congealing process place the bowl with the slightly cooled gelatin into a larger bowl with ice water. It will take about 10 minutes to start congealing.)

Remove 1/2 cup of the slightly congealed gelatin to another bowl. Fold in the thawed dessert topping. Then spread this mixture into the graham cracker crust. Add the strawberries to the remaining gelatin and spoon on top of the pie. Chill for 3 hours. Serves 6.

Watermelons

Large and Full of Juice

Watermelon is quite a distinctive fruit and unique among melons. The watermelon plant is a native of Africa and has a long history of cultivation. Watermelons were grown and consumed in Egypt before 2000 B.C. As the large green fruits are very refreshing, it is not surprising that the Israelites, wandering in the desert after their flight from Egypt and regretting the fruits they had left behind, thought wistfully of watermelons. (The Bible only mentions melons and does not specify which type of melon.)

The watermelon has one great advantage that encouraged its spread to lands around the Mediterranean and eastward into Asia. It is very useful as a source of potable liquid, especially where water supplies are polluted. However, in some places, where watermelons are sold by weight, one must beware of the practice of injecting additional water into the melons. Food writers tell us that this was a problem in Egypt, particularly Cairo, at one time. Watermelon seeds were sold along the ancient Middle East and Mediterranean trade routes.

Watermelons can be grown in the hotter parts of southern Europe, but have never gained the importance in Europe as other melons. In America watermelons gained early popularity. Watermelon seeds were brought to this country from Africa by the slaves and were soon growing in many Southern gardens.

Modern improved varieties, including seedless watermelons, have been developed mostly in the New World. By 1822 watermelons were grown as large as twenty pounds. Today a sixty pound watermelon is not uncommon and hundred pounds ones are not unknown. There are a number of contests throughout the country each year to find the largest watermelon.

Numerous varieties of watermelon exist today. They are of various shapes, colors, and sizes. Small ones are generally round and one of the best known of these is the Sugar Baby. It is dark green and is an early-ripening variety. "Baby" is a comparative term, as the fruits average seven-to-nine pounds. Wild watermelons are typically only the size of an orange.

"Sugar" and "sweet" are names that are merely wished onto many varieties of watermelons. No watermelon has more than a faintly sweet taste, that is why it is so refreshing. One of the largest and most common watermelons is the Charleston Gray, an elongated fruit with a pale green, marbled skin. Striped varieties are also widespread. Most have pink or red flesh, although there are also yellow-fleshed varieties, such as the Yellow Baby.

In the United States pickled watermelon rind has long been a favorite relish. When Amelia Simmons published her "American Cookbook" in 1796 many called it truly a book of American cookery because it included a recipe for Spiced Watermelon Pickles. Cooks in the southern states also liked to fry cubes of the rind, minus the skin. In some European countries, pieces of rind were often candied.

For years watermelon has been one of the favorite fruits of the South. In years past it was probably the only time when dignified ladies could let their manners "go to pot" so to speak. They along with the men would sit out under the trees on a hot day and enjoy the slurpy cold melon. They would also engage in the rather ungenteel pastime of seed spitting. This was hardly refined dining.

However, in the nineteenth-century South, watermelon also had a place at the more gracious table. Simple sliced watermelons with their brilliant red flesh were considered showy and were frequently served as dessert.

The recipe for watermelon ice that appeared in "Housekeeping in Old Virginia" published in 1879 has a unique touch: "A few of the seeds interspersed will add greatly to the appearance," suggests the cookbook. It probably never occurred to the hostess that there might be a problem of what to do with the seeds and she probably did not want them as black accents on her carpet.

At most outdoor food events in the summer watermelon-eating is a highlight and there are numerous watermelon eating contests around the country. The seventy-year old contest in Hope, Arkansas attracts some of the nation's top watermelon eaters.

Tipsy watermelon was a popular dessert before Prohibition. The liquor content varied from region-to-region — champagne, bourbon, rum, applejack, or cognac. All were good and made a special melon for a picnic or garden party.

To make tipsy watermelon, cut a deep plug about 2 inches square in a ripe watermelon. Remove the plug and through the incision make several deep stabs into the flesh of the melon with an ice pick or similar tool. Slowly pour in the liquor of your choice, as much liquid as the watermelon will take. Replace the plug and seal with tape. Refrigerate the watermelon for 24 hours, turning it four or five times to allow the liquor to permeate the melon evenly.

One of my favorite ways to serve watermelon in the summer is in the form of a cold soup. It is simple to make. I often serve it in the hollowed-out watermelon shell.

Watermelon Soup

1 medium elongated watermelon

Cut the top third off the watermelon. Scoop out the pulp of both sections, removing the seeds. Puree the pulp in a food processor. It will become quite watery. When 9 cups of pureed pulp have been achieved, save the extra pieces of watermelon flesh for other uses, such as fruit salad.

Cut zigzags in the top of the larger piece of scooped-out watermelon shell. Refrigerate until ready to serve.

Soup

9 cups watermelon pulp
1 1/2 cups buttermilk
2 tablespoons chopped fresh mint leaves
Mint leaves, for garnish

Combine the watermelon pulp, buttermilk, and chopped mint leaves in a large bowl. Refrigerate for 4 hours before serving.

To serve, pour the soup into the cold watermelon shell and garnish with mint.

Serves 10.

Other Fruits

Guava

Archaeological sites in Peru have established that guava was being eaten there in 800 B.C. Although native to Peru the guava tree had spread north to Mexico by 200 B.C. Europeans first encountered the fruit when they landed in Haiti. Spanish and Portuguese mariners spread the guava tree to other tropical regions. In the seventeenth century it was well established in India and Southeast Asia and has remained popular there ever since. Guavas are also grown in Hawaii, southern Florida, and southern California.

Guava fruits range in size from that of an apple to that of a plum and in shape from round to pear-shaped. They have a rough or smooth skin and can be greenish-white, yellow, or red. Large, pear-shaped white ones are considered to have the best taste. The fruit has an outer and inner zone, the latter containing many small gritty seeds. Seedless varieties are also available, however.

Guavas taste acid with sweet undertones and have an unusual aromatic quality. Apart from being eaten fresh, guavas are used in custards, ices, and cool drinks. They are also made into a popular jelly.

Lychee

The lychee or litchi is the best known of a group of tropical fruits native to China and Southeast Asia. Canned lychees have achieved a notoriety as the prime dessert in Chinese restaurants outside of China.

Lychees are the fruit of a large evergreen tree that has been cultivated in southern China since antiquity. During the first century A.D. lychees were considered the finest of southern Chinese delicacies. A special courier service with swift horses was established to bring fresh lychees from Canton north to the Imperial Court.

Today lychees are cultivated in a narrow climatic band from China through Thailand to northern India and Pakistan. The Pakistan region is especially productive with a crop larger than China. Lychees are also grown in South Africa, Hawaii, and Australia.

Lychees are a round fruit, about one and a half inches in diameter, with a tough, knobby skin which is red when the fruit is ripe and turns brown during shipment. Inside this fruit is a whitish pulp surrounding a large shiny, dark brown seed. Only the pulp is eaten. It has a flavor reminiscent of Muscat grapes. The fruit travels well if it is picked just before fully ripe.

Papaya

The papaya is one of the tastiest tropical fruits and looks somewhat like a pear-shaped melon. It is native to the lowlands of eastern Central America, but even before the arrival of the Europeans it was being cultivated beyond that area. The Spanish and Portuguese invaders took to papaya and quickly spread it to their other settlements in the West and East Indies. It was also taken to the Pacific islands as Europeans discovered them, and by 1800 was grown in all tropical regions. Hawaii and South Africa are now the main exporters of papaya.

The papaya plant is large, reaching heights of 20 feet. It is shaped like a palm tree but with big fingered leaves. The fruits hang from the top down in large clusters. The plant bears twelve to thirty fruits within a year, continues to fruit well for another two years, and is then cut down. Seedlings are planted in threes and the males, which bear no fruit, are used only for pollination. They are thinned when out they flower and their sex becomes apparent.

Papayas commonly weigh just over a pound, although much larger ones have recently appeared in the markets. They are pear-shaped, pale green when unripe and blotchy-yellow or -orange when ripe. A papaya is ripe when it begins to soften to the touch. The pulp inside is either creamy orange or yellow. It is delicately scented and sweet. The taste is slightly lacking in acidity and is enhanced with a squeeze of lime juice.

At the center of the fruit is a mass of black seeds encased in a gelatinous coating. These are edible, although generally discarded. They are crunchy and have a slightly peppery taste, like mustard and cress.

Papaya fruits and their leaves contain an enzyme, papain, which has a powerful tenderizing effect on meat. Wherever papayas are grown, tough meat is cooked in a wrapping of papaya leaves or mixed with chunks of papaya before cooking. Commercial meat tenderizer, available in powder form, is made from papayas.

Pomegranate

The pomegranate has an interior of surprising beauty, like an ovoid Fabergé jewel-case opened to display a mass of rubies within. Pomegranates have been the subject of paintings and porcelain decorations for many centuries.

Pomegranates are natives to Persia (Iran), southern Russia, and regions of Afghanistan near the Himalayas. The fruit was known to the ancient Greeks, and reached the Romans in a round-about way via North Africa. Pomegranates have been cultivated and enjoyed since remote antiquity. They were known in Egypt. Moses had to assure the Israelites on their flight from Egypt that they would find pomegranates in the Promised Land.

The pulp of the pomegranate which surrounds the seeds is encased in a honeycomb of interior membranes. The name pomegranate, taken from the Spanish, refers to many grains or seeds. The seeds themselves, although edible, are intrusive and require a decision whether or swallow them or spit them out.

This problem is well illustrated by a classical legend. Persephone, daughter of Demeter, goddess of fruit, was carried off to the underworld by its god, Pluto. She vowed not to eat in captivity, but eventually succumbed and ate a pomegranate, spitting out all the seeds, except six, that she swallowed. Demeter begged Pluto to return Persephone to her. When Pluto finally gave in to Demeter, he was allowed to keep Persephone in the underworld for six months of every year. Due to those six seeds she swallowed, six months became winter.

After the fall of the Roman Empire, pomegranates disappeared until the ninth and tenth centuries when the invading Arabs brought them to Sicily and then to Spain. Spanish sailors took the pomegranate from the Mediterranean region to America. It was a useful fruit for sea voyages as its hard skin helps to preserve it. It is now cultivated in parts of South America, Mexico, and California.

Wild pomegranates contain a high portion of seeds and are quite astringent. In contrast, cultivated pomegranates have juicy pulp with a sweet sharp flavor that is only slightly astringent. The pulp can be eaten from the half-skin with a spoon, or may be delicately separated and placed in a dish.

Pomegranate juice makes a refreshing drink and is also used in cooking, particularly with lamb. Grenadine is a concentrated syrup made from pomegranate juice.

Meat and Poultry

Meat

Beef	109	Lamb	118
Bison	113	Pork	121
Game	114	Veal	126

Poultry

Chicken	129	Turkey	135
Duck	133		

Meat and Poultry

Meat

From the earliest times, man has been carnivorous. He obtained most of his food by hunting. Wild meat was plentiful and provided protein as well as other nutrients. Cooking meat at that time was a simple matter. It was roasted on a spit over an open fire, or cut into pieces and cooked with water in a bag made of animal skins.

Today meat is still an important part of our diet. It comes from three main types of domestic farm animals — cattle, sheep, and pigs — providing us with beef and veal, mutton and lamb, and pork. Regional preferences, religion, and climate influence the type of meat most prevalent in the diet in various parts of the world. For example in China it is pork, in the Middle East it is mutton and lamb, and in Europe and America it is primarily beef. This was not always true in America as pork was more prevalent until the beginning of the 1900s.

At one time beef and mutton were very tough, fatty and strongly flavored. Candles were made from beef and mutton fat so fatty animals were preferred. Sheep were bred for their leather and wool and were slaughtered only after their fleece was no longer productive. After the development of modern road and rail transportation, the choices of meat increased as animals could be swiftly brought to market in distant locations.

The meat we purchase at the butcher counter today is a product of selective breeding and feeding techniques. The present-day demand for lean and tender meat has made the meat of cattle, sheep, as well as pigs more compact that those of a century ago.

Poultry

The word poultry is used to describe all domestic feathered fowl bred as food. The term covers, chickens, ducks. turkeys, geese, guinea hens, and domestic pigeons or squabs. Chickens are descended from the wild jungle fowl of the pheasant family which were in the Indus Valley four thousand years ago. Records show that the farmers of ancient Mesopotania bred ducks and geese were popular in Germany as early as 1000 B.C. Turkeys were domesticated by the Aztecs of Mexico long before the Spaniards arrived. There were also wild Turkeys in New England.

Over the years poultry farming has become very sophisticated. The demand for selective breeding for meat and eggs has led to automated production techniques. Poultry has become more popular than any other meat.

Beef

King of Meats

Raising cattle as a source of food has been practiced as long as history has been recorded. Prehistoric cave paintings depict the bull as a symbol of strength and fertility in Sumerian and Semitic religions. For the Syrians the bull was the symbol for the god of storms. Bulls also show up in Roman mythology.

By 3500 B.C. cattle had been domesticated in Egypt. There are numerous references to cattle in the Bible and even in the Ten Commandments. Owning cattle in ancient times was the equivalent to owning great wealth. Although cattle did not serve as money they were very important barter items and were used to value merchandise. In ancient Greece a slave was worth four oxen and a concubine cost as much as twenty oxen.

Because cattle were expensive in ancient Greece, great feasts for heroes consisted primarily of beef. The host of such feasts could have served his guests game, which could be had for the taking, but serving beef meant that he was presenting wealth to the honored guest. The cow was killed by the host, himself, and roasted by the male members of the family over an open fire. In ancient Greece beef meat was considered too precious to be entrusted to women, whether for cooking or eating.

By medieval times beef became more common, but was still highly regarded. The common man ate salt pork and mutton infrequently and beef was only the privilege of the wealthy. The butcher's guild of Paris even had their own church with two carved bulls on the facade.

By the fourteenth century the cuts of beef numbered thirty with sirloin being the most popular. Beef was still popular when four centuries later Richelieu gave a banquet where most of the dishes consisted of beef. The animals

eyelids were included in one of the hors d'oeuvre dishes. Every part of the animal was used at this banquet except the feet.

Louis XVI was so fond of beef that when he was arrested while attempting to escape the guillotine, he had a supply of short ribs in his coach. It is reported that he munched on the ribs on his way to his death.

Beef became very popular across the channel in England, although not as popular as in France. Beef was widely available during affluent Tudor times. Most of the English middle class at that time ate their main meal at noon and beef was usually included.

By the eighteenth century the English became known as beefeaters. At mealtime tables were loaded with large dishes of meat, including boiled beef heaped with carrots, cabbage, and turnips. Massive roasts were cooked on spits over an open fire. However, smaller cuts of beef were available.

In London there was an event that could be called a culinary revolution — the introduction of the beef steak. Steak became so popular that clubs were formed to study beef under the most favorable circumstances, dining. One such club, founded in 1735, the "sublime Society of Beefsteaks" had as their motto "Beef and Liberty," and their emblem was a gridiron upon which steaks were broiled.

The availability of beef in England was partly due to the unique experiments conducted by Lord Townshend, known as "Turnip Townshend." He proved that cattle could be kept well in winter in barns by feeding them turnips. Townshend inspired Robert Bakewell, England's first commercial stock breeder, to develop hardier and weightier cattle in order to produce better beefsteaks.

In France, as in England, butchering techniques, particularly for steaks, were gradually improved. Only city butchers, however, could be relied on to cut a beefsteak for the grill. Steaks became part of the French cuisine and recipes were developed for it. One chef invented a recipe for strips of fillet steak with mushrooms and sour cream and dedicated it to Count Stroganoff. In the Café Anglais in Paris, the composer Rossini was honored with tournedos Rossini, a filet mignon served with a truffle sauce.

By the nineteenth century, the English had been outdone by the Americans as beefeaters. In the mid-1800s Americans were eating twice as much beef per person as the English. An article in "Harper's Weekly" noted that the most common meal in America was steak. In the East most of the beef came from the Carolinas and Georgia. By 1854 Texas Longhorns became the main source of beef in the East.

The cattle raised by Mexican ranchers in Texas became known as Texas Longhorns. When these ranchers fled south after Texas independence in 1836, they left the Longhorns, descendants of the Andalusian cattle the Spanish had brought with them to Mexico, to roam free. When the Americans settled Texas they inbred the Longhorns with other species, such as Herefords. These cattle were herded a thousand miles to railroad centers for shipment east.

Texas cattle were driven north to railheads in the Midwest and shipped East by rail. The Shawnee Trail, the first of the great cattle trails opened from Brownsville on the Gulf through Dallas to Missouri in 1840. The most heavily traveled was the Chisholm Trail to Kansas. Half of all of the cattle moved from Texas followed it. The heyday of the cattle drives lasted about twenty years, from 1865 to the mid-1880s. During this period five million cows were moved from Texas to rail heads in Kansas and Missouri. The great cattle drives came to an end with the expansion of the railroads into Texas. Eventually refrigeration made it possible to slaughter closer to the cattle ranches and ship meat instead of live cattle. In addition to supplying Americans with their favorite meat, the cowboys who herded them popularized a new way of cooking — the barbecue.

In the latter part of the 1800s South Dakota became known for its cattle raising. In 1876, when the gold fever was at its height in South Dakota, there were no cattle on the lush prairies. Only a few remaining buffalo and a few oxen, abandoned by settlers moving west, roamed the vast grazing lands. Two years later when the value of the grazing land became apparent, however, there were 100,000 head of cattle in South Dakota. Five years later the number had risen to 800,000.

The new cattle industry appealed to European investors as there was money in food. The Scottish acquired large land holdings and hired hundreds of cowboys on their payrolls. In the late 1800s a Scottish accent was all that was needed as collateral for a mortgage to start a ranch and raise cattle in South Dakota.

Along with the Scots came their cattle—Scottish Highlanders, Aberdeen Angus, and white faced Herefords. Many returned to Scotland as meat. In 1883 South Dakota shipped 50,000 dressed beef carcasses on ice to Glasgow. Even with all of the cattle on the range, however, the majority of the American population mainly ate pork. At the time beef steak, like store-bought bread, was a luxury that few could afford. Today Americans eat more beef than any other country in the world. The average consumption of beef is sixty-five pounds per person per year in all types of beef dishes.

Many of the early American beef dishes have survived and are still a part of American cuisine. Corned beef was eaten by generations of Americans who otherwise would have been without beef meat in winter. Meat pies introduced by early English settlers made good use of leftover roasts and could be baked in the fireplace. Pot roasts were named for the vessels in which they were cooked, primarily Dutch ovens of the early New Englanders. Even the hamburger is a twentieth-century update of the minced beef first eaten by the early colonials without the benefit of forks.

Beef recipes often reflect the ethnic heritage of the people who settled this country. They have often combined cooking techniques and ingredients from other countries. For example, a grilled steak of English origin is seasoned with oriental flavorings in the Oriental Flank Steak recipe. Italian Beef Stew is cooked with wine and olives and may be served with mashed potatoes or polenta.. Also influenced by English cookery is my Beef Fillet in Puff Pastry, which tops the beef filet with sautéed mushrooms instead of the traditional liver pâté.

Oriental Flank Steak

1 large flank steak, about 2 pounds
2 tablespoons oil
1/4 teaspoon sesame oil
1/2 teaspoon garlic powder
1/2 teaspoon onion powder
1/8 teaspoon ground cloves
2 teaspoons fresh chopped ginger
5 tablespoons soy sauce
5 tablespoons orange juice concentrate
5 tablespoons brandy
Coarsely ground pepper, to taste

Score the flank steak on both sides and place in a shallow pan. In a small bowl combine the remaining ingredients and pour them over the steak. Marinate at room temperature for 2 hours, or in the refrigerator for 4 hours, turning the steak occasionally. Broil 3 to 4 inches from the heat or on the grill for 4 to 5 minutes per side for medium. Slice thinly across the grain at a 45° angle. Serves 4.

Beef Stew with Olives

5 tablespoons olive oil
2 1/2 pounds boneless beef chuck,
    cut into 1 1/2-inch cubes
1 medium onion, chopped
2 carrots, chopped
6 ounces crimini mushrooms, sliced
3 tablespoons chopped parsley
1 garlic clove, chopped
Few sprigs fresh thyme, or 1/4 teaspoon
    dried thyme leaves
Pinch of ground nutmeg
1 cup red wine
1 (14 ounce) can diced tomatoes
1/2 cup beef broth
1 (3 and 1/4 ounce) can black olives,
    halved
Salt and pepper, to taste
1 large red pepper, cut into strips

Heat 3 tablespoons of the oil in a large, heavy saucepan or Dutch oven. Brown the meat, a little at a time, turning it to brown all sides. Remove meat from the pan when it is browned.

When all the meat has been browned and removed, add the remaining oil, onion and carrots. Cook over low heat until the onion softens. Add the mushrooms, parsley, and garlic, and cook for 3 to 4 minutes more.

Return the meat to the pan, increase the heat to medium and stir well to mix the vegetables with the meat. Stir in the thyme and nutmeg. Add the wine, tomatoes, beef broth, and olives, and mix well. Season with salt and pepper. Bring to a boil. Cover the pan and place it in the center of a preheated 350° F. oven. Bake for 1 and 1/2 hours. Remove the pan from the oven. Stir in the strips of pepper. Return the stew to the oven and cook, uncovered, for another 15 to 20 minutes. Peppers should be crisp-tender. Serves 6.

Fillet of Beef in Puff Pastry

1/2 ounce dried porcini mushrooms
1 sheet frozen puff pastry (from
 a 17 1/4 ounce package)
2 tablespoons olive oil
12 ounces crimini mushrooms, sliced
6 ounces shiitake mushrooms, cut in strips
1 medium onion, chopped
Salt and pepper, to taste
Flour for rolling pastry
1 1/2 pounds fillet of beef
1 egg yolk, beaten
1/2 cup beef broth
2 tablespoons whipping cream

Put the porcini mushrooms in a bowl, pour 1 cup boiling water over them, and let them soften for at least 30 minutes. Then defrost the pastry.

While the pastry is defrosting, heat the olive oil in a large skillet over medium heat, add the crimini and shiitake mushrooms and onion, and sauté them for a few minutes. Squeeze as much liquid as possible out of the porcini mushrooms, reserve the liquid. Then cut the porcini into strips and add them to the mushrooms in the skillet. Add salt and pepper, to taste. Continue sautéing the mushrooms until all of the liquid has evaporated. Set aside and let cool while preparing the pastry.

Roll out the pastry so that it is large enough to fit around the piece of beef and long enough to generously seal the ends. Salt and pepper the beef. Place the pastry on a baking sheet. Then put a layer of mushrooms the same width as the beef down the center of the pastry. Place the beef on top of the mushrooms. Pack the remaining mushrooms on top of and around the sides of the beef, using your hands to press them onto the meat. Quickly fold the pastry across the top and brush the overlap with some of the beaten egg yolk. Then fold the ends of the roll to close it and seal it with the egg wash. If there are any pieces of dough remaining, use them to make a design on top, sticking them on with the egg wash. Brush the top of the pastry with remaining egg wash. (It may be necessary to use an additional egg yolk.)

Bake the pastry in a preheated 375° F. oven for 22 to 25 minutes for medium rare. Insert a meat thermometer to test the doneness. It should register 140° F.

While the beef is baking combine the reserved mushroom liquid and the beef broth in a small saucepan and reduce by half. Just before the beef is ready, stir in the cream and heat through.

To serve, slice the beef, divide among 4 plates, and spoon some of the sauce over each serving. Serves 4.

Bison

Extremely Lean Meat

It's a "he-man" piece of meat according to many food writers. This hunk of meat with virtually no fat comes from the American buffalo, the official designation of which is bison. The name was selected by Congress to differentiate the American Buffalo from the Asian Water Buffalo and the African Cape Buffalo. For years historians have used these terms interchangeably.

More and more chefs are featuring a bison dish on their menus. It is a regular menu item at the Four Seasons restaurant in New York and the Red Sage restaurant in Washington. Many upscale supermarkets are selling bison meat. It is usually available by specific cuts in vacuum-sealed packages.

Aside from the novelty, buffalo meat is good for you. It is extremely low in fat, even the ground meat is ninety-seven percent fat free. It is lower in cholesterol than skinless chicken breast. The demand from the general public for lean meat continues to grow and bison meat is probably the leanest being sold commercially.

Before the settlers came to the Great Plains, buffalo were the main sustenance for the Plains Indians. The animals provided food, clothing and shelter for these native Americans. At one time buffalo roamed the plains in such numbers that as one writer described the sight as "the plains were black and appeared as if in motion."

It has been estimated that as many as forty million buffalo roamed the plains prior to their rapid decline in the middle-to-late 1800s. With the coming of settlers, the growth of sheep and cattle ranches, and the coming of the railroads the buffalo gradually disappeared.

Hunters frequently killed buffalo for the fur and left the meat, except for the tongue which was considered a delicacy. By the turn of the century less than a thousand buffalo were left in the United States and Canada.

Through the efforts of conservationists, producers, and native Americans the buffalo has been saved from extinction and they are no longer an endangered species. There are now more than 150,000 buffalo in public and private herds in the United States and Canada. Many of the buffalo in private herds are being raised as meat animals, just like cattle.

The meat cuts of bison are similar to beef, although they tend to be smaller. All of the steaks and filets are smaller as they come from the rear quarter of the bison which is much narrower than beef cattle. Another factor that contributes to the smallness of the cuts of meat is that there is only 1/8 inch fat covering on the bison as opposed to 2 inches of fat on beef.

Compared to beef most bison cuts are almost double in price. However, because the meat is very dense, typical serving portions are smaller.

Any beef recipe can be used for bison. Bison steaks are usually grilled and should be served medium-rare due to the density of the meat. Moist cooking, cooking with some liquid, is best for the larger roast-type cuts of bison.

Game

Early Food of Man

Through the centuries man has hunted game to provide food for his family. The art of hunting and rules governing it have changed over the years, but the purpose of providing food is still the same.

Until the seventeen century hunting in Europe was restricted to the nobility and aristocrats. In the early 1600s many of the European countries passed laws governing hunting and the sale of game, if it was not used in the household of the hunter.

Poaching was a persistent concern in Europe at that time. Only legally obtained game could be sold during specific hours in public markets and in front of town halls. Laws also specified who was permitted to buy and sell game. If a stall at a market sold cooked foods, such as meat pies, the owner was not permitted to sell any game, although he was allowed to sell meat from domesticated animals.

Peacocks were one of the prized game animals, until the seventeen century when they were domesticated. From then on they were only occasionally eaten at elaborate banquets.

At that time, after any game was killed it was hung by its feet so that the blood would drain, making the meat more tender. Most game was hung in a cold place for eight to ten days before skinning and butchering.

In this country deer, squirrel, and rabbit were the most common wild meat for the early settlers. However, early diaries indicate that anything that ran and could be caught was regarded as a potentially edible item.

Early Virginia explorers recorded that beaver was generally tough and dry, except for the tail. Polecat had a sweet taste. The meat of a raccoon was highly regarded not only as food, but was also good to rub on swelling and inflammations of the body. Wildcat was favorably compared to young beef, though sweeter and more delicate. Otter was only eaten in times of near famine,

Buffalo, occasionally roamed through some of the northeast. Their roamings helped to clear footpaths in the dense forests. Buffalo were much sought-after targets for the hunter's bow and gun until the burly animals moved west toward the open plains.

The most highly prized game meat in colonial times was bear meat. It was very tasty and supposedly easily digestible. Both the Indians and the white man praised bear not only for its flavor, but because they believed that great sexual powers were given to those who ate it. The bear was also hunted for its oil, which was used as a mosquito repellent.

Wild meat pies and hashes helped to sustain hundreds of settlers until vegetable crops could be planted and harvested. Before the colonists' first century in America had passed, however, a shortage of game developed. Towns began to legislate game laws regulating the hunting and trapping of larger animals. As early as 1646 Portsmouth, Rhode Island, closed deer-hunting season for six months of the year. Other areas soon followed suit.

These game laws helped in part to preserve the number of game animals that were rapidly being diminished by commercial trappers hunting for pelts.

During the early eighteenth century, thousands of carcasses from wild animals were left behind, while their valuable skins were sent to Europe for clothing and other manufactured items. Nearly one million deer skins were reportedly sent from South Carolina to England during the first fifteen years of that century. A century before, America's woods teemed with white-tail deer. During the first years of

Jamestown an estimated 200,000 deer roamed nearby and herds of fifty were common.

The Atlantic coast Indians had their own hunting and cooking rituals. Most hunted food on a day-to-day basis. Both legend and sacred taboos influenced the cooking techniques of almost every tribe, particularly those that depended heavily on hunting.

One widespread belief was that if the dinner pot contained both the meats of the ground animals and the birds of the air, then the forest gods would be provoked into driving away all game. Thus most Indians rejected the mixed pots, or hotchpots, which were favorite dishes of the white settlers.

Many tribes worshipped gods who periodically appeared in animal form such as snakes and rabbits. These meats were, of course, taboo. Young braves on their first hunt dared not consume the first animal they slew, for it was understood that the penalty for such an act would be permanent bad luck at hunting.

Probably the most frequently held belief of many of the Indian tribes was the existence of the animal soul that could communicate with other wildlife both before and after death. As a result, detailed rituals were observed in the hunting, killing, and eating of wild game. The idea was that if an animal's carcass was treated without respect, its soul would warn the other living game to flee the Indian hunters. Elaborate ceremonies where braves praised the beauty, valor, and goodness of the kill were aimed at prompting the animal's soul to pass a message to other beasts that, if killed, they would be treated fairly.

Some tribes developed a system that assured food for members of the community who were not good hunters. On a mass tribal foray, the brave who brought down the kill was allowed the prime parts. The first hunter to ac-tually touch the animal received the next best share. In this way a poor marksman, if he was swift on foot, could still provide for his family.

Mass hunting matches were held by the Indians during the severe winter months. Unlike the fair weather season when game abounded in the forests near permanent villages, Indians in cold climate were forced to travel great distances to obtain food. Bows and arrows and spears were the most common hunting implements until guns were obtained from the settlers. Often packs of Indian dogs, a cross bred between domesticated species and wolves, cornered small animals or attack a deer or bear.

Bows and arrows are still used for hunting local deer during a specified period preceding the hunting season with guns.

In many of the European countries hunters can take their deer to the local butchers for processing as well as for sale. Maybe one of these days with FDA approval and inspectors this may also happen in this country. For now those of us who like venison have to depend on our "favorite hunter" or purchase farm raised venison which is scarce and expensive.

Each fall hunters from throughout the nation flock to South Dakota to hunt pheasants. The sport is so popular that game farms stock local hunting areas through government contracts. Pheasants are also commerically available from game farms in many states.

One of my favorite recipes for venison is of German origin. The meat is first marinated in buttermilk to remove some of the gamey taste. It is then roasted in the oven and served with a delicious gravy and Spätzle.

In the pheasant recipe the pheasant breast is covered with bacon to provide additional moisture during roasting. The juniper-flavored cabbage is a flavor contrast to the tarragon and slightly sweet glaze on the pheasant.

Roast Loin of Venison with Spätzle

1 fillet of venison (about 2 pounds)
2 cups buttermilk
1/4 pound bacon
Salt and pepper
4 tablespoons butter
6 juniper berries, crushed
1/2 cup fresh or frozen cranberries
1 cup sliced crimini mushrooms
1 cup beef broth
1/2 cup sour cream
2 tablespoons red currant jelly

Marinate the venison in buttermilk for 2 days in the refrigerator. Turn the meat several times each day. Remove the meat from the buttermilk and pat dry.

Lard the loins with small pieces of bacon at intervals of about 2 inches (Use either a larding needle or make small slits in the meat and insert bacon). Rub loin well with salt and pepper.

Melt the butter in a roasting pan and brown the venison in it on all sides. Add the juniper berries, cranberries, mushrooms, and beef broth to the pan. Cover and place in a preheated 375° F. oven, for 18 minutes per pound for medium. It should be pink inside to be at its best.

Remove the meat to a carving board and cover with aluminum foil to keep it warm while making the gravy. Skim excess fat from the pan juices and stir in the sour cream and currant jelly. Heat for a minute or two and serve gravy with sliced meat. Serve with mashed potatoes or Spätzle. Serves 4 to 6.

Spätzle

3 eggs
1 1/2 cups all-purpose flour
1/2 cup milk
Dash each of salt, pepper, and nutmeg

In a bowl combine the eggs, flour and milk to form a medium-thick batter. Add the salt, pepper, and nutmeg. Bring lightly salted water to a boil in a large pot. When the water is boiling, place some of the batter on a small cutting board. Cut slivers of the dough and push them into the boiling water. Continue until all of the dough has been used. When the spätzle rise to the surface, cook for an additional minute or two. With a slotted spoon remove them from the water to a plate to dry.

The spätzle may be kept warm in a low temperature oven. After cooking place the spätzle into a shallow pan and drizzle a little melted butter over them to keep them from drying out.

Roasted Pheasant
with
Savoy Cabbage

1 pheasant (2 to 2 1/2 pounds)
1/3 pound sausage
1/2 tart apple, peeled, cored, and chopped
2 tablespoon chopped onion
3 large mushrooms, chopped
1/4 cup golden raisins
1/4 cup chopped walnuts
1/4 cup chopped parsley
1 egg, beaten
1/2 teaspoon celery seeds
Salt and pepper, to taste
1 large sprig tarragon or 1 teaspoon dried
*   tarragon*
3 slices bacon
1/2 cup dry sherry
2 tablespoons red currant jelly

Rinse the pheasant and pat it dry. Combine the sausage, apple, celery, mushrooms, raisins, walnuts, parsley, egg, celery seeds, salt, and pepper. Stuff the bird with the sausage mixture.

Place the pheasant in a shallow roasting pan. Put the tarragon sprig on the breast of the bird or sprinkle it with dried tarragon. Then place the bacon slices over the breast and roast the bird in a preheated 350° F. oven for 1 hour, or until the bird is almost tender. Pour off the fat. Combine the sherry and jelly, mixing well to blend. Baste the bird several times with this glaze and continue roasting it for another 15 minutes, or until the pheasant is tender.

To serve, spoon some cabbage on each of two plates. Cut the pheasant in half and place each half on top of the cabbage. Serves 2.

Savory Cabbage with Juniper Berries

1/2 medium head Savoy cabbage
2 tablespoons butter
1/3 cup chopped onion
10 juniper berries, slightly crushed
1/4 cup chicken broth
1/4 cup white wine
Salt and pepper, to taste

Shred the cabbage. Melt the butter in a medium-size saucepan, add the onions, and sauté them until they are a light brown. Add the rest of the ingredients. Cover and bring to a boil, then cook over low heat for 15 to 20 minutes, or until the cabbage is done.

Lamb

"Wool on a Stick"

Archaeological digs in the Middle East have found domesticated lamb bones dating back to 9000 B.C. According to archeologists the majority of these bones came from sheep that had been killed before reaching the age of one year. Early man preferred lamb to the stronger taste of mutton from older sheep.

Lamb as a domesticated animal for food became popular in the Middle East in Biblical times. As sheep flourished in the arid lands of the Middle East, they figured prominently in the folklore and religions of that area. The ancient Israelites were shepherds and lamb played an important role as ceremonial meat.

Before the flight of the Jews from Egypt the Lord instructed them to kill lambs and mark their doors with the blood. This exodus of the Israelites from Egyptian bondage is commemorated each year with the feast of Passover. In the Christian religion lamb is considered a symbol of Christ. Lambs also symbolize innocence and peace.

Sheep were also raised in prehistoric Greece where lamb is still the favorite meat. The Romans, too, raised sheep and lamb eventually became a favorite meat of most Mediterranean countries.

One of the first cookbook writers, Apicus, a Roman who lived in the first century A.D., wrote about recipes for lamb stew which included ginger, parsley, and honey. A Muslim, writing twelve centuries later, records a recipe for lamb cooked with pistachio nuts. This dish was popular among the Persians and Arabs and is mentioned in The Arabian Nights.

In India, lamb is an important meat, especially in Moslem areas where beef and veal are not eaten and pork is forbidden by religion. Lamb is also favored by the Hindus. A traditional Hindu feast, such as a wedding, consists of seven dishes — all made with lamb. The Chinese also include lamb in their cuisine.

In France the enjoyment of lamb has had its ups and downs. In the Middle Ages, the French did not care for the meat of young animals, which they thought insipid, but they made an exception for lamb.

Lamb declined in popularity in France when veal was accepted and suckling pig began to replace suckling lamb. However, the custom of blessing a lamb at Easter kept alive the tradition of serving whole lamb on that holiday until the time of Louis XV.

During the reign of Louis XV the first hybridization of sheep occurred. He imported Merino sheep from Spain on the hoof. These sheep, which were valuable for their wool were crossed with Rambouillets, valuable for their meat. The king was determined to have the best of both worlds. King Louis XVI always referred to lambs as "walking cutlets."

The monarchistic associations of lamb made that form of meat lose favor during Napoleon's reign. Once when lamb was served at a Napoleonic dinner party critics said the menu was vulgar and the reputation of Napoleon suffered greatly in public opinion.

Today lamb is held in high esteem in France. One of the best classic French dishes is a leg of lamb, seasoned with garlic, roasted, and accompanied by white beans. The prime French lamb is raised in the lower Alps or Provence where the animals feed on pungent wild herbs.

Until the 1970s few Americans ate lamb. It was not a highly publicized meat and was not a featured item on restaurant menus. Traditionally Americans have preferred beef.

Part of the American distaste for lamb seems to have stemmed from the conflict between cattle raisers and sheep herders in the West. In the late 1800s there were various skirmishes between sheep raisers and cattlemen, as there was not enough grass to sustain both types of animals and sheep were not usually fenced in. While sheep could graze after cattle they grazed too low for the remaining grasses to provide subsequent grazing for cattle. Now both are fenced into separate grazing lands.

For years Americans disdained lamb because it was mutton. Not until we began processing sheep of one year of age or younger, usually weighing around thirty-five to forty pounds, did the American public start eating lamb in quantity. Texans still refer to lamb chops as "wool on a stick."

According to the United States Department of Agriculture standards, the age of the lamb is not as important as its weight in determining marketability. Lambs are usually processed when they weigh between 105 and 115 pounds. Some markets and restaurants prefer 135-pound animals, which have larger chops.

In determining if the animal is lamb or mutton USDA inspectors check what is called the break joint, comparable to a human's wrist. If the joint will break, the meat is stamped lamb; if not, it is mutton. Spring lamb meat is really a myth since most lambs are born between January and March and are slaughtered between August and October. However, we also get what is called year-round lamb which runs eleven to twelve months in age. This is considered mutton by European standards.

I frequently use shoulder pieces of lamb for stew or ground lamb for meatballs, but prefer leg of lamb for Shish Kebobs. Cinnamon, cloves, coriander, and a hint to citrus flavorings enhance the Spicy Lamb Stew. Green and black olives and thyme, all typical flavorings of Provence, are used in the following meatball recipe inspired by a dish we enjoyed in a small bistro in Provence. Do not overcook the Lamb Shish Kebobs, as they are best when the meat is still quite pink on the inside.

Spicy Lamb Stew

2 tablespoons olive oil
2 pounds lamb stew, carefully trimmed and
    cut into 1 1/2-inch cubes
1 medium onion, chopped
1 garlic clove, minced
1/2 cup diced carrots
1 cup thickly sliced mushrooms
1/2 small orange, seeded and cut
    into 8 pieces
1 large strip lemon peel, cut in 4 pieces
1 cup red wine
1 cup tomato juice
1/2 teaspoon ground cloves
1/2 teaspoon ground cinnamon
1 teaspoon coriander
2 tablespoons all-purpose flour mixed with
    1/3 cup water, optional

Heat the olive oil over in a medium-size Dutch oven medium-high heat. Add the lamb and brown it. Add the onions, garlic, and carrots and sauté briefly. Then add the remaining ingredients. Cover and bake in a preheated 325° F. oven for 1 and 1/2 to 2 hours or until the meat is tender. Check occasionally to see if more liquid is needed; if so add equal parts of wine and tomato juice. Remove any fat that may have accumulated on top of the stew and thicken with flour and water, if desired.

Serves 4

Lamb Meat Balls al la Provence

1 pound lean ground lamb
1 teaspoon thyme
1 teaspoon coriander
1/4 teaspoon cayenne pepper
Salt and pepper
1 egg
3 tablespoons olive oil
2/3 cup beef broth
1/3 cup dry white wine
2 medium onions , chopped
2 medium carrots, sliced
3 medium tomatoes, sliced
4 medium potatoes, sliced
10 green olives, pitted
10 black olives, pitted
1 lemon, sliced
Finely chopped parsley

In a bowl combine the ground lamb with the thyme, coriander, cayenne pepper, salt, pepper, and egg. Mix well and form into small balls. Heat oil in a large skillet over medium-high heat. Add the meat balls and brown them on all sides. Stir in the beef broth and wine. Cover the skillet and simmer over low heat 20 minutes. Add the onions, carrots, tomatoes, potatoes, green and black olives and lemon slices. Cover and simmer an additional 35 to 40 minutes or until the vegetables are tender. Sprinkle with parsley and serve. Serves 4 to 6.

Lamb Shish Kebobs

3 pounds boneless lamb,
    free of fat and gristle
1/2 pound onions, thinly sliced
3/4 cup dry sherry
2 tablespoon olive oil
3/4 teaspoon salt
1 teaspoon oregano
1/2 teaspoon black pepper
12 cherry tomatoes
12 pearl onions
12 mushrooms
1 green pepper, cut into 1-inch pieces

Cut the lamb into 1 and 1/2-inch cubes. In a large bowl combine the sliced onions, sherry, olive oil, salt, oregano, and pepper. Add the meat and marinate for several hours (preferably overnight), turning occasionally.

Thread the lamb onto skewers alternately with the cherry tomatoes, pearl onions, mushrooms, and green pepper. Broil over charcoal until brown on all sides. Do not overcook. Serve on a bed of rice. Serves 6.

Pork

Pigs Will Eat Almost Anything

Pork is the world's most widely eaten meat despite the fact that two of the four leading religions, Judaism and Islam, forbid eating it. In addition there are pockets of non-pork-eaters around the world, such as the Navaho Indians in North America,, Guiana Indians in South America, Laplanders in northern Europe and Yakuts in Turkey. The Japanese also did not partake of pork until recently.

In Hawaii, women were forbidden to eat pork until 1819, and even today they are not supposed to prepare and cook the "alua (roast pork), which is the main dish at a luau.

The origin of the common pig is mysterious. Some food writers say that it was the invention of man. In the zoological sense there has never been such an animal as a wild pig (except for those that might have escaped from domestication). Most historians agree that man domesticated the wild boar and evolved it into a different family of animals as distinguished from its ancestor. The pig had no tusks, as does the boar.

The oldest pig remains have been found from the Mesolithic period in the Crimea. This was also the likely place of origin of the wild boar. Historians tell us that the wild boars of that region are descents of two distinct species — the Celtic boar of northern Europe and the Chinese boar. Where the African boars, like the warthog, fit in no one apparently knows.

About 5000 B.C. writings and art in Egypt and China depicted pig raising in two widely diverse regions. The popularity of pork in China never waned. Marco Polo and later Jesuit missionaries were impressed with the quality of the pork. Even today everyone in China eats pork on New Year's Day and on as many other days as they can afford it.

In Egypt and the Middle East pig consumption started a drastic decline about 2400 B.C. This was attributed to the ecological changes which decreased the wooded areas of the region necessary to the self-feeding of pigs. The arrival of nomadic pig-hating peoples a half millennium later further reduced the consumption of pork. Then religious taboos and laws followed, ending the eating of pork among those of the Jewish and Islamic religions.

In ancient Greece meat was too expensive for most people, except for pork, which was more readily available in the countryside than in the cities. At the time the raising of livestock was more important than cultivating crops. Ancient Greek pigs fed primarily in the woods where acorns were plentiful.

In Italy there was also a great interest in pigs, which continued through Roman times. Roman armies sometimes brought pigs with them to provide fresh meat in the field. Although mutton remained the common daily dish of the Romans, pork became the delicacy, especially the intestines.

By the time of Nero, the Romans separated the pork butchers from the butchers of beef and mutton, housing them in separate buildings. This segregation is still followed in some areas of France today.

The Gauls and Germans were avid pig raisers, as the animals could feed on acorns in the thickly wooded areas of northern Europe. At one time the Gauls exported sausage and smoked hams to Rome.

In the Middle Ages, the principle meat of the upper classes was game. Butcher's meat was not welcomed with one exception — the suckling pig. For those less well off, pork was the basic meat and it was usually in the form of salt pork. Fresh pork was dangerous, given the sanitary conditions of the times. In medieval

Paris meat inspectors were called "tonguers" because their inspections consisted of lifting a pigs tongue to see if there were white ulcers under it. If so, the animal was condemned of spreading leprosy and was unfit for sale.

For centuries pork was the sole meat of European peasants, as the animals needed little care. If the pigs were allowed to feed in the forests their meat was more palatable. Acorn-fed pigs were prized despite the fact that sometimes the meat tended to be on the bitter side. This could be corrected by feeding the pig something else shortly before slaughtering. Chestnuts produced the tastiest pork, but the fat of these pigs when boiled down to lard became an unattractive black oil.

City folks also ate pork from foraging pigs, who were turned out on city streets to feed themselves on urban garbage. This pork was a gourmet's delight and had nutritional value, yet the feeding of these pigs cost nothing.

Pigs had roamed city streets since ancient times in Greece and Rome. In medieval times they obstructed traffic on busy thoroughfares of London, even though the authorities tried from time-to-time to get rid of them.

The situation was the same in Paris where pork was the food of the poor as well as the affluent. Most Parisians kept two or three pigs and allowed them to roam the streets by day, locking them up at night. The Paris authorities had a love-hate relationship with the pigs — at times trying to banish them as a nuisance.

In 1131 a street pig in Paris ran between the legs of the horse carrying Crown Prince Philip. The animal so frightened the horse that it threw the Prince, who died from a fractured skull. Pigs were ordered off the streets for a time, but they were soon back.

Naples was the last European city to permit pigs to feed in the city streets because until recent modern times it had no other street cleaning service. The custom there, however, was not to give the animals free run of the streets. Each home owner who had a pig tethered it on a twenty-four-foot rope. This was just the right length to permit the pig to clean off the street in front of its own premises.

The roving city pig was also prevalent in New York in the nineteenth century. The poor notched or marked the ears of their pigs, hoping that no one would take them. When the city authorities decided to get rid of the pigs and sent out carts to round them up, they were met by angry housewives who clubbed them with broomsticks and scratched with fingernails to defend their porkers.

Pigs first came to what is now the United States in 1542, having been brought by Hernando de Soto when he landed near Tampa, Florida. The first pigs brought to the Americas, however, earlier by Cortez when he conquered Mexico. Records show that he and his men gave a feast for the Indians outside of what is now Mexico City. The Indians enthusiastically welcomed the European pig as it provided them with fat to enrich their fat-poor diet.

The Pilgrims in Massachusetts and the settlers of Virginia soon started importing English pigs after coming to the New World. By 1640 the Massachusetts settlers were carrying on a profitable trade in salt pork. Four years later the pig was responsible for an important development in the colony's government. A neighborhood dispute over a stray sow snowballed into such a major conflict that it caused the General Court, the colony's governing body, to split into two houses.

In Virginia's mild climate with pastures and forest rich in feed "Hogs run where they list, and find their own support in the Woods, without any Care of the Owner," wrote Robert

Beverly, a plantation owner in 1705. William Byrd, another prominent Virginian, complained that Virginians ate so much pork that they were becoming "extremely hoggish in their temper and prone to grunt rather than speak."

In colonial times the safest way to slaughter the half-wild hogs was to shoot them. In order to catch the semi-wild pigs "trail dogs" were used to run the hog down and then bark to give its location for the "catch dogs." These dogs would then hold the pig down by its ears until it could be lassoed and penned. Later the pigs were caught alive and penned up for a final fattening before killing them.

In America the pig had a close association with several historical events. In Pennsylvania during King George's War, the pacifistic Quakers balked at providing pork to the army.

In Virginia voters electing members of the House of Burgesses were urged to make the right decisions with large quantities of barbecued pork offered to them by the candidates.

In the early days of this country pork was the prime meat, because it could be butchered in the fall and salted, smoked or made into sausage which would keep for months. Every southern plantation had a smoke house for hams. Most had their own unique recipes for curing hams.

Thomas Jefferson imported fine Calcutta hogs and invited his neighbors to breed their sows with his boars to improve the hog breed. The involvement with pigs proved not to be one of Mr. Jefferson's better moments. It was reported that he cornered the pig market and charged the butchers an enormous price. This annoyed the butchers so much that they draped the fence around his house with pig entrails and nicknamed him "the hog governor."

The army's need for meat during the Civil War doubled pork production in the North.

The government opened twenty-five million unexploited acres of land to homesteaders to encourage civilians to raise pigs. One reason the South lost the war was the shortage of land and farmers to raise meat, especially pork.

At the end of the Civil War pork prices fluctuated widely. This enabled Philip Armour to make the then incredible profit of two million dollars slaughtering and processing pork, thereby starting the modern meat-packing industry.

America was built by pioneers who relied on meat from the pig. Covered wagons, which started west even before the Gold Rush of 1849, usually carried seventy-five pounds of bacon per adult. Lewis and Clark started out their expedition with fifty kegs of pork. The guides and fur traders who traversed the northern part of this country and Canada in canoes were called "pork eaters," as salt pork was the only meat in their diet. Salt pork was also frequently the only meat of the slaves who worked the Southern plantations.

Immigrants to America from pork-eating countries brought their techniques for treating the meat and recipes for cooking pork with them. German immigrants who settled Cincinnati in the 1830s and '40s caused the city to be nicknamed Porkopolis.

The quality of American pork improved greatly with the advent of the railroads. Pigs which had formerly been bred tough enough to walk to market were now being transported by rail. Pork breeders started developing flesh which would be more tender and tastier.

Marvin Harris, a well-known writer once remarked that pigs were good for nothing but food. "They can't be milked or ridden, can't herd other animals, pull a plow, or a carry cargo, and don't catch mice."

That's not entirely true. The ancient Egyptians used pigs to tread seeds into the mud of the flooding Nile. Pigs provide fertilizer. They are scavengers and even today are used to root out prized truffles in Italy and France. Pigs are easily trained. They provided entertainment between courses of ancient Roman banquets, and they were dressed in human clothing to entertain at the court of Louis XIV.

Over the years one of my favorite pork recipes has been for a casserole with pasta that can be prepared early in the day and baked just before dinner time. It is ideal for an informal meal when accompanied by a green salad. Another favorite is spareribs cooked in a Chinese style. They are baked in the oven and are flavorful and juicy.

The fruit stuffing of the pork roast has a pleasing contrast of sweet prunes and tart apple, flavored with ginger. Cooking the roast in a combination of apple cider and the juice from the prunes adds yet another flavor component.

Zesty Pork Chop Bake

1 cup elbow macaroni
4 loin pork chops, about 3/4- inch thick
1/2 teaspoon salt
1/4 teaspoon pepper
1 tablespoon olive oil
2 tablespoon minced onions
1/4 cup chopped green pepper
1/4 cup chopped red pepper
2 tablespoons all-purpose flour
1 tablespoon brown sugar
1/2 cup water
1/2 cup chili sauce
1 tablespoon vinegar
1 (11 ounce) can cream-style corn

Early in the day cook macaroni until al dente, drain. Season chops with salt and pepper. Heat the oil in a skillet and brown the chops well on each side; then remove. Add onion and green and red pepper to the skillet and sauté lightly. Stir in the flour, sugar, water, chili sauce, and vinegar. Cook, stirring, until thickened. Then mix in the macaroni and corn. Pour the mixture into a 2-quart casserole and arrange the chops on top. Cover and refrigerate until 1 and 1/2 hours before serving.

Bring the casserole to room temperature and bake in a preheated 350° F. for 1 hour.
Serves 4.

Chinese Spareribs

1 side pork spareribs
1/2 teaspoon pepper
1/2 cup light soy sauce
1/2 cup water
1/4 cup finely minced fresh ginger
1 teaspoon garlic powder
1 cup orange marmalade

Cut the side of spareribs into 2-rib pieces and place them into an oblong baking dish. Sprinkle the ribs with the pepper. Bake in a preheated 350° F. oven for 1 hour. Drain any accumulate fat from the pan.

Combine the soy sauce, water, ginger, garlic powder, and orange marmalade in a small bowl. Baste the spareribs with the sauce. Continue to bake the ribs basting them every 15 minutes three more times for a total cooking time of 2 hours. Serves 2 to 3.

Note: If finishing the ribs on a grill, bake them in the oven as above, but only grill them for 45 minutes, basting them 3 times.

Roast Loin of Pork
with
Prune and Apple Stuffing

8 ounces pitted prunes
1 cup hot water
1 large tart apple, cut into 1/2-inch cubes
1 whole boneless pork loin
1 teaspoon ground ginger
3/4 teaspoon salt
1/2 teaspoon pepper
3 tablespoons butter
1 cup apple cider
2 tablespoon all-purpose flour dissolved
    in 1/3 cup water

Quarter the prunes and soak them in the hot water for 30 minutes. Drain and reserve the liquid. Combine the prunes and apple.

Cut the pork loin open lengthwise, but do not cut through. Sprinkle the meat with the salt, pepper, and ginger. Arrange the fruit down the center of the meat. Roll the roast and tie it with kitchen string in several places.

Melt the butter in a heavy skillet or roasting pan. Add the pork loin and brown it on all sides. Then add the apple cider and the reserved prune liquid. Cover the pan and bake in a preheated 350° F. oven for 1 and 1/2 to 1 and 3/4 hours, or until the roast is done. Remove the roast to a platter and thicken the gravy with the flour and water combination.

Serves 8.

Chowders first became a part of American cooking in New England where they were made with fish. Later in the Midwest chowders were created with readily available smoked pork, potatoes, and other vegetables.

This chowder is a good way to use the last of a ham and the ham bone. Small pieces of fresh green beans are added at the end of the cooking time. For a variation add fresh corn kernels during the last 7 minutes of cooking.

Ham and Potato Chowder

5 large carrots, diced
4 stalks celery, diced
1 medium onion, diced
5 large potatoes, diced
6 cups water
1/4 teaspoon pepper
1/2 teaspoon dried thyme
1 ham bone
3/4 cup 1-inch pieces of green beans
2 cups diced ham
1/3 cup half and half

Place the carrots, celery, onion, and potatoes in a stock pot and add the water, pepper, and thyme. Bring to a boil and cook over medium-low heat for 25 minutes, or until the vegetables are tender. Mash about half of the vegetables with a potato masher. Add the ham bone and bring the soup back to a boil. Then continue simmering for 2 and 1/2 to 3 hours. Remove the ham bone. Add the green beans and cook on medium-low heat for 15 to 20 minutes, or until the beans are done. Add the ham and the half and half to smooth and thin the soup. Heat through and serve. Serves 6.

Veal

Meat of Young Cows

Veal is the meat from young dairy calves, usually slaughtered between four and seven months of age. The meat is much lighter in color than beef, more tender, and subtle in flavor. It is not baby beef which is from calves slaughtered at one year of age. Veal is usually in limited supply as many of the animals are completely milk-fed.

Over the centuries milk and veal have had a close association. This goes back to Norman times when chefs prepared *blanc mange*, which is veal cooked with milk and almonds. The medieval English version of this dish was made with veal, eggs, milk, and spices. It later became known as *blanquette de veau*.

During the Renaissance in Europe veal was usually the outcome of calf mortality, as cattle were too precious to slaughter so young. Nevertheless, in France and Italy veal was highly prized meat. King François of France was said to have demanded veal daily. The popularity of veal in France was due to the influence of Italian cooking, introduced to the Court by Catherine de Medici, wife of King Henry II.

One particular cut of veal, the scallop, has had a curious military history. It probably originated in Spain, and was introduced in Milan when that city was part of the Spanish Empire in the sixteenth century. The *scallopine Milanese* may have been named after the scallop shell, the emblem of Spain's patron saint, St. James, and was served in Milan homes as a delicacy brought to Italy by the Spanish. The Italians quickly made it their own dish.

When Milan was later occupied by Austrian soldiers under Marshall Radetsky, the Marshall introduced the *scallopine* to the Imperial kitchens of Emperor Franz Jaséf in Vienna, where it became the famed *wiener schnitzel*.

Veal has long been a favorite meat of Europeans. The champion veal-eaters of Europe, have traditionally been the Italians, although the French also want to claim the honor. Today's typical Italian eats sixteen pounds of veal per person annually. This compares with four pounds for the typical American.

Italians, particularly, like veal because it is a mild meat whose neutrality blends with their sauces. A prime example of this is the famous Vitello Tonnato, veal with tuna sauce. The dish was created at a time when tuna was very scarce in Mediterranean waters. The veal taste was considered sufficiently neutral that it served as an extender of the tuna flavor.

Austria has a great variety of schnitzels. Schnitzel is a flat piece of veal from the leg that is breaded and sautéed with various flavor enhancers. There is Paprika schnitzel made with paprika, Rahm schnitzel served with a cream sauce, and my favorite, Holsteiner schnitzel which is breaded veal topped with a fried egg, a pair of anchovies, and some lemon slices.

In America the most common form of veal served in restaurants is veal scaloppini. In the late nineteenth century in the United States less-expensive veal was often substituted for more expensive chicken in such popular dishes as Chicken a la King. Today it is the other way around, as chicken and turkey have become less expensive than veal.

Veal shoulder, a less expensive cut and the same as a chuck roast in beef, makes a very tasty roast. In the following recipe it is cooked with sautéed mushrooms, fennel, tomato, and wine. Part veal and part beef is used in my Meat Loaf in Puff Pastry. It is simple to make and elegant for a dinner party.

Each region of Italy has its own version of Osso Buco (veal shanks) and I use an adaptation of the Lombardy style. Porcini mushrooms, tomatoes, and lemon zest flavor the veal shanks.

Shoulder Roast of Veal
with
Fennel and Mushrooms

1 (4 pound) shoulder roast of veal
Salt, pepper, garlic powder, to taste
2 tablespoons olive oil
1 tablespoon butter or margarine
1 large fennel bulb, trimmed of stalks and
*   greenery*
1/2 cup sliced shiitake mushrooms
3/4 cup sliced white or crimni mushrooms
1 leek, white part only, thinly sliced
1 carrot, chopped
1 small onion, chopped
1 large fresh tomato, finely chopped
1 cup dry white wine
1/2 cup chicken broth
1/4 cup freshly chopped basil
1 tablespoon of dry Italian seasonings
1/4 cup cream, optional

Sprinkle the roast on both sides with salt, pepper, and garlic powder, to taste. Heat the oil and butter in a large deep oven proof skillet over medium heat until the butter starts to foam. Add the roast and brown it on both sides over medium heat.

Trim the tough end off the fennel, cut it in half and then slice it thinly. When the roast has browned remove it from the skillet and add the fennel, mushrooms, leek, carrot, and onion. Sauté over medium heat until the vegetables start to become limp. Add the tomato

and sauté for a few minutes longer. Then add the wine and chicken broth and mix well. Push some of the vegetables aside in the center of the pan to make room for the roast. Return the roast to the pan, baste with some of the juices, and sprinkle the basil and herbs on top. Bake, covered, in a preheated 325° F. oven for 1 and 3/4 to 2 hours or until the meat is tender.

Remove the meat to a warm platter. Skim any fat from the pan juices. Add the cream, if desired, and reduce the gravy slightly over medium heat. Cut the meat into slices and serve with pasta or mashed potatoes and spoon some gravy and vegetables over the meat. Serves 6.

Meat Loaf in Puff Pastry

1 (17 and 1/4 ounce) package
*   frozen puff pastry*
1 hard or Kaiser roll or 3 slices day-old
*   French bread*
1 red pepper, chopped
1 medium onion, chopped
4 large mushrooms, chopped
3/4 pound ground beef
1/2 pound ground veal
1/4 pound ground pork
2 large eggs
1 1/2 tablespoons fresh thyme leaves or
*   1 teaspoon dried*
1 1/2 teaspoons Dijon mustard
Salt and pepper, to taste
1 tablespoons milk

Thaw the puff pastry at room temperature (takes about 20 minutes). Tear the roll into pieces, place it in a small bowl, and cover it with warm water. After 10 minutes of soaking, squeeze all of the water out of the roll.

In the meantime, combine the red pepper, onion, mushrooms, ground meats in a bowl. Add 1 of the eggs, thyme leaves, mustard, salt, pepper, milk, and the soaked roll to the meat mixture, combining it well. Use your hands, if necessary. Form the meat mixture into an ob-long meat loaf.

In a small bowl beat the remaining egg with 1 teaspoon cold water for an egg wash. Overlap the two long sides of the pastry sheets and roll them to a little more than double the length and circumference of the meat loaf. Place the dough on a cookie sheet and then carefully place the meat loaf on it. Brush one of the long edges with the egg wash and fold the dough over the meat, making sure that there is an overlap at the top and using the egg-brushed side as the sealer. Fold the ends onto the dough. Use the egg wash to brush the edges of the pastry and seal the ends.

Use any leftover dough to make a decorative design, such as a twisted rope, and adhere it to the top of the meat loaf with some of the egg wash. Then brush the entire top of the pastry with the egg wash and bake in a preheated 375° F. oven for 50 minutes to 1 hour.

Serves 4 to 6

Note: The meat loaf may be prepared and shaped early in the day and then placed in the refirgerator. Then after 2 to 3 hours of refrigeration, the meat loaf can be placed in the puff pastry and refrigerated until time to bake it.

Osso Buco à la Lombardy

1/2 ounce dried porcini mushrooms
6 veal shanks, about 8 ounces each
3 tablespoons extra virgin olive oil
2 medium onions, chopped
1 stalk celery, finely chopped
1 small carrot, finely chopped
1 pound plum tomatoes, peeled and pureed
1/2 cup dry white wine
Zest of 1/2 lemon
Salt and pepper, to taste
2 tablespoons chopped Italian (flat-leaf)
  parsley

In a small bowl soak the mushrooms in hot water to cover for 30 minutes. Drain and squeeze out any excess water, reserve liquid. Then chop the mushrooms and set them aside.

Heat the olive oil in a roasting pan over medium heat. Add the veal shanks and brown them on both sides. Then remove them from the pan and set them aside. Add the mushrooms, onions, celery, and carrot. Sauté just long enough to soften the vegetables. Then add the tomatoes, wine, and lemon zest and season with salt and pepper. Return the veal shanks to the pan, pushing them down into the vegetables and sauce. Bake, covered in a preheated 325° F. oven for 1 and 1/2 hours, checking occasionally to see if more liquid is needed. If so add a little more wine and some of the reserved mushroom liquid.

Serve each veal shank covered with some of the vegetable mixture and pan juices and sprinkled with a little parsley. Serves 6.

Chicken

Popular in Every Country

Man and chicken have lived in close proximity since about 2000 B.C. Today chicken is probably the most universally eaten of all meats, including beef. Although food historians say that chickens originated in tropical climates, this feathered fowl has become acclimated to almost any climate except for the very coldest regions of the world. Chickens are easily and inexpensively raised and are available in areas where other meats are too expensive.

Man's first association with chicken reportedly occurred in India, where the wild red jungle fowl was first domesticated. It was not used for food but as a sacred bird in religious ceremonies. Priests of olden times ate the remains of the sacrificial animals after offering their less edible parts to the gods.

From India, chicken made its way to China and the Pacific Islands. Magellan reported that the natives of the Philippine Islands possessed many cocks, presumably an outgrowth of the India chicken. These cocks were only used for fighting, however.

Chickens made their appearance in the Mediterranean region around 1350 B.C. at which time they appeared in Egyptian art. Before that date Egyptian paintings show only ducks and geese. The Hebrews of the Old Testament apparently had no chickens as there is no reference to them. There are, however, lengthy lists of other birds in ancient Hebrew literature.

In the fifth century B.C. chickens became common in Greece. The Greeks prized the birds for the eggs, but not for the meat. The chickens were given no food except what they could scratch up for themselves and consequently the meat was too scrawny to be eaten. Chickens became part of the Roman diet around 185 B.C. It is believed that chickens came to the Roman Empire from Greece by the way of the island of Cos. The inhabitants of this island had learned the art of fattening poultry for table use. A century later chicken was given the place of honor on the menus of Pompeii. By the beginning of the Christian era chicken had become a part of Roman cuisine and was prepared in a variety of ways.

Chicken was at one time considered a luxury in most countries. Frequently legislation was passed to curtail over-indulgence in it. In 817 the Council of Aachen (Germany) ruled that chicken was a dish too sumptuous for fast days and forbade monks to eat it except during four days at Easter and four days at Christmas. Five centuries later St. Thomas Aquinas stated that chicken was of aquatic origin and could thus be consumed on the same terms as fish. The Catholic Church later decided that St. Thomas had underestimated the chicken and ruled that it was definitely too good for fasting.

Henry IV of France agreed with the Church and as an incentive for the country's prosperity promised his subjects would eventually have a chicken in every pot. Halfway around the world the Chinese classified chicken as one of "the four heroes of the table."

During the Middle Ages chickens were the favorite meat of the inhabitants of northern Europe. The Germans used the fowl for chicken stew, while the people of the Italian peninsula stuffed and roasted their chickens. In the mid-1200s the French rulers issued directions for constructing hen houses. The king's own poultry yard became one of the most famous in France.

Chickens came to America with the first colonists and were staples of most farms from the beginning of colonial times. They were prized for the eggs as well as their meat. Most chickens were grown to "a ripe old age" and heavy weight (five to seven pounds) in order to provide the most meat.

Following the Civil War, farmers became interested in breeding better chickens for egg production and began to house chickens in laying-houses. Until that time chickens had fended for themselves in the farmyard. Farmers built clean, ventilated chicken houses with windows covered by wire (hence the term chicken wire) and cotton curtains. Calcium-rich meal was provided for food and crooks held drinking water. The laying-houses were built close to the farmer's house so that the housewife could take care of the chickens and gather the eggs.

The modern poultry (or broiler) industry was started in Delaware in the 1920s and '30s. Poultry became so important for the state that in 1939 the state legislature designated the "Blue Hen Chicken" to be the official state bird.

Delaware's broiler industry was started by accident in 1923 by Cecil Steele of Ocean View. She had ordered fifty chicks to provide eggs and meat for her family. Due to a mix-up, five hundred chicks arrived, so she built a chicken house for them and sold them commercially.

Mrs. Steele decided to market her chickens at age sixteen weeks, when they weighed approximately two and a half pounds. This was a younger age than customary and eliminated any of the diseases older chickens tended to have at that time. (Today, broilers reach maturity at seven weeks and weigh up to four pounds.) Mrs. Steele called these young chickens "broilers," because they could be cooked quickly. The Cecil Steele chicken house is on the National Register of Historic Places in recognition of her pioneering efforts.

In 1938 Jacob Udell of Frankfort, Dela-ware, started the first large poultry-dressing plant. Prior to this time, farm families who wanted chicken for dinner had to slaughter their own. Even city dwellers had to buy live chickens. The slaughtering and plucking was traditionally done by the female of the family, who chopped off the head, plucked the feathers, and then cleaned and prepared the bird for cooking.

All of the chickens in the world, billions of them (they outnumber the human race by far) are descendants of the wild red jungle chickens that were domesticated in India four thousand years ago. The Brahma is probably the best known of the Asian chickens in the Western World.

In France the most prized chicken is the Bresse, whose white flesh is a result of a diet of rice and white corn. A chicken of the Mediterranean region is known all over the world is the Leghorn. It is a better egg producer than a meat bird, however. The Jersey White giant is the heaviest American bird and is raised almost exclusively for meat. Other well-known American chickens are the New Hampshires and Wyandottes, both of which yield eggs and meat. The Plymouth Rock is a popular broiler.

Rock Cornish game hens, which were developed in the 1940s, are a hybrid of Cornish and White Rock chickens. These miniature chickens weigh up to two and a half pounds and are usually 4 to 6 weeks old when slaughtered

Chicken is a very versatile meat and lends itself to a great variety of preparations from many ethnic influences. Many recipes utilize only the chicken breast as in the South-of-the-Border Chicken., which has the spiciness of a Mexican dish, enhanced by black beans, corn, and salsa. Boneless chicken thighs are stuffed with Italian sausage and cooked in a tomato-based sauce to be served with pasta.

In the Moroccan-style Cornish Game hen recipe oranges, olives, and dates provided a unique flavor. This easy-to-prepare dish should be marinated overnight. For an authentic Moroccan meal serve it with Bulgar.

South-of-the-Border Chicken

1 teaspoon chili powder
1/2 teaspoon Mexican seasonings
4 boneless, skinless chicken breast halves
1 tablespoon olive oil
1 (15 ounce) can black beans, rinsed and
*   drained*
1 1/2 cups canned or frozen corn
3/4 cup chunky-style, medium hot salsa
1 large tomato, chopped
2 tablespoon chopped fresh cilantro
1/3 cup chicken broth

Mix the chili powder and Mexican seasoning and sprinkle over both sides of the chicken breast halves. Heat the oil in a 10-inch skillet over medium heat. Cook the chicken in the oil for 8 to 10 minutes, turning occasionally, until juice of chicken is no longer pink. Do not over cook the chicken.

Stir the remaining ingredients into the skillet. Heat to boiling, reduce heat to low. Place chicken breasts on top of the vegetables. Cover and cook for 3 to 5 minutes or until the vegetables are heated through. Serve with boiled white rice. Serves 4.

Stuffed Chicken Thighs

4 ounces sweet Italian sausage, casing
*   removed, meat crumbled*
1/2 cup fresh bread crumbs from day-old
*   French bread*
1/2 cup freshly grated Parmesan cheese
1 large shallot, minced
1 large egg
2 tablespoon chopped fresh parsley
2 teaspoon chopped fresh thyme or
*   1/2 teaspoon dried thyme*
1/4 teaspoon salt
1/8 teaspoon pepper
8 large skinless, boneless chicken thighs

Mix the first 9 ingredients in a bowl. With a tablespoon fill area where bone was removed from each chicken thigh with about 2 tablespoons of the stuffing. Wrap the thigh meat around the filling and tie the thigh with kitchen string to hold it together. Sprinkle the thighs with salt and pepper.

Sauce

2 tablespoon olive oil
1/4 cup chopped pancetta or lean bacon
1 medium onion, chopped
2 cgarlic loves, minced
1 and 1/2 cups red wine
1 cup chicken broth
1 (14 ounce) can diced tomatoes,
*   Italian-style*
1 (8-ounce) can tomato sauce
1/2 cup chopped fresh basil or 1 teaspoon
*   dried basil*
1 pound fettuccini

Heat the olive oil in a Dutch oven or large skillet over medium-high heat. Add the pancetta and sauté until light brown and fat is rendered, about 5 minutes. Transfer pancetta to paper towels to drain.

Add the chicken thighs to the pan and cook until golden on all sides, about 8 minutes. Transfer to a plate. Then add the onions and garlic to the pan and sauté until tender, about 5 minutes. Return the pancetta to the pan and add the wine; boil until reduced to 1 cup. Add the chicken broth, tomatoes, tomato sauce, basil, and chicken thighs. Bring to a boil; reduce to simmer and cook covered for about 35 minutes or until chicken is done. (May be prepared ahead to this point, refrigerated, and reheated.)

Transfer chicken to a bowl and cover to keep warm. Simmer sauce until slightly thickened. Meanwhile cook the fettuccini until al dente. Drain and transfer to a large platter. Top with chicken and sauce and serve.

Serves 6 to 8.

Moroccan-Style Cornish Hens with Bulgar

1 large orange, thinly sliced
4 Cornish game hens, cut in half
   lengtwise along the back, backbone
   removed
6 tablespoons chopped fresh cilantro
1/2 teaspoon garlic powder
1 1/2 teaspoons ground cumin
1/2 cup tawny port
1/4 cup olive oil
2 tablespoons balsamic vinegar
2 tablespoons honey

12 whole pitted dates
10 large pitted green olives

Arrange orange slices in bottom of 9x13-inch glass baking dish. Top with the game hens. Mix the cilantro, garlic, cumin, port, and olive oil together in a bowl or measuring cup. Gently spoon the mixture over the hens. Tuck dates and olives between the hens. Cover and refrigerate overnight or 24 hours.

Then bake in a preheated 375° F. oven, basting occasionally for 50 minutes. Transfer hens, dates and olives to a platter. Pour pan juices into a small saucepan, remove fat and reduce slightly over medium heat. Spoon some sauce over the hens and serve with Bulgar.

Serves 4.

Bulgar

1 1/2 tablespoons olive oil
4 mushrooms, coarsely chopped
3 green onions, finely sliced
1 1/4 cups bulgar
2 tablespoons dried currants
1 1/4 teaspoons curry powder
2 1/2 cups chicken broth

Heat the olive oil in a skillet over medium heat. Add the mushrooms and onions and sauté for 2 minutes. Stir in the bulgar, currants, curry powder, and chicken broth. Mix well. Bring the bulgar to a boil, cover and simmer for 20 minutes. Fluff with a fork before serving.

Duck

The China Connection

Food critics agree that duck is one of the most delectable forms of poultry, but man has not been in any hurry to domesticate the bird. Hunting aficionados prefer wild duck and until recently wild ducks were plentiful.

The ancient Egyptians ate duck before they became acquainted with chicken. The rush-bordered banks of the Nile attracted all types of wild birds and supplied the Egyptian table with wild fowl.

The Romans were fond of duck and kept them in net enclosures. They were probably wild birds, however, and were held captive until they were wanted for a meal. The Romans ate only the breast meat and sometimes the brains, as they felt that the rest of the duck was not worth bothering about.

Food historians assume that the Chinese were the first to domesticate ducks. According to some food experts they were also the first to incubate duck eggs. Others claim that the Incas were the first to domesticate ducks. The Aztecs also ate duck. It seems more likely that the American Indians also ate wild duck.

During the Renaissance in Europe people believed that ducks were born from the decomposition of leaves. They were so cheap in England during Elizabethan times that they were thought to be domesticated.

When the Europeans reached America they found great numbers of wild ducks. Captain John Smith wrote about their abundance in 1608. Wild ducks were still so plentiful in the first half of the nineteenth century that Charles Dickens visiting in Philadelphia remarked that nearby waters were blackened with flights of canvas-back ducks.

The canvas-back duck was America's tastiest wild duck because it fed primarily on tape grass, otherwise known as wild celery. The chef of Delmonico's, New York's famous restaurant, called it the king of birds. These ducks also became delicacies in Europe.

However, it was not the canvas-back or any other wild bird that became the most widely eaten domesticated bird in the United States. It was the Peking duck with its sturdy, tender, juicy meat that became the favorite of Americans. Nine of these ducks were reportedly brought here in 1873 from China by a Yankee Clipper ship captain. From these few birds nine million domestic ducks have been produced, creating a multi-million dollar business. Over the years this species of duck has became known as the "Long Island duckling."

French duck connoisseurs say that the tastiest duck in France is the Rouen duck. It is the species used in the famous French dish "pressed duck." The duck juices when squeezed ceremoniously at the table in a silver press are red and so is its flesh. It also has a gamey flavor. Both color and flavor are due to the manner of the duck's death. It is strangled, not decapitated, so that all of the blood remains in the body.

The other favorite American duck is the Muscovy duck, which is sold in many gourmet markets. At one time it had a very musty strong taste due to the glands in its rump. Over the years crossbreeding with French ducks have made the Muscovy an acceptable bird, but the Long Island still is the preferred domesticated duck for American tables.

Maple Leaf Farms of Milford, Indiana, is the largest producer of ducklings in the United States. Founded in 1958 on a farm two miles south of Milford, Indiana, the company began producing processed ducks at the rate of fifty-four hundred birds per week. In 1981 Maple Leaf Farms purchased its largest competitor, C & D Foods in Wisconsin.

Over the years the breeding, hatching, feeding, and growing of ducklings has become a sophisticated business. In recent years Maple Leaf Farms has also bred a species of ducks from the French Muscovy duck, which today is lighter in taste and leaner. They have named the breed Barbarie.

The company operates two hatcheries, which are capable of producing 270,000 ducklings per week. At one day old the little ducklings are delivered to forty-seven grow-out farms located in Indiana and neighboring states. The ducklings arrive at the farms weighing two ounces each and reach full growth in forty-nine days, with an average weight of five to six pounds. In order to support its feed requirements, Maple Leaf Farms owns and operates two feed mills, which produce the specified mix of feed.

This method of roasting a duck eliminates most of the fat during cooking. The crisp skin is basted with an orange-maple glaze and pineapple flavors the wild rice stuffing.

Duckling with Wild Rice Stuffing

1 duckling (about 5 pounds)
Wild rice stuffing (recipe follows)
1/2 teaspoon salt
1/4 teaspoon pepper
1/4 teaspoon garlic powder
1/2 teaspoon onion powder
1/4 teaspoon ground marjoram
1/2 teaspoon dry rosemary leaves
1/3 cup orange juice
1/3 cup maple syrup

Cut the wing tips off the duckling. Rinse the bird and pat it dry. Fill the cavity with the stuffing, packing it in rather tightly. Fold the rear skin flaps over each other and secure with metal skewers.

Place the duckling in a 13 x 9-inch glass baking dish. Sprinkle with the salt, pepper, garlic powder, onion powder, and marjoram. Crush the rosemary leaves as they are being sprinkled on top of the duckling. Bake in a 325° F. oven for 2 and 3/4 hours. About every 45 minutes, remove the accumulated fat with a bulb baster and loosen the back of the duckling if it has gotten stuck to the pan.

Combine the orange juice and maple syrup and generously baste the duckling. Increase oven heat to 350° F. and continue baking the bird for another 30 minutes, basting every 10 minutes (2 more bastings). Remove the duckling to a warm platter and cut into serving pieces. Serve with the wild rice stuffing.

Serves 4.

Stuffing

3/4 cup wild rice
3/4 cup coarsely chopped mushrooms
1 small onion, chopped
1 stalk celery, chopped
1/3 cup chopped parsley
1/2 cup small fresh pineapple chunks
1/4 teaspoon pepper
1 egg, lightly beaten

Place the rice in a small-holed colander and then put the colander in a bowl. Pour hot water over the rice, submerging it completely. Let the rice stand for 30 minutes, then drain. Repeat this process 2 more times. The rice kernels should begin to open.

Combine the rice with the rest of the stuffing ingredients.

Turkey

An American Bird

Turkeys are native to America. It was not until the Spanish conquistadors reached the mainland of North America that turkeys became known to Europeans. Cortez found that the turkeys had been domesticated by the Aztecs in Mexico. He noted that many of the Indian pueblos had a fenced area for turkeys. The bird was so popular that pre-prepared turkey dishes could be purchased in the Mexican markets. On festive occasions the Aztecs served turkey with chocolate molé sauce.

In the New World the Spanish priests who accompanied the conquistadors began raising turkeys for their own food as well as for the soldiers. When they returned to their native land the padres brought back turkeys, which were eventually raised in the monasteries. Not long afterwards French monks also began raising turkeys.

The French took a great liking to turkey as it was similar to peacocks, which were popular domestic fowl in the sixteenth century. At that time turkeys, like peacocks, were roasted with their feathers on and brought to the table with great fanfare as a "piece de resistance."

In France turkeys became so popular in the 1600 and 1700s that a little known profession in Paris at the time was a "varnisher of turkey legs." The age of a turkey can easily be determined by the condition of its legs. Young birds have smooth and black legs. As they age the legs become white and peeled. Thus to deceive the buying public turkey legs of the older birds were varnished black.

In the eighteenth century, France was swept by a wave of turkeymania. Intensified by the American Revolution, Frenchmen sympathetic to the American cause ate turkey as a symbol of solidarity. A favorite stuffing for the roasted bird was truffles — at least a dozen or two. The truffles were left in the body cavity of the turkey overnight to impart their fragrance to the bird and then were thrown away before cooking. At today's prices of truffles, it would be more economical to throw away the turkey and eat the truffles.

Food historians have disagreed for years as to whether turkey was served at the first Thanksgiving. Many say "no," because William Bradford, then governor of the Plymouth Colony, did not mention turkey in his account of the feast. Others believe that this was strictly an oversight and are amazed that any records exist of the meal at all.

There are, in fact, records of turkeys being served at the first Thanksgiving. Edward Winslow, one of the original Mayflower passengers, wrote that turkeys had been hunted successfully for that first dinner. Also the ninety Indian men who accompanied their chief, Massasoit, the invited guest, probably brought turkeys along with other foods to the feast.

The Pilgrims had no hesitation about eating turkey. The bird was not strange for them, as it had reached Europe a century earlier and was already a common dish. In the New World turkeys were plentiful and easy to hunt.

New settlers in New England hunted the turkey so vigorously that by 1672, a half century after the Pilgrims arrival, New Englanders were complaining that "tis very rare to meet with a wild turkie in the woods." By the early 1700s some of the New England colonies restricted hunting of turkeys and turkeys became domesticated.

In the early 1800s Vermont farmers drove their turkeys to the Boston market. At the time, the state was growing more turkeys than could be consumed by the local population. Since the turkeys were too bulky and perishable to cram into wagons, the farmers literally walked the birds to market, 10,000 at a time. They employed a team of a hundred drovers to keep them together on the 200-mile journey. That may have been the original turkey trot!

In the South, the first colonists found the land teeming with turkeys. The bird was so popular that the Natchez Indians named their eighth month of their thirteen-month calendar, "the Moon of the Turkey." Captain John Smith told of the Indians bringing him turkeys when he first arrived at Jamestown.

For a considerable time after the colonists arrived in America, all the turkeys were wild. The Indians had never bothered to domesticate the bird as it was easily harvested with a bow and arrow. In the Southwest, on the other hand, the turkey was domesticated by the Indians, who were not as nomadic as the eastern and Plains Indians.

For several years after Independence, Benjamin Franklin advocated that the turkey become our national bird instead of the eagle. "I wish the eagle had not been chosen as the representative of our country," he wrote to his daughter Sarah Bache in 1784. "He is a bird of bad moral character. Like those among men who live by sharpening and robbing, he is generally poor, and often very lousy. The turkey is a much more respectable bird, and withal a true original native of America."

The American turkey-raising industry was initiated on the production of feathers, rather than meat. Several Indian tribes raised turkeys primarily for their plumes, which were used in headdresses and clothing ornamentation. Even until the middle of the last century turkeys were judged at agricultural fairs for their plumage. The raising of turkeys for decorative feathers spawned another business in Monticello, Iowa, where William Hoag invented the turkey-feather duster in 1872.

There is no better way to enjoy a turkey than at Thanksgiving with family and friends. The stuffing has become as important to the meal as the bird itself.

Turkey with Pecan and Apple Stuffing

4 cups bread cubes
8 tablespoons (1 stick) melted butter,
* plus extra butter for basting*
2 onions, chopped
2 large apples, chopped
2 tablespoons butter
1/2 cup brandy
3/4 cup chicken broth
2 cups toasted pecans
1/2 cup dried currants
2 tablespoons fresh chopped sage
Salt and pepper, to taste
1 (15 to 17 pound) turkey
Melted butter

In a large bowl combine the bread cubes and 8 tablespoons of melted butter. Sauté the onion and apple in the 2 tablespoons of butter until soft. Add the onion to the bread cubes along with the brandy, chicken broth, pecans, currants, sage, salt, and pepper and toss lightly.

Stuff the turkey, being careful not to pack the stuffing, and truss it. Season with salt and pepper. Place the turkey in a preheated 450° F. oven and immediately turn the heat down to 325° F. Roast the turkey for about 20 minutes per pound, basting with the pan juices and additional melted butter every 30 minutes.

Serves 20.

Fish and Seafood

Fish

Seafood

Fish and Seafood

Fish

There are more than twenty thousand species of fish in the seas, rivers, and lakes of the world. About fifty percent are commercially unfeasible and of the remainder only about a dozen and a half regularly appear in the markets of the world. Japan uses a greater variety of fish and its fishing boats scour the oceans to bring home the national daily average of about seven thousand tons of fish, most of which is eaten raw as sashimi.

Ocean and freshwater fish were an important part of man's diet even before ancient societies learned to cultivate vegetables and domesticate animals. Fish provided necessary nutrients and were easy to catch and prepare. In all likelihood much of the fish and shellfish were eaten raw.

In ancient Egypt fish were abundant and cheap, even less expensive than bread. In addition to sea fishing, the Egyptians raised fish in ponds. The fish were spit-roasted over charcoal and served with eggs on top. Fish such as carp, barbel, bleak, and loach came from Egyptian rivers and lakes. Gray mullet and tuna were obtained from the sea.

The early people of the Iberian peninsula caught anchovies, sardines, and cod. They salted these fish and exported them as far away as Asia Minor.

In Europe fishing for pike provided both sport and feast. In Scotland in the seventeenth century salmon was so common that a law was passed forbidding employers to give it to their servants more than three times a week. Carp, a fresh water fish that grew very large, was raised in the ponds and lakes throughout Europe, the Middle East, China, and Japan. It provided inspiration for Asian poets and cooks alike.

The commercial prominence of certain fish species had been well established by the time fishermen learned to navigate the open seas. Nations argued over who had the rights to fish what and where. One of the most valuable fish at one time was herring, which yielded one-third of the world's catch. In the 1600s and 1700s this silvery, oily fish was the center of the commercial and economic history of northern Europe. It is said that Amsterdam was built upon herring bones. Today cod and tuna are the most prevalent fish caught commercially.

Bass

Many Varieties

The term bass encompasses a number of unrelated species of fishes, both fresh water and salt. The group known as bass includes, Atlantic rockfish, an important food along the East Coast in colonial days; grouper; black sea bass; white sea bass; and sand bass. Black sea bass is available from Cape Cod to Florida.

The most important fresh water bass are American. They are usually caught by sport fishermen. Most of the commercial bass in the markets are white bass and sea bass from Chile, a favorite of restaurant chefs.

American fresh water bass were first fished by French colonists in the St. Lawrence River valley in the 1660s. The bass were called "archigan," the Algonquian word for ferocious, which was not a true description of this fish. The northern Indians ate bass as did the Seminole Indians in Florida, who fished them with lures made of deer hair.

One of the historical fishing grounds for black sea bass was about twelve miles from New York Harbor. Until the mid-1800s commercial fishermen who supplied the Fulton Fish Market in New York seldom ventured further out because they could easily and quickly fully load their boats with black sea bass and return to home port. Skilled navigation was required to find the exact location of these fishing grounds — Middle Ground, Sandy Hook, and Angler Banks — because landmarks on the shore were not available.

Party boats for sport fishing came into vogue with the birth of our nation. When the nation's capital was in New York, President George Washington was one of the first to charter a boat to fish Sandy Hook. Sport fishing for bass became so popular that woodcut posters were distributed around New York depicting men carrying great strings of sea bass. Police boats usually met the charter fishing craft in order to expedite the unloading of the fish.

The Portuguese are renowned as commercial fishermen. The cuisine of Portugal reflects the bounty of the sea. Sea Bass Lisbon-Style consists of chunks of sea bass cooked with tomatoes, spices, red wine, and cream.

Sea Bass Lisbon-Style

4 pounds sea bass fillets, cut into chunks
1 tablespoon olive oil
2 tablespoons chopped onion
4 large ripe tomatoes, peeled, seeded, and
*   chopped*
1 garlic clove, minced
1 tablespoon chopped parsley
1/4 teaspoon dried marjoram leaves,
*   crushed*
3/4 cup red wine
1/2 cup cream
1 tablespoon butter and 1 tablespoon all-
*   purpose flour kneaded into asmooth paste*

Heat the olive oil in a heavy oven proof skillet. Add the onion, tomatoes, garlic parsley, and marjoram and sauté for 5 minutes. Lay the bass pieces on top of the vegetables. Combine the wine and cream and pour it into the skillet. Cover, and cook in a preheated 325° F. oven for 20 minutes.

Transfer the fish and the vegetables to a warm platter, allowing the juices to drain back into the pan. Bring the juices to a gentle simmer in the pan. Add the kneaded flour mixture, a little at a time, stirring until each bit has dissolved. Let the sauce simmer for 5 minutes. Pour the sauce over the fish and serve with steamed rice. Serves 4 to 6.

Catfish

Thousands Raised in Ponds

The United States leads all other nations in the consumption of catfish. Millions are caught each year, principally in the southern and central states. The sport catch is augmented by a commercial catfish industry involving hundreds of thousands of acres of ponds in 34 states under the leadership of the Catfish Farmers of America.

Catfish, after being harvested, are marketed through modern processing plants under strict state and federal controls. Some of the larger operations handle ten thousand pounds of fresh and frozen catfish per week, which are sold to supermarkets and restaurants.

There are twenty-eight species of catfish in North American waters, varying in size and weight up to 120 pounds. The largest catfish in the world are found in the Amazon Basin and in European rivers east of the Rhine, where they have been recorded weighing more than 600 pounds. The largest catfish was caught in Russia. It was sixteen feet long and weighed 660 pounds.

The three most popular species of catfish in the United States are the channel, white, and blue catfish. These are all commercially farmed. Big catfish are fished with gill nets and trotlines (a series of baited hooks strung out on a long line). Among catfish aficionados, half-pounders that can be crisply deep-fried and eaten out of hand are preferred.

Catfish is a mild-flavored, lean, moist fish with white-to-pink meat. Whole pan-dressed small fish, as well as fillets and steaks from large fish are generally available, either fresh or frozen, throughout the country. The white-meat catfish is more popular than the pink-meat or "red cat."

Skinned and filleted catfish are delightful whether fried or broiled. Small fish or steaks are delicious baked in a sauce or in foil, in casserole dishes, and in stews.

For a crisp catfish entree, try Oven-Fried Catfish with Sesame Seeds. Very quickly dip the fish in the egg mixture, so as not to saturate it and make the fish soggy.

Oven-Fried Catfish with Sesame Seeds

2 pounds catfish fillets, cut 1-inch thick
Salt and pepper
2 tablespoons milk
Dash of cayenne pepper
1 egg, beaten
1/2 cup cornmeal
1/2 cup sesame seeds
All-purpose flour
4 tablespoons butter
4 tablespoons vegetable oil

Wipe fillets with a damp cloth, sprinkle with salt and pepper. In a wide dish beat the milk and cayenne with the egg.

Mix the cornmeal and sesame seeds in a pie plate. Dust fish lightly with flour, dip in egg mixture, then turn in sesame mixture until evenly coated.

Set fish pieces on waxed paper to dry for 30 minutes; turn once after 15 minutes.

Preheat oven and cooking pan at 500° F. for 5 minutes. Then, melt butter and oil in hot pan and lay the fish in the hot fat, turning it so both sides are coated and return pan to the oven. Oven fry fish, uncovered, for about 10 minutes until cooked. Serves 4.

Cod

Prime Food for Centuries

Cod is a mainstay in American food history. Even before the discovery of America by Columbus, the Vikings came to American shores to fish for cod. The period from the end of the eighth to the beginning of the eleventh century might be called "The Age of the Cod," for cod provisioned and financed the Viking voyages and made their conquests possible. Cured cod gave the Vikings unspoilable provisions which permitted them to make lengthy sea voyages without having to land to take on food.

The demand for fish was great in medieval Europe where people ate more fish than meat and more than we do today. This was because religious fast days were strictly observed and there were more of them. Cod was particularly welcome among the poor during the long Lenten fast in the Middle Ages. The rich, if they were not too far from the sea, could pay to have fresh fish brought to them by fast relays of horses.

The Nordic (Scandinavian) countries prospered from cod because they popularized it throughout Europe. However, they soon lost their monopoly to competitors, particularly the French. The French, like the Noresemen, dried cod, but soon found that the fish would keep better if it was salted and then dried. By the fifteenth century salt cod had become a common French food.

The Basque fishermen of northern Spain were also major providers of cod. For a long time the Basques kept the source of their cod a secret. They were whalers and by following the whales they were led to the Great Banks of Newfoundland where there were tremendous quantities of cod. Somehow these fishermen must have known that a great continent lay beyond their fishing grounds. Historians say that they talked to Columbus and told him of the existence of the New World.

By 1602 when Bartholomew Gosnold ventured south of Newfoundland and Nova Scotia he discovered a great hook of land jutting out into the sea where fish were in great abundance. He named the land Cape Cod. The sea around it is part of the Great Banks extending from Newfoundland south to east of Massachusetts. The cold Labrador current and the warm Gulf Stream create thermal conditions ideal for plankton upon which fish depend as a food source. Thus the Great Banks became one of the prime fishing areas of the world.

The New England fishing industry began with the settlement of Gloucester in northeastern Massachusetts in 1623. By 1630 Boston had become the main port of this fishing industry. Men were willing to risk their lives to harvest the fish that at one time was a food mainstay of Europe and the American colonies. Cod was virtually the "beef" of centuries past. It could be cooked in a variety of ways or preserved with salt and stored for months.

In 1640 the Pilgrim colonists exported more than 300,000 dried codfish, mostly to England. The colonists, however, found their fish trade limited by restrictive English laws. In 1677 Massachusetts sent King Charles II a handsome gift of ten barrels of cranberries, two barrels of cornmeal mush, and three thousand dried codfish. Along with this gift was sent the request that His Majesty's Massachusetts' subjects be represented in Parliament and that there be relief from the restrictive trade laws. These requests were not granted, but the king did give the colonists permission to sell dried cod in the Mediterranean and Caribbean, as well as to the Southern colonies.

Beginning in the mid-1600s, and for the

next 80 years, cod supported the world's slave traffic as one of the three valuable cargoes. Ships out of Boston would deliver salt cod to Spain or Portugal, then sail to West Africa to take on slaves. The ships then proceeded to the West Indies where the slaves were sold for sugar and molasses to supply the New England rum distilleries. This became known as the triangle trade.

For centuries cod was such a popular item of commerce that it appeared symbolically on stamps, legal documents, letterheads, crests, and wind vanes. The huge white-pine carving of the "Sacred Cod" which was hung in the Massachusetts Hall of Representatives in 1784 is a tribute to the fishing industry and to the great sea power of U.S. ships built in that state.

Also part of the cod story is "scrod," which may or may not be cod. There is no such fish as scrod. The name "scrod" was invented in the nineteenth century by the maitre d' of the Parker House in Boston to assure his clientele that they were eating the freshest fish possible.

At that time fishing vessels spent up to ten days at the Great Banks off the coasts of Maine and Massachusetts. The first day's catch was gutted and iced down in the bottom of the boat. Subsequent days' catches were put on top until the vessel was full. The ship then sped to the Boston Fish Pier, where the catch was auctioned.

The Parker House chef insisted on buying the freshest fish from the top layer. Since the maitre d' had to get his menus printed a day in advance, and since he could not predict what fish would be on top, he coined the word "scrod." Today, scrod has come to mean a fish of the cod family, including haddock, hake, or pollock.

The following recipe for cod (scrod) includes peppers and cheese for an additional flavor to the usually mild fish.

Cod with Peppers

1 1/2 pounds cod fillet, in one piece,
  if possible
2 tablespoons lemon juice
3 tablespoons butter or margarine
1 small onion, sliced
1/2 red pepper, cut into 2-inch cubes
1/2 yellow pepper, cut into 2-inch cubes
1/2 green pepper, cut into 2-inch cubes
Salt and pepper, to taste
3 tablespoons all-purpose flour
1 cup vegetable broth (available canned)
1 cup milk
4 ounces Gouda cheese, grated
1 teaspoon paprika

Rinse the cod and pat it dry. Then lightly sprinkle it with the lemon juice.

Heat 1 tablespoon of the butter in a small skillet. Add the onion and sauté until golden. Add the peppers and continue sautéing for 2 more minutes. Season the mixture with salt and pepper and place it in a flat oven-proof dish. Place the fish on top of the vegetables, pushing some of the peppers to the side to surround the fish.

Melt the remaining 2 tablespoons of butter in the skillet. Add the flour and mix until smooth. Gradually add the vegetable broth and milk, stirring constantly, and cook until smooth. Add 3/4 of the cheese and season the sauce with salt, pepper, and paprika. Pour the sauce over the fish and vegetables, sprinkle with the remaining cheese, and lightly dust with paprika. Bake the fish in a preheated 375° F. oven for 20 minutes or until fish flakes easily with a fork. Serve with rice or boiled potatoes. Serves 4.

Flounder

Some Like Rivers

Flounders are abundant in America as well as Europe, where they have been eaten since Paleolithic times. Flounders range from Scandinavia to the Mediterranean, although are not prevalent in that sea, except in the waters around Turkey.

Flounders are the only flatfish that will swim up a river and may even stay there. They lay their eggs in salt water close to the mouth of a river where salinity is low. If flounders remain in fresh water they do not grow as large as those in the sea — usually about a pound which is the minimum weight at which a salt-water flounder may be taken.

American flounders are firm-fleshed and have a delicate flavor, much more so than their European counterparts. There are winter and summer flounders, each with different in colorations and habitat. The winter flounder is prevalent in the colder waters off of New England, Canada and Nova Scotia. They usually weight about two pounds.

The summer flounder, commonly known as fluke, occupies the warmer waters of the Chesapeake Bay and of the Carolinas. However, as soon as the waters begin to get cold the summer flounder disappears to the ocean floor. Summer flounders weigh an average of three to five pounds, but twenty-pounders are not uncommon.

Characteristically flounders ripple through the water, glide to the bottom, flip sand on their backs, and lie buried in sandy mud with only their eyes sticking out. Most flounders are deep-water fish out of the range of anglers. They are commercially caught with trawl nets. Flounders are often filleted and sold under the catch-all name of "fillet of sole."

One of the most elegant fish dishes is Flounder and Crab in Patty Shells, an excellent choice for a luncheon or as a first course for a dinner party. The delicate flavor of flounder pairs well with crab meat. Patty Shells are available frozen.

Flounder and Crab in Patty Shells

1 pound flounder fillet
Slice of lemon
1/2 cup sliced mushrooms
2 tablespoons minced green onions
4 tablespoons butter
3 tablespoons dry white wine
3/4 cup crab meat, picked over
2 tablespoons all purpose flour
1 1/4 cups chicken broth, heated
1/3 cup heavy cream
1 egg yolk
Salt and pepper, to taste
1/4 cup grated Parmesan cheese
6 patty shells

Poach the flounder in salted water with a slice of lemon. Then drain and cut fish into cubes. Sauté mushrooms and onions in 2 tablespoons of the butter until tender. Add the wine and simmer for 1 minute, then gently stir in the flounder and crab meat; set aside while making the sauce.

In a saucepan heat the remaining 2 tablespoons of butter, whisk in the flour, then pour in the hot chicken broth and whisk until the sauce boils. Reduce heat to very low. Mix the cream with the egg yolk and beat it into the sauce. Stir in the fish mixture, season with salt and pepper; stir in the cheese and heat through. Spoon mixture into patty shells and serve.

Serves 6.

Halibut

"Chickens" or "Whales"

In fishermen's language halibuts are "chickens" if they weigh up to ten pounds, and "whales" from 125 pounds and over. Halibut have been known to weigh as much as seven hundred pounds, but today a 300-pounder is rare. Commercial fishermen also refer to halibut as the King of the sea. It is bigger and more powerful than any of the other flatfish.

Part of halibut's mystique is that it is rather inaccessible as it lives on the ocean floor often at a depth of twelve hundred feet, and rarely comes above two hundred feet. However, it migrates into bays closer to shore to spawn from May through July.

Halibuts are found in the cold waters of the north Atlantic and Pacific and infrequently off the coast of Virginia. They were favorites of the Northwest Indians, who preferred halibut to the more plentiful, easily-cacheable salmon. Unfortunately over the years, halibut has become fished out in many areas, but is still plentiful in the Arctic Ocean.

Another part of the halibut family is the California halibut, a warm water fish. It is much smaller in size, weighing four to twelve pounds, and is harvested from the central California Coast to northern Mexico.

The eye and mouth are the least distorted in the halibut compared to other flatfish. It is also the biggest of the flatfish, running twelve feet in length. Plumper in form and proportionately longer in body than the sole or flounder, halibut has an easier time of procuring food by simply gliding over the sea's bottom, instead of rising to attack other fish.

Fishermen say that halibut simply club smaller fish to death with their tails, giving them a reputation of ferocity. This action probably inspired the U.S. Navy in the 1950s to name its first submarine equipped with missiles the USS *Halibut*.

Halibut has firm white meat with a delicate flavor. It is usually sold as fillets or steaks. The smaller halibuts, three to four pounds, are sold whole. Halibut steaks are ideal for grilling, broiling, or poaching and served with a sauce.

Even though the Alaskan halibut season is a short one, a million pounds are caught in a matter of days. The fish is shipped fresh by plane to wholesalers all over the country.

This recipe for Halibut Steaks with Caper Sauce is typical of the Pacific Northwest.

Halibut Steaks with Caper Sauce

2 (8-ounce) halibut fillets, 1/2 inch thick
1/2 cup all-purpose flour
Salt and pepper, to taste
2 eggs, well beaten
5 tablespoons butter
2 tablespoons vegetable oil
1/2 cup dry white wine
1 tablespoon lemon juice
1 tablespoon capers

Dip the halibut fillets into the flour mixed with salt and pepper, coating both sides of the fish. Then dip in beaten eggs. Heat 2 tablespoons of the butter and the oil in a skillet over medium heat. Sauté the halibut until golden and cooked through, about 3 to 4 minutes on each side. Transfer the fish to a heated platter.

Pour off the cooking oil from the skillet. Pour in the wine and bring to a boil for 1 minute. Remove from heat and stir in remaining 3 tablespoons of butter, lemon juice, and capers. Pour sauce for the fish. Serves 2.

Mahi Mahi

The Fish Dolphin

Mahi mahi is a member of the dolphin family. There are two different kinds of dolphins dwelling in the same area of the seas. The mammal called dolphin was named by ancient Greeks, who considered the animal friendly and included it in their legends. The fish dolphin was so named later by fishermen who confused the two because of their similar shape and jumping habits. We eat only the fish dolphin. Mahi mahi is the Hawaiian name for fish dolphin.

Fish dolphin are beautifully colored. They are predominately turquoise blue with silver bellies and yellow-orange pectoral fins. When threatened they light up with their colors changing in rapid succession. They lose the color with death. Their foreheads are high, bodies long slender and gracefully tapered with a dorsal fin that runs from head to forked tail.

Mahi mahi are warm water fish who prefer blue waters and are mostly found in Hawaiian waters, although in late summer they swim in the warm currents from Oregon to Baja.. They are fast swimmers and are not usually caught in nets. In Hawaiian waters mahi mahi are usually an additional catch for the vessels taking tuna and marlin with long lines. Only a little more than 100,000 pounds of mahi mahi are harvested annually.

At the daily fish auctions in Honolulu, mahi mahi are among the last fish auctioned each day because they do not keep well outside of refrigeration. Buyers prefer the females as they have more meat per pound of undressed fish.

The meat of mahi mahi is full-flavored and moderately rich with firm, meatlike texture. It is traditionally marketed as steaks or fillets.

Mahi mahi is the featured fish in many West Coast and Hawaiian restaurants. The following recipe for Mahi Mahi with Macadamia Nuts and coconut milk is typical of Hawaiian cooking. Coconut milk is the traditional liquid used in Hawaiian cooking.

Mahi Mahi with Macadamia Nuts

1 1/2 pounds mahi mahi fillet,
  cut into 4 servings
Salt and pepper
1 cup whole salted macadamia nuts,
  coarsely chopped
1 cup unsweetened coconut milk

Rinse the mahi mahi fillet and pat it dry. Place the fish in a 13 x 9-inch glass baking dish in a single layer. Season with salt and pepper. Sprinkle half of the macadamia nuts over the fish and pour the coconut milk around it. Bake the mahi mahi in a preheated 350° F. oven for about 18 minutes or until the fish flakes easily. Place fish on a platter and sprinkle with the remaining nuts. Serve immediately with the coconut milk as the sauce. Serves 4.

Monkfish

Mister Ugly

Monkfish are very ugly. They are often discarded by American fishermen, but are highly prized by Europeans. Along the East Coast monkfish are common from Newfoundland to North Carolina. They swim close to the tide line in winter and move into deeper water during warm weather. They are usually brought in as an incidental catch.

Their bizarre appearance, odd method of attracting food, and notorious gluttony make monkfish very unique.

Monkfish typically has a big, round, flattened head with tiny eyes and an enormous tooth-filled mouth. Its body, designed for hugging the sea bottom, is quite flat and the brown skin, lacking scales, is thin, pliable, and slippery. The pectoral fins are thick and fleshy handlike-structures sticking out of the side of the head.

Just behind the upper lip is a long spine with a bait-like tip which serves as the monkfish's "fishing lure." The hungry monkfish flutters its "fishing lure" to attract prey. When a curious fish investigates the fluttering "bait," the gluttonous monkfish opens its vast toothy mouth and in goes the victim.

The monkfish's appetite is insatiable. It can swallow a fish almost its own size. Monkfish can be two to four feet long and weigh more than thirty pounds. Flounders, skates, eels, herring, cod, sea bass, squid, and crab, as well as ducks, gulls, and other birds are part of the monkfish diet.

Only the tail meat of monkfish is eaten. It is light, delicate, firm, and without bones. Its texture and taste is similar to lobster. Monkfish is delicious baked with vegetables, poached, or steamed and served with a creamy sauce. Grilling or broiling tend to toughen and dry out the meat. Monkfish requires a little longer cooking than most fish. If underdone, it has a gelatinous taste.

Monkfish is in season in the summer at the same time as sweet, golden ears of corn come to market. Together they make a delightful chowder.

Monkfish and Corn Chowder

5 strips of bacon, cut into dice
1 small onion, chopped
1 medium potato, diced
2 cups fresh corn kernels (about 2 ears)
12 ounces monkfish, cut into 1/4-inch thick
  slices and cut in half, if very large
2 1/2 cups milk
1 cup whipping cream
Salt and pepper, to taste
1/4 cup finely chopped red pepper

Render the fat from the bacon in a medium-size saucepan over medium-high heat. When the bacon is crisp remove it from the pan. Drain on paper towels and reserve it.

Add the onion to the bacon fat and sauté until translucent, about 3 minutes. Stir in the potatoes, reduce heat to medium, and add just enough water to cover the potatoes. Cover the pan and cook, stirring occasionally, until the potatoes are almost soft, about 10 minutes.

Add the corn and cook, stirring, for 2 to 3 minutes. Then add the monkfish and cook until nearly opaque, about 4 minutes. Add the milk and cream and cook, stirring, until very hot. Do not let the soup boil. Season with salt and pepper. Serve in warm soup bowls garnished with red pepper and bacon bits.

Serves 4.

Orange Roughy

Deep, Deep Down in the Sea

Orange roughy is a deep water fish found in cold waters around the world, although is most prevalent off the coast of New Zealand. Until 30 years ago orange roughy managed to survive away from human intervention. Modern technology, however, has enabled fishermen to reach more than three thousand feet under the sea to harvest this fish.

Reddish-orange skin and fins are characteristic of orange roughy. It has a large, bony head with large eyes. Below the skin there is an oil-rich, waxy layer used in cosmetics.

This fish was virtually unknown in New Zealand waters until the 1970s. Commercial fishing for orange roughy did not develop until 1979. Today it is fished of the coasts of New Zealand, Australia, the United Kingdom, France, and Namibia. Some are also being caught off the coast of Norway.

The main fishing season for orange roughy is from June to August during the spawning season when fish aggregate and are easier to catch. It is only with the use of high technology and the use of sonar equipment that orange roughy can be located and caught.

Orange Roughy is a slow-growing, long-lived fish that is thought to live up to 150 years. Most of the fish caught are twelve to sixteen inches long and weigh between three and four pounds. They feed primarily on prawns, smaller fish, and squid.

Orange roughy do not begin to breed until they are 25 to 30 years old at which time each female carries about 11,000 eggs per pound of body weight. This is less than ten percent of the average of other fish. Orange roughy like rugged underwater terrain with hills and canyons for their spawning ground.

The delicate pearly-white, boned and skinned fillets of orange roughy have a subtle shellfish flavor. This taste makes them one of the world's most desirable white fish. The fillets may be breaded and deep-fried, oven baked, grilled, sautéed, broiled, or pan fried.

Snow peas and leeks flavor a poached orange roughy.

Orange Roughy with Snow Peas

2 pounds orange roughy fillets, cut into
   1-inch-wide strips
Salt and pepper, to taste
1/4 cup all-purpose flour
6 tablespoons butter
2 leeks, white part only, cut into 2-inch
   long fine julienne (about 2 cups)
1 cup clam juice
1 cup dry white wine
1 1/2 cups whipping cream
2 cups snow peas, cleaned and cut in half

Season the fish strips with salt and pepper and dust lightly on both sides with flour.

Heat 3 tablespoons of the butter in a large skillet over medium-high heat. Add the fish strips and sauté them for about 1 minute on each side. Remove from pan and set aside.

Clean the pan, heat, and add the remaining 3 tablespoons of butter. Add the leeks and sauté them for 3 to 4 minutes, until limp. Do not brown them. Add the clam juice and wine, bring to a boil and cook until the liquid is reduced by half, about 10 minutes. Add the cream and continue cooking, about 10 minutes more, to reduce the sauce until it coats a spoon thickly. Add the cooked fish and the snow peas. Cook just until the fish is heated through and the snow peas are softened, about 2 minutes. Remove from heat. Serves 6.

Salmon

Ancient Gourmet Food

Salmon is the most ancient gourmet food. Its bones have been found in the caves of Stone Age man in Southern Europe, dating back to 25,000 B.C. Cave paintings and sculptures of that time depict salmon in taxonomic detail.

Radiocarbon has dated artifacts from the Columbia River watershed in what is today Oregon which show that Indians were living there in 11,000 B.C. They not only worshipped salmon as food but gave the fish an elaborate role in their mythology.

By the Middle Ages in Europe, salmon was no longer merely a source of nourishment, but a spectacular display at banquet tables, where it was served whole on silver trays to the sound of trumpets. Salmon was typically served as a middle course between two meat courses.

During the reign of Louis XV salmon cookery reached incredible heights, with the fish almost lost under varieties of pastry, sauces, and assorted accompanying seafoods. This trend was reversed by the French chef, Escoffier, who advocated that salmon be served as plainly as possible. He even suggested it be fried in butter. Even though salmon was favored by the wealthy it was plentiful enough that it could also be enjoyed by the middle class.

In Colonial America indentured servants benefited from a clause in their contract that stipulated they were not to be fed salmon more than once a week. This was an outgrowth of an English law that prohibited apprentices from being served salmon more than three times a week. Similar laws existed in many European countries. Monks in at least one French abbey revolted when they were served salmon more than once a day.

At one time the great rivers of Europe, the Rhine, Seine, Loire, Thames, and the Adour in the Pyrenees, teamed with salmon. Pollution subsequently eliminated these spawning grounds of salmon.

There is only one kind of salmon native to the Atlantic ocean. Five others — the Chinook, sockeye, coho, pink and chum — are native to the Pacific. The Atlantic salmon and three Pacific species — the Chinook, coho, and sockeye also occur as landlocked fresh water fish, depending on availability of their food supply.

Atlantic salmon were once abundant in America from Nova Scotia to the Delaware River. With the exception of the Hudson River, which offered few tributary streams essential to spawning, the most important Eastern rivers for salmon spawning were the Connecticut, Merrimack, Androscoggin, Kennebec, Penobscot, and St. John. Many Dutch and English settled in these river valleys in the beginning of the seventeenth century.

Although salmon was not the favorite food of the Eastern Indians (striped bass and sturgeon were more highly esteemed) the spring run of salmon was a time for great celebration for the settlers. At that time marriages were consummated, political speeches were made, and treaties were formed.

By 1815, however, the proliferation of dams and pollution from sewage and textile mills wiped out salmon spawning on most of the above mentioned New England Rivers. Fortunately Pacific salmon has fared better.

Salmon was the principal food of the Indians living near the Columbia River. Edible roots, plants, and berries contributed to their diet, but "pemmican" of dried and pulverized salmon was their staple. These Indians were not avid hunters before the white man supplied them with guns. Killing an elk or a deer with a bow and arrow required far more effort than taking salmon in baskets or dip nets.

In 1792 a Yankee trader, Robert Gray, sailed into the mouth of the Columbia River, which he named after his ship. This vast river system, over twelve hundred miles long with a large tributary system, was and still is this country's greatest spawning ground for salmon. At one time, salmon on the Columbia river were so dense that locals claimed they could walked across the river on their backs.

The settlers on the Columbia River first preserved salmon by salting them in barrels. This salmon kept so well that it was exported to London, Valparaiso, and the Hawaiian Islands in the early 1830s.

The Hudson's Bay Company had a monopoly on Colombia River fishing until 1860. With the completion of the transcontinental railroad tons of salted salmon were sent to Chicago, New York, Boston, and by ship to Europe. In 1899 six cold-storage and freezing plants were operating on the Columbia River and Pacific salmon was being shipped either frozen or salted all over the world.

There are several stages at which salmon is the most desirable. Fortunately the first stage, when the salmon are starting their journey up the fresh water rivers to the spawning grounds, is now spared by law. It is at that time that the salmon flesh is firm and red, and packed with fat to gain strength for the long trip and the ordeal of breeding which awaits them at the end. Until recent times this is when most salmon have been caught.

The second best stage is when the salmon are in the ocean, where they feed on crustacean-like constituents in the plankton. This gives them their distinctive color. Taken then the salmon are also prevented from spawning. The third most desirable stage is when the young salmon swim toward the sea, which also prevents them from reproducing.

As a result, salmon has been over-fished in all areas of the world, hence most of the salmon in our markets today are farm raised. Farm or pond raised salmon does not have the taste of its sea-going twins.

Many salmon aficionados agree that the best wild salmon is the Atlantic salmon, with those taken near Scotland being superior. Although the species is the same on both sides of the ocean, Greenland, Nova Scotia, Maine, and Canadian salmon are rated below the European for taste.

Pacific salmon are generally ranked below Atlantic salmon for flavor, although I have found Pacific salmon to be excellent. The Indians along the Colombia River told of five tribes of salmon, which we today know as the five species of Pacific salmon.

The Chinook salmon is the tastiest as it spends the longest time in the ocean — eight years compared with four-to-five for other salmon. It also swims up stream further, having been found as far as 2250 miles away from the ocean. It is the largest salmon and the gamiest fighter when hooked by sport fishermen. The Chinook is also known as king salmon.

The sockeye salmon stays in the ocean almost as long as the Chinook. It is favored by canneries because of its dark red flesh and is rich in oil. It is also known as the red salmon.

The coho salmon spends two to three years at sea and moves only a short distance up stream to spawn. It is also called the silver salmon.

The pink salmon matures more quickly than any other salmon, at two years, and is the smallest. It is most often canned because it is the commonest.

The chum salmon is little valued for its flesh, which is yellowish or an unappetizing pale pink and is primarily fished for its roe. It is also called the dog salmon, a name given to it by the Athapaskan Indians of the Yukon, who eat choicer species and give the chum to their dogs. This greatly annoys the Eskimos of the Arctic Northwest, who have no other kind to eat than the chum salmon.

Dill and salmon have an affinity for each other as the dill masks some of the richness of the fish. Serve this salmon entrée with small boiled red potatoes and green beans.

Alaskans frequently grill their salmon over alderwood and charcoal, however, any aromatic wood may be added to the charcoal to impart extra flavor. The basting sauce, which caramelizes during cooking, adds a slightly sweet flavor to this Grilled Salmon.

Salmon with Dill Sauce

4 salmon steaks
1 small onion, sliced
1/2 lemon, thinly sliced
3/4 cup dry white wine

Place the salmon steaks in a large skillet; cover with the onion and lemon slices. Add the wine and sufficient water to barely cover the fish. Cover the skillet and bring to a boil. Reduce heat and simmer for 10 minutes, or until the fish flakes easily with a fork.

In the meantime, prepare the dill sauce. When the salmon is done, remove it to 4 warm plates and top with the sauce.

Dill Sauce

3 tablespoons butter or margarine
1 1/2 tablespoon all-purpose flour
2 teaspoons Dijon mustard
1 1/4 cups milk

1/4 cup chopped fresh dill
1 egg yolk
3 tablespoon lemon juice
Salt and pepper, to taste

Melt the butter in a medium-size saucepan over medium-low heat. Stir in the flour and then the mustard. Gradually add the milk, stirring constantly. Cook until the sauce is smooth and then add the dill. Beat the egg yolk, stir a little of the hot sauce into it, then add the egg mixture to the dill sauce. Blend in the lemon juice and season to taste with salt and pepper.

Serves 4.

Grilled Salmon

5 tablespoons butter or margarine
1/2 cup brown sugar
1 teaspoon dark rum
Lemon juice
4 salmon steaks
Vegetable oil

Very lightly brush the steaks with oil so that they will not stick to the grill. Combine the butter, brown sugar, and rum in a small saucepan. Cook over low heat until the butter melts and the ingredients are combined. Add enough lemon juice to the mixture to cut the sweetness and make it the consistency of a sauce.

Grill the salmon steaks on a charcoal grill until just done, about 5 minutes per side, depending on thickness of steaks. Just before the steaks have finished grilling, brush one side with the sauce and continue grilling for another minute or two. Turn and brush the other side with the sauce and grill for another minute.

Serves 4.

Snapper

Red Snapper, Most Prized

Snappers are an important fish family of tropical seas. They number about 250 species of which fifteen are found in U.S. waters from North Carolina to the Gulf of Mexico. The most prized is the red snapper.

The first red snapper industry began in 1870 at Pensacola, Florida, where the first fish house was built by an enterprising New Englander, S. C. Cobb. Mr. Cobb sent his boats out into the Gulf and the snappers caught in less than 20 fathoms could be kept alive in the wells of the ship until it returned to port. In time, artificially made ice permitted Cobb to send larger and longer ships to more remote areas, going out 600 to 700 miles west of Cuba. Today snapper is fished by modern fleets throughout the Gulf.

Snappers have several recognizable family characteristics — sloping flattened snout, elongated head, prominent eyes, and a big mouth.

Red snapper, the most popular of the species, resides in depths of sixty to two hundred feet primarily around Florida and the Gulf of Mexico. It grows to about thirty-five pounds, but the usual weight is four to six pounds. It is rose colored with deeper red fins and bright red eyes.

Other prominent snappers are the Atlantic gray, the schoolmaster, the lane, and the mutton snapper. Their habitat ranges from Florida to Texas, with the Atlantic gray inhabiting the bayous and streams of the Gulf coast.

Red snapper has pure white, lean, moist and firm meat. It has a mild but distinctive flavor. Red Snapper is marketed whole or filleted. Broiled, baked, steamed or poached it is a delicacy.

One of the most famous preparations for red snapper is in the Creole style. The following recipe is for red snapper fillets, but a whole fish may also be baked with the Creole sauce -- just bake the fish a little longer.

Red Snapper Creole

2 pounds red snapper fillets
2 strips bacon
2 tablespoons butter
1 small onion, minced
1 green onion, chopped
1 garlic clove, minced
2/3 cup sliced mushrooms
2 1/2 cups plum tomatoes, chopped
3 tablespoons tomato paste
1 bay leaf
1 teaspoon Worcestershire sauce
1 tablespoon lemon juice
2 tablespoons brandy or sherry
Salt and pepper, to taste

Fry the bacon in a skillet until crisp, drain, and set aside. Add the butter, onion, green onion, garlic, celery, and mushrooms to the skillet and sauté the vegetables in the bacon fat and butter until soft. Stir in the tomatoes, tomato paste, bay leaf, Worcestershire sauce, lemon juice, and crumbled bacon. Bring to a boil, then simmer, stirring occasionally, for 15 minutes. Mix in the brandy, season with salt and pepper, and simmer 5 more minutes. Keep the sauce warm.

Wipe the snapper fillets with a damp paper towel and place them in an oiled baking dish. Pour 1 cup of the sauce over the fish, or more if necessary. Bake in a preheated 400° F. oven for 15 minutes or until the fish flakes easily when tested. Serve the remaining sauce with the fish. Serves 4.

Sole

Chefs' Delight

No fish lends itself to such a variety of dishes as sole. One reason for its popularity is that sole does not have a "fishy" taste. Its texture and delicate flavor is ideal for the elaborate use of sauces, herbs, spices, fruits, and vegetables. It also contrasts well with seafoods, such as crab and shrimp. Few fish can tolerate such a myriad of additives without losing their identity. Sole is the traditional fish around which European chefs create their masterpieces.

Sole achieved a prime status in England in the days of horse transport when enterprising wholesalers hired fast carriages to convey fish from the South Coast of England to Billingsgate Market in London. The bulk of their catch was landed at the port of Dover and soon "Dover sole" became synonymous with prime quality.

When motor transport displaced the horse, inevitably all fresh soles earned the name "Dover." Subsequently, commercial fish dealers created new sole names, not simply because of the value placed on the original but to make some of the less-inspiring flatfishes more glamorous. For example, a witch flounder hardly generates gastronomic interest when purveyed under its correct common name, but when marketed as "white sole" as it is in Ireland, or as "gray sole" as it is in the United States, this very edible flounder becomes acceptable to the consumer.

Thus the term "sole" encompasses a number of flat fishes. Dover sole and English sole are even accepted common names for two Pacific flounders which bear no resemblance to true sole. Unfortunately some of these impostors are inferior in texture and flavor and do not lend themselves to sole recipes.

Much of the sole in the market today, such as rex sole, petrale sole, lemon sole, butter sole, sand sole, and yellowfin sole, are really flounders. They differ in taste but have been preferred by many over the costlier true sole.

There are four true soles in western Atlantic waters — the hogchoker, lined, naked, and scrawled soles. They are very small members of the sole family and seldom reach a length of more than eight inches. They also have little food value. Most of the time the true authentic Dover sole is only available in the United States as a frozen import from England and France. However, with air transport we are getting some fresh Dover sole.

Dover sole is found in the waters from the Mediterranean area to Denmark. Their thick-bodies produce a unique fillet of fine texture and flavor. Dover sole has a rounded snout, and a rounded, unbroken curve from back to belly. False soles have pointed snouts.

Among the sole substitutes, rex sole, the smallest Pacific flounder, is extremely delicate and of fine texture. It is also less numerous than other flatfishes and commands a higher price. Rex sole is too thin to fillet properly and is usually cooked whole.

Petrale sole, a large Pacific flounder, is ranked first among Pacific flatfishes. It is found in waters from the Mexican border north to Alaska. Lemon sole is the U. S. market name for a winter flounder weighing more than three pounds. It is found in the waters off of Massachusetts and Long Island. In France lemon sole denotes a true sand sole.

One of the most famous recipes for sole is Filet de Sole Florentine, a favorite of European chefs. This is a simple preparation for an elegant dish.

The Fillet of Sole with Mushrooms is an adaptation of an old German recipe. I have adapted it for microwave cooking which produces a very moist fish and a delicious sauce. Serve it with rice.

Filet de Sole Florentine

4 fillets of sole
2 pounds fresh spinach
1/2 teaspoon onion powder
1/2 teaspoon salt
Dash of white pepper
Dash of grated mace
1/2 teaspoon seasoned salt
2 tablespoons chopped parsley
2 tablespoons butter
2 1/2 tablespoons all-purpose flour
1/2 cup half-and -half
1/3 cup white wine
2/3 cup finely grated Gruyère cheese
Paprika

Wash the spinach well and remove any course stems. Cook the spinach in water that is clinging to the leaves just until wilted. Drain well and chop. Drain again, squeezing out all excess moisture.

Mix the spinach with the onion powder, 1/2 teaspoon salt, pepper and mace, and place in a shallow 5-cup baking dish.

Sprinkle the sole with the seasoned salt and parsley. Roll up the fillets, and place them on top of the spinach. Melt the butter in a saucepan and blend in the flour. Stir in the half-and-half and cook, stirring, until the sauce begins to thicken. Add the wine and cook until the sauce boils thoroughly. Remove from heat and stir in 3 tablespoons of cheese.

Spoon the sauce over the sole and spinach. Sprinkle with remaining cheese and some paprika. Bake in a preheated 350° F. oven for about 20 to 25 minutes or until the sole is cooked through. Serve at once. Serves 4.

Fillet of Sole with Mushrooms

1/4 cup butter
2 cups sliced mushrooms
1/2 cup sliced green onions
2 1/2 tablespoons all-purpose flour
1/4 teaspoon salt
1/4 teaspoon pepper
1/2 cup chopped fresh parsley
1 cup milk
3/4 pound sole fillets (4 fillets)

Place the butter, mushrooms, and onion in an 8 x 10-inch baking suitable for microwaving. Microwave on high for 3 to 4 minutes or until mushrooms and onion are partly cooked. Blend in the flour, salt, pepper, and parsley. Stir in the milk and mix well. Cover with plastic wrap, venting 1 corner. Microwave on high 4 to 5 minutes or until the mixture bubbles.

Stir the sauce and arrange the sole fillets in it, covering the fish with some of the sauce. As sole fillets can be very thin, it is advisable to put two on top of each other. Cover with plastic wrap and vent 1 corner. Microwave on high 5 to 6 minutes or until the fish is done. Serve with steamed rice. Serves 2.

Swordfish

The Sword Is His Weapon

The Latin name *gladius* is for the short sword carried by Roman legions, and the fish by that name sometimes uses it with stunning effects. Swordfish have rammed many ships, plunging deep into oak planking. During World War II when merchant ships were being sunk off the coast of Bermuda, broken bills of swordfish were frequently found in the wreckage.

Due to the fact that swordfish are not readily spooked by ships, most of the fish taken by commercial fishermen are harpooned, although in the Pacific many are caught on long lines. Some are trapped in tuna nets in the Mediterranean.

Most of the swordfish are harpooned as they bask on the surface in the morning sunshine. This is the same method that has been used for centuries to catch these fish.

Swordfish are deep water nocturnal feeders rising only to the surface in the early hours of the day after feeding. Deep water moonlight fishing for swords has become an exciting summer sport during the full-moon cycle.

Almost all big fish surface within the first hour of light to see what is going on. About one-third of the swords are chargers. Outmaneuvering a three hundred pound charging swordfish, capable of putting a hole through a three-inch plank, can offer a bit of excitement for the sport fisherman.

Swordfish are found throughout the world in tropical and temperate seas. In the western Atlantic they are prevalent from Newfoundland to Cuba. Swordfish are usually found off our East Coast from late June through the summer. They then move off shore into deep water along the edge of the Continental Shelf. In the eastern Atlantic swordfish occur from Scandinavia to the southern tip of Africa. They also reside in the waters of the Pacific along the West Coast and from Japan to New Zealand and Australia.

Cooking swordfish over charcoal is the best method for preparing it. Having a dry, firm, and lean meat, swordfish gains flavor by marinating it in herbs and oil. The rich smoke that results from the oil dripping on the hot charcoal greatly enhances the end result.

Grilled Swordfish

*6 swordfish steaks, about 8 ounces each,
    1-inch thick*
1 cup olive oil
1 tablespoon crumbled dried oregano
1 tablespoon crushed bay leaf
Juice of 1 lemon
3 garlic cloves, minced
2 tablespoons crumbled dried basil
1 teaspoon celery salt
1 teaspoon coarse black pepper
Melted butter
Finely chopped parsley, for garnish

Combine all of the ingredients except the fish and butter in a bowl and mix thoroughly. Swish each steak in the marinade to cover both sides and refrigerate for 2 to 3 hours. Turn once or twice to make certain the steaks are well coated.

With the grid about 6 inches from the fire, grill the steaks uncovered for 5 minutes, then turn and cook for 7 minutes on the other side. Baste the steaks with the remaining marinade, using a pastry brush. Arrange steaks on a platter and splash with melted butter. Garnish with parsley. Serves 6.

Trout

Favorite of Anglers

Trout are the most universally cultured fish both for angling and the commercial market. Their domestic propagation began in the fourteenth century when a French monk, Dom Pichon, discovered trout eggs could be artificially impregnated. During the next 400 years there were some minor contributions to trout culture, but the science did not gain momentum until 1852 when the first publicly owned trout hatchery was constructed in France.

The alarming decrease of trout in America due to the industrialization of our river valleys soon required their production by artificial methods. In 1864 Seth Green built the first American trout hatchery at Mumford, New York. He was a pioneer fish culturist and helped construct private and state hatcheries throughout New England and the Middle Atlantic states. Green originally reared only the native eastern brook trout in preference over the hardier rainbow trout of the West. In 1886 German fish culturist, Von Behr, sent the first brown trout to the United States.

By the early 1900s rainbow trout were a huge success and were being shipped all over the world to thrive in countries were natural populations of trout were unknown, such as New Zealand and South Africa. Today the red-sided rainbow trout is internationally esteemed. For example, the species is farmed throughout Denmark, where commercial production of trout is that nation's second largest industry.

There are numerous species of trout, each with distinct flavors and textures. Flesh color may range from white to brilliant red. The coloration stems from dietary fat-soluble carotenoids found in crustaceans in waters where trout consume large quantities of crayfish or shrimp.

With the exception of lake trout, and to a lesser extent, steelhead trout, all trout served in U. S. restaurants by law must be of hatchery origin. Wild fish do legally enter many European markets, although the vast majority are farm raised in Denmark, France, and Italy.

By the same token wild trout can be less than desirable if they feed on algal blossoms, causing a muddy taste. Those that are in rivers containing an abundance of organic material are also of poor quality. Generally fish taken from high, clear mountain lakes and swift-flowing clear streams are the best for eating.

This simple method of baking whole trout with some herbs enhances the flavor of the fish.

Baked Whole Trout

4 trout, cleaned and dressed
Salt and pepper
6 tablespoons butter
1/2 small onion, minced
3 tablespoon chopped parsley
1 teaspoon dried basil
1/4 teaspoon dried tarragon
1/4 cup dry white wine
4 tablespoons sour cream
1/3 cup bread crumbs

Wipe trout with a damp paper towel inside and out. Salt and pepper the fish and arrange them in a buttered baking dish.

Melt the butter in a small saucepan with the onion, parsley, basil, tarragon, and wine. Then pour the mixture over the fish. Cover the dish tightly with aluminum foil. Bake in a preheated 425° F. oven for 12 to 15 minutes. Remove the foil, spoon the sour cream over the fish, sprinkle with crumbs, and then broil until crumbs are browned. Serves 4.

Tuna

More Than Just Canned

Tuna is a favorite food in many cultures. The Italians, for example, use tuna in a variety of recipes. Tuna and white beans are the basis of a famous appetizer called, *Tonno e Fagioli*. Traditional pasta sauces made with tuna are numerous in the south of Italy, while in the north tuna is often used in a rice salad. Tuna is also used in the sauce for cold sliced veal in the well-known dish, *Vitello Tonnato*.

Italian food writers have compared tuna to pork, both for its fatty meat and because it has no waste. Sicilian cooking, in particular, includes an array of tuna recipes, some of which originated in Roman times.

Apicius, a famous Roman food aficionado who lived in the first century A.D., served tuna with sweet and sour sauces. These were based on a pounded mixture of honey, pepper, onion, vinegar, herbs, mustard, and oil. Nearly two thousand years later the Sicilians created the recipe, *Tonno alla Marinara* —meaning cooked the sailor's way. The dish consists of tuna fish steaks cooked in the oven in olive oil with black olives, tomatoes, capers, dried bread crumbs and basil. In the region of Calabria on the southern mainland, cooks add a fresh chili pepper to this dish.

The catching and eating of tuna goes back to the ancient peoples of the Mediterranean and Black Seas. They treated tuna as an epicurean delicacy, typically roasting it on a spit with olive oil and spices, as well as a staple food. Tuna was used as a trading commodity and was so prized that an image of the fish appeared on the most valuable coins of ancient civilizations of that area.

All along the northern coastline of the Mediterranean are steep cliffs where men could sight great migrations of tuna from elevated platforms and then give a shout inviting fishermen to row out and spread their nets. Many of the ancient civilizations such as those in Sicily, southern Italy, Greece, southern Spain, and Portugal depended on tuna fishing for their main food supply.

A number of ancient place names on the Mediterranean derive their origin from "cete," meaning a fish of great dimensions and locations where tuna were frequently caught.

According to early Greek writings fresh tuna was often seasoned with cinnamon, ground coriander, vinegar and honey, then cooked in olive oil with chopped onion. The Romans, on the other hand, favored cumin and mint as the principle seasonings for tuna. They also added mustard and raisins, along with wine, garlic, and onions.

The butchering of tuna was regarded as an art in Mediterranean cultures and continues to be so today. The only part of a tuna not utilized by ancient fishermen was the tail. However, even the dried tail fin had its purpose when nailed over a doorway to protect the home from evil spirits. Francesco Cetti, an eighteenth century historian, wrote this about tuna: "Every spot at which a knife penetrates is different; firm in one spot, tender in another; here it looks like veal, there like pork."

Tuna is a members of the mackerel family. There are six species of tuna on the market in fresh, frozen, or canned forms — each is distinctly different in color, texture, and flavor. The light meat used by the canning industry comes from the yellowfin tuna, skipjack, and small bluefin. The white meat tuna is derived only from the albacore. The flesh color of tuna reflects its quality. The darker the tuna the less delicate the flavor.

Americans are mainly familiar with canned tuna, a compacted and steamed product. It is only in the last ten years that fresh tuna caught commercially has become readily available in our seafood markets. Large quantities of tuna are caught by sport fishermen in northeastern waters and in the Pacific.

American commercial fishermen on the east coast did not pursue tuna in the western Atlantic until the early 1960s. Essentially tuna fishing in the Atlantic was done by Europeans, particularly French and Spanish fleets which, traditionally plied the waters off of west Africa. In the 1970s the Japanese spread their extensive tuna fishing operations all over the tropical and subtropical Atlantic.

The U.S. tuna fleet was mainly centered in the Pacific where it had been for over a century. With fierce competition from the Japanese in the Pacific, commercial American fishermen were encouraged to work the Atlantic waters. Now the American tuna catch is about equally divided between the two oceans.

The main feature of the Tokyo fish auction — the largest fish market in the world — is tuna. Depending on the season, frozen whole tuna, minus head and tail looking like huge bombs, are flown to the daily fish auction from the Mediterranean, the United States, and Mexico. In the very early morning thousands of tuna are spread out in a large shed that extends for several hundred yards.

The Japanese use tuna in their sashimi and sushi. The higher the fat content of each tuna the higher the price at the auction. The fattiness of the fish adds to its flavor, and also gives the raw fish a more delicate pink color.

The Pasta with Tuna and Tomato Sauce is typical of Sicilian cuisine with red pepper flakes. The Tonno e Fagioli is a traditional Italian antipasti. Tuna Steaks with Onion and Bacon is a California creation.

Pasta with Tuna and Tomato Sauce

1 tablespoon olive oil
2 garlic cloves, minced
1 medium onion, chopped
3 pounds fresh tomatoes
1 tablespoon tomato paste
1/2 teaspoon sugar
Salt and pepper, to taste

Heat the olive oil over medium heat in a large saucepan. Add the garlic and onion and sauté until the onion turns golden. Add the tomatoes, tomato paste, sugar, and salt and pepper. Bring to a slow boil and simmer over medium-low heat for 20 minutes, stirring occasionally. Remove from heat and puree the sauce with a hand-held blender or in a food processor. Set aside.

1 pound fresh tuna steaks
1 tablespoon olive oil
3 garlic cloves, chopped
1/4 teaspoon red pepper flakes
1 pound penne or other tubular pasta
Freshly grated Parmesan cheese, optional

Remove the skins from the tuna steaks and cut the meat off the center bone. Sauté the garlic in 1 tablespoon of olive oil in a skillet over medium heat for 2 minutes. Add the tuna and sauté, stirring the fish occasionally, for about 5 minutes or until the tuna has become light gray on the surface. With a large spoon break the tuna apart and add the tomato sauce and the red pepper flakes. Bring to a simmer and cook, stirring often, for 10 to 15 minutes.

While the sauce is simmering, cook the pasta in boiling water until as dente. Drain and toss with half of the sauce. Spoon onto warm plates and top each serving with the remaining sauce. Sprinkle with Parmesan cheese, if desired. Serves 6.

Tonno e Fagioli
(Tuna with Beans)

2 (15 ounce) cans cannellini (white) beans, rinsed and drained
1/2 cup coarsely chopped red onion
1 (6 ounce) can tuna packed in oil, drained
4 to 5 tablespoon extra virgin olive oil
1/4 teaspoon salt
1/2 teaspoon freshly ground black pepper.

Place the cannellini beans in a large serving bowl and add the onions. Break the tuna apart with a fork and mix it with the beans and onions. Add the oil and season with salt and pepper. Mix well. Cover the bowl and refrigerate until ready to serve. Serves 8.

Tuna Steaks
with Onion and Bacon

4 tablespoons olive oil
4 medium onions, sliced
1/4 cup red wine vinegar
1/2 cup balsamic vinegar
1/2 cup chicken broth
Salt and pepper
3 slices bacon, diced and sautéed until crisp
4 tuna steaks, about 6 to 8 ounces each

Heat 2 tablespoon of the olive oil in a skillet. Add the onions and sauté until golden brown, about 8 to 10 minutes. Add both vinegars and reduce until all the liquid has evaporated, about 4 minutes. Pour in the chicken broth, and cook for 5 minutes, until onions are very soft. Add salt, pepper and bacon pieces.

In a separate skillet heat the remaining 2 tablespoons of olive oil. Sauté the tuna steaks until medium, about 2 to 3 minutes on each side. Place on warm plates and top each steak with the onion mixture. Serves 4.

Some Other Fish

Bonita

Bonita, also known as skipjack, is classified as a tuna, but look different from other tunas. Dark green-blue to purple stripes run diagonally along their backs. It has red flesh and does taste like tuna. They are usually found in the warm waters of southern California.

Most of the bonita found close to the shore are young, weighing three to twelve pounds. They are heavily preyed upon by all predators. The older fish, weighing up to twenty-five pounds are found off shore. Bonita is a favorite of sport fishermen.

Hake

Hake's flesh is tender white and flaky and is almost as delicate as sole. Since it does not keep well it has not been heavily exploited. The part that first spoils is the long, transparent, gelatinous segment of the throat, which therefore is cut out immediately after the fish is caught. Although fishermen usually throw the throat away, the people of the Spanish Basque coast consider this morsel a delicacy. It is sold early in the morning at the dock where the boats come in from overnight fishing. Flash freezing has helped preserved hake for market.

Hake is the only member of the cod family that is found both in the northern and southern hemispheres, and also in the Mediterranean. Hake are smaller than cod and are often misnamed "codling" by Americans. Hake is often preserved by salting, similar to cod.

Hake can be ferocious for their large mouths contain unusually sharp teeth, which are hinged to bend backwards to let prey in. After the prey is caught the teeth snap back into position. Hake, a cannibalistic fish, takes twenty percent of its food in smaller hake.

Herring

Historians have argued as to whether herring or cod has been the most important food fish, historically. Both inhabit the northern oceans. Before the days of rapid transportation and refrigeration, cod and herring alike could be cured for delivery to the consumer far from where they were caught. Fresh herring, however, was usually available only in fishing ports.

Because of its fat content (about 6 percent of its weight) herring did not take well to drying and salt curing. It did not become popular until it was found that herring could be preserved by smoking.

Smoking herring began in the twelfth century and smoked herring quickly became a staple of the European diet. In Paris in 1170 Louis VII granted licenses to a guild of fish dealers. He divided them into two types — fishmongers who sold fresh water fish and those who sold herring. This meant that the herring sellers were superior to fishmongers. However, a century later due to the abundance of herring, it became a cheap food for the poor.

Herring quickly lost its snob appeal because of its relative cheapness and was considered suitable for those living on charity. In the 1300s in France 70,000 herring were donated annually to monasteries, hospitals, and plague houses.

On the other hand, the herring trade brought prosperity to a number of nations. The Danes were the first to exploit the herring trade, followed by the other Scandinavians and the English. The herring trade led to the development of the Hanseatic League in the thirteenth century. With a monopoly on the transport and sale of herring, the Hansa cities grew rich on this trade, which lasted for two centuries.

By the mid 1400s the Dutch with swifter and larger ships took control of the herring trade. They had also improved methods of preserving the catch. It was said jokingly that Amsterdam was built on herring bones. Large fishing fleets led to large navies and the English followed the Dutch in fishing for herring.

Today Great Britain dominates herring fishing in Europe. Herring has a much higher consumption than cod as the latter has been over-fished. While popular in Europe, fresh herring is seldom found in American markets.

The most enthusiastic consumers of herring are the Dutch. Each spring when the first fishing boats return there is celebration on the streets of Dutch villages and fresh herring is sold from flower-decked carts.

Herring is available in many forms — fresh, smoked, and pickled. Kippered (smoked) herring is the typical English breakfast food. When canneries came into being canned herring became a popular item.

A herring school is a shimmering, round, silvery mass that moves slowly clockwise. Herring spend their lives eating tiny plankton plants and animals. During the winter they come inshore to spawn and tend to return each year to the same spawning ground. Herring occupy the cold waters of the Atlantic and Pacific Oceans. They are an important link in the food chain, eaten by larger fish, birds, seals, and other mammals. Their abundance so far has enabled them to survive.

Mackerel

Mackerel was originally a Turkish fish, but now is found in almost every salt water habitat in the Northern Hemisphere. It is a fatty fish and thus tends to spoil quickly.

Mackerel has been eaten for centuries. Its bones dating back to the Stone Age have been found in northern Europe. The Romans used fermented mackerel to make a drink and a sauce.

Mackerel tastes best in the spring and early summer because at that time they are at their fattest. That is also the time when mackerels come closest to shore to spawn. On their way they devour everything in their path. Fishermen at that time are able to bring in tremendous hauls of mackerel and are almost able to scoop them up by their hands.

There are three different types of mackerel off of our coasts — the Atlantic and chub mackerel on the East Coast and the Pacific mackerel on the West Coast. All average between one and two pounds, are deep green on top with dark and silver stripes underneath. Spanish mackerel live in warmer waters and are prevalent in the Gulf.

Mackerel is a rich, firm textured fish that is best broiled, barbecued, or baked and served with a tart spicy sauce.

Pollack

A member of the cod family, pollack is favored by fishermen as they come closer to the shore than any other cod. Pollacks are not found on the West Coast, but are most plentiful in deep waters from Maine to Cape Cod. They are almost as versatile and often less expensive than true cod.

Pompano

Pompano are handsome slender, deep bodied, silver-blue fish with gold flecks. They typically weigh between one and four pounds, and are among the swiftest of all fish.

Atlantic pompano range from the Chesapeake Bay to the Gulf and Caribbean. They travel in schools along sandy beaches working their way in and out along with the tide. They are also found in bays and inlets where mollusks and crustaceans provide abundant food.

Pompano is served as an expensive delicacy in our country's finest restaurants and is considered by many to be the finest edible fish. Mark Twain once described pompano "as delicious as the less criminal forms of sin."

Pompano and sole are similar in taste and their methods of preparation are the same.

Turbot

Turbot is a member of the flatfish family. Many regard it equal to sole. The Atlantic turbot ranges from the Mediterranean to Norway and along our northeastern coast. Its body is diamond-shaped and its dark side is covered with tubercles. Turbot attain a fairly large size, over thirty pounds, although the average is considerably smaller.

The firm white meat of turbot has a delicate flavor. It is usually prepared very simply, either steamed or poached, and covered with melted butter or a simple sauce.

The following recipe is a classic preparation for a firm-fleshed fish. Soy sauce, ginger, and mushrooms add an Oriental flavor.

Halibut in Parchment with Ginger Mushrooms

4 halibut fillets
Soy-Ginger Marinade
3 tablespoons butter
1/2 pound shiitake mushrooms, sliced
1 pound white mushrooms, thinly sliced
2 tablespoons minced fresh ginger

1/2 tablespoon minced jalapeno pepper
6 scallions, green tops only, sliced, plus some for garnish
4 tablespoons butter
Hot cooked rice

Marinate fish in soy-ginger marinade for 10 minutes. Heat the 3 tablespoons of butter in a large skillet. Add mushrooms and sauté until most of the moisture has been absorbed. Add the ginger and cook until the mushrooms are cooked through, about 2 minutes. Add the minced jalapeno and cook for a minute longer.

Fold four 12 x 16-inch pieces of baking parchment or aluminum foil in half to make a triangle. Open each one out and place a marinated fish fillet above the crease. (Discard marinade.) Top with one quarter of the mushrooms and one quarter of sliced scallion tops. Dot with butter. Close packet by bringing top half over and crimping and folding edges together to make a tight seal. (Can be prepared ahead to this point and refrigerated for a few hours.)

Preheat oven and baking sheet to 375° F. Place packets on hot baking sheet and bake for 6 to 8 minutes, depending on thickness of fish. Place a packet on each plate and cut open. Sprinkle with more scallions and serve with rice.

Serves 4.

Soy-Ginger Marinade

1/4 cup low-salt soy sauce
1/4 cup water
3/4 cup lemon juice
1/2 teaspoon minced garlic
1 tablespoon minced fresh ginger

Combine all ingredients

Seafood

It has been written that Julius Caesar was the first emperor to serve a variety of seafood at a state dinner. However, oyster and mussel shells have been found in prehistoric dwellings throughout the world. This indicates that seafood has been a prime source of food since earliest times.

Seafood consists largely of "shellfish." The term includes edible freshwater and marine animals without backbones — crustaceans and mollusks. Crustaceans, such as lobsters and crabs, have a hard jointed exoskeleton or "crust" which they periodically shed and replace as they grow. Mollusks inhabit shells that are either hinged, like oysters and clams, or single like abalone.

For culinary purposes, other mollusks, such as land snails and shell-less marine animals such as squid, cuttlefish, and octopus are traditionally considered as seafood. This category also includes edible frogs, turtles, and terrapins

The shells of some crustaceans are renowned for their dramatic color change when cooked. This is because they contain red and yellow pigments that become activated by heat.

Shellfish are prized for their tender, fine-textured flesh which can be prepared in a variety of ways. However, they are notorious for rapid spoilage. Shellfish contain quantities of certain proteins, amino acids, which encourage bacterial growth. It is essential that they be extremely fresh or, if frozen, be consumed immediately after thawing, and come from unpolluted waters.

Fresh shellfish are available throughout most of the year, but some species reflect seasonal changes. For example, crabs shed their shells many times before reaching maturity from mid-spring to mid-autumn. That is when crabs are available as "soft-shells." Oysters, on the other hand, are traditionally eaten during cold weather months when they are fatter and have more taste.

Clams

Valuable Clam Shells

In 1641 the New Netherland Colony (later known as New York) passed a law governing wampum and its value. Wampum, Indian beads, was made from clam shells. Black wampum, actually deep purple, was made from the center of the quahaug clam shell and was more valuable than the white wampum made from conch shells. Wampum beads, strung into strands or belts served as money in the eastern colonies until the end of the seventeenth century. It continued to serve for trading with western Indians until two centuries later.

The consumption of clams, however, was and still is an American passion. Clams on the half shell swallowed in its salt fragrant glory is a gourmet's delight. All clams cannot be enjoyed on the half shell, however, as some species need to be cooked.

Along the East Coast the most prevalent clam is the soft shell which is found from the Arctic ocean to Cape Hatteras. The hardshell clam, more properly known by its Indian name "quahaug" (or quahog pronounced co-hog), inhabits the same area. The quahaug is usually eaten raw and in chowder. The soft shell clam is considered a delicacy when steamed or fried.

Hardshell clams (quahaugs), which occur in shallow water, can be scooped up with a clam rake or simply by digging for them. Commercial clammers often work in deep water using hydraulic dredge boats which unearth clams with high pressure jets. Most of the nearly 20 million pounds of quahaugs consumed in the United States annually come from Long Island's Great South Bay.

Quahaugs are marketed according to size, the smallest being the Little Neck clams, named after Little Neck Bay on Long Island. They are usually three to four years old. The next larger size are known as Cherrystone clams, named after Cherrystone Creek in Virginia. They are usually harvested when about five years old. Any quahaug bigger than a Cherrystone is simply called a chowder clam, as they are too tough to serve on the half shell.

There are two other large eastern clams that are not widely eaten. The razor clam has a very sharp shell and is difficult to dig for because of its injurious qualities. This "digger" sport is enjoyed more by people on the West Coast where the razor clam is washed ashore with the tide by the thousands. The other eastern clam, the bar clam, is fine bait for codfish and is too big and tough for anything but chowder.

Along the Pacific Coast, in addition to the razor and softshell clams, there are several species of so-called littleneck clams, which have no relation to the eastern ones. These are the most tender of the western clams and can be eaten on the half shell.

Probably the most unique West Coast clam is the geoduck. It grows to seven inches across the shell and comes with a siphon that may be six or seven times as long. Geoducks reveal their presence at low tide by squirting water in the air like a fountain. It takes two people to remove this huge bivalve from its burrow, one to grab the clam's "neck" and the other to do the digging.

The geoduck is not the largest clam ever eaten, however. Among his other conquests, Alexander the Great managed to extract and consume the giant "granddaddy" clams of the Indian Ocean. The meat of this species may weight up to twenty pounds and the shell a quarter of a ton. Later navigators traveling through the Pacific discovered giant clams of 4 feet in length on the Great Barrier Reef of Australia.

Clams have been a food of man since prehistoric times. They were easy to obtain for those living near the sea shore as the tide uncovered the clams twice daily.

Clams are marketed in three forms — in the shell, shucked, and canned. Clams in the shell are usually sold on location by the dozen and must be alive with their valves tightly closed when bought. Refrigerated at 40° F. they will stay alive for several days. Shucked clams are whole meat sold in pints or quarts. They should be refrigerated at all times and will stay fresh for about a week. Clam meat is canned for later use. Clams are also sold smoked, usually canned in oil.

Clam liquor extracted during the shucking operation is sold bottled in undiluted form as "clam juice" or when diluted as "clam broth."

Brightly colored and flavored with a hint of the sea, this Green Pea and Clam Bisque is a variation of the familiar clam chowder. The soup is best if made a day in advance, and reheated just before serving with the addition of the wine.

Green Pea and Clam Bisque

3 slices bacon, chopped
1 cup chopped onions
1/2 cup chopped carrot
3 cups chicken broth
1/2 teaspoon salt
1/4 teaspoon white pepper
1/2 teaspoon thyme, crumbled
3 cups (1 pound) frozen baby peas, thawed
1/2 cup chopped parsley
2 cups whipping cream
2 (10 ounce) cans baby clams, with juice
1 cup dry white wine

In a soup pot sauté the bacon until the fat is rendered. Add the onions and carrot and sauté over medium heat for 5 minutes. Do not allow the vegetables to brown. Add the chicken broth, salt, pepper, and thyme. Cover and bring to a boil. Reduce heat and simmer for 10 minutes. Add the peas and the parsley. Stir the mixture a little to incorporate the peas.

Remove from heat and puree in several batches in a food processor or a blender. (A blender will yield a finer puree.) Return the mixture to the soup pot and bring to a boil. Add the cream and the clams with their juice. Taste and adjust seasonings, if necessary. (If making soup ahead, cool and refrigerate at this point. Just before serving, reheat carefully, stirring often.) Continue heating until very hot, but do not allow to boil. Just before serving, stir in the wine. Serve with slices of French bread and butter. Serves 8; makes about 2 and 1/2 quarts.

Crab

Hard or Soft Shell

There are 4400 species of crab, each with immensely different habitats, but they have one thing in common — all true crabs are edible. They range in size from the tiny pea crab, which lives inside the shells of mollusks, to the giant Tasmanian crab which can weigh thirty pounds. Most crabs walk sideways because their wide body gets in the way of walking.

Crabs live in shallow water, deep water, fresh water, on the beach, and on land. The island of Borneo has two very unique crabs. One lives in caves and the other in the mountains at an altitude of 8500 feet. In spite of these two mavericks, most crabs live in the sea. Even the females of the land crabs wander to the sea to release their eggs.

Just as the crabs themselves are different so are their eating habits. Some are hunters and pursue their prey primarily shrimp. One species prefers oyster and establishes itself among the rocks where oysters dwell. The crab seizes a rock and when the oyster opens its shell it inserts the rock in the shell, enabling the crab to leisurely feast on the oyster. Some crabs prefer a vegetable diet. The robber crab climbs tall palm tress to pick coconuts for its dinner.

Crabs are found in most areas of the world. The most popular in the United States are the West coast dwellers — the Dungeness , the Alaska king , and the Tanner crab. The smaller rock crab has also recently become popular in California. In the East the blue crab is most prevalent in the Chesapeake Bay and along the Gulf Coast. The blue crab is also prized during the molting season when they shed their shells and are marketed as soft shell crabs. This delicacy is only available on a limited basis during the summer months. Stone crabs are native to Florida and the Gulf.

Crabs are caught in cages (pots) or hoop nets that are baited with fish and dropped overboard to sink to the bottom. A line attached to the cage connects to a surface float marking the position of the cage, allowing for subsequent recovery. Crabs have a very keen sense of smell and are attracted to the bait from a considerable distance. They walk into the cage on the tips of their pointed claws to consume the bait. The fisherman returns to the marker after a period of time and if he is lucky the cage is loaded with crabs.

Dungeness crabs are found from Lower California to Alaska on sandy, grassy bottoms, from shallow-tide zones to 300-foot ocean depths. The big fishing fleets for this crab run primarily from Monterey Bay, south of San Francisco, to the northern California border. The height of the Dungeness crab season is from November through March.

Dungeness crabs are the most favorite of California seafoods. These delicate crabs are usually steamed and then served cold. The meat is picked out of the crab shell and often topped with a Louis sauce. Dungeness crabs are also a favorite ingredient of *Cioppino*. During crab season, crabs are cooked in big caldrons on the sidewalk at Fisherman's Wharf in San Francisco. "Walk-Away Crab Cocktails" can literally be eaten as you stroll along the colorful wharf.

The king crab lives along the continental shelf in the Gulf of Alaska and north into the Bering Strait. Typically, gigantic male king crabs have legs two feet long.

With over-fishing of the king crab, Alaskan crab fishermen are now harvesting the Tanner, or snow crab, and the smaller and more delicately flavored Dungeness crab. The annual Alaska crab harvest is about 200 million pounds, with Tanner crabs predominating. Like the king crab, the Tanner crab has long spindly legs but a smaller body. To be harvested legally, it must measure five and a half inches across the body.

All of the crabs harvested off the coast of Alaska are caught in large traps dropped from fishing boats. The traps are usually baited with fish heads, and when the ship's sonar detects that the traps are full, they are raised by hydraulic lift. The crabs are then placed in holding tanks, where cold sea water is constantly circulated in order to keep them alive. Some of the larger ships process the crab harvest aboard ship. A large boat can butcher, clean, cook, box, and freeze 40,000 pounds of crab meat per day.

The Chesapeake Bay commercial crabbing industry began in the mid-nineteenth century with the advent of refrigeration and regular steamboat and rail transportation. Until then the highly perishable crabs could not survive shipments to markets outside the local area.

Chesapeake Bay's blue crabs are highly prized and have some special characteristics. The blue refers to the color on the underside of the large claws. Most of the crab's life is spent on the floor of the Bay. Each female blue crab produces about two million eggs, but only about fifty reach maturity. Eggs, which are hatched in June, mature in July or August of the following year.

The blue crab may shed its shell as many as twenty-three times during its natural life span of three years. Each molt increases the crab's size by one -third. Before molting the crab develops a soft, new internal shell. The old shell then cracks, and the crab wiggles out. This fresh "soft crab" draws in water to expand its wrinkled shell, and after two days the shell hardens. As the crab ages, molts are less frequent. There is only a 24-hour period when the shell is soft enough so that the whole body of the crab can be eaten.

With each summer dawn a Chesapeake Bay crabber loads his workboat with barrels, baskets, and frozen bait and heads out for the creek mouths or the open, choppy Bay. On a bright day he can easily spot the lines of floats that mark his line of crab pots. At the start of each line, he idles his engine, reaches over the side with a hooked pole, and catches the line under the first float. In rapid succession he raises the pot, dumps the catch into a basket, slashes a new piece of fresh bait and puts it into the pot's funnel neck, closes the pot, and drops it back. He may do this from twenty times or hundreds of times, depending on the weather, the market, and the size of his operation. Heavy gloves save his hands from the snapping crab claws.

One crab pot can trap up to fifty crabs. The Atlantic blue crab that ventures into the crab pot averages five to seven inches across the back of the shell. Crab potters will keep almost all forms of legal size crabs, although they prefer the crab with the hard shell. "Jimmy" crabs, or males, are the fattest and meatiest. Egg-bearing females are not harvested commercially and are thrown back.

As baskets or barrels are filled, the waterman keeps his wooden sizing gauge at hand to make sure the crab is more than the five inch minimum legal size. Then he heads to the picking house, where his baskets are weighed and their struggling contents are sent to be steamed, picked, graded, and packed.

Crab pickers are paid by the pound. It takes about twenty seconds to pick a crab, and they are never picked by machine. Professional crab pickers use a small sharp knife and their hands to break the crab into manageable pieces.

Soft-shell crabs are "peeler" crabs in a molting phase that shed their shells. Crabs, intended for market as soft-shell crabs, are often held in raft-like floats in creeks or in concrete tanks ashore until they shed their hard shells. As soon they shed and while their new shell is still soft and edible, they are quickly removed, packed in ice, and placed on a bed of eel grass on flat trays for shipment.

Blue crabs are the basis of crab cakes, cream of crab soup, and deviled crab. Soft shell crabs are usually served fried.

The crab cakes are of Maryland origin. The addition of baking powder to this crab mixture results in a light and fluffy crab cake. The citrus and olive flavors of the rice salad team well with sautéed soft shell crabs.

Crab Cakes

1 pound crab meat
1 egg, beaten
2/3 cup finely crushed saltine cracker crumbs
1 1/2 teaspoons Old Bay Seasoning
3 dashes Tabasco sauce
1/2 teaspoon dry mustard
1 teaspoon Worcestershire sauce
1 teaspoon baking powder
1 tablespoon lemon juice
3 tablespoons chopped parsley
3 to 4 tablespoons mayonnaise
Butter or margarine for frying

Pick over the crab meat, removing any loose shells. Place in a bowl and add all of the ingredients except the mayonnaise. Gently fold to mix, being careful not to break up the crabmeat. Fold in enough mayonnaise to hold the mixture together. Shape the crabmeat mixture into 8 three-inch patties.

Melt enough butter in a large skillet over medium heat to cover the bottom of the skil-

let. Add the crabmeat cakes and fry until brown on one side, about 3 to 4 minutes, then turn and brown the other side, also about 3 to 4 minutes. Serve at once. Serves 8

Soft-Shell Crabs with Orange-Rice Salad

8 soft-shelled crabs
All-purpose flour
Salt and pepper, to taste
3 tablespoons butter or margarine

Dredge the crabs lightly in flour and sprinkle them with salt and pepper. Heat the butter in a large skillet over medium-high heat. Add the crabs and sauté for 4 to 5 minutes per side, depending on size. Serves 4

Orange Rice Salad

1/4 cup orange juice
2 tablespoons lime juice
2 tablespoons chopped cilantro
1/2 tablespoon white wine vinegar
6 ounces rinsed, drained black beans
2 cups cooked rice
1/3 cup pimento stuffed olives, sliced
1/3 cup chopped red pepper
1 avocado, peeled and diced
1/2 large Valencia orange, peeled and diced

In a 1-cup measuring cup, combine the orange juice, lime juice, cilantro, and wine vinegar. Stir and set aside.

Combine the remaining ingredients in a mixing bowl and toss gently. Pour the dressing over the salad and mix gently. Refrigerate for 4 hours before serving. Serve on lettuce.

Crayfish

Freshwater Crustacean

The crayfish is a small lobster-like crustacean that inhabits freshwater on all continents except Africa. Some even burrow holes in ground dampened by fresh water.

Crayfish range in size from the inch-long crayfish of America to the 8-pound Tasmanian crayfish, a culinary treasure. More than 800 species are found throughout the world, of which more than 250 are known in North America. There are twenty-nine different crayfish in Louisiana alone. Despite this large number of crayfish, few grow to edible size. which is a body of three and a half inches long, but preferably over five inches.

Crayfish belong to a rare category of animals that do not have specific nocturnal or daytime habits. This is because they are blind. Some crayfish live in caves where there is abundant water but no light.

Crayfish are consumed more in Europe than in this country. There they have been popular since the Middle Ages, as it was easier for people to collect them than salt water crustaceans. At one time crayfish were very popular in Paris where they were fished out of the Seine.

By the 1830s Parisians were eating 150,000 pounds of crayfish a year and paying as little as three francs per hundred. By 1880 the price had gone up by five hundred percent and consumption dropped. Crayfish was no longer the star of Parisian tables, except for the affluent who served them as a status symbol.

Farm raising crayfish in ponds has become a rather large scale business in Louisiana with more than ten million pounds being produced annually. Crayfish are also being farmed in Missouri, Texas, Mississippi, Alabama, and Arkansas. Most of the Pacific Coast harvest of wild crayfish from Oregon, Washington, and California is utilized locally with the remainder being shipped to France and Sweden. Some Pacific Coast crayfish reach eight inches in length.

Four-fifths of the crayfish raised in Louisiana are consumed locally. The Louisiana legislature has declared Breaux Bridge, population 5,000, as the Crayfish Capital of the World. Every other year the town holds a crayfish festival featuring a crayfish eating contest. Record holders have eaten as much as thirty five pounds of crayfish tails in two hours.

Crayfish is also an honored food in Scandinavia where some insist that the only way to eat them is to alternate a swallow of crayfish with a swallow of *akvavit*. Reportedly the usual consumption of crayfish at parties averages twenty. No statistics apparently exist on the amount of *akvavit* consumed. In Norway and Sweden crayfish are typically served on a bed of greens with a light dressing as an appetizer.

Throughout the world a dish having a sauce *Nantua* is one that has crawfish in the sauce. The dish is named after the town of Nantua in France. Crayfish Étouffée, a famous dishes of Louisiana origin, consisted of steamed crayfish meat and is served with rice.

Lobster

The King of Seafood

Nine times out of ten the live lobsters in the tanks at our local supermarkets came from Maine. Although American lobsters exist on the East Coast from Labrador to the Carolinas, they are most plentiful in the cold waters of the Gulf of Maine. That is where most of the nation's lobsters are caught live and quickly transported to restaurants and markets all over the country.

Maine lobsters are often referred to as American lobsters to distinguish them from other lobster-like crustaceans. For example, the Mediterranean lobster is a spiny lobster with no large claws; the same is true of the Caribbean lobster. The latter has a larger tail than the American lobster. European lobsters are small in comparison.

In the 1930's a lobster's wholesale price was ten cents a pound. In the 1950's it went up to thirty-four cents a pound and by the 1970's a lobster fisherman could get two dollars and twenty-five cents a pound. Today it is four and a half to five dollars a pound, depending on the size of the lobster. Prices have changed over the years, but the basic method of lobster fishing has not altered in the last two hundred years. Lobster fishing is a very labor intensive occupation.

Maine is a word synonymous with American lobster because the cold waters of the Gulf of Maine are full of fish and crustaceans that are the natural food of lobsters. These ungainly nocturnal creatures live on the rocky bottom of the Gulf where there is abundant kelp to provide shelter.

Lobster, along with clams and oysters, was a favorite dish of the coastal Indians in New England when the first settlers arrived. The native Americans also used them for fertilizer and fashioned pipes from the larger claws. The Indians taught the settlers how to steam lobsters in a variation of the cooking method we know today as a clam bake. At that time lobsters were much larger than today, five to six pounds was the norm, with the largest reaching twenty five to thirty pounds.

Before the early 1800's, Maine lobsters were not harvested commercially. They were simply caught by walking along the shore at low tide, poking under rocks and ledges and picking up the big-clawed crustaceans by hand. They were also caught with an ordinary dip net. It is said that after a storm, lobsters used to be piled two feet high on the beaches of Maine and Massachusetts. At that time lobster was considered the food of the poor.

Commercial fishing of lobsters started about the mid-1840's. Due to inadequate transportation for shipping live lobsters, the canning industry started a few years later. By 1854 canned Maine lobster meats were being sent to foreign markets.

Today lobsters are still caught by the same traps or "pots" used over a hundred years ago. These wooden or mesh boxes are baited with fish or fish heads. The traps are attached to brightly painted styrofoam buoys with a nylon rope. Each fisherman has his own distinctive markings on his buoys. Usually there are two traps attached to each buoy, but larger fishing operations may have as many as one hundred traps strung together.

Each lobster fishing port has its own distinctive fishing territory in the Gulf of Maine which extends thirty to forty miles from shore in the shape of a cucumber. Each lobster man or woman (only nine percent of Maine's lobster fishermen are women) is an independent operator who owns his own boat and gear, and works on his own schedule. In Maine encroachment on another's territory is punishable by law.

A typical lobster boat is about thirty-five feet long and usually is operated by two people. They haul in and rebait about five hundred traps in a period of two to three days. After the typical two-to-three day fishing trip, the lobster catches are taken to a central market from where they are wrapped in seaweed and transported by air to local distribution points around the country. Lobsters can live in their "seaweed bed" for approximately eighteen hours, reaching their destination long before that time. Local supermarkets and restaurants put them into tanks where they survive for up to two weeks.

There is a famous lobster story relating to World War II. Just before the invasion of Normandy, the British sent reconnaissance teams in small fishing boats into the English channel. Each day the men hauled up lobster pots and removed rubber lobsters from them. After dark they lowered them back into the water to be pulled up again the next day. No one knows if this deception was successful in deceiving the Germans.

Boiling is the most common method of preparing lobster. Use a kettle large enough to hold the lobster, or lobsters and put about 3 inches of water in the bottom of the kettle. Add a little salt and bring the water to a boil. Place the lobster in the kettle and immediately bring the water to a boil again. Boil for 12 to 15 minutes for lobsters weighing under 1 and 1/2 pounds. If larger, cook for 18 to 20 minutes. Serve the lobster either hot or cold with drawn butter or mayonnaise. If using lobsters as an ingredient in other dishes, remember a 1 and 1/2 pound lobster yields about 1 and 1/2 cups of meat.

Lobster can enhance a wide variety of dishes, such as this Baked Brie with Lobster that can be served as an hors d'oeuvre with crackers or a first course. on lettuce.

Baked Brie with Lobster

1 1/2 cups cooked lobster meat
2 scallions, finely chopped
1/4 cup minced celery
1/4 cup minced red pepper
1/4 teaspoon white pepper
1/2 cup mayonnaise
1 small wheel of Brie, weighing
    about 14 ounces, at room temperature
Lettuce leaves, for garnish

In a bowl combine the lobster meat, scallions, celery, red pepper, pepper, and mayonnaise. Refrigerate until ready to serve. Place the Brie on a non-stick baking sheet and top with the lobster salad. Bake in a preheated 350° F. oven for 3 minutes or until the salad is lukewarm and the cheese begins to soften.

Serve on lettuce leaves. Cut the cheese into wedges and serve as an hors d'oeuvres with crackers or as a first course with mini slices of French bread. Serves 8 to 10 as hors d'oeuvres or 4 as a first course.

Mussels

European Specialty

Mussels have never enjoyed the great popularity in American cuisine as they have in Europe. The French consume more than 80,000 tons of mussels annually, with the British, Dutch, Belgians, Spanish, Portuguese, and Italians not far behind that number. The Spanish lead in the production of mussels, most of which takes place in the bays and inlets on the Galician (north) coast. France and Italy follow in mussel production with the United States being last with less than 5,000 tons.

When the first settlers landed on the Atlantic coast they found that the Indians were afraid to eat mussels because they regarded them as being poisonous. The Pacific coast Indians, on the other hand, ate mussels that were poisonous.

Wild Pacific Coast mussels are not edible from May through October. This is not the fault of the mussel, but of its food. When the water of the Pacific warms in the spring, plankton, a genus of dinoflagellates. proliferates in great quantities. This plankton contains a powerful poison, saxitoxin. Mussels eat this plankton and build up a poison level that can be dangerous to humans. This plankton also produces the phenomenon of phosphorescence in the sea. When the water began to glow, the Indians knew to stop eating mussels and when it returned to normal they ate them again.

This phenomenon is very rare on the Atlantic Coast because the waters are much colder. If it ever occurs the seas turn reddish. That may have been what frightened the Indians before the white man came, and kept them from eating mussels and other seafood. The Indians, however, did favor fresh water mussels. Today these mussels are pond raised not for food but for the inside of their shell, which produce mother of pearl for buttons.

The French claim to have started mussel farming in 1235, although the Romans established mussel beds years before along the coast of Italy. It was an Irishman, Patrick Walton, who started modern mussel farming in France as a result of a series of mistakes. He had become unpopular with the police in Ireland and was forced to leave in a hurry. Walton set sail in a boat too small for crossing the seas and became shipwrecked on the coast of France. In order to feed himself he tried trapping birds by driving stakes into the water at the edge of the beach and stretching nets between them.

While this experiment failed he noticed that mussels had attached themselves to the stakes and he began to harvest and sell them. Walton is also credited with inventing a flat-bottomed boat used to harvest mussels in their shallow-water habitat.

The story may or may not be true, but the stakes, called *bouchots*, are still in use in France as is the flat-bottom boat. Today the most prized and expensive mussels in France are *moules de bouchots*, named after the stakes. They are smaller, tenderer, and tastier.

France today has more than 600 miles of bouchots along its Atlantic coast, producing about 45,000 tons of mussels annually. The rest of their mussels come mainly from Spain.

Mussels are bivalve mollusks, and only certain species of sea mussels are edible. The most common is the blue mussel which occurs in Europe and eastern north America as far south as North Carolina. It has also been introduced on the Pacific Coast. The blue mussel has a smooth dark blue shell, which is covered by a black epidermis. These mussels are usually pear shaped and vary from two to five inches in length. The blue mussel is tangy, almost smoky in flavor.

There are two widely used methods of growing mussels — by suspension between the surface and the sea bottom, and on the sea bottom. In some coastal areas of France, Spain and along the coast of Maine and Washington state mussels are grown on ropes suspended from rafts or wooden frames built over the water. Although this method is more labor intensive, it yields mussels free of grit and pearls. The *bouchot* method invented by Walton is still used in much of Europe.

A light wine sauce and fresh spinach compliment the mussels in the Warm Mussel Salad. It may be served as a first course for dinner or as a salad for lunch. For an enjoyable mussel feast, try the famous Moules Marinière. In Belgium some heavy cream is frequently added at the end of cooking, just before serving.

Warm Mussel Salad

3 tablespoons butter
4 tablespoons minced shallots
3 cups dry white wine
2 1/2 pounds mussels, well scrubbed
1 small carrot, minced
1/2 cup heavy cream
Shredded spinach leaves
Butter lettuce leaves

Melt the butter in a saucepan over medium-low heat. Add 2 tablespoons of the shallots. Sauté for 5 minutes. Add the wine and the mussels. Cover and cook over medium-high heat until mussels open, about 3 to 4 minutes. Remove from heat and remove the mussels from the pan with a slotted spoon. When cool, shell the mussels and set them aside.

Strain the cooking liquid through a fine sieve into a frying pan. Add the carrot and the remaining 2 tablespoons of shallots. Cook over medium-high heat until reduced by half, approximately 15 minutes. Add the cream and simmer until thickened, about another 15 minutes. Five minutes before serving, add the mussels and simmer to warm them.

Place a bed of shredded spinach in each of 6 butter lettuce cups. Spoon mussels and sauce equally onto each. Serve at once. Serves 6

Moules Marinière

4 dozen mussels, well scrubbed
4 cups white wine
2 shallots, chopped fine
6 large basil leaves, julienned
3 parsley sprigs
1 tablespoon lemon juice
1/4 teaspoon salt
1/4 teaspoon black pepper
4 tablespoons butter
1/4 cup heavy cream
4 teaspoons minced parsley

Place the mussels in a large saucepan with all of the ingredients except the butter, cream, and minced parsley. Bring to a boil, then cover and simmer until the mussels open, about 4 to 5 minutes. Remove the mussels with a slotted spoon, discarding any that have not opened. Add butter to the liquid, increase the heat, and reduce the liquid by half.

Arrange the mussels in their open shells in warm bowls or soup plates. When the liquid is reduced pass it through a fine sieve into a smaller pan. Then add cream and warm again over low heat. Pour some liquid over each portion of mussels and sprinkle with 1 teaspoon of parsley. Serves 4.

Oysters

Prized on the Half Shell

In prehistoric times there was a great barrier reef surrounding Europe and was the habitat of an abundance of oysters. It lay off the coasts of Europe starting near Denmark, going south along the Mediterranean's north coast, under the Italian "boot," to Greece. Today only five meager islands remain of this reef and few oyster beds remain.

The ancient Greeks were eating wild oysters and made a meager attempt to cultivate them when they noticed that oysters had attached themselves to broken pottery that had fallen into the sea. The Greeks threw more pottery into the sea to encourage the growth of the oyster beds.

The serious cultivation of oysters began more than two thousand years ago when Romans collected the bivalves at Brindisi, located on the Italian "boot" near the mouth of the Adriatic Sea, and transplanted them further north. The Japanese are often credited with pioneering oyster culture, but their records only date the first attempt as recent as 1620.

The Romans had such a passion for oysters that they imported them from all over the Mediterranean and European coasts. They were shipped in special amphorae containing sea water. In the second century they began packing oysters in ice. The Romans ate oysters not as food but to encourage the stomach to make room for further eating. It was not unusual for wealthy Romans to eat one hundred dozen oysters a week.

After the decline of the Roman Empire the interest in oysters subsided. The barbarians who ended Rome's glory were not frightened of the Roman legions but were afraid that oysters were poisonous.

The French were the first to consume oysters during the Renaissance. King Henry IV often worked up an appetite for dinner by swallowing three hundred oysters. Louis XIV ate them by the dozens. His oysters came from his own private park.

European settlers in America were delighted when they found an abundance of oysters along the eastern shores. Oysters became the rage. By the mid-1800s express wagons carrying barrels of oysters packed in damp straw and ice made regular runs from the Chesapeake Bay to the large cities along the Eastern seaboard. They also traversed the mountains, changing horses at regular intervals. These express shipments of oysters permitted Abraham Lincoln in Springfield, Illinois to give oyster parties for his constituents. Oyster parties became the favorite way of entertaining. In the South they were held outdoors at tables covered in newspaper for easy clean-up.

By the end of the nineteenth century the United States found itself in the same situation as Europe. We were running out of oysters. Today all of our oyster production, including the Chesapeake Bay, is less than one-tenth the harvest of a hundred years ago. Farm raised oysters has become the only answer.

The oyster lives best in brackish water because in saltier waters it is subject to predators, such as starfish, and disease. Growth, however, is rather slow in brackish waters. Thus the oyster farmer plants his seed stock in low saline areas and then transfers the oysters to saltier waters. The average life span of an oyster is three years, although some survive for ten to twelve years. In northern waters where the growing season is shorter, the technique of "off-bottom" oyster culture is to suspend the bivalves on nylon strings which are attached to racks.

Natural oyster beds are found in varying depths and temperatures of the sea. They grow in the Caribbean, off the coast of Florida, in the Chesapeake Bay, off the coast of New England, and the Pacific Northwest. In Europe they are found in the Mediterranean Sea as well as the Atlantic Ocean.

The proximity to freshwater determines the flavor of the oyster. It is a vegetarian and its main food source is a minute one-celled plant known as diatom. In feeding, an oyster pumps and filters as much as twenty-five gallons of water every twenty-four hours. The diatoms provide flavor and color to the oyster. In France, oysters from the Seudre River estuary ingest large quantities of a type of diatom that tinges the meat green. The excellent flavor of these oysters brings the highest price in Paris.

Although all oysters are edible during their spawning season, the months without an "r" in them, the production of glycogen (an animal starch) is excessive. This gives the meat a milky appearance and a flat taste. Northern oysters are at their best in the fall and winter months, while Gulf and Caribbean bivalves are firm and ripe from December onward.

Only ten species of oysters are marketed throughout the world. In the United States the most common is the Blue Point. The Indian River Oyster is found off the coast of Florida. The tiny Olympia oyster of the Pacific Northwest, which is two inches in length is considered a real delicacy.

Oysters are marketed fresh in the shell, or as shucked meats iced in containers. They are also sold as frozen shucked meats, smoked and then canned in edible oil, and in the form of soup, stew, or bisque, either frozen or canned.

Although oysters on the half shell is the preferred method of eating them, Oysters Rockefeller has long been a traditional way of preparing them.

Oysters Rockefeller

36 large oysters, shucked
Rock salt
1 1/2 cups lightly packed fresh spinach
3/4 cup lightly packed parsley leaves
3/4 cup chopped scallions, including
* green tops*
6 shallots, chopped
3 tablespoons chopped fresh fennel leaves
8 tablespoons (1 stick) butter
2 tablespoons anchovy paste
Tabasco sauce
1 cup fresh bread crumbs
1/2 cup Pernod or Absinthe
Salt and black pepper

Drain the oysters. Strain and save the liquor. Scrub and dry half of the shells and arrange them in 6 pans filled with rock salt. Place an oyster in each shell. Puree vegetables in a food processor. Melt the butter in a large skillet over low heat, add vegetables and cook for 5 minutes. Stir in the anchovy paste, several dashes of Tabasco sauce, and bread crumbs. Cook, stirring, until well mixed and thick. Add oyster liquor or more crumbs to adjust thickness. Add Pernod, season to taste, and add more Tabasco sauce, if desired.

Spread sauce over the oysters. Bake in a preheated 450° F. oven for about 5 minutes and serve at once. Makes 6 servings.

Scallops

Patron Saint

In Greek mythology when Aphrodite rose from the sea she skimmed over the Aegean waves on a scallop shell. This traveling goddess had a team of six seahorses to take her to the island of Cythera, arriving in a scallop carriage. The graceful form of these shells have clearly been reflected in art and architecture since early times.

The scallop is the only bivalve to have a patron saint. The name coquille Saint-Jacque, or St. James shell, is not only a term for a variety of creamy scallop dishes, but it is also the name used for this mollusk in France. The apostle St. James wore the shell as his personal emblem and after being put to death by sword at the order of Herod I in 44 A.D., it became a badge for the pilgrims who visited his shrine in Santiago de Compostela, Spain, during the Middle Ages. Annual pilgrimages are still made.

Beauty is not just shell deep in the case of the scallop as the meat is sweet and nutlike with the fragrance of a refreshing sea breeze. The orange-colored coral is a delicacy in itself. Scallops should be eaten fresh from the water.

There are more than four hundred species of scallops found throughout the world but only a dozen are found in the commercial markets — mainly in Europe, North America, Japan, and Australia.

Some scallops have smooth shells, but most have radiating ribs. The shells may be orange, red, yellow, black, or even white in deep water. Nearly all scallops move freely in the water. Only one species attaches itself to rocks. Scallops leap in zigzag flights by forcefully opening their valve and expelling a jet of water which drives the mollusk in yard-long hops to avoid capture. This movement of the shell is achieved by the large muscle, called an adductor muscle.

Scallops like to live in eel grass. Those that live under the heavy pressure of deep water have heavier shells without fluting. The Canadian Digby scallop, which is found off the coast of Newfoundland, lives six fathoms down in the Bay of Fundy. Scallops develop their best flavor in the coldest waters.

The entire content of a scallop is edible, but only the tender adductor muscle is consumed in North America. Unlike other bivalves, a scallop cannot hold its shell firmly closed. Thus it quickly loses body moisture when removed from water and dies. Only the muscle is taken by the fisherman, iced, and quickly shipped to its destination.

Some commercial distributors put scallops in water for several hours to increase their bulk. This may improve the appearance of the scallop, but depletes some of its flavor. Another trick used by unscrupulous fishmongers is to buy a slab of inexpensive shark meat, and with the appropriate cookie cutter produce scallops of similar size and shape.

The commercial market for scallops today depends on the sea scallop, which is not only large, growing to five inches across the shell, but is the most abundant. It is concentrated off the coast of Maine, but can be found from Labrador to New Jersey.

The bay scallop, the tastiest of all scallops, occurs from North Carolina to around Florida and into the northern Gulf of Mexico. It is two to three inches across the shell, which has mottlings of brown, red and yellow on a white background. It is also found on the Pacific Coast. The calico scallop lives in deep water off the east coast of Florida. It is growing in popularity. Rock scallops which are four to six inches in diameter, are prevalent from Alaska to southern California.

This recipe for the famous Coquille

Saint-Jacque is prepared in the microwave oven. Scallops in Wine Sauce combines sea scallops with vegetables in a creamy wine sauce garnished with puff pastry and baked.

Coquilles St. Jacques

3 tablespoons butter
1 cup sliced mushrooms
2 green onions, sliced
1/4 cup chopped celery
2 tablespoons chopped red pepper
2 tablespoons all-purpose flour
1/4 teaspoon salt
1/4 teaspoon dried thyme leaves
1/3 cup white wine
1 pound scallops, cut in quarters, if large
1/4 cup half-and-half
1 egg yolk, beaten
2 tablespoons melted butter
1/4 cup fine dry bread crumbs
2 tablespoons Parmesan cheese

In a 2-quart microwavable casserole, place the butter, mushrooms, onion, celery, and red pepper. Microwave at high for 3 to 4 minutes. Then stir in the flour, salt, and thyme, mixing well. Add the wine and scallops and stir again. Microwave at high for 5 to 6 minutes, stirring after 3 minutes. Stir in the half-and-half and egg yolk. Microwave at low for 3 to 4 minutes, stirring after 2 minutes.

Divide mixture among 4 scallop shells or small dishes. Combine melted butter, bread crumbs, and Parmesan cheese until crumbs form. Top scallop shells with crumbs. Cover with wax paper. Microwave at medium for 5 to 7 minutes, until hot. Serves 4.

Scallops in Wine Sauce

1 sheet puff pastry from package frozen puff pastry sheets
2 tablespoons butter or margarine
2 medium zucchini, thinly sliced
1 carrot, cut into 1-inch julienne strips
5 large mushrooms, sliced
1/4 cup chopped red pepper
2 tablespoons all-purpose flour
1/2 cup whipping cream
1/4 cup milk
2 tablespoons freshly grated Parmesan cheese
1/4 teaspoon dried thyme
3 tablespoons dry white wine
1 egg white, beaten
Freshly grated Parmesan cheese, for garnish

Thaw the sheet of puff pastry and, with a glass or cookie cutter, cut it into 2-inch rounds. Refrigerate while preparing the scallops.

Melt the butter in a large skillet over medium heat. Add the zucchini, carrots, mushrooms, and red pepper and sauté for 3 to 4 minutes, until the vegetables are crisp-tender. Sprinkle the flour over the vegetables and stir gently to combine. Add the cream and milk and cook for 1 minute, stirring constantly. The mixture will be very thick. Add the scallops, Parmesan cheese, and thyme and cook over medium heat until the mixture comes to a boil. Remove from heat and stir in the wine.

Spoon the scallop mixture into an ungreased, 9-inch quiche pan. Stand circles of puff pastry around the edges of the dish. Lightly brush each pastry circle with beaten egg white and sprinkle with some Parmesan cheese. Bake in a preheated 375° F. oven for 25 to 30 minutes, until the pastry is golden brown and the scallop mixture is bubbling. Serves 4.

Shrimp

Americans Love Shrimp

Shrimp are our most valuable seafood. There are more than 500 million pounds caught by domestic commercial fishermen annually and we import an additional 250 to 300 million pounds. Shrimps are popular all over the world from the sweltering markets of West Africa to the finest hotels in Europe. Americans, however, are the largest consumers of shrimp.

The interchange of the names "shrimp" and "prawn" has no universal recognition. In India, which is the world's largest shrimp farming nation, all shrimp-like animals are called prawns. We should probably designate all fresh water species as prawns and all ocean species as shrimp. However, in the United States and the United Kingdom, prawn is used as a name for large shrimps. On the West Coast the tiny small bay crustaceans are called shrimp and all others are prawns.

People living close to the water have always enjoyed shrimp. In the ancient Mediterranean world, the Greeks preferred the larger shrimp to lobster, cooking them wrapped in fig leaves. The Romans made an exotic sauce from shrimp. As the European world expanded and people lived long distances from the sea, shrimps lost favor.

Nobody tried to preserve shrimp for those living inland except the Chinese. Their know-how came to the United States with Lee Yuen who settled in Louisiana. He was amazed by the abundance of shrimp on the coast and went into the shrimp-drying business. He built platforms on piles to dry the shrimp in the sun.

Lee Yuen's venture was so profitable that he was joined by more of his countrymen, who built similar shrimp-drying structures. The area became known as Chinamen's Platform.

Its products were sold all over the world until refrigeration surpassed drying.

In this country shrimp, both large and small, are commercially fished from the Pacific, Atlantic, and Gulf coasts. However, most of our shrimp comes from the Gulf of Mexico. In the Gulf, shrimp spawn in deep water and the young come inshore to live in creeks, canals, and bays until half grown.

By day the Gulf shrimp bury themselves in sand or mud, covering themselves completely by sweeping up sand with their antennae. After dark the shrimp climb out, walking on two pairs of their hind legs, and feeling their way with the front two pairs. They swim along the bottom using their tails as paddles and they can dart backward by suddenly bending their tails forward. When shrimp leave the coast on their migration to deep water, the males are the first to leave. The females then follow to the breeding grounds.

It was not until the early 1900s that shrimp began to appear commercially. Shrimp are very perishable and they die and decay quickly after being taken from the water. Consequently there was no commercial shrimp fishing until refrigeration and fast transportation became available. People living near the coast, however, could purchase shrimp from the boats of local fishermen on the docks.

The first step in mechanizing the shrimp industry was the development of large dragnets. These were pulled by horses along the shore in shallow water. Refrigeration, followed by deep freezing, made it possible to use large trawlers for shrimp fishing. Now the large nets stay in the water from 45 minutes to two hours, and bring up several hundred pounds of shrimp.

Like other seafood, the shrimp population is being depleted. They are now being farm-raised by two methods. One is to allow young shrimp to be carried by the tides into coastal ponds where they grow to market size. The other method, first used in India and now successfully duplicated in Texas and Louisiana, is to catch females at sea and allow them to spawn in ponds.

There are a number of species of shrimp that have commercial importance in our Atlantic and Gulf of Mexico waters — brown, pink, white, red, and tiger. Sometimes it takes an expert to distinguish one from the other. Brown and pink shrimp are similar despite their names. The brown shrimp has tinges of blue or purple on the tail and on some of the legs. Depending on their location, usually the Gulf of Mexico, pink shrimp can be light pinkish-brown.

White shrimp found in the Gulf of Mexico, Texas, and North Carolina are grayish-white with tail and legs tinged with pale green, red, or blue. Royal red shrimp, which are a pinkish-gray, are found only in deep water. Tiger shrimp, originally from the Indo-Pacific region and South America, are now being farm raised in the United States. They are gray and black striped.

Shrimp are sold according to how many constitute a pound. They range from very large shrimp at 10 to 15 to a pound to 31 to 40 to a pound, which are called medium.

Fresh shrimp are firm and smell fresh. A stale shrimp has an offensive ammonia odor. If there is one bad shrimp in a box you can assume that they are all bad. Sometimes shrimp may have an "iodine" taste because they were caught in brackish waters where their food is low in salt. They are not spoiled.

Pasta with Shrimp and Tomato is prepared with fresh tomatoes, mushrooms, and shrimps seasoned with Italian spices in a cream sauce.

Pasta with Shrimp and Tomato

5 tablespoons olive oil
1 cup sliced crimini (brown) mushrooms
3/4 cup julienned shiitake mushrooms
1/2 cup chopped red pepper
3/4 cup chopped celery
1 large ripe tomato, peeled and diced
3/4 cup dry white wine
1 cup whipping cream
2 tablespoons slivered fresh basil
10 ounces spaghettini
Salt and pepper, to taste
1 1/2 pounds (24 shrimp) large shrimp, peeled and deveined
1/2 teaspoon of dry Italian seasoning

Heat 3 tablespoons of the olive oil in a large skillet over medium heat and add the mushrooms, red pepper, and celery. Sauté for about 5 minutes or until the mushrooms begin to get limp. Add the tomato and continue sautéing for a few minutes. Add the wine and cook until some of the wine starts to evaporate. Then add the cream and continue cooking on low heat until the sauce starts to thicken. Add the basil and keep warm on low heat.

In the meantime, boil the spaghettini in salted water until al dente. Just before the pasta is done, heat the remaining 2 tablespoons of olive oil in another skillet over medium heat and add the shrimp. Sprinkle with the dry Italian seasoning and sauté for about 2 minutes on each side or until the shrimp are just done.

Drain the pasta and place into a warm bowl. Add the sauce and toss to combine. Divide the pasta among four warm plates. Top each serving with 6 shrimp. Serves 4.

Spices and Herbs

Spice Trade

Herbs

Spices

Spice of Life

Today we need only to go to our local supermarket to buy a vast array of spices that four hundred years ago cost a king's ransom and the loss of many lives.

Once valued as highly as gold, spices have changed the course of history. Countries vied to win control over their sources. Navigators attempted to discover new sea routes to the Far East. If it had not been the quest for spices, Columbus would not have discovered America.

The early civilizations around the Mediterranean got spices from India and other lands to the east, as well as Africa. Records exist of Egyptian spice expeditions to the east coast of Africa three and four thousand years ago. Particularly treasured were two aromatic barks, cinnamon and cassia. The Egyptians used them not only to flavor foods but in cosmetics, ceremonial functions, and burial rites.

Spices are mentioned in the Bible. One of the most well-known references to spices are the instructions to Moses in the book of Exodus telling him to take myrrh, sweet cinnamon, sweet calamus, and cassia with him on the journey out of Egypt. Myrrh was brought to Jesus by the wise men.

Geoffrey Chaucer, author of the Canterbury Tales, wrote "ginger green and liquorice pale, and cloves their sweetness offer, with nutmegs too, to put in ale, no matter whether fresh or stale." In Chaucer's time (1340 - 1400), all the cloves in the world came from a tiny group of islands on the equator called the Moluccas, or Spice Islands. All the world's nutmegs grew on an even smaller set of nearby islands known as Banda.

In the early 1400s the magnificent and powerful city-state of Venice ruled the Mediterranean spice trade, along with the Arab traders. All of the fabulous spices of the Orient flowing into Europe passed through Venice, as did the vast sums of gold and silver to pay for the spices. The Venetians grew rich, but the rest of Europe began to suffer balance of payment difficulties.

Far to the west, in Portugal, one man decided to challenge the supremacy of Venice. Ultimately, his decision changed the whole course of human events.

Prince Henry of Portugal's plan was a simple one: to find the end of Africa, sail around it to India, and buy the spices directly from the producers, cutting out the Venetians and the Arabs. Prince Henry was driven not only by his desire for spices, but his hatred of the Moslem Arabs and the hope of finding a fabled Christian empire in the East.

By the 1480s the Portuguese had rounded Africa and were ready to push on to India, which they reached in 1497. Their leader, Vasco de Gama, announced to the local population "I have come for Christians and spices."

This so worried Portugal's neighbor and rival, Spain, that the Spanish decided to finance an Italian navigator, Christopher Columbus, who claimed that he could reach India ahead of the Portuguese by sailing westward into the Atlantic.

While Columbus never did find India, he did find North America, which his fellow Europeans were quick to claim as their own. All in search of spices!

Columbus' discovery of the New World changed the eating habits of the old world, particularly Europe. This great navigator, however, caused everlasting confusion by calling all the peoples he encountered in the New World "Indians." Similarly, Columbus continued to muddy the linguistic waters by bestowing upon two different plants, allspice and chili, the name of yet a third — pepper.

Until chili peppers were introduced to Europe at the beginning of the sixteenth century, the spices used for pungency were pepper, mustard, horseradish, and ginger.

As chilies are easily cultivated, the little yellow, red, and green hot fruits flourished wherever the Spanish and later Portuguese sailors took them and planted them. It was a red-letter culinary day when chilies arrived in India. Today India is the largest grower of chilies and it is inconceivable to enjoy Indian foods without the heat of the chili.

The two "Christian" nations, Spain and Portugal, started to interfere with each other's conquests and search for spices to such an extent that the Pope was forced to draw an imaginary line down the center of the Atlantic ocean to separate their spheres of interest. Portugal was given all of the heathen lands east of the line while Spain was given those to the west.

The Spanish felt that their claim on the Spice Islands would be strengthened if they could be reached by sailing west, following Columbus' original plan. Thus an expedition of five ships and two hundred and thirty men set sail, led ironically, by a Portuguese, Ferdinand Magellan. Three years after it set out, only one ship with eighteen emaciated sailors returned to Spain. These were the first to sail around the world — all for cloves and nutmegs !

In the seventeenth century Spain and Portugal's influence over the spice trade declined and gave way to the more ruthless European empires — England, Holland, and France. Large companies were formed to procure the necessary capital to mount great expeditions. The Dutch, in particular, attempted to corner the world market in various spices by destroying all the clove and nutmeg trees, except for those they controlled. Ultimately clove and nutmeg trees were smuggled out and planted elsewhere, breaking the Dutch stronghold.

By the middle of the eighteenth century the desperate desire for spices slowed down. The choice of spices was changing. In the early years, cinnamon and cloves were most valued because the primary method of cooking in Europe was a single pot on the hearth in which various foods were cooked together.

There was no distinction between sweet, sour, and savory flavors. Both cinnamon and cloves are binding spices, bringing together the opposite flavors of sweet and sour. For example, apple strudel with sour apples and sweet sugar would be unthinkable without them.

The introduction of the cooking stove meant that everything no longer had to be cooked together. A new type of main dish arose, savory, and with it a different spice took prominence — pepper.

As spices became more readily available in Europe during the eighteenth century, it became fashionable to be spice-conscious. People carried their own nutmeg with little grinders in silver cases which they used when dining out. Pepper corn grinders were also used.

Today the United States is the world's largest importer of spices while Singapore is the largest exporter. India is still the leading producer of spices, followed by Indonesia, Brazil, and Malaysia.

Spices are just one of thousands of items of international commerce. However, for centuries the search for spices controlled the destiny of nations. In its time spices influenced the world every bit as much as communications, computers, and the internet do today.

Capers

The Little Green Bud

I had not used capers very much in my cooking nor, frankly, had I thought much about them until I visited Sicily. Capers grow wild on a vine-like bush in Sicily and other Mediterranean countries. Many of the stones of the Greek and Roman ruins on Sicily are interspersed with wild caper bushes.

The piquant, tasty little green beads known as capers are the pickled unopened flower buds of the caper shrub. The bush probably originated in the Middle East, although some food historians place its origin as Asia Minor. Many believe that the Sahara Desert was the first home of the bush known as "capparis spinosa," because it thrives in arid climates.

The caper bush remains green, its stems and small 2-inch, dark green leaves are juicy with sap, even when the soil around its roots is completely dry. I saw it growing on the hillsides in Sicily where there was very little other vegetation and no iirrigation. It thrives in full sunlight. Botanists believe that the caper bush absorbs moisture from the humidity of the night air, enough for its daily needs.

The ancient Greeks were the first to use capers. They flavored olive oil with them as early as the thirteenth century B.C. Later the Greeks and Romans ate capers with bread, and used them as seasonings for fish and meat.

The first reported attempts to cultivate the caper plant took place in the sixteenth century when poor peasants raised the caper bush in order to sell the much-prized buds to the households of the nobility. By that time capers had become a popular ingredient in Mediterranean cuisine. I found that in southern Italian cooking they are used in such dishes as caponata (a type of eggplant and tomato rel-

ish), vitello tonnato (cold roasted veal with a tuna-caper sauce), and various pasta dishes.

Although the wild caper bushes are still harvested in many regions of the Mediterranean, they are also cultivated. Some of the best capers come from southern France where the plants are grown on terraced land and are fully exposed to the sun. The buds are picked every two days in order to catch them at their prime edible stage.

The island of Pantelleria, off the southwestern coast of Sicily, also produces some of the world's finest capers on hillside terraces. The caper buds range in size from a quarter of an inch to about an half-inch. The volcanic soil of the island and the humidity from the sea are contributing factors to their big size.

The largest producer of capers in the world is Spain, with an annual production of about 1,700 tons. Most of the production is exported to Europe.

Caper buds vary in size, depending on when they are harvested. The early-picked ones are tight in texture and measure about a quarter of an inch in diameter. The larger ones, which are harvested just before they bloom, are about a half an inch in diameter and have a more leafy flavor. There are six recognized commercial sizes of capers between the smallest and the largest ones.

Capers cannot be used until they have been preserved because raw capers, like olives, have a very bitter flavor. After the capers are picked they are usually fermented in brine (salt water solution) for about two months. They are then rinsed, sized, and packed in jars with vinegar.

The Italians have a different method of curing capers which they claim brings out the more subtle flavors of the buds. They place the capers in large vats with dry sea salt for ten days. The salt extracts the moisture from the buds, creating a pickling brine.

If the caper bud is left on the bush it will eventually become a fragrant white flower, three-to-four inches in diameter, which grows on a long stem. When the flowers wither and fall off an inch-long fruit grows on the stem. Spanish caper producers are pickling these olive-like fruits for use in salads and as an accompaniment to pates and cold meats. They have also become a tapas item and a trendy addition to a martini, replacing the traditional olive.

The veal with caper sauce is a traditional Southern European dish. The eggplant recipe is a variation of the well-known caponata, however, this dish is served warm as a meat accompaniment.

Veal with Caper-Mustard Sauce

5 ounces bow-tie noodles
2 tablespoons oil
1 tablespoon butter or margarine
8 ounces veal fillet, cut into ribbon strips
1 medium onion, chopped
3 ounces cremini mushrooms, sliced
2 ounces shiitake mushrooms, sliced
4 cornichons, cut in ribbon-like strips
2/3 cup chicken broth
3/4 cup whipping cream
2 tablespoons capers, drained, reserve liquid
1 tablespoon Dijon mustard
Salt and cayenne pepper, to taste

Cook the noodles according to package directions. Drain them and mix them with 1 tablespoon of the oil.

While the noodles are cooking prepare the sauce. Melt the butter and remaining oil in a large skillet over medium-high heat. Add the veal strips and brown them quickly. Remove the veal; add the onions and mushrooms and sauté until all of the juice has evaporated. Then add the cornichons along with the chicken broth. Continue cooking until slightly reduced. Add the whipping cream, 1 tablespoon of the caper liquid, and the mustard and mix well. Season with salt and cayenne pepper, to taste. Reduce the liquid until the sauce is creamy, stirring occasionally. Then add the capers, and veal strips. Heat through and serve over the bow-tie noodles. Serves 2.

Eggplant with Tomatoes, Capers, and Olives

1 pound small eggplants
1 teaspoon salt
4 large plum tomatoes, skinned and
*   coarsely chopped*
Olive oil for frying
1 tablespoon tiny capers
8 large black olives
1 garlic clove

Peel the eggplants, removing all green pith. Cut them into 1/2-inch slices. Toss slices with the salt in a colander and let drain in the sink for 1 hour. Rinse eggplant, dry each piece with a paper towel, pressing to get out moisture.

Pour some olive oil into a heavy skillet over medium-high heat. Add the eggplant slices and fry them until golden brown on both sides. This may have to be done in several batches. Drain all oil except 1 tablespoon. Add the garlic and tomatoes and cook over medium-low heat for about 10 minutes until the tomatoes are softened. Then add the eggplant slices, capers and olives. Mix gently and cook for 5 minutes. Serve hot or warm. Serves 4.

Chili Peppers

From Hot to Sweet

Many of use think of chilies as the contributing factor to hot spicy food and shun away from them. However, the use of chilies in moderation can be a very pleasant addition to an often otherwise dull dish. Besides all chilies are not hot. They belong to the pepper family which includes many sweet varieties, such as the red pepper used to make paprika.

The world of chilies is a fascinating and sometimes confusing one. There are more than two hundred varieties of chilies, which grow primarily in Mexico, South America, and the Southwest. About twenty-five of these varieties are in common use. Even the spelling of the word chili is confusing, as it often appears as chile or chilli. Mr. Webster prefers the chili spelling, which agrees with that found in fifteenth century Mexican Indian records. The other two spellings designate the traditional dish with meat and beans or the commercial spice powder that contains ground chilies.

Another confusion concerning chilies dates back to when Columbus discovered the chili plant. Since it was a hot spice, he thought he had found the source of pepper. He christened the plant "pepper" and that misnomer has persisted ever since, particularly in Europe.

The first chilies were tiny wild berries that grew on vines beneath the forest canopy of the Amazon jungle in South America thousands of years ago. Chilies were one of the first plants to be cultivated and domesticated in the New World. (Beans, corn, and squash were other early crops.) There is archaeological evidence that chilies were used as a cooking ingredient at least 8000 years ago — around 6200 B.C. Traces of chilies have been found in burial sites in Peru dating from that time.

The plants proliferated and gradually spread northwards to Central America, the Caribbean, and eventually the Southwest. The seeds of the chili plants were spread by birds and also by trade between the peoples of South and Central America.

Chilies were common in the diet of the Incas, Toltecs, Mayans, and Aztecs. They were used to impart flavor and spiciness to the otherwise bland food of these Indians. The Mayans cultivated more than thirty varieties of chilies. The Aztecs, as well as the Incas, used them in almost every dish. Food research has shown that the Aztecs used chilies for their mole sauces and tamales — both derived from other pre-Columbian civilizations and which became part of modern Mexican cuisine.

From Mexico the chili pushed north to what is now the southwestern United States, where it was enthusiastically adopted by the Pueblo Indians. They used it in a green chili stew which was eaten with adobe bread (similar to a soft tortilla). Inter-tribal trade also brought various types of chilies to the region.

The Spanish colonization of the Southwest and the founding of the Missions, which encouraged the development of agriculture, particularly in what is now New Mexico, contributed to the rapid spread of chilies in that region. Today they are the major crop of the local Indian-Spanish farmers.

The Spanish and Portuguese explorers took chilies from the New World with them on their travels and the plant rapidly spread along the maritime trade routes to North Africa, West Africa, and India. The native populations incorporated chilies in their cooking and by 1550 chilies had reached western China, Southeast Asia, and the East Indies. Within a hundred years chilies had spread around the world. The Ottoman Turks brought them to such landlocked countries as Hungary and Tibet.

Today chilies are grown throughout the world. In this country they are cultivated in New Mexico, California, Texas, Arizona, and Louisiana, where they are an integral part of Cajun and Creole cuisine.

Chilies are best known for their heat. The fiery sensation is caused by capsaicin, a potent chemical that survives both cooking and freezing. Some chilies have a high "fire" content while others, such as the green, red, yellow, and violet bell peppers, have none. Also the thick-fleshed Hungarian chili as well as the heart-shaped pimento chili contain no hotness.

One of the chilies prevalent in our supermarkets is the Anaheim chili, which is an elongated medium green chili of mild hotness. It is most frequently used as a stuffed relleno. The two-to-three inch long green or red Jalapeno chili is quite hot and is used sparingly. The small Serrano chili is the hottest pepper available in the United States. Either the red or green is primarily used in salsas. There is also the Scotch Bonnet. It is a small round yellow chili, which grows in the Caribbean, and is extremely hot. This chili is used in Caribbean curries. In addition to the fresh chilies there are also many varieties that are sold and used only in their dried stage.

Regardless of which of the fresh hot chilies you choose to use, it is wise to start with a little and add more, as desired. When working with fresh hot chilies wear rubber gloves and avoid any contact of your hands with your face and eyes. Always wash any cutting boards and knives that have been used to cut chilies before proceeding with other food preparations.

Use either one or two Jalapeno peppers in the Mexican Chicken, depending on the degree of hotness you like.

Mexican Chicken Casserole

1 can (14 ounces) stewed tomatoes, Mexican style
1/2 teaspoon chili powder
1 teaspoon Mexican seasonings
1/4 teaspoon oregano
2 cups cooked chicken, cut-up
1/2 cup chopped green pepper
1/2 cup chopped red pepper
1 jalapeno pepper, seeded and finely chopped
3 green onions, chopped
1 can (12 ounces) whole kernel corn
1 can (2.2 ounces) sliced black olives
1 1/2 cups milk
2 tablespoons butter or margarine
1/2 cup cornmeal
1 cup grated Cheddar cheese
2 eggs, lightly beaten

Combine the tomatoes, chili powder, Mexican seasonings, and oregano in a saucepan. Bring to a slow boil and simmer for 10 minutes. Combine the chicken, peppers, onion, corn, and olives in a bowl. Add the simmered tomato mixture and pour into a 3-quart casserole dish. (May be prepared ahead to this point and refrigerated. Bring to room temperature before proceeding.)

Heat milk with the butter, then slowly add the cornmeal, stirring constantly to prevent lumps from forming. Cook over medium-low heat until thickened. Remove from heat; stir in the cheese and eggs. Pour over the chicken mixture, spreading it with a spatula to completely cover. Bake in a preheated 375° F. oven for 40 minutes or until the corn bread topping is done. Serves 4.

Cinnamon

The Curled Bark

Why do many manufacturers of breakfast foods use cinnamon as a flavoring in cereals, pop tarts, frozen waffles, and granola bars? Its use in these foods probably stems from ancient times when cinnamon was considered to be a stimulant and a tonic.

A tincture of cinnamon was used to deaden the nerve in a toothache. The spice has also been associated with sensuousness, warmth, and love. It could be that a touch of cinnamon gives extra pep to start the day.

Cinnamon has been used continually since ancient times, and was one of the oldest and most valuable items in the spice trade. The first known reference to cinnamon is in a treaty written by the Chinese Emperor Shen Nung in 2700 B.C. He was also the first to document the medicinal properties of plants.

Emperor Shen Nung called cinnamon "kwei." a variation of the Indian name for this spice, although it was not grown in India, but in Ceylon (Sri Lanka), at that time.

Early spice traders soon discovered that there are two types of cinnamon — one from Ceylon (cinnamomum zeylanicum) and the other (*C. cassia*) from China and other southeast Asian islands. The cinnamon from Ceylon is buff colored and quite mild. The cassia variety from China and Indonesia is reddish brown with an aromatic odor and a pungently sweet taste. It is the primary variety used today.

The ancient people of the Mediterranean area knew both kinds of cinnamon, but did not know where they originated. It assumed that they were grown in Arabia or Ethiopia, as the cassia leaves came from there. These leaves were used to sweeten the breath.

There were many myths about the origin of this spice merchandised in small sticks resembling a wood quill. One of the most famous myths by the Greek historian Herodotus (420 B. C.) is as follows:

"Cinnamon grows in high inaccessible mountains where certain large birds transport the twigs to more attainable regions to make nests. To entice the birds out of these nests the natives place large quantities of meat under the nests. As the birds are very fond of meat, they carry the meat back to their nests. The nests break under the weight of the meat and fall to the ground. Thus the natives only have to pick up the cinnamon."

Cinnamon was very rare in ancient Greece and what little arrived was used to flavor wine. The same was true in Rome. It was not used in cooking because it cost too much. in Roman times cinnamon was worth more than its weight in gold.

Only emperors could afford to keep a supply of cinnamon on hand for their own use. When the Empress Poppea died because Nero had kicked her in the stomach, he made amends by burning her body with more cinnamon than the spice merchants of Arabia could furnish in a whole year — possibly the most expensive funeral pyre in history.

Most of the spices the Romans received from the East disappeared from Europe when the Roman empire collapsed. They began to return in the ninth and tenth centuries when the Arabs moved to Sicily and to southern Europe, bringing their spices with them.

In the eleventh century when the Normans took over Sicily, they began using cinnamon, expensive though it was, to disguise the taste of tainted meat. Over the next hundred years the Crusaders returning from the East brought spices to Europe. Marco Polo came back from China at the end of the thirteenth century with spices from China, including cinnamon.

Cinnamon was used in sauces in the households of the nobility in the fourteenth and fifteenth centuries. In France it was used because of its pungent flavor in black sauces when pepper was not available. Cinnamon was still very rare and European white female slaves were often traded to the Arabs for it.

Cinnamon did not become widely used in Europe until the discovery of the Spice Islands (Indonesia) by Magellan. By the early 1500s, cinnamon was used in almost every dish in Italy. It also became one of the most important seasonings in English cooking.

Despite strong Portuguese competition, the Dutch were masters of the cinnamon trade, not only in Indonesia but also in Ceylon. The Dutch East India Company grew rich on spices and its most profitable one was cinnamon.

The Dutch were the first to cultivate the cinnamon tree. In the late 1500s a Frenchman, Pierre Poivre, smuggled some slips of the cinnamon tree out of Dutch-controlled territory and planted them in French tropical colonies. Thus Holland's monopoly was broken. Soon thereafter cinnamon was grown on British tropical islands.

The cinnamon tree, a member of the laurel family, grows to a height of about thirty feet and has willow-like branches with oblong leaves. Cinnamon is one of the few spices not obtained from the seeds, flowers, or fruit of the plant. Rather it is obtained from the inner bark of the young shoots and branches which are cut when they are about one inch thick. The branches are then dried in the sun. After drying the bark is easily peeled, wrapped around a thin rod, and the outer skin then scraped off. What remains are quills of cinnamon which can be used whole or ground into powder.

Cinnamon has remained an important spice in Spanish, Mexican, and English cooking. In Spain and Mexico it is used to flavor chocolate and chocolate deserts. In Mexico it is used in mole sauces. The English and Americans use it in apple pie. Cinnamon has become a part of Indian curries and Chinese five-spice powder. In many African countries cinnamon is used in fiery hot dishes.

Although cinnamon is used to flavor breakfast foods, most of it is utilized in baking and desert dishes. These Zucchini Spice Cookies are flavored with cinnamon, are simple to prepare, and stay moist for several days

Zucchini Spice Cookies

8 tablespoons (1 stick) butter or margarine
3/4 cup sugar
1 egg
2 cups all-purpose flour
1 1/4 teaspoon soda
1 1/4 teaspoon cinnamon
1/2 teaspoon cloves
1/4 teaspoon nutmeg
1 1/3 cups grated zucchini
1 cup chopped walnuts
1 cup raisins

Cream together the butter and sugar in a large bowl. Add the egg and beat well. Combine the flour, soda, cinnamon, cloves, and nutmeg. Gradually stir the flour mixture into the batter. The dough will be very stiff. Slowly add the grated zucchini, incorporating it into the batter, which will become lighter with the moisture of the zucchini. Stir in the nuts and raisins. Drop by heaping teaspoonfuls onto a lightly greased cookie sheet. Bake in a preheated 350° F. oven for 15 minutes. Makes 4 to 5 dozen cookies.

Cloves

The Dried Buds

A clove is the dried, unopened flower bud of the evergreen clove tree — a member of the myrtle family. The name originated from the fact that the flower buds resemble small nails, and clou is nail in French, in Latin, clavus.

The first reported use of cloves was in China. There is no evidence that the Chinese grew clove trees and it is a mystery where they originated. In the second century B.C. etiquette at the court of the emperor demanded that persons having an audience with the emperor should hold a clove in their mouth to perfume their breath. The Chinese also believed that cloves could relieve the pain of a toothache.

Very little is known about the early history of cloves. It was not until 1511 that the habitat of cloves were discovered by Francisco Serrano, serving under Magellan, on a Portuguese voyage. He found the clover evergreen on Ternate, one of the Spice Islands.

The Chinese exported cloves to India — the first reported use outside of China. By the fourth century A.D. cloves were known in the Mediterranean area, having been brought there by Arab traders. With the collapse of the Roman Empire and the trade routes, cloves disappeared from Europe.

The Portuguese tried for many years to keep the source of cloves a secret. They published false maps to confuse others seeking the spice. The Dutch arrived in spite of these obstacles and drove the Portuguese out of the Spice Islands in 1605.

The Dutch destroyed all of the clove trees except on two of the most easily defensible islands. They decreeded death to anyone trying to export cloves or seedlings of the trees.

Toward the end of the eighteenth century a Frenchman, Pierre Poivre (Peter Pepper) managed to get a few clove trees and planted them on Réunion and Mauritius in the Indian Ocean. Louis XV's enemies had the trees destroyed because they did not want France to have this source of riches. One tree, however, escaped the destruction and today all clove trees stem from this one survivor.

Cloves are now cultivated in many tropical areas with Zanzibar and Madagascar leading the world production. Even with increased production, cloves still remain an expensive spice due to extensive hand labor in picking and curing.

Rice with Lentils, a recipe from India, features cloves and some of the typical spices used in that country's cooking.

Lentils and Rice

1/2 cup lentils
4 tablespoons butter
1 medium onion, finely chopped
1/2 teaspoon cumin
1/2 teaspoon ground cinnamon
5 cloves
1/4 teaspoon turmeric
1 cup Basmati rice

Soak the lentils for 30 minutes, then drain.

Heat the butter in a saucepan over medium heat. Add the onions and sauté until lightly browned. Push the onions to one side of the pan and add the lentils and spices. Cook for 5 minutes, stirring constantly.

Add the rice and stir until well coated with the spices. Then add enough hot water to cover the rice mixture by 1 inch. Bring to a boil and simmer until the rice is cooked and the water is absorbed, about 18 minutes. Serves 4.

Coriander

Two for One

I frequently use cilantro when I prepare Chinese or Mexican dishes, but I rarely use coriander which is part of the same plant. Coriander is the seed of the coriander plant while the leaves are called cilantro.

Cilantro with its dark green, lacy leaves has a pungent flavor that blends well with highly seasoned foods. It looks similar to Italian parsley but the taste of the two are as different as night and day.

Coriander is made from the dried tiny (1/8 inch) yellow-tan seeds of the coriander plant. They are quiet fragrant and have an aromatic flavor akin to a combination of lemon, sage, and caraway. Depending on their use they can be sharply pungent in game, pork, or sausage dishes. On the other hand coriander used in cheese and egg dishes adds a very subtle flavor.

Whole coriander seeds are used in pickling and for special drinks, such as mulled wine. Ground seeds are used in many baked goods (particularly Scandinavian), curry blends, and soups.

To make matters even more complicated the coriander plant has two kinds of leaves and two kinds of flowers. As it belongs to the carrot family, one type of leaf is very thin like that of the carrot and the other rather massive like Italian parsley.

The word coriander is derived from the Greek "Koris," meaning bedbug. The ancient Greeks were of the opinion that both leaves and seeds smelled like that insect. In modern times the smell of coriander has been likened to that of rubber.

However, coriander is used in medicine to counteract the disagreeable smells or tastes of certain drugs. The inhabitants of southern France chew coriander leaves (cilantro) to sweeten their breath after eating garlic. Coriander is used in perfumes and soaps, imparting to them the fragrance of lilies of the valley.

Coriander was one of the first spices to be used by man. Its seeds have been found in Bronze Age ruins on the Aegean Islands and in the tombs of Pharaohs in Egypt. The Egyptians put it in wine to increase its intoxicating power and the ancient Hindus employed it in magic and religious ceremonies.

The Romans thought that Egyptian coriander was the best and used it in bread and stews, especially one made of greens. Ancient records show that the Romans used lightly crushed coriander and caraway seeds in vinegar to preserve meat throughout the summer. They also made an ancient version of a bouquet garni with cilantro leaves. The most commonly used spice mixture in Roman cuisine consisted of rue (an ancient woody herb with bitter leaves), savory, mint, wild celery, onion, thyme, coriander, and garlic. Apicius, the renowned Roman gourmet and cooking teacher, created a coriander-flavored dip for oysters and other shellfish.

In medieval times, coriander was cultivated along the shores of the Mediterranean and exported to northern Europe. Then it dropped temporarily out of favor. However, in the fourteenth century when all food tended to be bland, coriander and other seasonings made a comeback.

Coriander was grown in southern England and was quite cheap at that time when most spices were expensive. An account book dated 1265 showed that coriander cost four pence a pound while pepper and ginger were two shillings and saffron and cloves varied between ten and fourteen shillings. One of the specialties of Sussex cooks over the years has been ham cooked in milk flavored with coriander.

Shortly after the Spaniards discovered the New World they introduced coriander. It won instant favor with the Indians and eventually was passed on to the Indians of the Southwest. Coriander is still widely grown by the Zuni Indians who use its leaves for salad and flavor meat and chili with the seeds. Many Southwestern dishes, today, are garnished with cilantro. It is also used in salsas.

Although the coriander leaves, cilantro, are much more widely used than the coriander spice, the spice is still an integral part of almost every curry powder on the market. If purchasing ground coriander do so in small quantities as the spice looses its pungency more rapidly than other spices. Today the major exporters of coriander are Morocco, Russia, Romania, and Bulgaria.

Dishes consisting of black beans are one of the "in-foods." One of my favorites is Black Bean Chili. It is served with a salsa of tomatoes, peppers, onion, and cilantro. Serve Black Bean Chili with grilled meats or by itself with cornbread or crusty French bread for a meatless meal.

Black Bean Chili

3 cups black beans
2 small onions, 1 chopped, 1 diced
2 garlic cloves, chopped
Salt to taste
2 tablespoons olive oil
1 green pepper, diced
2 tablespoons minced garlic
1 can (16 ounces) tomatoes, crushed
1 1/2 cups chicken broth
1 tablespoon sugar
2 teaspoons cumin
1 teaspoon ground oregano
1/2 teaspoon cinnamon
3 teaspoons blueberry vinegar (or other fruit-flavored vinegar)
Salsa Cruda (recipe follows)

Soak the beans overnight. Drain the water, then place the beans in a saucepan and add enough fresh water to cover them. Bring to a boil and boil very gently for 20 minutes. Add the chopped onion, chopped garlic, and salt, to taste, and simmer, covered, for 1 and 1/2 hours.

Sauté the diced onion, diced peppers, and minced garlic in the olive oil until soft. When the beans have simmered for 1 and 1/2 hours, add the vegetables to them along with the remaining ingredients. Simmer very gently for another 1/2 hour or until the beans are tender. Serve with sour cream and Salsa Cruda.

Serves 8.

Salsa Cruda

3 to 4 large tomatoes, finely diced
1 small red onion, finely diced
4 green onions, chopped
1 Jalapeno pepper, very finely diced
1/2 cup chopped fresh cilantro
Juice of 1 lemon
1 1/2 teaspoons ground black pepper
Garlic powder and salt, to taste

Combine all ingredients in a bowl. Serve with Black Bean Chili.

Curry Powder

A Blend of Many to Make One

Today we refer to the main seasoning of curries as curry powder. The blend is actually composed of several spices, usually five to ten. Some Indian curry combinations use as many as forty.

Curries are the base of the traditional cooking of India. At the time the British ruled India they had problems feeding the native Indian troops. The Moslems did not eat pork, while some Hindus ate meat and some were vegetarians. Fortunately, curry sauce provided an easily adaptable seasoning for the basic rice or bread eaten by the troops.

Over time curry sauce rose in importance and became the name of the dishes seasoned with curry sauce. The spices were hotter and stronger in the extremely hot climates of southern India, while much milder spice combinations were prevalent in the cooler north.

Although curries did not become popular in Europe until the late 1500s, they are mentioned in the writings of India as early as 477 A.D. The word curry is an adaptation of "kari," which comes from the Southeast Asian dialect, Tamil. Curry appears in the English language in the sixteenth century when English explorers tasted curry while stopping in India on the way to the Far East.

Commercial curry powder, despite its popular association with India, is a Western invention. Some brands may be produced in India, but they are rarely used there. The idea of resorting to a commercially mass-produced powder, as opposed to a careful selection of specific spices to complement a particular food, is unthinkable for the Indian cook. He or she daily prepares his or her selection of spices into a paste with a little water. The ingredients and proportions are entirely dependent on the judgment of the cook and the kind of curry he or she is going to make. There are hundreds of variations of curry dishes in the various regions of India.

Certain spices are always used in curry powder. They include turmeric, fenugreek, cuminseed, coriander, and red or cayenne pepper. Beyond that curry powder may also include allspice, cinnamon, cardamom, cloves, fennel, ginger, mace, yellow mustard seeds and black or white pepper. The various combinations and amounts determine the flavor of the curry. I like both cinnamon and cloves in my chicken curry dishes.

Before the early sixteenth century, curries and curry powders were made without red peppers. When Columbus discovered America he also discovered many members of the great capsicum family — the pod peppers from which red pepper is made. Word of this new spice spread as fast as ships could sail and within a decade capsicums were brought to India by the Portuguese. It was at this time that curries became hot.

Curry powder is probably the world's earliest spice blend. Rare cook books from two hundred years ago call for curry powder in Indian-style dishes. The well-known Williamsburg cook book has a recipe for Gumbo dating from 1837 which calls for curry powder to season the chicken used in the gumbo. A century earlier a sea captain taught the women of Charleston, South Carolina, how to make Country Captain Chicken using his own curry spice blend.

The best known Indian spice mixture for curries is Garam Masala. It is not a powder, but a spice mixture whose name means "the warming spices." There is no set formula for this, as each Indian family determines the selection of spices and then grinds them. Before grinding, however, the spices are heated and slightly roasted to bring out their flavors.

Garam Masala is added to a dish near the end of the cooking process and is never the complete seasoning of a dish. Most curry powders, which contain hot spices such as red pepper and ginger, are added at the beginning of the cooking process so that the hot flavors permeate the dish.

Two other well-known curry mixtures are Bombay and Madras. Both contain hot chilies. The Bombay mixture includes cinnamon and both of the mixtures include ginger and turmeric. The ginger adds more hotness and the turmeric gives a slightly musty flavor to balance the sharpness of the curry. It also imparts a yellow color. Turmeric. like ginger is a rhizome, or knobby root, that is widely used in the cooking of India, Southeast Asia, and Latin America.

This chicken curry uses many of the spices of a traditional Indian curry with modern curry powder as a base. If you like the dish hotter add more curry powder, but remember that the chili pepper and ginger also add hotness. I suggest you taste the sauce mixture before putting the chicken pieces in the oven. Basamti or any aromatic rice is a good accompaniment.

Curried Chicken Legs

4 whole chicken legs
2 tablespoons olive oil
2 onions, chopped
1 garlic clove, minced
1-inch piece fresh ginger, peeled and chopped
1 jalapeno pepper, seeded and chopped
1/2 red bell pepper, chopped
1 1/2 tablespoons curry powder
1/4 teaspoon ground cinnamon
1/4 teaspoon ground cloves
1/4 teaspoon chili powder
3/4 teaspoon coriander
1 (14 ounce) can chopped tomatoes
1 cup chicken broth
2 tablespoons all-purpose flour mixed with 1/4 cup water

Skin the chicken legs and cut them apart at the joint.

Heat the olive oil in a skillet over medium heat. Add the chicken pieces and brown them on both sides. Then remove them from the skillet and set aside.

Add the onions, garlic, ginger, chili pepper, and red pepper to the skillet and sauté for 3 to 4 minutes. Then add the curry powder, chili powder, and coriander and continue sautéing for another minute, stirring constantly. Add the tomatoes with their juice and the chicken broth. Add the chicken pieces. Cover the skillet and bake in a preheated 325° F. oven for 35 to 40 minutes or until the chicken is tender.

Thicken the sauce with some of the flour-water mixture to the desired consistency. Serve with rice. Serves 4.

Garlic

The Powerful, Pungent Clove

I like and I don't like garlic. I like it when it is used as a subtle seasoning to enhance the flavor of a dish. I do not like garlic when its flavor overwhelms a dish to the extent that all you taste is garlic. And I do not like garlic when its smell penetrates a restaurant, or when someone's breath reeks of garlic.

However, millions of people love garlic while millions of others dislike it. Unfortunately, for me too many restaurant chefs have been taught to use garlic to excess.

Garlic has been cultivated for thousands of years. It is believed to have originated in Asia where the Chinese used it as early as 2000 B.C. for medicinal purposes. From there garlic was transported to the Middle East and Europe where other civilizations also used it to cure ills. In order to alleviate a toothache, a piece of garlic was placed in the cavity. Garlic was used to cure snake bites, dog bites, insect stings, and most intestinal disorders. Now it is believed that garlic can lower cholesterol.

A king of ancient Babylon grew garlic in his garden as early as 721 B.C., and the ancient Egyptian slaves who built the Great Pyramid in the fifth century B.C. are supposed to have lived on garlic and onions. Roman peasants ate garlic to give them strength for their work in the fields in the hot sun. Roman soldiers also ate garlic to give them strength. Upper class society at the time rejected garlic because of its strong smell so they looked down on garlic-eaters.

Garlic had a practical use in Greek and Roman times. Boiled garlic seeds were sprinkled by the farmers on their fields to help protect them from the birds. Birds would eat the garlic and fall asleep. Then the farmer could easily trap them, thus protecting the fields and also providing food for the family.

Through the ages garlic has acquired a mystical quality. In medieval times, it was believed that witches and vampires would flee at the sight of garlic. People wore wreaths of garlic around their necks to ward off the evil spirits. German miners took garlic with them into the mines as a charm against evil spirits.

In some European countries in the nineteenth century cloves of garlic were put into the wool stockings of children suffering from whooping cough. A little later, bruised cloves of garlic were mixed with lard and used as a liniment for bronchitis. I say, thank Good we now rely on modern antibiotics and cough medicine! During the Crusades, the Muslims who encountered the first European Crusaders were more terrified of the European's strong garlic smell than of their armor and weapons.

Wild garlic, a cousin of the present cultivated plant, was found growing in America by the Spanish explorers. They observed local Indians using the plant as a vegetable, and sometimes to season soups.

The early English settlers of this country did not readily accept native garlic as a culinary ingredient. In a 1808 cookbook, entitled "New England Cookery," the author comments "Garlicks, though used by the French, are better adapted to medicine than cookery."

In European cuisine, the use of garlic as a seasoning has been mainly confined to the southern regions of the continent. Southern France and southern Italy both included garlic in many of their dishes. Garlic was probably transported to Italy from Greece where it was eaten as a vegetable.

Today in the United States, garlic snobbery has been reversed. In the early part of this century you were looked down upon if you ate garlic — a food fit only for menial workers. In recent years you are not "with it" if you do not eat garlic. Today garlic is everywhere and is as popular as Reebok running shoes.

There are over three hundred thousand people who attend the Garlic Festival in Gilroy, California each year where they sample such delicacies as garlic wine and garlic ice cream. Although Gilroy is considered the garlic capital of the world, and does process a great amount of garlic, most of the California garlic is actually grown in the neighboring state of Nevada.

One of the most famous recipes for garlic is Bagna Caoda, a garlic sauce which is served like a fondue. The name means hot bath, since this sauce from the Piedmont region of Italy, must be kept hot in order to cook the food being dipped into it. Raw bell peppers, celery, cabbage, and fennel are preferred in Piedmont. In some other areas onions, carrots, potatoes, and turnips are pre-boiled and dipped into the sauce. When there is only a little sauce left, eggs are broken into it and scrambled.

Bagna Caoda is a very old sauce, which has been popular since its creation in the sixteenth century. It is now served on festive occasions, particularly Christmas Eve. It should be kept hot in the same way as a fondue, preferably in a chafing dish.

Bagna Caoda

!/2 cup butter
4 garlic cloves, peeled and very finely sliced
1/2 onion, finely chopped
10 anchovy fillets, rinsed
2 cups olive oil
Salt
1 white truffle, optional
Vegetables, such as cabbage, carrots, cauli-flower, green beans, mushrooms, cherry tomatoes, bell peppers, radishes, turnips, squash, zucchini
Strips of lean beef
Shrimp
French bread

Melt the butter in a small deep earthenware pot or a very heavy-based saucepan (or a chafing dish) over the lowest heat. As soon as the butter has melted, add the garlic and sauté for a few seconds. The garlic should not color.

Add the anchovies to the pot and pour the olive oil in very gradually, stirring constantly. Cook for about 10 minutes, always on the lowest heat and stirring constantly. The dip is ready when the ingredients are well blended and smooth. Add slivers of truffle and serve. Provide skewers or fondue forks ti dipthe vegetabes, meat, and shirimp into the sauce. Chunks of French bread are used at the end to scoop up any leftover sauce. Serves 4 to 6.

Ginger

The Ugly Root

One of the most pungent and delightful spices comes from a rather ugly, gnarled, light brown root — ginger. It is one of the world's oldest spices and can be found in the specialty produce section of most of our supermarkets.

Ginger is the sharp, spicy ingredient in many different dishes — soups, cakes and cookies, pickles, drinks, confections and ice cream. It is the basis of gingerale, ginger bread and is one of the main ingredients in curry dishes.

In the Far East it is also eaten raw in a salad or cooked as a vegetable. The Chinese have long considered ginger a great delicacy and use it extensively in their cooking.

Ginger was one of the first true Oriental spices. For centuries it was transported overland from the ginger fields of Southeast Asia across Persia to Europe, where it was in great demand for its pungency and aroma. Ginger made the long trip in greater abundance than other exotic spices from Asia as it was shipped in root form and was thus less perishable.

In early times ginger had great medicinal uses. During Biblical times it was used in a "refresher cup" to renew a person's vitality. In Arabia it was said to have aphrodisiac properties as described in the stories of The Thousand and One Nights. The Greeks used ginger in combination with other ingredients such as black pepper and honey as an antidote for sickness. Historians report that the first recipe for gingerbread came from the ancient Greeks.

The Romans introduced ginger to Europe. Since it came by the way of Alexandria and the Red Sea they assumed ginger was grown in Southern Arabia or India. With the collapse of the Roman Empire, ginger disappeared from Europe and was not re-introduced until the 1400's when Marco Polo rediscovered it in China and India. Even though the Romans were avid ginger users, the spice is absent from modern Italian cookery.

During medieval times in Europe ginger, although cheap to cultivate was very expensive. A pound of ginger was equivalent to the cost of a sheep. As the French palate became more accustomed to more delicate flavors and as French cooking became more refined, the use of ginger declined in that country.

England, however, remained wedded to ginger. Queen Elizabeth I is said to have invented the gingerbread man when she ordered little cakes flavored with ginger be baked in the shapes and likenesses of her favorite people. The conquest of India by the British insured a constant supply of the spice and also helped keep its price low.

For centuries ginger was used in the English taverns where customers would help themselves from a jar on the bar to spice up their tankards of porter or ale. These Chinese ginger jars have since become collectors' items. The practice of keeping a jar of ginger on the bar in English taverns ceased just before the Second World War.

The English settlers carried their love of ginger to America. In colonial Virginia ginger cookies were among the treats passed out to the voters to induce them to choose the right candidates for the House of Burgesses. Ginger was included in the rations of the American soldiers during the Revolution.

The speed of the Yankee Clipper ships in the early nineteenth century brought an abundance of ginger and other spices to the eastern shores of America with Salem, Massachusetts becoming the leading spice port. In New England ginger ice cream is still popular. Until the mid-1900s, it was a common practice in the Eastern states to pass candied ginger around after a meal to aid in digestion.

The Dutch, who had close relationships with Indonesia since the 1600's, have also used ginger as a prominent cooking ingredient. Besides using ginger in dishes of Indonesian origin, the Dutch use it raw in rice dishes, combine candied ginger with Gouda cheese and pineapple for a cocktail snack, and also use it in meatballs.

Today fresh ginger is an integral part of our cooking. With the popularity of Asian restaurants and at-home-stir frying, ginger has become a common cooking ingredient in America.

Ginger is still grown in Southeast Asia, but it is now also grown in other tropical regions — Africa, the Caribbean, and Australia. In recent years if has become a successful agricultural product of Hawaii. India, however, is still the largest ginger producer in the world, growing half of the world's production.

The fresh ginger we eat is the root of the ginger plant. It has a white, pungently aromatic rhizome which is covered with a light brown scaly skin. When buying fresh ginger, I try to select a firm, heavy-feeling piece. The wrinkled, light feeling ones tend not to be fresh.

I try to keep a piece of fresh ginger root in my refrigerator to have it available as an additive to a variety of dishes. It adds extra zest to soup, is wonderful in curries, and gives an Oriental flavor to most meat dishes.

The Gingerbread with Apricot Glaze makes a delightful, light dessert. It keps well for several days.

Gingerbread with Apricot Glaze

1/2 cup sugar
1/2 teaspoon ground ginger
1/4 teaspoon cinnamon
1/4 teaspoon ground cloves
1/4 teaspoon nutmeg
1/2 cup vegetable oil
1/2 cup dark molasses
1 teaspoon baking soda
1/4 cup boiling water
1/4 cup cream sherry
1 1/4 cups all-purpose flour
1 egg, beaten

Combine the sugar and spices in a bowl. Stir in the oil and molasses. Mix together the soda, and boiling water and stir into the sugar mixture. Then add the sherry and pour in the flour in a gradual stream, stirring constantly. Add the beaten egg and mix well. Pour the batter into a well-greased 8-by 8-inch pan and bake in a preheated 350° F. oven for 30 to 35 minutes. Spoon the glaze over the warm cake and serve at room temperature. Serves 10 to 12.

Glaze

1 cup apricot jam
1/3 cup water
1 teaspoon sugar
1 teaspoon grated orange zest
2 tablespoons cream sherry
1/2 chopped walnuts

Combine the apricot jam, water, sugar, and orange zest in a small saucepan. Bring to a boil; simmer for 5 minutes, stirring constantly. Remove from the heat; stir in sherry and nuts.

Mustard

Brown and Yellow Seeds

Ninety percent of the world's brown and yellow mustard seeds are grown in Canada along its border with the United States and in North and South Dakota and Wisconsin.

Food historians tell us that man first cultivated mustard in 8000 B.C., in the Indus Valley of what is today India. This early civilization cooked some of their foods in sesame oil and seasoned them with mustard seeds. At that time mustard grew wild, its seeds being scattered by the birds. From there mustard seeds were carried by ancient Arab traders to China and the Middle East. The Arabs sold mustard seeds to the Egyptians, Greeks, and Romans. The Egyptians and Chinese created medicines as well as seasonings from mustard.

Mustard seeds have been found in the Great Pyramids and the tombs in the Valley of the Kings. The Egyptians used mustard as a condiment by popping a few of the seeds into their mouths as they chewed cooked meat. The Greeks claimed that eating mustard seeds helped retain memory.

Alexander the Great once communicated with his enemy via mustard seeds. In 331 B.C. before a battle, the Persian emperor sent a bag of sesame seeds to Alexander, symbolizing how numerous his troops were. Alexander replied with a similar bag filled with smaller, more numerous mustard seeds. The mustard seeds also indicated his army was very ferocious.

Persian noblemen, exhibited their swordsmanship by putting a mustard seed on a block and slicing through it with a single stroke of the sword. Quite an accomplishment when the seed is only .064 inches in diameter.

Eventually the Romans tired of paying the Arabs high prices for mustard seeds, so they began cultivating the mustard plant. Like the Egyptians, the Romans also enjoyed chewing mustard seeds with their meats. They became so fond of this spice that they ordered their invading legions to carry mustard seeds and plant them in all of the conquered territories, from North Africa to Great Britain. Mustard became established in Burgundy when the Romans planted it on the hills surrounding Dijon.

The defeat of Rome and the Dark Ages put an end to the spice trade. It was not revived in Europe until the Muslim Empire spread from North Africa into Spain. Mustard which grew wild as well as being cultivated, became one of the most esteemed seasonings of the Middle Ages, brightening that era's drab cuisine.

By the ninth century, mustard was being grown on convent grounds near Paris and sold to provide revenue for the church. Charlemagne in 812 decreed that mustard be grown on all imperial farms in central Europe. The French not only used the seeds as a spice, but also added the leaves of the plant to their stews and salads.

The Norman invasion of England in 1066 brought with it some innovations in cooking. The Norman palate, being more sophisticated, introduced many spices, including mustard, to England, where it became the prime ingredient in English cooking. However, its primacy was short-lived, when the Crusaders brought black pepper back to England. Pepper quickly became the essential cooking spice in England, even in the tiniest farmhouse kitchen.

Mustard, however, remained popular in France. By the seventeenth century Dijon had become an important center for European and Asian merchants trading in spices. Until 1634 Dijon mustard manufacturers merely ground the mustard seeds and compressed the powder into bricks, tablets, or pellets. The cook then mixed the mustard brick with liquids and other spices to suit. In 1634, the French government allowed the mustard manufacturers of Dijon to purchase vinegar from the vinegar makers and gave them the exclusive right to make the finished product.

The Dijon mustard industry was strictly regulated by the government. The workers had to wear clean and modest clothing and they had to conduct themselves properly. The manufacturers could own only one shop and had to mark their names on all casks and stone jars of mustard mix. Seeds were ground by hand and workers who shed the most tears received a bonus for their finer powder.

Today France produces about 50 percent of all prepared mustard exported from Europe. About 4,four thousand tons of Dijon mustard are sent to the United States annually. Even though the French prefer a straight mustard they are exporting more than fifty varieties.

Although we, in the United States consume more than 30 million gallons of mustard each year, we use very little as a spice in cooking. As a condiment, mustard is king from the ball park to the dining table.

Even today, the American mustard market is still dominated by the bright-yellow spread known as French's Classic Yellow. It first came into being at the 1904 St. Louis World's Fair, where the yellow mustard teamed up with the hot dog for the first time. French's Yellow mustard was the creation of George Dunn, the plant superintendent for George French.

Attuned to the American palette, George French and his brother, Francis, concluded that Americans were not consuming much mustard because it was too hot. Americans, at that time, preferred bland food, a throwback to their English ancestors. The French brothers decided to produce a milder mustard with a yellow color, which soon became the new gourmet rage. The color comes not from the mus-

tard seed, but from the addition of turmeric. By 1915 the French Company had made a million dollars profit.

Today, the French Company processes more than 30 million pounds of mustard seeds each year. The Classic Yellow is a staple in American households. The company also produces a milder version of Dijon-style mustard.

The Grilled Chicken recipe combines two mustards, one sharp, the other mild for a pleasant piquant flavor

Grilled Chicken
with Mustard-Orange Glaze

1 (3 1/2 to 4 pound) chicken, split for broiling
Salt, pepper, garlic powder, and onion powder, to taste
1/4 cup fresh orange juice
3 tablespoons maple syrup or maple flavored pancake syrup
2 teaspoons honey-orange mustard
2 teaspoons coarse-grain mustard

Rinse the chicken and pat it dry. Sprinkle the outside with salt, pepper, garlic powder, and onion powder. Grill the two chicken halves over medium hot coals for 30 minutes.

In the meantime, combine the orange juice, maple syrup, and the two mustards in a small bowl. After 30 minutes of grilling time baste the chicken with the orange mixture and grill for another 10 minutes, then baste again and grill for another 10 minutes,. Repeat the basting process one more time for a total of 3 bastings and 30 more minutes of cooking time. Remove the chicken from the grill and cut it into serving pieces. Serves 4.

Nutmeg

The Nut and Its Netting

There was a time when nutmeg was not readily available and smugglers of this aromatic spice were put to death. According to food historians, the Portuguese so prized their sixteenth-century monopoly of nutmeg that they distributed phony maps of the seas surrounding the Spice Islands. They hoped to steer foreign vessels away from the islands and onto dangerous unknown reefs.

Sixteenth-century Europe's passion for nutmeg and other spices stemmed from the blandness of the daily diet, particularly vegetable cookery. Before Magellan's crew discovered Indonesia's Molluccas (Spice Islands) in 1521, even the affluent dined on boiled vegetables and mutton, followed by more bland vegetables and tasteless meats. The spice trade transformed the taste of everyday foods.

However, the aromatic qualities of nutmeg were known for several centuries previously. Nutmeg's heavenly scent may have contributed to its popularity. In 1190 the soon-to-be Holy Roman Emperor Henry VI visited Rome and found that the streets had been fumigated by a then little known spice — nutmeg.

During the centuries that followed, fashionable ladies carried sachets of nutmeg. Some suspended whole nutmegs caged in silver filigree from chains around their necks. In an age graced with poor personal hygiene and open-air slaughterhouses, the pleasant scent of nutmeg was welcomed. There was a certain romantic aspect to the nut's success stemming from the fact that it came from exotic lands many, many miles away from the everyday drudgery of medieval life.

Men and women of all backgrounds continued to crave nutmeg well into the eighteenth century. While relaxing at private clubs and taverns, well-dressed gentlemen reached into their pockets for their own personal nutmeg graters (the little silver graters now bring enormous prices at auctions) and shaved a few grains into their beer or grog. In America the rage for nutmeg was just as big. Food historians tell us that early American cookbooks mention nutmeg more than any other spice.

The evergreen nutmeg tree known by its botanical name "Myristica fragrans," produces two spices — nutmeg and mace. Mace is the waxy scarlet net that encases nutmeg's outer shell. Mace and nutmeg are ready for harvesting when the peach-like fruit that encases them both ripens and splits. The nutmeg tree varies in height from twenty-five to forty feet. At maturity each tree can yield as many as fifteen hundred nuts annually.

Mace is a traditional ingredient in pound cake. It is more pungent than nutmeg and historically has been more costly. In the twelfth century a pound of mace was worth three sheep or half a cow.

Most of the nutmeg and mace used in America today comes from Grenada. In 1843, a merchant ship called on this small island in the Caribbean on its way back to England from the Spice Islands and left some nutmeg trees. These became the foundation of Grenada's third most import export. Today, Grenada produces about forty percent of the world's nutmeg.

Frugal Grenadians waste no part of their favorite tree. The peach-like flesh of the fruit is made into jam or a soft candy called nutmeg cheese. The shell that houses the nutmeg is ground for oil, and the cracked casings become "gravel" for driveways that emit a wonderful aroma after a gentle rain.

In Grenada ice cream is flavored with nutmeg and cooks use it in pumpkin soup and most vegetable cookery. Nutmeg is widely used in Indian and Southeast Asian cooking. It is also utilized in a variety of spice mixtures.

In America we add a pinch of nutmeg to white sauce to give it mellowness. A sprinkle of nutmeg over any type of squash or creamed spinach enhances otherwise bland vegetables.

The following recipe for Parsnip and Sweet Potato Tart uses a little nutmeg for additional flavoring. It is a tasty accompaniment to ham or grilled meats and is also a nice luncheon dish when served with a green salad. Mace in the Pear Tart adds spiceness.

Parsnip and Sweet Potato Tart

*3/4 pound parsnips, peeled and cut
    into 3/4-inch dice*
*3/4 pound sweet potatoes, peeled
    and cut into 3/4-inch dice*
*1/2 (17 and 1/4 ounce) package frozen puff
    pastry sheets, thawed*
3/4 cup whipping cream
3 large eggs
*6 ounces Emmanthaler or Swiss cheese,
coarsely grated*
1/4 teaspoon pepper
3/4 teaspoon ground nutmeg

Place parsnips and sweet potato dices in a 2-quart saucepan with just enough water to barely cover them. Bring to a boil and then cook on medium-low for 8 to 10 minutes or until just tender.

Unfold the thawed pastry sheet on a lightly floured surface and roll out into a 11-inch circle. Fit the pastry into a 9-inch pie pan or fluted tart pan with removable bottom.

Spread the vegetables in the bottom of the pastry-lined pan. Sprinkle with half of the cheese. Whisk together the cream, eggs, pepper, and nutmeg. Add the remaining cheese. Gently pour the cream mixture over vegetables, spreading it over the top with a spatula.

Bake the tart in a preheated 375° F. oven for 40 minutes or until golden brown. Cut in wedges and serve. Serves 6.

Early American Pear Pie

1/3 cup sugar
2 tablespoons all-purpose flour
1/2 teaspoon ground mace
1/2 teaspoon ground cinnamon
6 cups thinly sliced peeled ripe pears
Pastry for 2-crust, 9-inch pie
2 tablespoons butter

In a large mixing bowl combine the sugar, flour, and spices. Add the pears and mix lightly. Line a 9-inch pie pan with half of the pastry. Add the filling and dot with butter. Top with remaining pastry and crimp the edges together. Cut several slits in top of pastry. Bake in a preheated 425° F. oven for about 50 minutes. Serve warm or cool with vanilla ice cream.

Serves 6.

Paprika

Red, and Sometimes Hot

Hungary and paprika are nearly synonymous. Although Spain produces more paprika and California's paprika is redder, no country is more closely identified with this spice than Hungary. The deep blush of paprika tints every widely known Hungarian dish.

This association of country and spice results from history, climate, and soil. Paprika, a member of the pepper family, originated in the New World. It was transported to Spain by the Spanish explorers. From Spain the peppers were taken to Hungary by the Turks after they invaded Spain in the sixteenth century.

Paprika was a spice of the common people. In the sixteenth century most spices imported into Europe were very costly and used only by the affluent. Paprika, however, worked it way up the Hungarian social scale from peasant to nobility.

Hungarian peasants first used paprika as a medicine to treat the malaria they contracted from swamps on the Great Hungarian Plain. Many centuries later, in 1937, a Hungarian scientist, Dr. Albert Szent-Gyorgyi, received a Nobel prize for discovering that paprika peppers are one of the world's most potent source of Vitamin C, and contain a substantial amount of Vitamin A. Most of the Vitamin C is lost, however, when the peppers are processed into powder.

By the eighteenth century paprika had reached the kitchen. For centuries previously, Magyar shepherds had stewed meat with onions in pots hung over open fires, dried the stew in the sun and carried it with them in bags made of sheep's stomachs. Reheated with water, the stew made a nourishing meal. With the addition of paprika, it became delicious and the foundation of Hungarian cooking. The Magyars, original inhabitants of Hungary, called the stew "Gulyas" (now known in the rest of the world as goulash).

By the middle of the nineteenth century, paprika had been accepted in many upper-class kitchens of Europe. Restaurateurs in Hungary featured peasant dishes containing paprika on their menus. Eventually paprika dishes spread to the restaurants of nearby countries, particularly Austria where chicken paprika became a household and restaurant staple.

The word paprika in Hungary refers both to the bell peppers and the spice. The peppers, Capsicum annum, are a species related to many other peppers grown throughout the world. The paprika plant is very sensitive. With a change of soil and climate, the same plants will produce peppers with different character and taste.

The sunny Great Plain around the cities of Szeged and Kalocsa, south of Budapest, is ideally suited to the paprika plants. There are more than thirty thousand acres devoted to growing paprika. In September the fields glow red with the ripe peppers. Farm houses in the area literally drip with red peppers, as farmers hang them on strings under the eaves to dry.

The pungency or heat of the paprika peppers comes from their ribs, or veins, not their seeds, as commonly believed. Seeds are hot only because they rub against the ribs, picking up a chemical compound called "capsicin." The quantity of capsicin determines how hot a particular variety of pepper is.

Processing of paprika began on a large scale in the nineteenth century when two brothers in Szeged invented a machine to separate ribs and seeds from the peppers' flesh, permitting the grading of paprika by the amount of heat it contained. There is virtually no difference among comparable grades of Spanish, California, and Hungarian paprika.

Most of the Hungarian paprika imported into this country is of the mild variety, or what the Hungarian state-owned trading companies call "noble-sweet." Sweet paprika has no pungency. Its principal use is for coloring processed foods such as salad dressings. Today most of the sweet paprika comes from California where the paprika plant has been bred to produce peppers of bright red color but with no taste.

The hotter varieties of Hungarian paprika are available in the gourmet section of our grocery stores. Even the hottest paprika, however, does not rival cayenne in bite, so paprika, unlike other spices, is added to food by the spoonful rather than by pinches. Adding flavor to the sweeter grade of paprika generally available in the U. S. may be achieved by the addition of a pinch of cayenne for every tablespoon of paprika. I also sprinkle paprika on meats when I want them to brown nicely.

The secret of any Hungarian goulash is to slowly sauté the onions until they are a deep golden brown. Always cook the goulash slowly, as was done traditionally by the Magyars over their camp fires. The following recipe for Beef Goulash is known as Bogracs Gulyas in Hungary. Bogracs means iron pot, the kind Hungarian shepherds hung over the fire to prepare their gently simmering stew.

Chicken Paprika (Csirke Paprikas in Hungarian) is different from goulash in that the meat is braised in very little liquid. Chicken, veal, and lamb are usually used for "paprikas" and sour cream is added.

Beef Goulash

2 tablespoons butter, olive oil, or bacon fat
1 cup finely-chopped onions
2 garlic cloves, minced
3 tablespoons paprika
2 pounds beef (chuck), cut in 1-inch cubes
1/2 teaspoon caraway seeds
Salt and pepper, to taste
Beef broth
2 medium potatoes, cut in 1-inch cubes
2 medium tomatoes, peeled, seeded and chopped
2 medium green peppers, seeded and chopped

Melt the butter over medium heat in a heavy pot. Reduce heat to low, add onion and garlic and sauté about 10 minutes, until golden, stirring frequently.

Add the paprika and stir thoroughly. Then add the beef, caraway seeds, salt and pepper, and beef broth to cover. Bring to a slow boil, partially cover, and simmer 1 to 1 and 1/2 hours or until beef is nearly tender. Add potatoes, tomatoes, and peppers and more broth if necessary. (Goulash should be like a stew, not a soup.) Partially cover and cook over low heat for about 30 minutes, until potatoes are tender. Serves 4 to 6.

Pepper

Dried Berries

Pepper has been used since the earliest times of civilization. The word pepper comes from the Sanskrit "pipali." Until the arrival of chilies from the New World, pepper was used in India and southeast Asia to make foods spicy and hot. Pepper was the world's first spice because peppercorns (the dried berries of the pepper vine) store well without losing their flavor. This was essential to the success of the spice trade.

At one time pepper was a most precious commodity and as negotiable as gold or silver. In England "peppercorn rent" is a term still used in legal documents to signify a nominal payment which does not represent the real value of a piece of property.

In the Middle Ages tenants paid rent for land to their feudal lords in the form of a pound of peppercorns, which was equivalent to two to three weeks' salary for a farmhand in England. In France a pound of peppercorns bought a serf's freedom. Both in ancient and medieval times a pound of peppercorns was worth a pound of gold.

Peppercorns were also used to make international payments as they represented a more stable medium of exchange than gold or silver. Rulers who struck their own gold coins were often in the habit of clipping or scraping some of the gold from their coins. This habit continued as the money passed from hand to hand. The peppercorn standard therefore became safer than gold.

The use of pepper as money spanned a period of about two thousand years. In ancient Greek and Roman times it was also used as a means of paying tribute. Rome saved itself from Attila the Hun in 452 by "presents" of cinnamon and pepper. In the twelfth century several French cities imposed a tribute of two pounds of pepper per head instead of taxes.

Peppercorns were used not only to pay rent for land but also to buy it. Pepper provided rewards for Genoese soldiers who participated in battles in the Middle East. They were given two pounds of pepper per man. Court fines were imposed in the form of peppercorns. It is reported that King John III of Portugal paid part of his sister's dowry in peppercorns when she married Charles I of Spain in 1524.

In medieval times pepper was also used as a measure of wealth. One measure of a person's wealth was the amount of pepper in his pantry. One way of saying that a man was poor was to say that he lacked pepper. The wealthy kept large stores of pepper in their homes and let it be known that it was there. It was a guarantee of solvency.

Food historians claim that pepper first reached the Mediterranean area from India. European sailing vessels used to sail to India in the summer and come back in the winter with prevailing winds bringing Indian products in the winter, pepper being the most important.

The Romans were so avid for pepper and other spices that they built a great market for spices. When Venice gained control of the salt trade, it also had a monopoly on the pepper trade. During the years of the Crusades, Venetian ships carried men to the Middle East and came back laden with pepper and other spices.

After Portuguese ships began trading with the Far East that country quickly became the leading importer of pepper, selling it throughout Europe. The Dutch East India Company subsequently wrested the pepper monopoly from Portugal. England, not wanting to be left out, formed the British East India Company. With all of this competition the world price of pepper quickly declined.

Traders from Salem, Massachusetts, became known for pepper imports into this country and also sold pepper to Europe. In 1791 the United States re-exported only 500 pounds of pepper to other parts of the world, By 1805, however, 7.5 million pounds were re-exported. This increase in America's role in the spice trade, particularly the importance of Salem as an export center was due to the fast American clipper ships. They were able to bring the pepper harvest from Sumatra, where most of the world's pepper was grown at the time, faster than their European competitors.

Pepper does not grow on trees, but on a vine that clings to trees. They can grow up to thirty feet in height. Most of the pepper is grown in tropical areas near the equator. The small grains, no more than a quarter of an inch when full grown, are green at first and then become a yellowish red as they ripen.

Black peppercorns are the dried berries of the pepper vine. White peppercorns are the same berries with the darker outer layer, the scented layer, removed by soaking the peppercorns. Some chefs prefer using white pepper for pale sauces so that no dark specs appear.

Green peppercorns have become popular in the last twenty-five years since France started importing them from Madagascar. Green peppercorns are juicy and much hotter than dried peppercorns. They are preserved in a light vinegar and are sold in glass jars.

Today there are various grades of ground pepper on the market, ranging from fine to coarse grinds. Many cooks prefer grinding their own pepper as needed.

And

The Grainy Substance

While salt is not a spice, it is used to flavor food and contributes to our well being. Salt is essential to life because the body requires a constant presence of three and a half ounces of salt in the system in order to function properly. Various health authorities have different theories as to how much salt is lost by our bodies every day and how much needs to be replaced.

The word salt comes from the Roman god of health, Salus, whose name is also the origin of "salutary" and "salute" both originally a wish for good health for the person saluted.

Salt is the oldest seasoning. It came into use when Neolithic man's existence changed from a nomadic way of life to an agricultural existence. His food source changed from hunting to herding and cultivation. He began eating less game and more vegetables, whose bland flavor required a seasoning — salt.

Some salt was obtained from burning salty plants and extracting salt from the ashes of burned grasses. Neither of these methods produced enough salt, however.

At the same time that man settled down, cooking pots resistant enough to be placed over a fire came into being. Before this time early man's meat was roasted on a spit or in a hole in the ground lined with heated stones. Now he could boil his food, a more convenient way of cooking requiring minimum attention from the cook. But while roasting conserves the salt content of meat, boiling leaches it out. Thus it became necessary to find salt.

The earliest salt mines were in Austria at Hallstein and Hallstatt. Around the latter a rich community developed as evidenced by the vast archeological treasures found at the site. In Austria the salt mines are still a tourist attraction and can be visited from Salzburg.

Salt mines were not the only source of salt. The oceans, the deltas and the mouths of rivers flowing into the ocean provided and still provide the majority of salt. In Roman times the Via Salaria was a pair of worn ruts leading from Rome to the Adriatic Sea. The Romans extracted so much salt by evaporation from the sea that they became the major suppliers of salt to the neighboring lands around the Mediterranean. The flag followed the trade and as the Roman legions marched along the various salt roads the empire expanded.

When we think of Venice we think of the spice trade which came to that port from the Middle and Far East. In reality it was salt extracted from the sea around Venice that was the go-between for spices. Ships laden with salt traveled to Constantinople where the salt was exchanged for spices from the East.

In the thirteenth century caravans with as many as forty thousand horses were sent to Venice from Hungary, Croatia and eastern Germany to buy salt. For many years there was intense competition between the principality of Venice and its neighbor, Cervia, for the salt trade. Venice annexed Cervia to stop the competition, but today Venice produces no salt and Cervia is one of the leading Italian salt producers.

Throughout history salt has been a symbol of well-being. The ancient Greeks believed that bread and salt were gifts to the gods. For them and for the Romans salt appeared on altars in the same place of honor as incense. It appeared on Hebrew altars, too. Moses ordered that every sacrificial offering of meat be sprinkled with salt.

For years there was a superstition that the partaking of salt drove away demons. In the Middle Ages it was thought that people thought to be witches did not eat salt. In France it was tradition to place a saucer containing salt and a piece of bread on a corpse during the wake.

There are a number of other superstitions connected with salt, one of which was that it was unlucky to spill salt. This was illustrated in Leonardo da Vinci's "Last Supper," where Judas is shown upsetting the salt. In France, a farmer taking his cow to market for sale still places half a pinch of salt between her horns and puts the other half in his pocket. This assures a good price for the cow. Also in France, salt is thrown into the fire to protect a house from being struck by lightning. In Russia strangers are welcomed into the home with a piece of bread and salt.

Salt is a symbol of respect and in former days salt cellars were often monumental pieces of very ornate silver placed in the middle of the table. The expression "below the salt" originates from the fact that places of honor at the table were designated by their position in regard to the salt. The most revered guests were seated above the salt, towards the head of the table, while those who were less favored were below the salt.

Saffron

The Most Expensive Spice

Considered to be the most expensive spice in the world, saffron is extremely labor-intensive to produce. It sells for about $40 per ounce, varying according to quality. The cultivation of the plant, the harvest of the stigmas, and the production of the spice is done completely by hand. Each plant has from two-to-nine blossoms, three-to-four being the more usual. Efforts to mechanize the operations have failed.

There have been many imitations of saffron in recent years, particularly in Middle Eastern markets where ground turmeric (also orange) has been sold to unknowing customers for saffron. Some have brought the used stigmas, only to find that they were infused with yellow food coloring and sold at bargain prices.

Although small amounts of saffron are produced in other countries, Spain is the largest producer and the only country that exports saffron to any significant extent. The saffron crocus grows abundantly in the dry, central La Mancha and Valencia regions of Spain. There the crocus plant thrives in tiny arid plots on which nothing else will grow.

The saffron crocus no longer exists in the wild as it does not propagate through seeds. In order to create new plants, two or three cromlets (bulb-like structures on the roots) are separated from the main bulb and replanted. As the plant is very susceptible to disease, the crocus is disposed-of after four harvests and after removal of the new cromlets.

The beautiful, pale purple saffron crocus blooms very briefly in the autumn during about a three-week period. The flowers must be picked immediately upon blooming since they do not close up again, and rough weather can destroy the harvest. In La Mancha and Valencia saffron crocus harvesting is usually a family af-fair, as cultivation of these plants is often a side-line to other farming. Entire families share the tasks of picking the flowers, separating the stigma, and curing and bottling the spice.

Within hours of blooming the stigma must be removed as the flowers deteriorate quickly and this deterioration effects the quality of the saffron. The stigmas are then placed in piles on baking sheets, and put in low-heated ovens. This roasting removes excess moisture and releases the full flavor and aroma of the saffron. As saffron-crocus growing is a cottage industry, most of the roasting is done in small local facilities.

Why is saffron so expensive? It takes two hundred man-hours from planting through curing to produce one pound of saffron. It takes a hundred thousand fresh flowers to produce eleven pounds of fresh stigma, which dry down to 2.2 pounds of saffron. Spanish saffron is considered to be the best. Mostly saffron is sold in gram quantities (there are 28 grams to an ounce) and there are usually forty threads to a gram. Most cooks use just a few threads of saffron per dish.

It is believed that the crocus plant is native to Asia Minor and that saffron was first developed and used in Persia. It was well-known and much-used by the Greeks and Romans.

Saffron grew wild in Italy at one time. However, the Romans, not wanting to work at gathering the flowers, preferred to buy saffron from Greece. Both the Greeks and Romans used saffron as a fumigant, perfume, and bath oil, in addition to its numerous culinary uses. In some cultures saffron continues to be prized for ceremonial foods. In fact the name saffron comes from the Arabic word for yellow. It was also used as a fabric dye.

After the collapse of the Roman Empire saffron cultivation declined sharply, but it still grew wild in Greece and Italy. The less refined civilization that followed the Romans could not be bothered with cultivating a plant that basically gave color to foods and only a little flavor.

The Moors brought saffron to Spain. When the Arabs entered Europe in the eighth and ninth centuries they introduced many new and forgotten food items. They planted saffron primarily in Spain. The word saffron is Arabic, while in Greek it is called crocus.

After its introduction into Spain saffron became popular throughout Europe. During the Middle Ages it was grown as a crop in England for more than three hundred years. There is even a town in western England named Saffron Walden in Essex where saffron buns and teacakes are still very popular. During the Renaissance saffron was very expensive. There were times and places when a pound of saffron would buy a horse.

The industrial revolution and the development of synthetic dyes, as well as changes in food preferences, caused the decline of saffron production. Except on the rocky plateaus of La Mancha and Valencia in Spain, the arrival of other spices from the Far East in the sixteenth century brought an end to major European saffron cultivation,

The Pennsylvania Dutch still grow some saffron for use in many of their dishes. England, Sweden, eastern Europe, southern France, northern Italy, and of course Spain have continued to value saffron as a culinary ingredient. Spanish paella, French bouillabaisse, Italian Risotto, English saffron buns, and Pennsylvania Dutch chicken dishes get extra pizzazz from saffron.

The following Mussel and Saffron Soup is typical of Mediterranean cooking with its inclusion of tomatoes, saffron and thyme.

Mussel and Saffron Soup

2 pounds mussels
3 tablespoons olive oil
2 medium onions, chopped
2 garlic cloves, chopped
1 (14 ounce) can tomatoes, diced
1 teaspoon saffron threads (about 3)
1 sprig fresh thyme, chopped
1/2 cup dry white wine
Salt and pepper, to taste
3/4 cup half and half
2 tablespoons chopped fresh parsley

Rinse the mussels in cold water and scrub each shell well, removing any beard. Place the mussels in a large saucepan and set over high heat for 2 to 3 minutes, or until the shells have just begun to open, but the mussels are still firmly compacted and not fully opened. Discard any mussels that do not open. Remove from heat and rapidly remove the mussels from their shells, straining the mussel liquor into a bowl. Reserve liquid and mussels separately.

Heat the oil in a large saucepan; add the onions and garlic and sauté over medium heat for 5 minutes until soft and lightly colored. Add the tomatoes with their juice, breaking them up with a large spoon. Simmer for 3 minutes.

Add the saffron, thyme, and wine and stir to mix. Then cover and simmer for 5 minutes. Stir in the mussel liquor and season to taste, remembering that mussels are salty.

Five minutes before serving add the mussels and cream to the soup. Stir to mix, then reheat gently without boiling until the mussels are heated through. Sprinkle with parsley. Ladle into heated soup bowls and serve with French bread. Serves 4.

Tabasco Sauce

A Drop or Two Will Do

A drop or two, a dash, or at the most a teaspoon of the sauce that is the best kept secret in the United States enhances many a dish. What would a Bloody Mary, a Creole Gumbo, or even a pot of beans be without a dash of Tabasco Sauce?

Manufactured for more than 125 years on remote Avery Island, 120 miles west of New Orleans in the swampland of Louisiana, Tabasco Sauce has gained an international reputation in more than 100 countries where it is sprinkled on all types of foods from chili to chop suey. The labels for Tabasco Sauce are printed in fifteen languages, and the second biggest users are the Japanese, although half of the sauce's production is sold in the United States.

Tabasco Sauce has been produced by the McIlhenny family since shortly after the Civil War. Shortly before the War, Edmund McIlhenny, a self-made New Orleans banker and founder of the McIlhenny Company, married Mary Eliza Avery, the eldest daughter of a Baton Rouge judge. The Avery family owned a 2300 acre island on which a salt mine was located in the swamp lands of Louisiana.

The salt mine became a strategic target of the Union Army in 1863. They seized it, flooded it, and forced the Avery family to flee the island. When the family returned in 1865, the only thing on the island that had survived was a small Capsicum pepper plant that Edmund McIlhenny had grown from seeds given to him by a friend returning from Mexico.

McIlhenny took the tiny red peppers from the surviving plant and mixed them with Avery Island salt to age. Later vinegar was added and the result was a unique pepper sauce. He poured it into small cast-off cologne bottles and called it Tabasco pepper sauce, after the name of the river and town in southern Mexico from which the peppers originally came. McIlhenny continued to experiment and perfect his sauce. The first year he produced 350 tiny bottles of sauce.

In 1868, McIlhenny obtained a patent for his unique formula. In 1870 he received orders for thousands of bottles of Tabasco Sauce at the unheard of price of $1.00 per bottle. Two years later, he opened an office in London to meet the increasing demand for Tabasco Sauce from European countries.

Succeeding generations of the McIlhenny family have operated the firm and have personally supervised the production of Tabasco Sauce. Family members oversee the planting, the harvesting, the wine-like fermentation of the peppers, the final blending of juices, and the bottling of the sauce.

Today the peppers are still picked by hand as they were a century ago. However, to meet the great demand for Tabasco Sauce, the peppers are now grown in Mexico, Colombia, Honduras and Venezuela. There is not enough acreage or manpower on Avery Island to keep up with the demand for the peppers and consequently the sauce. However, all of the seed used on the contract farms in Latin America comes from Avery Island.

Each spring, seedlings are transplanted from seedbeds to the fields. As the plants develop, each branch becomes almost like Joseph's coat of many colors with beautiful peppers that range from green to yellow to orange to bright red.

Toward the end of the summer only the bright red peppers are picked. This involves many pickings since the peppers do not ripen simultaneously. The freshly harvested peppers must be processed the same day they are picked to retain their flavor. They are ground with a small amount of Avery Island salt and the fresh "mash" is put into white oak barrels for fermentation and aging.

After years of fermentation, the mash is appraised by a member of the McIlhenny family to determine if it is good enough to go into the sauce. The mash that passes the test is blended with high grain, distilled vinegar. The mixture is then gently stirred by hand periodically with wooden paddles for four weeks. The seeds and skins are removed and the resulting sauce is bottled and labeled TABASCO.

In the years since the first production of Tabasco Sauce many recipes have been developed that include either a dash or a teaspoon of it. The Chicken Au Cognac was a particular favorite of Walter McIlhenny, grandson of the founder of the company. Mr. McIlhenny was recognized as an extraordinary gourmet who enjoyed cooking until his death in 1985 at the age of seventy-five.

Chicken Au Cognac

2 whole chicken breasts, cut in half
1 teaspoon Tabasco sauce, divided
Salt, to taste
2 tablespoons vegetable oil
1/2 cup cognac
1 cup thinly sliced onions
2 tablespoons tomato paste
1 can (28 ounces) tomatoes, drained and
  coarsely chopped
1 teaspoon sugar
1/2 teaspoon dried thyme leaves
1/3 cup whipping cream

Season the chicken with 1/2 teaspoon Tabasco sauce and sprinkle with salt, to taste. In a deep skillet heat the oil over medium-high heat. Add the chicken and brown on all sides. Pour the cognac over the chicken and heat it slightly. With a long match, very carefully light the mixture and let it flame. After the flames have died down, remove the chicken and set it aside.

Add the onion to the skillet, and saute it for about 5 minutes or until almost tender. Stir in the tomato paste and cook 1 minute. Add the tomatoes, sugar, thyme and remaining 1/2 teaspoon of Tabasco sauce. Stirring occasionally, bring the mixture to a boil, reduce heat and simmer for 10 minutes.

Return the chicken to the skillet. Cover and cook over low heat 15 to 20 minutes or until the chicken is tender. Remove the chicken to a serving platter and keep it warm. Gradually stir the cream into the sauce mixture and cook over low heat until heated through, but do not let it boil. Serve the sauce over the chicken. Serves 4.

Vanilla

The Flavorfull Bean

Vanilla is one of the most frequently used flavorings in baking. The other is chocolate. Some early food historians claimed that vanilla originated in Africa, while others said Asia. In fact it is a native of the New World. The vanilla plant, a member of the orchid family, originated in southeastern Mexico. It has probably been in use for at least a thousand years.

Its discovery as a flavor is unknown. Some food historians say that the native Mexican Indians observed monkeys chewing fermented ripe vanilla beans. Others contend that some adventuresome native tasted a fermented bean, liked it, and vanilla was incorporated into the tribal diet.

When the Aztecs conquered the native tribes of southeastern Mexico, they found the local Indians processing the beans using crude techniques. The Aztecs were quite enchanted with the vanilla flavor and required that the local tribes grow the beans for them. The beans were then used as a method of paying tribute to the Emperor.

In the beginning, vanilla's role was to enhance the flavor of chocolate. It masked some of the bitterness of the chocolate as no sugar was used with chocolate at that time. The first cup of chocolate given by the Aztec emperor, Montezuma II, to Spanish explorer Cortés in 1520, reportedly was laced with vanilla.

Cortes and his entourage became aware that vanilla was an essential part of the flavoring of chocolat (as the drink was then known). Cortes took some cuttings of the vanilla plant back to Spain and introduced vanilla as a flavoring for chocolate.

During the latter part of the sixteenth century vanilla became quite popular among the royalty and affluent of Europe. In 1602 Hugh Morgan, apothecary to Queen Elizabeth I of England, suggested using vanilla as a flavoring. During the following year, the last year of her life, Elizabeth would only eat and drink foods prepared with vanilla. As a result of this royal patronage, vanilla suddenly grew in demand in England.

When vanilla was first introduced to Europe, it was extraordinarily expensive. Sugar, a white treasure, was selling for as much as $270 per pound (in present dollars). One vanilla bean cost that same amount.

In the 1700s the pressure was on to increase the production of vanilla in Mexico, the only place where it grew at the time. The efforts were hampered by the lack of melipona bees, natives of Mexico, which were the only insects capable of pollinating the vanilla plants.

During the eighteenth century Europeans smuggled vanilla plants out of Mexico and Central America with hopes of growing the vine in Europe or in the tropical colonial outposts of various European countries. Cuttings were started and would grow but seldom flowered and never produced any fruit. It was rumored that there was a curse placed on the plants by Montezuma, and that they would never fruit in areas other than their native habitat.

In the mid-1800s Edmund Albius, a former slave from the island of Réunion (in the West Indian Ocean) came up with a practical version of the process of pollination, which became known as the "mariage de vanille." It consisted of piercing the membrane of the flower of the vanilla plant with a bamboo skewer to collect pollen and transferring it to another flower. This method of pollination had been known and used by the Totonac Indians of Mexico hundreds of years before. With the ability to produce flowering vanilla vines, production increased and the price came down and demand for the beans increased dramatically.

Fortunes were soon made in the growing of vanilla. Vanilla plantations appeared on every island with a warm humid climate and rich soil that the vanilla vine requires.

The vanilla plant is a first cousin of the orchid and the only one of more than twenty thousand orchid varieties that is edible. It takes three years from the planting for the first flowers to appear on the vine.

When it finally does bloom, if not pollinated by that same afternoon, the orchid begins to wilt and by nightfall is dead. The next morning, the process of blossoms begins again and continues every morning for two months. The vanilla vine must be visited daily and the blooms hand-pollinated.

A skilled laborer can pollinate about seventeen hundred blooms a day. The production of vanilla is almost as labor-intensive as that of saffron. Unfortunately the demand for vanilla beans and pure vanilla extract far exceeds the supply and has for centuries.

Unfortunately the pods do not all mature at the same time. Thus each plant must be harvested daily. If a ripe pod is missed and splits open, it cannot be sold whole but is used for extract.

Before the pods can be cured they must be "killed" by either blanching for twenty seconds in hot water or roasted in a slow oven. Then, they go through a fermenting process that takes up to three months.

Finally. the beans are spread on ventilated racks in a storehouse for several months to complete the curing and drying. Just before shipping, the beans are sorted, with the biggest and best saved to be sold whole, the rest used for vanilla extract. The extraction of vanillin from the beans is similar to perking a pot of coffee.

As there is not a great amount of vanilla used in any recipe, I recommend pure vanilla extract or beans. In the following recipe you may use either. Crema Espanola is a light vanilla custard which holds its shape with the addition of gelatin. Top it with fresh berries.

Crema Espanola

1 (2-inch) piece of vanilla bean or
*   1 teaspoon vanilla extract*
2 cups milk
1 envelope unflavored gelatin
1/4 cup cold water
3 eggs, separated
1/3 cup sugar

In a small saucepan, soak the vanilla bean in the milk for 20 minutes. Then heat the milk until bubbles form around the edge. Keep the milk hot.

In a small bowl, sprinkle the gelatin on the cold water and let it soften. In a large bowl with an electric mixer, beat the egg yolks with the sugar until well blended. Remove the vanilla bean from the milk and discard it. While still beating, very slowly add the hot milk to the egg yolks. Transfer the mixture to a saucepan or top of a double boiler and cook until it thickens and barely coats a spoon. Remove from the heat immediately and pour back into the mixing bowl. Add the gelatin, mix well, and let cool. If using vanilla extract, add it at this time. Chill. When the mixture begins to jell, beat the egg whites until stiff and fold them into the mixture.

Pour the Crema into six individual molds or a 1 and 1/2-quart mold and chill until set, at least 3 hours. Turn out the molds and serve with crushed berries. Serves 6.

Herbs

Pungent Leaves

The history of herbs is as benign as that of spices is exciting. In past centuries marching armies have blindly passed fields of wild thyme and other herbs. No nations sent out daring ships in search of basil, although basil is not without a sinister history.

In western society herbs have been used as medicine, food and flavoring, drinks and decoration. They have cured diseases and they have kept away snakes, fleas, witches, and some of the stenches of medieval living.

Basil

One of the oldest member of the mint family, sweet basil is the only one not from the Mediterranean area. It originated in Thailand or India and was brought west by the early traders, first to the Middle east and then to the Mediterranean area. Today there are more than 150 varieties of basil, including purple basil.

According to legend, Helena, the mother of the Roman Emperor Constantine was told in a vision that she would find the sign of the Cross in a place where the air was sweet with perfume. She found it under a patch of basil in Bethlehem, and years later she built a Church near that spot.

Basil was regarded as a sacred plant in India and was used in religious services. The Egyptians also included basil in religious offerings and used it to embalm the dead. The Greeks regarded basil as a sign of mourning.

It was also a sign of love, particularly in the springtime. After her gruesome dance, Salome hid John the Baptist's head in a pot of basil, where she could give it loving care. A similar story about basil exists in Keat's poem, "Isabella."

Basil is related to the mint family. It is a rather pungent herb and has been used in cooking since about 400 B.C. The Greeks used it for seasonings. The Romans included it in their mix of cooking herbs and to flavor sauces.

In the Middle Ages basil became popular in France. In the nineteenth century it was sold in the streets of Paris, although today it is primarily used in southern France. Basil was popular for several centuries in England, but its use has deminished and today is only used today in English turtle soup.

Italians claim that the best basil is grown in Liguria where it became the basis of pesto.

Marjoram and Oregano

There is very little difference between marjoram and oregano and in some Mediterranean cooking they have been used interchangeably. Both are native of the Mediterranean area, but oregano is the hardier of the two, even growing wild in England.

In ancient times marjoram was used in baths, before people stopped bathing in the Middle Ages. Then marjoram became more valued as an air-sweetener, although it was also used in cooking. Stephen, king of England in the early twelfth century created the post of "Strewer of Herbs to his Majesty," His favorite herb was marjoram which continued in favor for centuries until the post of Strewer was eliminated in the twentieth century.

The coronation of James II of England in the middle of the fifteenth century smelled lovely. The Strewer of Herbs had six women scatter eighteen bushels of marjoram and other sweet herbs on the floor under the ceremony.

Today marjoram is primarily used in poultry cooking, and what would pizza be without oregano?

Parsley

Not Just a Pretty Sight

Don't discard that piece of parsley decorating your food, instead eat it. Parsley is loaded with protein, carbohydrates, calcium, phosphorus, iron, vitamin A, thiamin, riboflavin, niacin, and vitamin C.

People of early civilizations considered parsley to be a symbol of joy and festivity. "I'm feeling full of parsley today," they probably said. An English botanist writing in the mid-1500s said that "parsley seeds help those who are light-headed to resist drink better."

For thousands of years parsley has been nourishing man as well as horses. Like so many of our valuable food plants, it originated in the Mediterranean area on the island of Sardinia. From there it spread all over the world and became so common that we hardly appreciate it as a food, seasoning, or decoration.

In ancient Greek times parsley was used as decoration. Homer, the Greek poet, used a combination of parsley and roses as decorations at his banquets. The ancient Greeks did not eat parsley and some regarded it as a symbol of death to be used only in funeral rites.

The ancient Egyptians sprinkled parsley on the graves of their dead. The association of parsley with death continued through Greek and Roman times and for many centuries thereafter. There is an old English proverbial expression "to be in need of parsley," which meant to be at death's door.

The Romans did eat parsley and wore garlands of it at feasts to absorb wine fumes and prevent intoxication. They liked the light, peppery taste of parsley so much that it became a common breakfast food with a piece of bread.

The Romans knew five kinds of parsley and so do we, although they are not the same five.

At that time, Rome was strategically located to receive parsley from all over the Mediterranean region. For years parsley grew wild in southern Europe and northern Africa.

Parsley was grown in Charlemagne's gardens in 800 A.D. as well as in French monasteries during that period. One of the favorite dishes in France in the 1300s was boiled leeks seasoned with parsley.

The curly forms of parsley became popular in medieval England and were associated with many stories of black magic and superstitions, most of which were connected with parsley's reputation for slow germination. The English believed that the parsley seeds had to go to the Devil and back seven times before the plant would grow. They also believed that the plant would only grow successfully where the woman was master of the household and that to transplant it would bring bad luck.

The first sighting of parsley in America is rather confusing. It has been reported that Verrazano, the Florentine navigator, saw parsley growing on the coast of Massachusetts about 1524. Most food historians insist this is not true as parsley is an Old World plant.

However, it could be true. There were Norsemen in the area of Massachusetts five hundred years before Verrazano. There were also Basque fishermen who came from parsley country to the Grand Banks to fish years before Columbus. These fishermen came ashore to dry their catch and could have left a seed or two of parsley.

Unfortunately, there is no written record of parsley being grown in Massachusetts before 1806 when both plain and curled varieties were being cultivated. By 1828 there were three kinds of parsley and by 1881 there were four.

Our five kinds of parsley today are the plain-leafed, the curly-leafed, the fern-leafed, the celery-leafed, and the turnip rooted. Of these the plain-leafed is probably the original form. It is tastier than the curly-leafed, and is therefore extensively grown in Europe, but has almost disappeared commercially in the United States. It seems that in parsley, as in many of our fruits and vegetable, Americans prefer prettiness to tastefulness.

Curly parsley has edged its way into favor because of its decorative quality when used to garnish dishes, from which it is usually pushed aside uneaten. This parsley was hybridized from the plain variety by a Roman botanist as early as 42 A.D.

Fern-leafed parsley was developed by the French and is not grown in abundance anywhere today. Celery-leafed parsley was a Neapolitan discovery and is now commonly known as Italian parsley. It has lighter stalks and a much stronger, sharper flavor.

Turnip-rooted parsley is grown for its foliage and its root, which looks like a small parsnip but tastes like celeriac. It is grown and used primarily in northern Germany and Holland.

Parsley could well be designated as first among leafy seasonings, for whenever a combination of herbs is used, others may be omitted, but parsley. is always included. A "bouquet garni" nearly always starts with parsley. A French "omelette fines herbes" always contains parsley and sometimes only parsley.

The exact taste of parsley is hard to describe. Some say it tastes somewhat like onion, others say licorice, and still others say it has a piney characteristic. Parsley blends well with other seasonings or it can stand along. However, it is seldom used as the sole seasoning in a dish.

One of my favorite dishes using parsley is a pasta dish from Tuscany. The Red, White, and Green Pasta (the colors in Italy's flag) can be served hot or at room temperature. It pairs well with grilled meats. Sprinkling lemon juice over the avocado slices prevents their discoloration and adds to the flavor of the dish. Be sure to use the Italian parsley which is much more flavorful.

Red, White, and Green Pasta

6 ounces fusilli (short twisted pasta)
1 avocado
2 tablespoons lemon juice
1/2 teaspoon chili powder
4 tablespoons olive oil
2 tomatoes, peeled and chopped
3 tablespoons chopped parsley
6 Basil leaves, cut julienne

Cook the pasta in boiling water until al dente.

In the meantime, peel and cut the avocado in slices. Then cut the slices into 1-inch pieces. Place the avocado in a bowl and sprinkle with lemon juice, chili powder and 1 tablespoon of olive oil.

Drain the pasta, place in a bowl, and add the 3 remaining tablespoons of the olive oil. Toss to combine. If serving warm, place the pasta in a warm oven, 150 degrees, for 5 minutes.

Just before serving add the avocado pieces, tomato, parsley, and basil. Toss to combine and serve immediately.

If serving at room temperature, do not place the pasta in the oven, but combine all ingredients with the drained pasta and serve.

Serves 4.

Rosemary

Rosemary is also a native of the Mediterranean region and grows best along the rocky seashore or in an arid area where there is a lot of dew.

At one time rosemary had two symbolic meanings, which were opposites. In Athens and Rome it stood for love, but it also stood for death. Maids of honor carried sprigs of rosemary at weddings, and branches of rosemary were laid on coffins.

In the Middle Ages, rosemary was in great favor as an air purifier and was planted in many private gardens. Sprigs of it were offered to ladies to gain their favor. Some of the other myths about rosemary are that it will ward off evil, stave off nightmares and prevent baldness.

Rosemary became very popular in England in the early 1600s. It was imported from southern Europe and was first used for medicinal purpose, later gaining favor as a food herb.

Some of the foods enhanced by rosemary are lamb, and chicken. In Italy it is frequently sprinkled on focaccia, just before baking this crusty bread.

Sage

Sage is another herb that is native to the Mediterranean area, where it thrives on arid hillsides. There are more than five hundred varieties of sage, including those used only for ornamental purposes.

The ancient Greeks said that sage was the most health-giving herb. Many in the third and fourth centuries believed that it could resuscitate the dead. During the time of the Crusades, sage was thought to ward off snake venom and poison.

During the reign of Elizabeth I in England, sage was used to flavor meat pies. By the early 1700s, sage had lost some of its appeal. However, the English still use sage to flavor their Derbyshire cheese. They also mix the leaves with cottage cheese and use it as a sandwich spread. Sage is used to flavor leek tarts, baked tomatoes, sausage meat and baked beans.

Today the northern Europeans use young sage leaves in salads. They also pickle the leaves and use some of the leaves in dessert fritters. In Provence sage is boiled with chestnuts and is sometimes added to garlic soup.

In the United States, what would Thanksgiving turkey be without a sage stuffing. Sage was a great favorite of the Pennsylvania Dutch who used it in scrapple. Other Germans who settled in Texas used sage in their sausage making. Italian-Americans spread sage on buttered bread and cook white beans with the herb. Although sage is grown in the United States, we import almost two million pounds a year.

Tarragon

Food writers have sung the praises of tarragon as a replacement for salt, pepper, and vinegar. Through the centuries tarragon has been used as a cure for various intestinal ailments.

Tarragon is the only important herb that was unknown to the ancient Greeks and Romans. Its land of origin is not exactly known, but believed to be the steppes of Asia. It was brought to Middle East by the invading Mongols and came to Europe with the Crusaders.

By the sixteenth century, the Europeans found tarragon to be a pleasant addition to salads. The young leaves were also cooked and eaten as a vegetable. Eventually tarragon was used in sauces (Béarnaise and Hollandaise), soups, stews, and salads. It was a good compliment to Romaine lettuce. In the Middle East tarragon was served as an appetizer to welcome a guest to dinner.

Tarragon came to the United States with the French settlers. Thus, today, tarragon is widely used in cooking.by chefs in French restaurant s and by cooks of French extraction.

Thyme

Thyme is almost everyone's friend. It gives a lift to many dishes — meat, fish, cheese, eggs, stuffings, and bland creamy foods. It is the cornerstone of the French bouquet garni.

A native of the Mediterranean area, thyme was used before the Romans by the Summerians, whose civilization dates from 3500 B.C. It is a member of the mint family and has numerous varieties.

The Egyptians used thyme for embalming. The Romans thought that eating thyme would make them brave. In the Middle Ages knights wore scarves on which ladies had embroidered sprigs of thyme. Thyme also dispelled melancholy or depression. Many warriors put thyme among the straw of their beds to give them protection from the enemy.

Thyme was the first herb planted by the colonists in Virginia in 1610, in New Netherlands in 1653, and in gardens of New England in 1672. Some of the crop was reserved for the bees, as thyme was always regarded as excellent raw material for honey. But the kitchen also got its share of thyme for usage in various pot pies and puddings.

In the Shaker communities, the Sisters kept giant vats of thyme-scented lard next to barrels of meat scraps. They transformed these into loaves of head cheese, scrapple, and jellied meat dishes. They also used thyme in their herb dumplings and herbed breads. Thyme has also been used extensively in the cuisine of Louisiana.

Even with warm weather, I usually wait until the 10th of May to plant my herbs so that they will not be killed by a late frost. I am really anxious particularly to plant my basil, as I use it in so many dishes.

Fresh Cream of Tomato Soup

2 tablespoons butter
2 tablespoons olive oil
1 medium onion, chopped
2 medium carrots, chopped
5 large red tomatoes, skinned, seeded,
  and chopped
2 tablespoons chopped parsley
2 long sprigs fresh thyme
  (or 1/4 teaspoon dry)
Salt and pepper, to taste
1 cup cream

Heat butter and oil in a saucepan. Add the onion and carrots, cover and cook over medium-low heat until tender, about 10 minutes. Add the tomatoes, parsley, thyme, and salt and pepper.

Bring to a boil, lower heat, cover and simmer until tomatoes are tender, about 12 to 15 minutes.

Remove from heat. When the vegetables are cool, puree in a food processor or use a hand blender. Return the mixture to the saucepan and set aside until just before serving. Then add the cream and reheat without boiling. Or refrigerate and serve cold. Serves 6.

Nuts

Nuts

The nut has a huge family tree with some branches dating back to prehistoric times. Forty thousand years ago, nuts and fruits were an important part of the diet of early man and a source of oil. Man gathered nuts in the wild long before the advent of agriculture.

Nuts are single-seeded, hard-shelled fruits that have to be cracked to open — for example, chestnuts and hazelnuts. However, the term nut is also used for any seed or fruit with an edible kernel in a hard or brittle shell, such as almonds, walnuts, and coconuts. The peanut also falls in this category, although technically speaking it is a legume.

Long before the advent of flour or cornstarch, pulverized nuts were a thickening agent for sauces and gravies. When animal milk was scarce or unavailable, "milk" was made by soaking ground pulverized nutmeats in water until a milky-looking liquid developed. Several kinds of nut butters long predated our contemporary favorite, peanut butter.

Nuts were used extensively by the Greeks and the Romans, both as food and as a symbol of fertility. As early as the second century sugared almonds were distributed by the Romans on special occasions, such as births and marriages.

In India nuts were a food staple and were converted into flour for fritters and to enrich many dishes. Marzipan, the world's oldest candy is of Arabic-Egyptian origin. Made from pulverized almonds, it has been produced for two thousand years. Nuts such as almonds, pistachios, walnuts, hazelnuts, and pine nuts were part of the foods of ancient Persian and China and appear frequently in the Bible.

Medieval Europe learned to use nuts in cooking from the Arabs, who used them in sauces with meat and poultry as well as in marzipan, nougat, and other sweets. Spaniards, occupied for almost eight centuries by the Moors, adopted the use of nuts in cooking. They brought the technique to the Americas but found the Aztecs were already using pumpkin seeds, peanuts, and possibly pecans, as thickeners for poultry and fish sauces.

Some nuts such as pecans and peanuts, are relative newcomers and were popularized in the United States. The peanut, one of the newest, is not even a true nut, as mentioned earlier. It starts its growth on a small bush and ends it with the pod ripening underground.

Nuts have special affinities to other foods. They go well with grains and fruits. Early in the history of Persia and India, they were part of a popular trio — fruit, nuts, an wine. Indonesian, Far Eastern, and African cooking also contains nuts.

Almonds were used extensively in Scandinavian cooking. Traditionally an almond was insrted into the Christmas Eve pudding. It was a tradition that whoever found it would be the first to get married.

Nuts have been prized for their flavor, crunch, texture, and interesting appearance in primitive cooking as well as in elegant sophisticated haute cuisine. The use of nuts is clearly universal and are present in every aspect of cooking from hors d'oeuvres to desserts.

Almonds

Ancient Nut

The almond is a native of Asia Minor. It was known long before Biblical times and was one of the two nuts mentioned in the Bible -- the other being pistachio. The almond started its westward migration before historic times as evidenced by archaeological findings in Crete and other Mediterranean islands.   In two of its ancient habitats, Israel and Syria, the almond tree is not only prized for its beauty and delicious fruit, but because its blossoms in January are considered a symbol of rebirth.

The Romans were very fond of almonds and indicated the direction from whence this nut came by calling it the "Greek nut." Over the years almonds have become the basis of many modern Italian desserts.

Almonds are also the basis of marzipan (a sweet pliable mixture of almond paste, sugar, and unbeaten egg whites) which originated in Sicily more than two thousand years ago. Through the centuries nobody has surpassed the confectioners of Palermo in modeling and coloring marzipan to make life-like facsimiles of fruit, salami, cheese, and other enticing edible items.

During the Renaissance the Italian banquet tables held centerpieces of elaborate marzipan sculptures. The leading sculptors of the day were commissioned to create these "triumphs of the table," as they were called.

For some unknown reason the migration of almond trees from the Middle East westward bypassed Egypt. However, Egyptians imported almond oil and used it as a cosmetic — a practice that is still being followed today.

Food historians used to believe that almond trees were not planted in France until 1548, but further research has found that Charlemagne (742-814) ordered them grown in this gardens. The first French cookbook, written about 1300, mentions almond milk as a basic sauce ingredient. By the seventh century, the city of Nancy in France was famous for almond macaroons, which were made by an order of nuns who later became known as the Macaroon Sisters

At about this time the English also used almonds in cooking. They tried unsuccessfully to grow almonds along England's southern coast but were finally forced to import them from warmer climates.

The Moors (Arabs) brought cuttings of almond trees to Spain and Portugal when they occupied the Iberian Peninsula in the mid-800s. There is a charming Portuguese legend that tells how almond trees came to that area. It seems that a Moorish prince of the Algarve, the southern part of Portugal, married a Scandinavian princess who wished for the snow of her homeland in this land of eternal sun. Her prince tried to cure her homesickness by thickly planting the entire coast with almond trees, whose white blossoms covered the land each spring with a snow-white blanket.

Almond trees bloom in the very early spring, thus making them vulnerable to spring frosts. In the United States certain varieties of almond trees grow as far north as Ohio and Pennsylvania. Unfortunately the nuts of these trees are of poor quality.

California is American almond country as it provides ninety-nine percent of this country's almond crop — more than two hundred million pounds of shelled almonds annually. Half of all the almonds grown in the world are from California. Thirty percent of our almonds are exported to Europe, even though Italy and Spain produce bumper crops each year for their own use and export.

Today there are trees that bear either bitter or sweet almonds. In Europe, more so than in the United States, almonds are frequently classed as sweet or bitter. Bitter almonds are tastier, but contain prussic acid, which should not be consumed in quantity. in Europe many cooks add a few bitter almonds to the sweet ones in baking to bring out the flavor. Bitter almonds grow primarily in north Africa.

This almond tart is one of the specialities of Santiago in northern Spain. Marzipan is avaiilable in the super markets.

Tart de Santiago

Crust

1 1/2 cups all purpose flour
1 tablespoon sugar
10 tablespoons butter or margarine
1 egg yolk
3 tablespoons ice water

Combine the flour and sugar in a bowl. Cut the butter into small pieces and then cut it into the flour until the mixture resembles coarse bread crumbs. Mix the egg yolk with the water and add it to the flour mixture, a tablespoon at a time. A little more water may be needed to work the dough into a ball. Sprinkle a little flour onto a pastry board and quickly, but gently, knead the dough four or five times to distribute the butter. Wrap the dough in plastic wrap and refrigerate it for at least one hour.

Roll the dough on a floured board to fit a 10-inch tart pan allowing for a 1/2-inch overhang. Press the dough into the tart pan and fold the overhang back under the dough, pressing it into the side of the pan to form a fluted edge. Prick the bottom of the tart and bake in a preheated 375° F. oven for 12 minutes. Remove the tart pan from the oven and allow it to cool slightly while preparing the filling.

Filling

3 1/2 ounces marzipan
9 tablespoons butter or margarine, softened
1/2 cup sugar
4 eggs, separated
7 tablespoons Amaretto
7 ounces almonds, ground
1 cup slivered almonds

Place the marzipan, butter, and sugar in a bowl and with an electric mixer beat the mixture at low speed until well combined. Then beat in 1 egg yolk at a time and the Amaretto. Fold in the ground almonds. Beat the egg whites until stiff and gently fold them into the batter.

Pour the batter into the partially baked tart shell and smooth the top. Sprinkle the slivered almonds on top of the filling. Then bake in a 375° F. oven for 30 to 35 minutes or until a cake tester inserted in the center comes out clean. After 20 minutes of baking, lightly cover the top of the tart with aluminum foil to prevent the almonds from getting too brown. Serves 10 to 12.

Note: The marzipan may be softened in the microwave oven at very low power for about 2 minutes.

Cashews

Kidney-Shaped Nut

There are two well-documented conflicting theories as to the origin of cashews. The dominating theory is that the cashew is a native of Brazil and was distributed by early Portuguese and Spanish explorers. They carried it around the world, particularly to India, where the Portuguese planted them in Goa. Today India is the leading producer of cashews.

The other theory traces the origin in the exact reverse. It claims that the Portuguese found cashews in Asia and brought them to Brazil. These historians claim that the Brazilian name "acaju" is a derivative of the Asian "acajoba."

The cashew tree is highly prized for its nut, fruit, and wood. It grows well in dry areas and is found extensively in the tropics. The cashew tree grows twenty to forty feet in height.

The fruit of the cashew tree, known as the cashew pear or apple, is red, yellow, or sometimes white. The kidney-shaped nuts hang like a multi-pendant from the flower end of this fruit . The cashews are olive colored or almost a greenish-tan. The nuts are housed in a double shell and are cushioned by membranes containing a caustic acid which irritates and burns if touched before the nuts in the shell are treated. The ultra careful harvesting of cashews contributes to their high price.

The next step in preparing the cashews for consumption is roasting, which is done immediately after harvesting. The roasting process dissipates the thick caustic liquid in the shell and makes the nuts safe for handling, shelling, and eating. The plus side of the caustic acid is that it protects the nuts from insects while they hang from the cashew apple. The acid is sometimes used in the manufacture of varnishes and insecticides.

After roasting the second shell is discarded. As cashews do not have an inner skin, they do not need to be blanched.

The cashew nut is about one inch long. It has a sweet, creamy, mild almond-like flavor. Cashew nuts are always shipped shelled because of the safeguard treatment needed for the raw nuts in their shells. They are available raw or roasted, usually the latter.

The cashew apple is eaten as a fruit by the natives where the trees grow. The apples are also fermented to produce a liqueur. In India cashew liqueur and a nut vinegar, called Anacard, are popular. Brazil produces a famous wine from the cashew fruit. The nut yields a light-colored oil popular in the West Indies. It is used to flavor Maderia wine.

Cashews are used extensively in Oriental cooking because of their mealiness, which is enhanced by cooking. This mealiness, however, limits the use of cashews in pastries and cakes. Cashews lack crunchiness which is an attribute of most nuts. Nevertheless they are a desirable nut for eating out-of-hand, salted or unsalted.

Coconuts

Food for Many People

For one-third of the earth's population the coconut is one of the most important foods. It is even more important in the humid and tropical countries than the date is in the arid tropical regions of the world. The coconut is a prominent food in the vast Asian-Pacific region stretching from Thailand to Hawaii. It is also an essential food in West Africa.

The coconut has played a significant role in the lifestyle of the Asia-Pacific region. In Bali, women are forbidden to touch coconut palms because the belief is that the fertility of the coconut palm will be drained off and transferred to the fertility of the woman.

In Thailand, the first solid or semi-solid food a baby is permitted to eat is three spoonfuls of the soft, custard-like meat of an immature coconut. This is fed to the infant by a priest. In the Philippines, rival gangs no longer fight each other for coconut oil, as they used to, but they still commemorate those ancient battles with a dance called "magla-latik."

In Samoa, visitors are told not to pick up a stray coconut along the road. Someone knows it is there and has a right to it. It is believed that if the law does not get the coconut thief, the magical force that protects the fruit will punish the offender by striking him down with lightning or afflicting him with an incurable disease.

"He who plants a coconut tree," according to an old South Sea's saying," plants food and drink, vessels and clothing, a habitation for himself and a heritage for his children."

The origin of the coconut is unknown, although some food historians say that it originated in tropical South America and was carried across the Pacific to the South Sea Islands. Other food historians claim that the coconut originated somewhere in the Indo-Malaysian region. Coconuts float, taking root wherever they happen to be washed ashore.

The coconut was not known to the Western world until about the sixth century A.D. At that time it was eaten in Egypt, as Arab merchants had brought coconuts to Egypt from islands of the Indian Ocean. Nothing else was recorded about coconuts until Marco Polo encountered them in India and Sumatra. He was aware of their Egyptian past, for he called them the "Pharaoh's nut." Magellan (1480-1521) found coconuts growing on the island that is today Guam.

Neither Columbus (1492) nor the explorers who came after him into the Caribbean region found coconuts growing there. However, there were coconut palms in the New World before Columbus. They were on the Pacific side of South America as evidenced from their representation in pre-Columbian-Peruvian pottery. In northern Chile the Indians sweetened their food with boiled-down coconut sap.

Coconuts will grow anywhere in the tropics where temperatures never fall below 68 degree F. and where there is an annual rainfall of fifty to seventy inches. The chief producing areas lie within 22 degrees of the equator.

Coconuts are slow ripeners and take a year to reach full maturity from the time they first take shape. To make up for this slow ripening, ten to thirteen times a year a new flower spike appears from the crown of the tree and develops into another cluster of six to twelve nuts. Coconuts grow in bunches, but ripen one at a time. They fall to the ground when they are fully ripe.

As Vasco da Gama brought the first coconut to Portugal from India in 1500, its present name stems from Portuguese and Spanish, where it was known as "coco," which refers to ghost or bogeyman. The strange appearance of the coconut in its shell with its "eyes" (indentations) might have seemed like a bogeyman to early explorers.

Other historians say that the word coco means grimace, and pushing its meaning even further, monkey. The coconut was so named because it resembles a monkey's face. Another theory is that the Portuguese word for monkey, "macaco." could have some bearing since monkeys were professionally trained to climb the trees to harvest coconuts in Brazil, a Portuguese colony at one time.

The coconut is the same species the world over, except for the "coco de mer." For centuries this coconut was a mystery. It was picked up from time to time at sea or was washed up on beaches in East Africa. The French found these huge coconuts growing only on the island of Praslin in the Seychelles and only in what they named the Vallée de Mer. This valley has been referred to romantically as the Garden of Eden.

The coco de mar, or Maldive coconuts as they are known, are believed to be the largest coconut in the world. They may weigh up to forty-five pounds as compared to an ordinary coconut which weighs three to six pounds. The Maldive coconut takes ten years to ripen. It is sometimes called a double coconut because it is two-lobed as if a pair of coconuts had grown together. In carefree moments the coco de mer is referred to as the "buttocks coconut."

In the tropical areas where the coconut grows, it is often eaten before it fully matures. At the age of six months when the pulp begins to form and the nut is still green its soft flesh can be eaten with a spoon. It has a fresh, fruity flavor, but is too perishable to ship at that point.

In all the diverse cuisines of the vast Asia-Pacific region coconuts are one of the unifying factors in their cooking. Coconut milk is frequently used as the cooking liquid and shavings of the nut are often added as an ingredient or a condiment. The rarest food of the coconut is coconut honey, which is made by bees dividing their time between coconut and banana groves. In Paris, a fourteen-ounce jar of this coconut honey sells for $150.

Although most people use canned or packaged grated coconut when baking a coconut cake, the fresh is more delicate and moister. When using fresh coconuts, it is wise to buy two in case one is not sweet enough. Select large coconuts that are heavy and contain a lot of liquid. You can hear the liquid when you shake the coconut.

Pierce the eyes of the coconut with an ice pick. Then crack the shell in several places, using a hammer or hatchet. But be careful! Pry out the flesh with a blunt knife and pare away the dark skin. Grate the coconut in a food processor or on a grater.

Dried coconut is available in our markets in cellophane packages or in sealed cans, sweetened or unsweetened. The domestically processed is usually sweetened and is labeled "southern style." It is exceptionally moist and most closely resembles fresh coconut. Coconut milk is available in cans.

Fresh coconuts are available in most supermarkets and health food stores. They are seldom seen with their outer husk except during the Christmas holidays.

Hazelnuts

Divining Rods

The name hazelnut and filbert are used for the same nut, with hazelnut being preferred. At one time the English referred to this nut as filbert if it was a long nut, cobnut if it was of medium length, and hazelnut if it was short and round.

The hazel tree is a bushy shrub dating back to 4500 B.C. It is said to have mysterious legendary qualities. The words "hazing" and "hazy" are supposed to be derived from this tree. A Y-shaped branch of the hazel tree, grasped by hand at each end with the point kept toward the ground, is the divining rod of classical history. It was thought to find hidden springs and locate water that no one could have dreamed existed.

A hazel rod was used by Moses to smite rocks to bring forth water. Medieval sorcerers were never without their hazel wand. In recent history, its most famous role has been as an integral part of the caduceus of Mercury. This hazel branch is entwined with two serpents and is the well-recognized symbol of the medical profession.

Hazelnuts were the second most widely eaten nuts in the Stone Age — acorns being the first. According to a manuscript found in China dating back to about 3000 B.C., the hazelnut was classified as one of five sacred nourishments the Deity bestowed on mankind. In classical times, the Greeks used hazelnuts for a variety of medicinal purposes. Both the Greeks and Romans cultivated hazelnut trees.

During the Middle Ages the Europeans gathered wild hazelnuts and used them to make puddings. In the New World pre-Columbian Indians were making crisp cakes of cornmeal flavored with pounded hazelnuts.

American wild hazelnuts were inferior in quality to those of Europe. In the 1700s European hazel trees were transplanted to the eastern United States where wild hazel trees were doing well. However, the transplanted hazel trees did not flourish.

Ninety-eight percent of the hazelnuts used in this country are now grown in Oregon. The first American hazelnut trees were planted in 1858 in Scottsburg, Oregon, by David Gernot, a Frenchman. When he arrived in the lush Willamette Valley, he found it very similar to his native Loire Valley in France. Gernot planted the fifty young hazelnut seedlings he had brought with him, and from these trees a major agricultural commodity developed in Oregon. Today, there are more than 1,100 hazelnut growers in the state.

Unlike other nut trees, hazelnut trees bloom and pollinate in mid-winter. Nuts begin to form in June, then mature, and are harvested in the early fall. After the nuts have fallen to the ground, mechanical harvesters sweep the nuts into boxes. They are then picked up by another machine and taken to processing plants.

Hazelnuts are used to a greater extent in European cuisine than in American. Green, unroasted, hazelnuts are frequently added to salads in Europe. Toasted hazelnuts are used extensively in tortes, pastries, and cookies. They have a natural affinity to chocolate. In France *beurre de noisette*, a hazelnut butter is used to season vegetables and meat.

Macadamia Nuts

Major Hawaiian Crop

Production of macadamia nuts last year in the State of Hawaii exceeded 100 million pounds, with most being grown on the Big Island. This nut is the third largest agricultural commodity in Hawaii and acreage continues to expand.

The macadamia nut, was first brought to Hawaii from Australia in 1881 by William H. Purvis, a Hawaiian sugar-plantation owner. However, the first commercial trees were not planted until 1949. Since it takes seven years from the planting for the grafted tree to bear its first crop, the first macadamia were not commercially harvested until 1956. Macadamia trees do not reach full production until they are at least 15 years old.

Today, there are more than nine hundred macadamia nut growers in Hawaii, making the state the world's leader in both the growing and processing of these nuts. The leading processor is C. Brewer and Co., which has been marketing these nuts under the Mauna Loa brand from their plant outside of Hilo on the Big Island.

The macadamia nut grows on an evergreen tree that can easily reach forty feet in height and width, has bright green foliage, and likes a lot of moisture. The tree flowers in the early spring with long racemes of creamy white flowers that hang down like tassels from the tree's branches. Although there can be several hundred flowers on a raceme, very few set fruit.

The macadamia tree need not be shaken as the nuts fall to the ground naturally. On the tree the macadamia nut is encased in a thick green-colored leathery husk. At maturity the husk falls to the ground and splits open, thereby exposing the hard-shelled nut. The nuts start falling from the tree in late July, and harvesting continues until the next March. To avoid mildew the husks must be removed promptly. On the larger plantations the shells are cracked by machine in the field, and then the nuts are sent to the processing plants.

The nuts in the shell are small, shaped like a marble, and have a smooth brown cover. The harvested nuts are first husked, then dried and cured. This is to separate the kernel from the shell, making it possible to shatter the shell without damaging the nut. It takes three hundred pounds per square inch of pressure to break the shell.

After shelling, the nuts are color-sorted electronically to select the light, uniformly colored ones to be roasted. Only the perfect nuts are roasted and lightly salted for retail distribution. Others are set aside for commercial use. Most of the macadamia nuts are sold to tourists. They are very expensive, ranging from $15 to $20 per pound.

Macadamia nuts enhance this easy-to-prepare ice cream dessert.

Macadamia Ice Cream Delight

1 1/4 cups plain chocolate wafer crumbs
1/2 cup butter, melted
1/2 gallon chocolate ice cream
1 1/2 cups chopped macadamia nuts

Mix the chocolate crumbs and butter thoroughly. Press the mixture into a 13x9x2-inch baking pan. Cut the ice cream in 1 and 1/2-inch thick slices. Lay the slices close together over the crumb crust, blending slices together with a knife as ice cream melts slightly until it is spread evenly over the entire pan. Top with nuts. Freeze for 2 hours. Cut in squares and serve. Serves 8.

Peanuts

Ground Nuts

Peanuts originated in Peru, according to historians who have excavated pottery of that area dating back 3500 years. Jars found in Inca graves were made in the shape of peanuts. Drawings of peanuts also decorated these ancient containers. Portuguese explorers in the sixteenth century found peanuts growing wild in Brazil.

By the time the Spanish began their explorations of the New World, peanuts were being grown as far north as Mexico. The explorers took peanuts back to Spain from where traders took them to Africa and Asia. In Africa the natives regarded the peanut as a sacred symbol. They believed it possessed a soul.

The African slaves brought peanuts with them to the South. One of the earliest documented records of peanuts being grown in the United States dates from 1791 when Thomas Jefferson recorded he cultivated them. Records also indicate that peanuts were commercially grown in South Carolina by 1800.

The Civil War increased commercial production of peanuts as they were used for food by the northern and southern soldiers. By 1900 peanuts were being eaten regularly as snacks as well as a basic food ingredient. Soon thereafter, equipment was invented to plant, cultivate, harvest, shell, and clean the nuts. With mechanization, peanuts came into great demand for oil, peanut butter, candy, and snack food.

Development of large-scale peanut production techniques is credited to the famous botanist, Dr. George Washington Carver, at Tuskegee Institute. At the turn of the century cotton crops in Georgia and the South were being destroyed by the boll weevil and the land had been stripped of its nutrients by the continuous planting of cotton. Dr. Carver proposed that the southern farmers turn to other crops, especially peanuts. In order to encourage peanut production he invented 300 usages for the nut from oils to soups to ice cream.

The peanut is an unusual plant because it flowers above ground, but its fruit is created below the ground. Peanut seeds grow into small green bushes about eighteen inches tall that develop delicate yellow flowers. As the flowers begin to lose their petals, "pegs" begin to develop which eventually drop down into the soil. These pegs or embryos turn horizontal to the soil and mature into a peanut. It takes four to six months. depending on the variety, to plant and harvest a crop of peanuts. Since peanuts grow underground they have also been called "ground nuts."

Today peanuts are planted and harvested with special machinery. The peanut seeds are planted in rows, usually in sandy soil. When the plant has matured and the peanuts are ready for harvest, a mechanical digger is driven up and down the rows. The mechanical digger's long blade cuts the tap root, lifts the plant from the soil, shakes the dirt from the peanuts, and lays the plant back down in rows, peanuts up. The peanuts are left on top of the rows for two days to dry. Then a mechanical combine drives over the rows, lifts the plants, separates the nuts and blows them into a hopper at the top of the machine. The peanuts are then dumped into wagons and dried with forced hot air.

The individual farmers sell their peanuts to peanut buying stations where the nuts are stored. The peanuts are cleaned, sized, and some are sold in the shell. The shell is corrugated-looking, straw colored, and soft. When the nuts are roasted in the shells, the salt is easily absorbed into the kernels. The smaller peanuts are shelled, graded and then the skins are removed by blanching in a water or steam bath.

Half of all edible peanuts consumed in the United States are used to make peanut butter. It was in 1890 that a doctor in St. Louis, looking for a high-protein food that could easily be digested by his patients, tried an experiment. He put roasted shelled peanuts and some salt through a meat grinder. The result was peanut butter. Soon hospitals were serving it for ailing and undernourished patients. In the 1920s peanut butter emerged from the health food category into the popular spread.

In the Orient peanuts are used in soups, sauces and to accompany curry. Indonesia has its peanut specialty, saté, which consists of pieces of grilled meat with a peanut sauce. Peanuts are often sprinkled on top of a finished dish. Peanut meal and flour are used by bakers and candy-makers, and the peanut has even become a coffee substitute. Whole nuts and less desirable parts of peanuts are used as animal food. Hams from peanut-fed pigs have a sweeter taste and command a higher price.

The following recipe for Chicken in Peanut-Tomato Sauce has a sweet and sour flavor as well as the spiciness of chili powder. Serve this chicken dish with rice and a green vegetable. The Peanut Soup is a traditional Virginia dish often served in Williamsburg.

Chicken in Peanut-Tomato Sauce

1 (3 to 3 1/2 pound) frying chicken, cut-up
Salt and pepper
2 tablespoons vegetable or olive oil
1 medium onion, chopped
1 clove garlic, chopped
1/2 cup chopped green pepper
1/4 cup peanut butter
1 can (8 ounces) tomato sauce
1/3 cup dry white wine

1/3 chicken broth
1 tablespoon sugar
1 tablespoon vinegar
1 teaspoon chili powder

Wash and dry chicken and sprinkle with salt and pepper. Melt the oil in an oven-proof skillet, add the chicken pieces and brown them on both sides. Remove the chicken and add the onion, garlic, and green pepper. Sauté until the onion is lightly browned. Blend in the remaining ingredients and add the chicken pieces. Cover and bake in a preheated 325° F. oven for 50 minutes. Serve chicken with the sauce. Serves 4.

Peanut Soup

4 tablespoons butter or margarine
1/3 cup very finely minced onion
1/3 cup very finely minced celery
1 1/2 tablespoons all-purpose flour
1 cup smooth peanut butter
5 cups chicken broth
1/2 cup half and half
Salt and pepper, to taste
1/4 cup chopped peanuts, for garnish

Melt the butter in a large saucepan over medium-low heat. Add the onions and celery and sauté until soft, but not brown. Stir in the flour and blend until smooth. Lower heat to simmer and stir in the peanut butter. Slowly add the chicken broth, bring to a slow boil, and simmer the soup for 20 minutes. Add the half and half and heat the soup just to the boiling point. Add salt and pepper, to taste. Ladle the soup into bowls and garnish each serving with some chopped peanuts. Serves 4 to 6.

Pecans

A Southern Nut

The pecan is strictly an American nut. It is a species of the hickory nut family, whose existence goes back to early man.

Pecans are the fruit of a big tree that originally grew wild throughout the Mississippi Valley and the river valleys of its tributaries. The tree is also found in the river valleys in Texas and northern Mexico. The pecan tree is the largest of its species and is often 150 feet in height and its trunk up to eight feet in diameter. Mature trees can yield up to six hundred pounds of nuts annually.

Long before the advent of the European explorer, Indian tribes used pecans as food, even making flour from the nuts to thicken stews. They also pressed oil from the nuts and seasoned cooked fruits with it. The Indians carried roasted pecans with them on hunting trips as a quick energy "pick-me-upper." The word pecan is an Indian word that appears in varied forms in all the Indian languages where wild pecan trees once grew.

Although many pecan trees are still wild in the South, today the cultivated pecan industry is centered in Georgia, Texas, and Southern California. There are no records as to when domestic cultivation of the pecan started. George Washington planted them at Mount Vernon in 1775, as he had been given some trees by his friend, Thomas Jefferson. More than 300 varieties of pecans have been propagated from wild seedlings.

The shell of the pecans are smooth and the nuts in the shells are oblong-shape. They are brown and have a thin, clinging inner skin, which is not easily removed. Various species of pecans range in shape and color, from long and pointed to almost rectangular. For marketing purposes some of the shells are artificially colored a reddish brown and even polished. The shells range from being very hard to "paper-shelled," the latter are often a grayish beige or tan.

The shell of the paper-shell variety is especially easy to crack, although all varieties of pecans crack easily. They can come out of their shell whole with a thin layer of brown fibrous material between the two halves. When this inedible material is removed, the pecan becomes two halves — frequently perfect halves. When sold the halves are graded and priced according to size.

The pecan has a very sweet, oily, rich-tasting meat and a warm, lovely brown color. The pecan tree is considered the most valuable of the nut trees in the United States, for the wood is used extensively in furniture.

Pecans are delicious right our of the shell and are prized for their taste and texture in cakes and candies. They are also used in all kinds of cooking, whether in halves, chopped, ground, and/or roasted.

While the pecan does not have as glamorous or romantic history as other nuts, the name pecan has a aura of its own, conjuring up visions of southern dishes. A delicious nut, sweet and yet mild, it blends in and enhances many foods without dominating them. Its fame as part of pecan pie and New Orleans's famous praline family has endeared it to Americans.

In recent years there have been numerous variations of the time-honored southern pecan pie. Some include bourbon, others have chocolate added to the custard, and others place the pecans on the bottom with a chocolate mixture on top. This traditional Pecan Pie is a little less sweet and includes more pecans than most modern recipes. The richness of this less sweet filling is due to the use of some brown sugar.

Pecan Pralines

2 cups sugar
1/2 cup light corn syrup
1/2 cup water
2 cups pecan halves
1/4 cup (4 tablespoons) butter
1 tablespoon vanilla extract

Heat the sugar, syrup, water and pecans in a saucepan until the sugar is dissolved. Bring the mixture to a boil, stirring occasionally, until it reaches the soft ball candy stage (240° F. on a candy thermometer). Remove the saucepan from the heat and add the butter and vanilla.

Let the candy cool. Whip by hand until the mixture gradually changes to an opaque color and becomes creamy. Drop by tablespoons onto a buttered cookie sheet and allow to harden. Makes 2 dozen.

Pecan Pie

4 tablespoons butter or margarine, at room
  temperature
1/4 cup sugar
1/4 cup light brown sugar
1 cup light corn syrup
3 eggs
1 1/2 cups pecan halves
Pastry for 9-inch pie (recipe follows)

Cream the butter and the two sugars in a medium-size bowl until light and fluffy. Add the corn syrup and beat well. Then add the eggs, one at a time, beating well after each addition. Fold in the pecans.

Pour the filling into the prepared pie shell and bake in a preheated 350° F. oven for 50 minutes, or until a knife inserted halfway between the center and the outside of the filling comes out clean. Serves 6 to 8.

Pastry

1 cup all-purpose flour
3 tablespoons butter or margarine
3 tablespoons solid vegetable shortening
3 to 4 tablespoons ice water

Place the flour in a bowl. With a pastry blender cut in the butter and shortening until the solids are the size of very small peas. Fluff the mixture with a fork. Add the ice water, one tablespoon at a time, tossing the mixture with the fork until the dough sticks together and can be formed into a ball. Wrap the dough in plastic wrap and place in the refrigerator for at least one hour.

Remove dough from the refrigerator, place on a floured board, and roll 1 inch larger in diameter than the top surface of the pie pan. Place dough in pie pan; crimp the edges.

Pine Nuts

From Pine Cones

The pine nut is the fruit of the pine tree. The very small nuts inside the pine cone have a smooth, brown shell. When harvesting these nuts the cones are often heated to spread their scales so that the nuts can be easily dislodged.

The pine nut comes in many sizes and shapes and has a variety of names. The nut is white and is smaller than a tiny white bean. It varies between a quarter and three-quarters inch in length and can be compared to a single kernel of puffed rice, only solid. It has no inner skin. The largest pine nuts come from the Araucanian pines of Brazil and Chile. They often grow to two inches in length.

The tall stone pine of Italy furnishes most of the pine nuts for that country's domestic market and also for export to many parts of the world. France is also a large exporter of pine nuts, as well as a user in its haute cuisine. In France these nuts are known as pignolias.

Among the Indians and Mexicans, pine nuts are known as pinons or pignolas, Indian nuts, or stone nuts. These names are applied to a variety of nuts from all species of pine trees. They are described as stone nuts in the Bible and as coming from the green fir tree.

The ancient Greeks added pine nuts to their grape leaf recipes for flavor to complement the lamb filling and for thickening.

When the colonists arrived in the United States, they found most Indian tribes using pine nuts as a salted, roasted snack and food staple. The Indians also used them in soups, meat dishes, for flour, and for baby food. Pine nuts are now frequently a part of South American and Mediterranean cooking.

The Italians fry pine nuts in butter as an appetizer and also use them in fish and meat dishes. In China, the city of Soochow specializes in pine nut confections. The nuts are made into a brittle with caramelized sugar.

The pine nut is sweet and only slightly mealy. Pine nuts are sold shelled. Although they are expensive, they are very light in weight.

Pine nuts abound in Mediterranean cooking as in this pasta dish from Tuscany.

Pasta with Eggplant and Pine Nuts

2 (16 ounce) eggplants, cut into inch cubes
2 tablespoons olive oil
1 medium onion, chopped
2 garlic cloves, minced
3/4 cup pine nuts, toasted
3/4 cup dried currants
1/2 cup drained capers
2 (14 ounce) cans diced tomatoes
Salt and pepper, to taste
1 pound fusilli pasta
1 cup freshly grated Romano cheese
3/4 cup chopped fresh basil

Place the eggplant cubes in a colander. Sprinkle with salt and mix. Let stand 20 minutes. Rinse, drain, and pat the eggplant dry.

Heat the olive oil in a large skillet over medium-high heat. Add the onion and sauté until golden, about 4 minutes. Add the garlic and sauté 1 minute. Add the eggplant and sauté until tender, about 10 minutes. Stir in the pine nuts, currants, and capers; sauté 1 minute. Add the tomatoes with juices and bring to a simmer. Season to taste with salt and pepper.

Meanwhile, cook the pasta in a large pot of boiling water until al dente. Drain. Return the pasta to the pot and add the eggplant mixture, 1/4 cup of cheese, and basil. Toss to combine. Transfer to a large bowl. Serve and pass the remaining cheese separately. Serves 6 to 8.

Pistachios

Appealing Color

The pistachio nut is probably the most elegant of all the nuts. The name alone has an exotic connotation of a special food. Its green beauty adds to its distinctiveness, although some pistachios are creamy yellow in color, particularly those from Iran.

Food historians say that pistachios were in existence 20,000 years ago and made their way from Persia to China at that time. Archeological excavations in Iraq have revealed pistachio nuts from 6750 B.C. No one paid attention to pistachios again for more than three centuries when there was a shortage of food in the Middle East and the populace turned to lesser important fare. At the time almonds were considered superior as food.

Pistachios were grown in the hanging gardens of Babylon in about 700 B.C. The Bible mentions pistachios in the Old Testament as the nuts referred to by Jacob. Many of the rocky parts of Lebanon and Israel are still planted with pistachio trees.

At the beginning of the Christian Era, pistachios were introduced to Mediterranean Europe as green almonds. They were brought to ancient Rome at about 50 A.D.

The Arabs were introduced to pistachios by the Persians who used them lavishly in their cuisine, particularly ground ones to thicken sauces. The Greeks prized pistachios and believed that they were not only delicious as appetizers, but also were an effective way of promoting the desire for drink. In Rome the nuts were layered in special pâtés. Eye-catching Persian pilafs were studded with whole pistachio nuts. Even today some of the world's finest ice creams contain whole pistachios.

The Arabs introduced pistachios to the lands they conquered between 700 and 1100 A.D., such as Sicily, parts of North Africa, and the Iberian Peninsula. They were used sparingly in Sicily and Spain due to their cost. Chefs preferred the less-expensive almond.

In the Middle Ages in Europe pistachios were ground and mixed with cereal. Pistachios were also preferred for nut butter over other nuts because of their lovely color. Pistachios are still a favorite of the Italians. Much of that country's pistachio crop is grown on the slopes of Mt. Etna in Sicily.

Pistachio nuts were introduced in the United States through vending machines. Red pistachios were conceived by vendors as a colorful and appealing snack. As the cuisine of this country became more sophisticated in the 1970s, natural pistachios were preferred and used in a variety of dishes.

Native to Asia and Asia Minor, pistachios are cultivated in the warm arid countries of the Mediterranean and California. Pistachio cultivation started in this country in the late 1960s in California. It is the only state where the tropical pistachio tree will grow. Florida is warm enough for pistachios, but has proved to be too humid. Although California production of pistachios has increased in recent years, many of the nuts consumed in America are still imported from Italy and Turkey.

Pistachios grow on a small, 20-foot tall, deciduous tree. In their natural state, the nuts come from the tree in a gummy husk, which is removed by a special soaking process. In this crude state, they can be kept safely for two years, but they are not exported this way. Pistachios do not leave their native habitat until they are out of the husks and roasted in their shells. They are sold mostly in the shell.

Prized for its looks, taste, and texture, the pistachio is equally at home in simple sausages and elegant baked goods. French pâtés are more desirable when pistachios are included. The pistachio adds luster wherever it is used and is truly a nut of distinction.

This easy-to-prepare Pâté may be served as an hors d'oeuvre at a cocktail party or as a first course at a dinner party. Penne with Pistachios is of Sicilian origin.

Vineyard Pâté

2 tablespoons olive oil
1 onion, chopped
3/4 cup brandy
2 garlic cloves, chopped
1/2 teaspoon salt
1/2 teaspoon pepper
1 teaspoon thyme
1/4 teaspoon sage
1/8 teaspoon nutmeg
1/4 teaspoon allspice
3/4 pound ground pork
1/2 pound ground veal
1/4 pound ground ham
2 eggs, lightly beaten
3/4 cup chopped pistachios
8 to 10 thin slices of bacon

Heat the oil in a skillet over medium heat. Add the onions and sauté them until lightly golden. Remove the onions to a large bowl. Add the brandy to the skillet and simmer on low heat until reduced to 1/3 cup. Pour the brandy into the bowl with the onions and add the garlic, salt, pepper, thyme, sage, nutmeg, and allspice. Then add the meats and the eggs. Add the nuts and mix well.

Line an 8-inch loaf pan with the bacon slices, arranging them crossways so that the ends will overhang the sides of the pan. Spoon the meat mixture into the pan, smoothing out the top. Fold the bacon ends over the meat.

Place the pan in a 13x9x2-inch pan and add water to come up 1 and 1/2 inches on the loaf pan. Bake in a preheated 350° F. oven for 1 and 1/2 hours or until the center of the pâté registers 180° degrees on a meat thermometer.

Remove the loaf pan from the water and pour off any liquid that has accumulated on the pâté. Cover it with aluminum foil and place a smaller pan filled with heavy objects such as a brick on top. Chill the pâté overnight and then slice and serve with French bread and cornichons (small pickles). Serves 8 to 10.

Penne with Pistachios

3 tablespoons butter
2 tablespoons olive oil
1 medium onion, finely chopped
3/4 cup coarsely ground pistachio nuts
1 cup heavy cream (or half and half)
Freshly ground pepper
8 ounces penne
Freshly grated Parmesan cheese

Place the butter and oil in a medium skillet over medium heat. Add the onion and sauté until the onion is translucent. Then stir in the ground pistachios and add the cream. Season with pepper to taste. Bring the cream to a boil and then simmer the sauce until thickened, about 5 minutes.

While the sauce is simmering, cook the penne in boiling salted water until al dente. Drain and add pasta to the skillet with the cream sauce, mixing well to coat the pasta with the sauce. Sprinkle with Parmesan cheese and serve immediately. Serves 6 as a first course.

Walnuts

Historic Nut

The Persians and Phoenicians used walnuts for barter. The Greeks dedicated the walnut to the goddess Diana, whose feasts were held beneath walnut trees. There are many myths about the magical properties of walnuts and the walnut tree. It was believed that both could cure or at least ward off diseases. Because walnuts were thought to make a couple fertile, they were strewn at wedding parties. The Bible refers to walnuts growing in King Solomon's garden. Today walnut trees grow profusely in Israel.

For the ancient Romans the walnut was a portrait of the human brain. The outer green husk, which we usually do not see, was likened to the scalp. The hard shell of the walnut was considered the protective skull while the thin, paper-like, skin inside the shell with its cardboard-like partition between the two halves, was the membrane. The convoluted nut represented the two hemispheres of the brain.

The Romans concluded that eating walnuts would cure headaches. This theory was believed for many centuries as people thought that the shape of a plant was a signal from nature to man as to the purpose the plant or food could serve. During the Middle Ages, however, the interpretation was reversed and walnuts were said to cause headaches.

The history of the walnut goes so far back that nobody knows where it originated. Some food historians claim it is a native of Persia as ancient Roman writings call it the Persian.

The walnut probably originated somewhere in the Middle East. Walnuts growing in the wild were in evidence from southeastern Europe to Asia Minor. They even grew in the Himalayas at 8,000 foot elevation.

The first historic reference to walnuts is from Babylon in the fifth century B.C. The ancient Greeks, in about the fourth century B.C., pressed walnuts for their oil. Records show that a century later the Romans paid high prices for walnuts and they were served by the nobility along with fruit for dessert.

Excavations at Pompeii show that some of the populace had reached the last stage of their meal on that bright sunny day of August 24, 79 A.D. when Vesuvius erupted, as evidenced by nuts preserved on the table.

The Romans are credited with spreading the walnut to the rest of Europe. However, some historians say that walnuts were being eaten in Switzerland in the Stone Age, long before the Romans invaded Middle Europe. There is also the theory that the Romans brought the walnut to England, but the first record of walnuts in the British Isles date one thousand years after the Romans departed.

The word walnut comes from the Old English "Walh-hnuta," meaning foreign nut. Today we refer to this nut as the English walnut. Except for use as an accompaniment to port and Stilton cheese, walnuts were not used extensively in England until after World War I when they were commercially produced domestically for the first time.

On the European continent only the rich could afford cultivated walnuts until the early 1900s. The poor were forced to gather wild ones. During medieval times wild nuts, including wild walnuts, were often the only food for much of the European populace.

In the Middle Ages many of the chefs serving the nobility used finely ground nuts to thicken stews and soups. The Arabs who occupied Spain in the ninth and tenth century introduced this method of cooking with the lavish use of almond-flavored sauces. Cooks in Northern Europe used walnuts, as almonds were only available in the warm climates where they grew.

There are more than fifteen species of walnuts, one of which is native to North America — the black walnut. Archeological finds in the upper Great Lakes area have shown that the Indians had been eating black walnuts since at least 2000 B.C. They used both the nut and the tree's sap in their cooking.

The early English settlers had to depend on the native black walnut because the English walnut tree seedlings they planted did not adapt to the new environment. Despite its availability, the black walnut did not and does not have as pleasing a taste when eaten raw. However, it retains more of its flavor when cooked. The greatest obstacle to the black walnut is its tough outer and inner shell.

The Franciscan fathers brought the English walnut trees to the shores of California in the early 1700s from Mexico. Through their efforts, walnut trees were planted in the courtyards of the California missions where they flourished. It was about 150 years later when walnut trees became a commercial entity in California and Oregon. Today California produces 98 percent of all the walnuts grown commercially in this country.

Walnut trees are prized for their beauty and majesty as well as their tasty nuts. They bloom in May and small fruits appear in July. The wood of the walnut tree is used to make fine furniture. Many European countries produce a fine liqueur from walnuts. Walnut oil is especially prized in Germany and Switzerland. The oil is used in the production of paints because it promotes fast drying.

The nut or kernel of the walnut has a tightly attached inner covering or skin, which is brown and somewhat wrinkled. The nutmeat is cream colored. Its wheat-colored hard outer shell is further covered in the growing stages by a heavy rubbery green husk, known as the shuck. The shell itself is partially bisected and appears to be in two parts, but the parts are not separated.

Today walnuts can be found as an ingredient in all types of cooking. Walnut-stuffed chicken is an Italian specialty while in China walnuts are often added to stir-frys. In Eastern Europe walnuts are combined with cucumbers in a cold soup. In the Middle East walnuts are often used in a lamb stew along with pomegranate juice and cardamom. Walnuts are particularly delicious as a spiced appetizer and as a sugared sweetmeat after dinner.

Walnut Pie is a variation of the traditional pecan pie, but has a less-sweet taste.

Walnut Pie

Pastry for a single 9-inch pie (see p, 229)
4 tablespoons butter or margarine, at room
temperature
1/4 cup sugar
1/4 cup light brown sugar
1 cup light corn syrup
3 eggs
1 teaspoon vanilla
1 1/2 cups walnut pieces

Cream the butter and the two sugars in a medium-size bowl until light and fluffy. Add the syrup and beat well. Then add the eggs, one at a time, beating well after each addition. Add the vanilla and fold in the walnuts.

Pour the filling into the prepared pie shell and bake in a preheated 350° F. oven for 50 minutes, or until a knife inserted halfway between the center and the outside of the filling comes out clean. Serves 6 to 8.

Pulses, Cereals, and Pasta

Pulses, Cereals, and Pasta

Pulses

Pulses are the edible seeds of certain plants of the legume family. They include beans, peas, and lentils. Some, such as green beans, fava beans, lima beans, and green peas are eaten fresh, although lima beans are also dried. Others are eaten dried and in that form have been a staple food in many parts of the world for thousands of years.

Archeological research into plant origins has shown that beans were among the first plants cultivated when agriculture began. The common bean, which includes the kidney bean and its many varieties such as pinto and black beans, was first cultivated in Mexico. Lima beans were first cultivated in Peru and chickpeas, which are really beans, in the Middle East. Black beans have their origins in Africa.

Through the years pulses have remained popular in the cooking of the Middle East, Asia, the Caribbean, Mexico, and Central and South America. In America and Europe there is a renewed interest in them due to the high cost of meat and an increasing popularity of vegetarian cooking. Pulses can serve as a substitute for meat as they are also high in protein.

Cereals

Cereals are actually the fruit (seeds) of cultivated grasses. Cereals, also called grains, are named after Ceres, the Roman goddess of agriculture. They comprise edible grains such as wheat, rice, and corn, as well as foods prepared from these grains.

When agriculture, first started by women, began in the Middle East and Central and South America in about 7000 B.C., cereals were a prominent part of the diet. Wheat and barley were the crops of the Middle East and corn in the Americas. Rice has supported the life of populations in the Far East.

The starchy carbohydrates of cereals are essential to humans. Rice, being high in starch, is a staple food for half of the world's population. The other half consume wheat, oats, corn, barley, millet, and other grains. These cereals contain both carbohydrates and proteins in varying amounts, the basic elements required by the body.

Pasta

The word pasta simply means dough. It is the staple diet of Italy and is essential to the Italian kitchen. In Italian cuisine, pasta is far more popular than its rivals — bread, polenta (made from corn meal), and rice. Pasta falls into two categories — dry pasta, usually sold in packages, and fresh pasta made with flour and eggs in individual kitchens to be consumed immediately.

Dried Beans

A Wide Variety

Dried beans are a gourmet's delight and a budget-conscious cook's best friend. They can be used as a main dish or in a casserole, soup, or salad. Almost every country in the world has a favorite dried bean dish. For centuries beans have been the principal ingredient in delicious French cassoulets, Italian bean soups, Greek bean stews, Spanish rice and bean combinations, Boston baked beans, chili, and Mexican refried beans.

Historically, beans have become a source of energy and a cooking ingredient dating back to prehistoric times. Historians report that American beans date back 7,000 years, while the Asian soybean has only been cultivated for 4,000 years. Fava beans, Italian favorites, have been found in Stone Age and Bronze Age archaeological digs, in the ruins of Troy and Rome, as well as in the tombs of ancient Egypt.

Just as with grains, the bean was critical to the evolution of prehistoric tribes from a hunting society to that of an agricultural one. It took vast areas of land to feed one prehistoric family by hunting, while a much smaller area of land planted with beans could feed multitudes. There was also an added advantage in bean cultivation as it returns nitrogen to the soil, which allowed crops to flourish year-after-year.

Beans were crucial to the survival of the ancient Indians of the Americas, both in the northern and southern hemispheres. Dried beans frequently saw those peoples through harsh winters. The Hopi Indians of the Southwest still celebrate an annual bean festival.

Although there are more than 14,000 species of the legume (bean) family only twenty-two major ones are grown for human consumption. Many of the dried bean species we know today originated in South America. When the Europeans came they carried back home seeds of the various bean varieties that flourished in South America. It was soon discovered that most beans can be grown in relatively poor soil. The bean yield per acre is high compared to many other crops.

In past years, beans were shunned as "food for the poor" or "poor man's meat." This low state of appreciation created the expression "not worth a hill of beans." The ancient Romans, who cultivated the broad green bean we know today as Kentucky wonders, were often cautioned to "eat no beans," as they believed that the dried seeds or bean contained the soul of the dead.

The American bean includes, round beans, oval beans, fat beans, flat beans, long beans, and kidney-shaped beans. There are white beans, yellow beans, tan beans, green beans, pink beans, red beans, purple beans, black beans, and mottled beans. Their pods are flat or round, smooth or irregular, straight or curved, short or long, and the outsides may be green, yellow, red, purple, or splashed in different colors.

One of the most popular native American bean varieties is the kidney bean. First domesticated by the Incas of Peru, these beans were used extensively by the Indians of South and North America. The Indians appreciated the fact that beans could be cultivated in poorer soil than corn, that they could be dried for easy storage, and that they contained high-energy. When the meat supply dwindled, beans became an excellent source of protein, particularly during winter months.

The early colonists found that the Indians were growing a wide variety of beans. The Indians taught the colonists how to grow beans in the same hill where a corn seed was planted.

As the corn and beans grew the bean plant would entwine itself on the corn using it as a pole. They also taught the colonists how to bake beans in pots in the earth, how to cook them green in the summer, and how to dry them for winter storage. The Indians taught the settlers that beans and corn have an affinity for each other and could be cooked together. The settlers called the dish "succotash," a variation of the original Indian name "msickquatash."

In 1620 the Pilgrims saw the Indian squaws baking beans with deer fat and onions overnight in clay pots resting on hot stones lining a hole in the ground. The Pilgrim women adapted this method of cooking dried beans, but replaced the deer fat with pork and added maple sugar or syrup.

Baked beans became a Massachusetts food tradition and provided the typical Saturday night supper in Puritan Boston. The Sabbath started at sundown Saturday and, according to Puritan belief, no work was to be done until sundown Sunday. Therefore, the bean pot was put in the low heat of the brick oven beside the open hearth on Saturday morning so that the beans would be ready by supper time. The slowly baking pot of beans gave off fragrant aromas of onions, salt pork, and maple sugar or syrup all day. The leftovers were kept warm in the fireplace and served for Sunday breakfast.

When American trade with the West Indies developed, less-expensive Caribbean molasses replaced the maple sugar or syrup in baked beans. Many continued to use maple sugar, however, because too much molasses tended to make the beans tough. Others claim that molasses keep the beans from becoming too soft during the slow cooking process.

When settlers moved westward, dried beans were one of the staples they took along. As each region of the country developed, the basic bean recipe changed. In the Midwest, tomatoes were added. In Texas, hot chilies were added and instead of a ceramic bean pot the beans were cooked in a big black iron pot, often over an open fire on the range.

Beans had another use besides food. In the Massachusetts Colony in the seventeenth century the saying "Counting Beans" meant counting votes. White beans were used for a "yes" vote and black beans for a "nay" vote.

Although early colonists were growing beans in their vegetable gardens and drying them for winter use, beans did not become a farm crop until 1836 when several acres were planted on a large farm in the eastern part of New York State. The cultivation of beans for drying expanded when the government started to buy beans for the army during the Civil War. Teddy Roosevelt once claimed that the battle of San Juan Hill was won on beans.

Until the growing interest in American cuisine, which started in the late 1970s with California cuisine, beans were considered to be a mundane ingredient. The old-fashioned cooking of ethnic American recipes, which became popular in the early 1990s, further enhanced the status of beans, particularly dried ones. In addition to renewing interest in such dried bean varieties as kidney, pinto, navy, black-eyed peas (which are really beans), and black beans, chefs and home cooks also seeki out the old fashioned varieties such as soldier beans, tongues of fire, and Spanish tolasanas beans. As the versatility of dried beans have become recognized, sales of dried beans have soared.

Beans have been a staple of Southwestern, Indian, Italian, Middle Eastern, American and Thai cuisine, and even French country cooking. With the rapid growth of ethnic restaurants, chefs are including bean dishes on their menus, even in the most sophisticated and expensive restaurants. Consequently, the much overused word "gourmet" has now been attached to the once lowly bean.

In recent years black beans have gained in popularity. This 5/8-inch long kidney-shaped bean is shiny black with a white keel. It is a native of South America and is used throughout South and Central America and the Caribbean, where it is a staple that is boiled, spiced, or mixed with rice. Black beans have a slightly mushroom flavor and in Cuba, Puerto Rico, and Spain are traditionally made into black bean soup . In Brazil the black bean is the basis of feijoada, the national dish, which contains roasted pork, oranges, and black beans.

Rice and beans have long been a favorite dish in the south and southwestern part of the United States, as well as in Mexico and the Caribbean Islands. The following recipe for Rice Cake with Southwestern Sauce combines the two for a vegetarian entree.

Rice Cake
with Southwestern Sauce

1 3/4 cups medium-grain rice
3 1/2 cups water
1 cup grated Monterey Jack cheese
1 large jalapeno pepper, seeded and minced
8 green onions, white and green parts
  chopped separately
1 (16 ounce) can black beans,
  rinsed and drained
1 (14 ounce) can tomatoes,
  diced and juice reserved
1 (8 ounce) can tomato sauce

2 1/2 teaspoons chili powder
1/2 teaspoon dried oregano leaves
1 (16 ounce) can yellow corn kernels,
  drained
4 tablespoons chopped fresh cilantro
1 large egg, beaten
1 tablespoon olive oil

Combine the rice and water in a medium-size saucepan and bring to a boil. Reduce heat to low, cover and cook rice until tender and water has been absorbed, about 20 minutes. Remove the rice from the heat and stir in the cheese and jalapeño pepper. Cool to room temperature.

In another saucepan combine the white parts of the onion, beans, diced tomatoes with their juice, tomato sauce, chili powder, and oregano. Bring to a boil, reduce heat, and simmer for 10 minutes until the mixture thickens a little. Add the green parts of the onions, corn, and 2 tablespoons of the cilantro. (The sauce and rice mixture can be prepared 4 hours ahead and let stand at room temperature. Rewarm the sauce before serving.)

Mix the egg into the rice mixture. Heat the olive oil in a 10-inch skillet over medium-high heat. Add the rice mixture to the skillet and using a spatula, press the mixture into an even layer. Reduce heat to medium, cover and cook until the bottom of the rice cake is brown and crisp, about 12 minutes. Turn the rice cake onto a platter, brown side up. Spoon the warm sauce over the cake and garnish with the 2 remaining tablespoons of cilantro. Cut into wedges and serve. Serves 4 as a main course, or 6 as a side dish.

Lentils

Ancient Round Discs

Lentils look like tiny pebbles and are used dried. They have been consumed by mankind for more than eight thousand years and were one of the first vegetables brought under cultivation. Lentils are small flattened biconvex seeds that grow in a pod on a fern-like plant. Today there are more than fifty varieties of lentils grown around the world — the brown, green, and red being the most popular.

The birthplace of lentils is unknown. Some historians say that their place of origin was Southeast Asia, in the area of the fertile lands bordering the Indus River. Other historians have concluded, however, that since lentils were found in archaeological digs in Iraq and Turkey dating back to 6750 B.C., they probably originated in the Middle East.

Lentils are mentioned in the Old Testament. Esau sold his birthright for a mess of "pottage of lentils." This is thought to be an ancient Middle Eastern dish of lentils and onions simmered slowly in sesame oil. Even today the French word for lentil soup is "Potage Esau," and in classic French cooking the word "Esau" usually signifies a dish whose main ingredient is lentils.

Lentils came to Egypt around 2000 B.C. Remains of a lentil puree were discovered in the Twelfth dynasty (around 1750 B.C.) tomb at Thebes. Several food historians have speculated that it was the consumption of protein-rich lentils that gave the Egyptians the strength to build the Pyramids.

From Egypt lentils were brought by ship to Greece and Rome. The Greeks considered them food for the poor. Some of the Greek philosophers ate them to prove that they were not subject to any class distinction. By the time Athens had reached its height of civilization, lentils had become a staple. Hippocrates, the father of medicine, prescribed them with small slices of boiled egg for liver ailments.

The Romans gave lentils the name "lens culinaris." The name was inspired by astronomers and physicists who found a similarity between lentils and disk-shaped double convex optic glass. As Roman food became diversified with many cultivated vegetables being served at the banquets of the rich, lentils were left to the plebeians. However, lentils did find their way to the banquet tables in rather sophisticated dishes such as lentils with chestnuts, lentils with mussels, and barley soup enriched with lentils and chickpeas (garbanzo). One of the Roman noblemen, Heliogabalus, served lentils mixed with topazes. This offered his guests the possibility of finding a fortune — although possibly losing a tooth at the same time.

The Roman's demand for lentils was so great that there was a constant stream of ships carrying lentils from Alexandria in Egypt to ports near Rome. At the time the small red Egyptian lentils were considered to be the best. Historians claim that the obelisk which stands in front of St. Peter's cathedral in Rome was created in Egypt and made the voyage to Rome buried under its main cargo -- Egyptian lentils.

By the Middle Ages even the poor considered lentils unworthy of human consumption since physicians claimed they were difficult to digest, inflamed the stomach, weakened eyesight, and caused nightmares. Only the poorest of the poor and the monks ate lentils. Lentils became popular among Catholics who could not afford fish during Lent.

But the French had other ideas. In the eighth century Charlemagne ordered lentils planted in his gardens. French physicians used lentils against smallpox. During the reign of Louis XIV lentil soup became popular. Louis XV's Polish wife, Maria Leszczynska, helped to popularize green lentils, which were considered to be the country's best and were renamed "lentilles a la reine." These lentils were being grown in the queen's native Poland.

The phrase often applied to the lentil is "the poor man's meat." It is only derogatory if the emphasis is on "poor man's" instead of on "meat." Of all dried vegetables, lentils and soybeans are the best substitute for meat. One hundred grams of lentils contain the same amount of protein as 134 grams of beef. In addition there is less cholesterol and more beneficial fiber in lentils than beef.

The majority of Americans have never really taken to lentils. The first Americans who encountered them were the Iroquois Indians when they were introduced to lentils by the Jesuit missionaries. These missionaries planted lentils along the St. Lawrence River, but they did not grow well there.

The only place where lentils are grown today in the United States is in a fifty-mile wide strip of land along the Washington-Idaho border. The arid climate of this region makes it possible to dry lentils in the field before harvesting. The majority of this lentil crop is sold overseas.

There are about fifty different types of lentils grown throughout the world. The people of India are the greatest lentil consumers in the world. There is an interesting Indian dish called "Dahnsak," in which up to nine different kinds of lentils of various flavors, colors and textures are combined.

Although chili is traditionally made with red eat and beans, this is a lighter version with lentils and chicken. Pineapple chunks give the chili an additional flavor.

Lentil Chili

2 boneless, skinless chicken breast halves
2 tablespoons olive oil
Salt and pepper
1 tablespoon chili powder
1 onion, chopped
4 tablespoons tomato paste
4 cups chicken broth
1/2 pound lentils, rinsed
1/2 teaspoon dried thyme
1 small red chili pepper, seeds removed
  and chopped
1 medium green pepper, chopped
1 medium red pepper, chopped
1 (8 ounce) can pineapple rings,
  drained and cut into chunks

Cut the chicken breasts into 1-inch wide strips.

Heat the olive oil in a medium-size saucepan over medium-high heat. Add the chicken strips and brown them on both sides. Sprinkle with salt and pepper. Remove the chicken to a plate and cover with aluminum foil. Add the onion to the pan and sauté it until it is soft. Add the tomato paste and the chicken broth and mix thoroughly. Then add the lentils and thyme. Bring to a boil and cook, covered, over low heat for 40 minutes.

After 20 minutes of cooking add the chili pepper, green and red pepper and continue cooking. Five minutes before the end of cooking time add the chicken pieces and the pineapple chunks. Adjust seasonings and finish cooking. Lentils should be tender, but not mushy. Serve with boiled rice or taco chips.

Serves 4.

Barley

Not Just for Beer

For centuries barley has been prized as a brewing ingredient in both beers and whiskies. Barley is also the prime ingredient in Scottish broth, a rather thick soup made with vegetables, barley, and chunks of lamb. It is also frequently used in Irish lamb stew. Today about half of the barley grown in this country goes into the brewing of beer, while most of the remainder is used for animal feed.

Food historians believe that barley was one of the first food plants raised by pre-historic man. It originated in the highlands of Ethiopia and was taken from there by caravans into Egypt, the Middle East, and eventually as far as northwestern Europe. Egyptian hieroglyphics dating from 5000 B.C. depict barley cultivation. The Chinese cultivated barley as early as 2800 B.C. and considered it to be one of the five sacred cultivated plants of China — the others being rice, soybeans, wheat, and millet.

The ancient Sumerians (3500 B.C.) used barley as the basis of their monetary system. The Babylonian Code specifically stated that barley was to be used as the means of monetary exchange.

Barley was the chief grain used by the ancient Hebrews to make bread. The first chapter of Exodus describes one of the Egyptian plagues where the bombardment of hailstone caused "the barley to be smitten." Barley is mentioned throughout the Bible. The story of the miracle of the loaves and fishes specifies that the five loaves of bread Christ used to feed five thousand people were made of barley.

The Greeks regarded barley as a sacred grain and used it in many of their secret religious ceremonies in adoration of their gods. The Romans made a gruel from barley. Often this gruel was left to harden and can be considered to be the forerunner of bread. Roman historians mention that barley was used to make a porridge that was flavored with coriander.

Barley was the chief bread grain in Europe until the sixteenth century, when it was surpassed by wheat and rye. Historians say that the grain was first brought to the Americas in 1543 by the Spanish governor of Columbia. The Pilgrims planted barley in Massachusetts without much success. However, it later flourished in Pennsylvania where the barley seeds were combined with the area's limestone water to make whiskey.

With the advent of modern leavening agents, barley lost its importance for bread making because its low gluten content weakens the action of yeast. Its high protein content, however, is still a valuable food for man. The northern European countries, Israel, and the land of its birth, Ethiopia, still regard barley as a principal grain. Here in the United States, it is gaining popularity as an ingredient in multi-grain cold breakfast cereals.

With the trend toward healthy foods barley is also finding its way to our dinner tables. When cooked, barley has a delectable nutlike flavor and an attractive chewy texture. Although the traditional cooking time for barley is 45 to 50 minutes, there is also quick-cooking barley on the market which takes about 10 minutes of cooking time.

The "pearl" in pearled barley is not a description of the grade or quality, but refers to the whiteness and rounded shape of the grain after milling. When harvested, barley grains are enclosed in three-layered husks that are milled away from the kernels, leaving "pearls."

Rice

Rice Feeds Millions

Rice is the staple food for more people than wheat. A third of the world's population is nourished by rice exclusively and it is considered to be the main item in the diet for six out of every ten people in the world. Asians have become so accustomed to the presence of rice in their meals, that regardless of how much they eat of other foods, they feel hungry if they have not had rice.

Historians do not agree as to where rice was first cultivated, but it is certain that it was in a region with plenty of rain and flat farmland. Today modern irrigation extends its cultivation to regions with moderate rainfall.

Traditionally rice plants were started in small plots for about four weeks and then transplanted into larger plots covered with shallow water(paddies) until they matured in about four months. Rice is still cultivated this way in Japan, China and Southeast Asia. Historically only one type of climate provided these growing conditions — areas with a monsoon season where up to 160 inches of rain might fall during the season. The monsoons are then followed by a dry period when the waters recede and the rice finishes maturing.

There is still a debate among food historians which of the countries with a monsoon season was the first to cultivate rice. Most have narrowed the beginnings of rice to three countries — China, India, and Thailand. Traditionally, China had the earliest written documents mentioning rice cultivation, dating from about 2800 B.C. In the 1970s, however, archaeologists found actual rice grains in an excavation site in northern Thailand dating from 3500 B.C. The earliest documents in India mentioning rice date from 2000 B.C.

Rice was not a popular grain at that time as it was easier to cultivate tubers such as taro. The raising of tubers was much less labor intensive than the back breaking irrigated cultivation of rice . The cultivation of rice increased, however, as mankind found it contained a greater variety of healthy ingredients.

The Persians brought rice plants from India to the Middle East in the Euphrates Valley. Rice plants were rare to the Greeks and Romans who used the grains primarily for medicinal purposes. However, the Arabs and Turks took rice and its cultivation by irrigation very seriously. To them rice, like wheat in Europe, meant life.

There was probably no rice grown in Europe until the Moors brought it to Spain and cultivated it in Andalusia in the ninth century. From there it traveled to Italy and was planted in the Po Valley where it is still grown. One of the most famous Italian dishes, Risotto alla Milanese, was created with rice from the Po Valley in the late 1500s. Eventually rice was grown in the Rhone Valley of France.

The British did not acquire their liking for rice from the continent, but from India when it was part of the British Empire. One of the favorite English dishes during the height of that country's imperialism was a derivative of the Indian "kitcherie." The original dish was made with curry-spiced rice and lentils. The British replaced the lentils with leftover smoked fish, hard-boiled eggs, and a cream sauce and made it a breakfast dish, called "kedgeree."

Rice was eaten very sparingly in England, as it was very expensive. It was used as a special ingredient in puddings, along with sugar and powdered spice. At the time four tablespoons of rice were enough to make a pudding for eight to ten people.

Although the British were not consuming much rice when they started to colonize

America, they nevertheless called upon the new colonies to produce it. Sir William Buckley sowed half a bushel of rice seed in Virginia in 1647 and reaped fifteen bushels. Seventeenth century colonial planters, however, did not develop an interest in raising this grain because tobacco was much more profitable.

Rice growing did take hold in colonial times, however, in the area surrounding Charleston, South Carolina, which became known for its rice production. Sea captains had first brought seed rice from Madagascar to South Carolina. The local plantation owners found that the Madagascar rice flourished in the Carolina low country environment, and South Carolina began growing and exporting rice to England in the early 1600s.

The entire rice production of South Carolina was lost during the British occupation of Charleston during the American Revolutionary War. The British shipped all of the rice back to England, including the portion that should have been withheld for the next year's seeds. When Thomas Jefferson served as ambassador to France, he managed to smuggle two bags of rice out of Italy in 1887 and gave it to South Carolina to restart their rice industry. This rice from the Piedmont area of Italy was of a superior quality and the Italians had tried to prevent its export.

Rice cultivation was back-breaking work in those early years. It was planted by hand in very poor soil and under very poor working conditions, given the hot and humid climate of the coastal region. White indentured servants, who worked to pay back their passage money, refused to work in the rice fields. Negro slaves became the answer, and the plantation system was soon established in South Carolina. To work a 500-acre rice field required as many as 2,000 slaves.

The end of the Civil War marked the decline of rice cultivation in South Carolina, mainly because the freed slaves no longer wanted to work in the rice fields. Immigrant Irish and Italian workers from the north were brought to work in the rice fields, but they proved to be unsatisfactory. Cultivation of rice declined very rapidly at the beginning of the twentieth century, and subsequent hurricanes permanently demolished many of the low-lying coastal rice fields.

After the Civil War large tracts of land in Louisiana were planted with rice and it became one of that state's major crops in the late 1800s. Rice had also been brought to California in the 1760s, but it did not become a viable crop until 1912 when it was planted in the upper Sacramento Valley. In the last fifty years Texas has also become a prominent rice producer. Texas farmers produce not only regular and brown rice, but also an aromatic rice similar to the basmati rice of India. Texas growers have labeled this aromatic rice Texmati.

There are three types of rice found in our supermarkets. Long grain refers to rice three times longer than it is wide. Medium grain is about twice as long as wide, and short grain is less than twice as long as its width. Both medium and short grain rice are high in starch and after cooking the grains tend to stick together and have a very creamy texture. Thus both of these are frequently used for rice puddings. The grains of long grain rice remain separate and fluff up while cooking.

Other forms of rice on our grocery store shelves include, Italian arborio, which is considered to be medium grain and cooks fairly firm to the bite, al dente. Brown rice, which has recently become very popular, is rice with the hull removed and the bran layers left clinging to the grains. It has a nutty flavor and is slightly chewy. Wild rice, primarily from Minnesota, is not a rice but the seeds of a grass.

The Rice Camargue, seasoned with rosemary, is typical of the Rhone Valley of France. Serve it with grilled lamb. The Orange and Rice Creme Caramel is similar to a flan. As the pudding bakes, the rice settles to the bottom and absorbs the caramelized sugar.

Camargue Rice

3 tablespoons extra virgin olive oil
1 medium onion, halved and thinly sliced
2 garlic cloves, minced
1 large ripe tomato, chopped
1 bay leaf
1 1/4 cups long grain rice
Salt and pepper, to taste
1/3 cup sliced black olives
1 cup chicken broth
1 1/2 cups water
Leaves of 1 small sprig fresh rosemary
1/4 teaspoon cumin
1 leek, white and tender green parts, sliced
1/2 stalk celery, sliced
1 small carrot, sliced
Grated peel of 1/4 lemon

In a large saucepan heat the olive oil over medium-high heat. Add the onion and sauté until soft and golden, about 4 minutes. Then add the garlic, tomato, and bay leaf and stir. Add the rice and sprinkle with some salt and pepper. Add the olives, chicken broth, and water, and stir well. Bring to a boil. Add the rosemary, cumin, leek, celery, carrot and lemon zest. Cover the saucepan, reduce heat to low and cook for 25 minutes or until rice is done.

Serves 6 to 8.

Orange and Rice Creme Caramel

1 1/2 cups sugar
1 cup half-and-half
1 cup milk
2 pieces (2 x 1/2 inch) orange peel
2 eggs
2 egg yolks
1 cup cooked medium-grain white rice
1 tablespoon Grand Marnier
1 teaspoon vanilla extract

Over medium-low heat warm 1 cup of sugar in a 10-inch skillet until the sugar begins to dissolve. Cook the syrup without stirring until it turns a golden caramel. Pour the caramel in each of 6 (4 ounce) custard cups.

Scald the half-and-half, milk and orange peel in a medium saucepan; remove from heat. Whisk the eggs, egg yolks, and remaining 1/2 cup of sugar in a bowl until light in color. Gradually whisk in half of the scalded milk. Add the remaining milk slowly. Strain the mixture into the saucepan, discarding the orange peel. Add the rice and cook over low heat, stirring constantly, until the rice is heated and the mixture thickens slightly. Remove from the heat and let stand for 10 minutes. Stir in the Grand Marnier and vanilla.

With a slotted spoon remove the rice and divide it among the custard cups. Fill the cups with the custard. Place the cups in the baking pan and add enough boiling water to the pan to come halfway up the sides of the cups. Bake in a preheated 325° F. oven for 35 minutes or until the custard is set. Remove the custard cups from the hot water and let them cool on a wire rack. Refrigerate the custards until chilled. To serve, loosen the edges with a sharp knife and invert on dessert plates. Serves 6.

Wheat

Two Species of Wheat

There are two basic species of wheat grown — *Triticum durum* and *Triticum aestivum*. The latter is divided into two degrees of hardness — hard and soft. Each has its own unique kernel composition and particular culinary usage. The distinguishing factor is the hardness of the kernel, which is a measure of the wheat's protein content. The higher the protein content, the fewer the starch granules. Hard wheat breaks up into large chunks of protein with relatively little starch and forms a strong gluten when the flour is mixed with water.

Durum wheat is the hardest type of wheat grown. It is too hard for bread dough which must have some give to it. Durum wheat is usually milled into a coarse product called semolina, which is used principally to make pasta. *Durum* wheat is about five percent of the American wheat crop.

Hard *aestivum* is preferred for bread making and constitutes about seventy-five percent of the American wheat crop. Soft *aestivum has* a high starch content and low gluten. This wheat is suited for cake flours and other products that are tender and crumbly.

The familiar all-purpose flour is a blend of hard and soft flours and is used in a wide range of foods — particularly for home baking. It seldom gives the same results as commercially baked products which are made from specialized flours and often to the standards of specific bakeries..

Wheat has played an important role in the creation of civilization. The earliest settlements in Asia Minor arose where wheat grew wild. Archeologists have determined that Paleolithic man was consuming wheat in the upper Tigris valley in the ninth millennium B.C. They used primitive mortars and pestles to grind the wheat into a gruel. By 5000 B.C. wheat was being cultivated with the aid of irrigation in Babylon and Mesopotamia.

During this period Egypt was the world's largest wheat producer. Wheat became the basis of the Egyptian economy in ancient times. It was an ideal crop for Egypt as it had a growing period that matched the periodic rising and falling of the Nile River. Planted in time for the yearly flooding, it was harvested when the ground became firm and hard. Egyptian hieroglyphics depict wheat being cut knee-high with copper sickles, then being trodden by buffaloes followed by being winnowed by slaves.

The Egyptians were the first to make raised bread. Food historians say that they broke off a piece of the dough before baking for later use as a starter, as they did not know how to develop yeast. The Greeks, who imported wheat from Egypt, did not learn to make bread until the second century B.C.

Bread played a prominent role in Europe's social relations and hierarchy. One's bread was determined by one's rank. Starting with the Greeks, white bread made from refined flour was considered superior, and only the upper class enjoyed it. The poor and criminals ate course dark breads. Most of the bread originally made in Rome was made in the home by women. By 170 B.C., however, a cooperative of bakers had been formed. Storage bins of wheat and bakeries have been found in the excavations of Pompeii. Much of the wheat used in Roman bread making was imported from North Africa or other parts of the Roman empire as very little was grown in Italy.

In France at the time of Charlemagne, wheat had become the most prized grain. It remained a comparative luxury in England until the seventh century. In years of poor harvest in England laws were passed prohibiting the use of wheat in beer making. By the thirteenth century, the Baltic region had become the principal wheat-growing region of Europe.

When the first settlers came to America they tried to raise European wheat and were only successful in certain regions along the east coast. New York state, Delaware, and Maryland became major wheat producers.

Although tobacco was the mainstay of Maryland's economy in the seventeenth and eighteenth centuries, wheat became an important crop as more overseas markets developed. At one time wheat was grown in the Shenandoah Valley in Virginia and during the Civil War that area was nicknamed the "Bread Basket" of the Confederacy. Mills abounded in the Valley, grinding both wheat and corn. Cyrus McCormick lived near Raphine, Virginia, where he invented the reaper, which helped improve wheat harvesting. Wheat did not to grow well in the Virginia, however, because much of the land's nutrients had been depleted with tobacco cultivation.

In the 1750s John Stevenson, an Irish immigrant who settled in Maryland, sent the first cargo of wheat to Ireland and began trading in that commodity. The Baltimore economy soon centered around the wheat trade with Great Britain, the West Indies, and southern Europe. Water provided the necessary power for milling the grain grown in northern and western Maryland. In 1804 there were fifty mills within eighteen miles of Baltimore.

Delaware also played a role in the history of flour milling along the east coast in the early days of our nation. Oliver Evans, originally a Delaware farmer, automated flour milling with the invention of a continuous conveyor belt. Many millers were skeptical of the Evans mill and did not readily accept it. By 1792, however, his inventions had been licensed to more than a hundred mills. At that time large quantities of milled wheat were shipped overseas, and many mills ceased grinding small amounts of grain for local families, claiming it was uneconomical.

The opening of the Erie Canal in the mid-1820s greatly reduced the cost of shipping wheat and flour from western New York state to the ports along the coast. As the country expanded westward, so did wheat production and the eastern states eventually ceased large-scale wheat cultivation. For a time Ohio became the largest producer of wheat, shipping flour via Lake Erie and the Erie Canal to the East. However, Ohio's wheat farms could not compete with those of Kansas, Nebraska, and the Dakotas.

In the developing years of wheat farming in the eastern regions of the country, flour mills were the first signs of stability in a new settlement. Mills were meeting places where isolated farmers were glad to wait for their flour while enjoying gossip and companionship with other farmers. To avoid a long ride, many people settled near a mill, thereby forming communities.

Even though the Midwest provided vast extensions of open prairies, the soil was not naturally conducive to the growing of wheat. It was the German Mennonites from Russia who pioneered wheat growing in the Midwest.

When German Mennonite immigrants from Russia arrived in Kansas in the 1870s, they found parched land. Local farmers, who were depending on wheat, were almost starving. Being frugal people, each Mennonite family had brought with them seeds of a special wheat that they had been growing on the steppes of Russia. These new wheat seeds flourished and made the American Midwest one of the major wheat producing regions in the world.

The Mennonites were originally pacifist Germans. Many had fled their native country to escape compulsory military service and had gone to Russia in 1783 at the invitation of Catherine the Great. She wanted them to settle in the Crimea, hoping they would be examples of industrious, hard-working people for the shiftless Tatars, then predominating the region.

Ninety years later, the Crimean Mennonites realized that their century of military-conscription exemption in Russia was about to expire so they began searching for a new home. They sent scouts to Canada and the United States and as a result, five hundred families moved to Kansas. The first twenty-four families arrived in 1874 -- others soon followed.

While living in the Crimea, the Mennonites had found that the Turks grew a dark, hard wheat that was excellent for baking. Over the years, with careful selection of seeds, the Mennonites improved the wheat strain and named it Turkey Red. Each family brought a small amount of Turkey Red seed with them to Kansas. Since the Mennonites could carry very little on the long journey, each seed was hand-picked, a grain at a time, to insure that none but the finest was taken to the new land.

These new immigrants bought inexpensive land from the newly-built railroads, and proceeded to plant Turkey Red. It proved successful where no other variety would grow. Neighbors started buying seeds from the Mennonites, and Turkey Red spread all over the plains. With the aid of the new inventions such as the stainless steel plow, the reaper, and milling automation, the United States became one of the world's greatest wheat growing countries.

Quick breads, such as muffins, biscuits, and fruit breads, have been popular for a long time. They use either baking powder or soda as a leavening agent. The following recipe for Italian Herb Biscuit Loaf is a great accompaniment to soups or salads.

Italian Herb Quick Bread

1 1/2 cups all-purpose flour
1/4 cup freshly grated Parmesan cheese
2 tablespoons cornmeal
2 teaspoons baking powder
4 tablespoons margarine
2 eggs
1/2 cup whipping cream
3/4 teaspoon dried basil
3/4 teaspoon dried oregano
1/8 teaspoon garlic powder
Additional Parmesan cheese, optional

Combine the flour, 1/4 cup cheese, cornmeal, and baking powder in a bowl. Cut in the margarine with a pastry blender until mixture resembles coarse crumbs. Beat the eggs in another bowl. Add the cream, basil, oregano, and garlic powder and beat well until blended. Add the cream mixture to the flour mixture and stir until the dough forms a ball.

Turn the dough onto a floured surface and knead 10 to 12 times. Place the dough on a lightly greased cookie sheet and pat it out into a 7-inch round. Score the top of the dough into 8 wedges, being careful not to cut through the dough. Sprinkle with additional Parmesan cheese, if desired. Bake in a preheated 425° F. oven for 25 minutes or until a toothpick inserted into the center comes out clean. Serve warm. Serves 8.

Pasta

More Than 500 Shapes

The old myth that Marco Polo brought pasta back from China is just that, a myth. Historians now say that he brought back a thinner noodle made from rice flour. Records show that Italians in Rome, Genoa, and Padua were eating ravioli and fettuccine in the 1270s. Marco Polo did not return from China until 1295.

There is still a controversy about the origin of pasta. Some believe it started in Mesopotamia a millennia ago. Others say that pasta was first made in what is today Ethiopia in about the eleventh century. A third version relates its origin to Greece on the theory that the word macaroni came from the Greek word "makar," meaning "blessed" as used when referring to sacramental food.

The consensus seems to be that pasta came from somewhere in the Middle East. Since it is light in weight and can be stored for long periods of time in dry climate, historians believe that the desert nomads carried pasta with them as a major source of protein.

By the fourth and third centuries B.C. many cultures were eating some form of pasta. An Italian bas-relief of that time shows people making pasta with a rolling pin and cutting the dough into strips with a pastry wheel.

The most common name for pasta in Europe during the Middle Ages was "maccari" or "maccaroni." The word maccari relates to the Italian and means to pound, as in making a paste of flour and water.

The Middle Ages were also a time of great experimentation in making pasta. At first the pasta dough was kneaded in a large wooden trough by men who trampled the dough with their bare feet. Eventually a rotating wheel was invented that replaced this foot power. A perforated mold was also constructed which by means of a screw mechanism forced the flour-and-water dough mixture through the holes. This permitted long strings of pasta to become available. Tubular pasta, now called macaroni, was made from a very thin dough and rolled around knitting needles to create the hole in the middle. Other pasta were put through a hand press to shape them into the "pasta of the day." Today there are more than five hundred different shapes of pasta being produced in Italy.

For centuries *maccheroni con la ricotta* (macaroni with ricotta, sugar, and cinnamon) was the traditional dish of Rome. During the Middle Ages and the Renaissance this dish was served as a first course.

Naples became famous for its pasta. The population's appetite for macaroni, as pasta was then called, was enormous from the start. Street vendors fished macaroni from boiling cauldrons, and sold it sprinkled with a little grated cheese and black pepper. Neapolitans ate the pasta with their fingers, throwing back their heads, raising their eyes to heaven, and lowering the strands of pasta into their mouths. Foreign visitors marveled at the sight and assumed that the poor were thanking God for their daily food.

Italians at all levels of society preferred to eat pasta with their hands. For this reason it was not served at court. Finally, Ferdinand II protested at this deprivation, and his advisors invented the short four-pronged fork (like our dessert forks) to allow their sovereign to eat his pasta with dignity. French chefs, who were imported by the richest families, had to learn how to embellish pasta and invented many of the sauces we regard as Italian today.

In Italy durum wheat (see wheat section) was grown around Naples in the early sixteenth century, and Naples consequently became the center for pasta making. The ancient streets and courtyards of old Naples were habitually strung with pasta hung out to dry, along with the day's wash. The southwestern area of the city became the center for pasta manufacturing, because the combination of hot winds from Mt. Vesuvius and cool breezes from the sea provided ideal temperatures to dry pasta.

Pasta was introduced to France in 1533 when Catherine de Medici married the Duke of Orleans who later became King Henry II of France. However, pasta did not gain the popularity in France as it enjoyed in Italy.

Between 1700 and 1785 pasta became the rage in Italy and the number of pasta shops in Naples alone increased from 60 to 280. Pasta of every shape dried on the roof-tops and hung over fences in that city. Gioacchino Rossini, the well-known nineteenth century Italian composer, spent much of his earnings trying to invent a commercial macaroni machine.

Macaroni, spaghetti, and all the other pasta shapes were considered food for the poor in the late eighteenth and nineteenth centuries in both Europe and America. However, that was not always the case. The natives of Naples considered pasta a great luxury.

By the eighteenth century when travel to Italy became popular with the Europeans, the word macaroni became firmly established. Young tourists to Italy upon their return home, became known as "macaronis." In England, just prior to the American Revolution, the term "macaroni" was a synonym for perfection or elegance. The most popular slang expression of the day was "That's Macaroni," meaning "That's great."

Many Italians who came to the United States during the Gold Rush of 1849 became restaurant proprietors and cooks. Their simple spaghetti with tomato sauce caught on rapidly. Between the end of the nineteenth century and the beginning of World War II spaghetti became a popular American dish. With Italian neighborhoods in large cities such as New York, Boston, Philadelphia, and San Francisco, local non-Italian residents started tasting the exotic inexpensive fare of their Italian neighbors. At first pasta could only be purchased from gourmet grocers who sold imported pasta, cheese, and sauces.

The first American pasta factory was opened in Philadelphia in 1798 by a Frenchman. But, it was Thomas Jefferson who really brought pasta to America when he brought back a simple macaroni machine from one of his visits to Italy. His daughter, Martha, prepared the first macaroni and cheese dish, using Parmesan cheese.

With the advent of World War I imports from abroad were cut off and local production of pasta became essential. By the end of the war there were 557 pasta manufacturers in America. Pressure from the ever-growing group of domestic pasta manufacturers, forced the Department of Agriculture to encourage farmers in the Midwest to grow durum wheat. This is the hard wheat needed for firm pasta dough. Today North and South Dakota are the leading states providing durum wheat.

Over the years pasta products have become a staple of the American food market. Most of our supermarkets have large sections of pasta along with a myriad of ready-made sauces. Today the average annual per capita consumption of pasta is approximately twelve pounds (slightly higher in the East). One of the largest manufacturers of pasta in this country, The American Italian Pasta Company of Excelsior Springs, Missouri makes about 50 different sizes and shapes of pasta.

For a Naples pasta recipe, see page 57.

Other Foods

Baking Powder and Yeast

Gives Rise to Baked Goods

Few of us have really given much thought to the subject of leavenings, those necessary elements that make baked goods rise. There is much confusion over the difference between baking powder, baking soda, and also where yeast fits in.

Baking soda, technically called bicarbonate of soda, is used as a leavener in baked goods. When combined with an acid such as buttermilk or yogurt, baking soda produces carbon dioxide gas which causes the dough or batter to rise. Because baking soda reacts immediately when moistened, it should always be mixed with other dry ingredients before adding liquid to the batter.

Baking powder is a combination of baking soda; an acid, such as cream of tartar; and a moisture-absorber, such as cornstarch. It combines the separate ingredients needed when using baking soda alone. When mixed with liquid, baking powder releases carbon dioxide gas that causes a bread or cake to rise. Today the most common baking powder is double-acting, which releases some gas when it becomes wet and the rest when exposed to oven heat.

When double acting baking powder replaced single-acting baking powder, so did having to tiptoe past the oven to prevent the cakes from falling.

Baking powder and baking soda were relative newcomers to baking. Before the turn of the nineteenth century, all leavening in baking was either by yeast or manually beating air into the dough or batter. Frequently beaten egg whites were folded into the dough to give it a lightness. At the time yeast was derived from alcoholic spirits, such as beer or wine.

Many recipes written in the eighteenth and nineteenth centuries called for beating dough for an hour or two. A Maryland biscuit recipe of the mid-1700s instructed the cook to beat the biscuit dough 300 times for family and 500 times for company. A hammer, a mallet, or an ax was used to perform this task which usually took about 30 minutes. These biscuits became known as Beaten Biscuits.

The breakthrough in leavening came in the 1790s in America when it was discovered that pearl ash, a refined form of wood ash, could make cakes rise. Within two years America was exporting pearl ash to Europe. The use of this form of leavening was restricted to highly spiced cakes, such as gingerbread, because the pearl ash had a soapy taste. Spices were required to mask this unpleasantness.

In the early nineteenth century it was discovered that bicarbonate of soda (baking soda) could be used as a leavener. Formerly known as saleratus, baking soda had been used in baking and cleaning butter churns and other household articles. It was made in this country as early as 1839 and created a formidable competition for the soda imported from England.

It was easy to see why homemakers preferred the American baking soda because it was packaged in a bright-red wrapper and each pound package contained a free recipe card. One of the most colorful traveling baking soda salesmen, Colonel Powell, had a brightly colored wagon drawn by plumed horses. He always arrived in a community with a jingle of bells and a trumpet blast. The Colonel, a former circus giant, stood nine feet tall with his high hat and thick-soled shoes.

Unlike our modern powdered version, bicarbonate of soda came in large lumps, was very coarse, and had to be dissolved in a little water before being added to dough or batter. Until 1979 the original recipe for Toll House Cookies called for 1/2 teaspoon of water to be added to the dough, a hold-over from the time when baking soda lumps had to be dissolved.

When single-acting baking powder came into common use, cakes could be quickly mixed by hand and then popped into the oven. All of this had to be done quickly because as soon as the baking powder came into contact with moisture the gases were released. If the batter was allowed to sit before baking, the carbon dioxide would dissipate and the cake would not rise during baking.

The widespread use of baking powder in the United States in the nineteenth century fostered the development of a large variety of "quick breads" and sweet breads, such as banana bread and applesauce bread. Baking powder biscuits became a popular item on the dinner table and strawberry shortcake was an important summer dessert.

One of the earliest successful forms of baking powder in the United States was developed after the Civil War by two Fort Wayne, Indiana, druggists, Biddle and Hoagland. They had spent several years experimenting with a chemical compound involving baking soda, an acid, and cornstarch.

The duo started their baking powder business in 1873. Two years later Biddle and Hoagland moved the business to Chicago and subsequently merged it with two other baking-powder firms. The resulting product became known as Royal Baking Powder.

Next to baking powder the most frequently-used rising agent is yeast. It is used in breads and many traditional European cakes. Until after the Civil War, yeast for bread baking was primarily made at home from potato skins or leftover beer. The result was a haphazard product that varied from batch-to-batch, producing a barely edible bread.

Fleischmann's yeast has long been a household name The company started with an idea from a young Austrian, Charles Fleischmann. He revolutionized the American baking industry with his high quality yeast. Fleischmann had come to the United States in 1865 to attend the wedding of a sister. Astonished by what he called the poor taste of American bread, he went back to Austria to collect samples of the yeast used in making Viennese breads.

When Fleischmann returned to America with his brother Maximilian, they took their yeast samples to James M. Gaff, a well-known Cincinnati distiller. The three went into business together and in 1868 began manufacturing the country's first standardized yeast. The advantage of the new yeast was that it was created under rigid controls and compressed into cakes of uniform size and effectiveness.

Two years after they started producing yeast, the partners used their expertise in the distilling field by forming The Fleischmann Distilling Company and started producing America's first gin.

After the second World War, Fleischmann began producing yeast in dehydrated granules. Each package was designed to contain the same rising agents as the original compressed cake of yeast. Since the packages do not need to be refrigerated, as did the cakes, they could be placed on the grocer's shelves alongside flour and sugar. This made it more convenient for the shopper to get all of the baking ingredients in one place.

Bread

The Staff of Life

Some ten thousand years ago man settled down from his nomadic ways. He domesticated animals and started to raise grains which he then ground and mixed with water to form a stiff paste. This was spread on a flat hot stone and baked in an open fire, creating the first unleavened flat bread. If stored in a dry place, this bread would keep for several months. Today, many of the world's population still eat flat breads such as Mexican tortilla, Pakistani chapati and Middle Eastern pita.

From the early cultivation of grains primitive man also learned to ferment beer. When the beer was mixed with crudely ground wheat grains and baked, the resulting loaves became leavened bread.

Later it was discovered that if the grain paste was set aside for a few days it would ferment and become aerated. When this paste or dough was baked it resulted in a raised bread. People liked the yeasty flavor and the variety of textures that could be produced. Archaeological evidence has shown that the first raised breads were developed in Egypt around 4000 B.C. By 300 BC yeast-making was a specialized profession in Egypt.

Historians say the Egyptians constructed the first bread ovens 2000 years before Christ. Egyptians were great bread eaters. It is said that they had forty-two types of baked goods and each Egyptian ate about a pound and a half of bread daily.

The Greeks were also great bread eaters. As early as the second century A.D. they produced fifty different kinds of bread, including a cheese bread, similar to the ones made today.

In the Middle East bread-making techniques were quickly developed. Throughout the Bible there are numerous references to bread, including the familiar saying of Jesus, "Man shall not live by bread alone."

The biblical-sounding phrase, "Bread is the staff of life," was a commonplace utterance from the English pulpit and a sign of the dominance of bread in everyday life.

Bread-making has not basically changed over the centuries. From the first commercial bread bakers of Roman times, to the baker's guilds of the Middle Ages, to the improved flours and ovens of the nineteenth century, the process has always been the same — ground grain (flour), combined with a liquid and a leavening agent (yeast) to form a dough which was then baked.

At one time the color of the flour and the resulting bread was a status symbol. White breads were the most prized since they signified that dirt free flour was used. In Roman times it also meant that the person who had white bread was affluent. Roman bakers often added chalk to make the dough white, enabling them to charge a higher price for their product. The poor ate unleavened barley cakes or course dark breads.

During the Middle Ages, Arabs brought the windmill to Europe from Persia and with that the profession of bread-making became firmly established. Bakers' brotherhoods, and then guilds, arose in the eleventh century. At first bakers were specialists, producing either brown or white bread. By the seventeenth century improvements in milling and in per capita income led to the dissolution of the brown (bread) guild as a separate body.

Bakeries were largely entities of the city. In the country, bread-making continued to be a domestic task. In the northern areas of Europe rye, barley, and oats were more common than wheat and cooks made these grains into coarse, heavy breads.

One odd use of a flat bread during the Middle Ages was the "trencher." It was a dense, dry, thick slice of bread that served as a plate at meals. Once the meal was over, the trencher was either eaten or given to the poor.

In America the early settlers where taught by the Indians to make a variety of breads from cornmeal. The variations of corn bread are many and include spoon bread, johnnycakes, corn sticks, and corn muffins.

Early English settlers brought with them the recipe for the traditional English "cottage loaf." It was originated to conserve space in the oven. The "cottage loaf" consists of two round loaves of unequal sizes, with the smaller one baked on top of the larger one.

In this country the first commercial bake shop opened in New Amsterdam (now New York) in 1648. By the 1700s every town in the East large enough to have an inn also had a baker. At that time there was strict price regulation by local governments based on the kind of bread — rye, white, or coarse — and its weight. Eight pounds was the standard weight of a loaf of bread as fixed by law.

Government officials were very watchful of the baking industry. Bakers were often required to initial their loaves, so that if the weight was short they could be reprimanded. This was a carry-over from England when London bakers cheated so consistently that they were made to give thirteen rolls to the dozen so that the customer could get his money's worth. Hence the name "baker's dozen."

In Philadelphia one of the duties of the mayor was the weighing of the bakers' loaves of bread once a month. In New York, a law was passed for some obscure reason that forbade a baker to sell sweet cakes unless he also had a variety of breads for sale.

A roll in colonial days, particularly in the northeast, was not the tiny dainty thing we know today. Two pennies bought two large fluffy rolls, big enough to carry under ones arms, wider around but similar to a French baguette. Bread, as well as rolls, were carried home under ones arms because paper was much too scarce to be used to wrap anything that did not have to be held together. If a customer wanted to keep his bread warm he brought along a large napkin for wrapping.

Some bake shops took in housewives' bread dough and baked it for them. These breads were marked with initials or some other marking to make sure that the baked bread was returned to the rightful owner.

The baker also had other custom jobs. If the wig maker had trouble curling certain hair that he had set on curlers, he sent it to the baker. At the bake shop the wig was encased in rye dough and baked, after which the dough was broken away to reveal the set curls. While the baker might set wigs, he did not bake pies. That was the job of the pie woman.

Bread has played a crucial role in American history. In the Revolutionary War it was such an important part of the soldiers diet that a Superintendent of Bakers and Director of Baking in the Grand Army of the United States was appointed by the Continental Congress. During the Civil War, the Senate wing of the Capitol was turned into a bakery to provide bread for the Union Army. More than ten thousand loaves of bread were produced every day. Some say that it was Congress' the most productive period.

In the 1800's almost every community in America had a mill to grind local grain for bread-making. Although America can be considered a late-comer into the history of bread-making, our bread varieties are endless.

Casseroles

One-Dish Meals

During the past century, casseroles have meant one-dish meals baked or stewed in a covered dish in the oven. Today, the word simply describes food that is prepared and cooked in a dish that can be brought to the table. For more sophisticated recipes preparation work, such as sautéing or browning, is done in another pan and the food is transferred to the casserole dish for baking.

Traditionally the English word "casserole" means a heavy, lidded pot used both in the oven and on top of the stove. The word has also been used to describe stews of meat and vegetables that are cooked slowly in the oven. All of this is confusing to the French, who originated the word. They used the word casserole to mean simply a saucepan or a stew pan. What the English call casseroles are generally described in France as "marmites" or "cocottes" — simply pots.

Clay pots are among the earliest utensils used for cooking. Their versatility is that when they are made they can be shaped to suit the food and the style of cooking, as per example a casserole dish in the shape of a chicken or a fish. The greatest virtue of these pots is the way in which they absorb heat and evenly transmit it to the contents. Thus the food on the top is cooked as thoroughly as the food on the bottom. Only a low heat is used in this type of cookery, almost eliminating the chances that the food might burn.

Since the first settlers arrived on the American shores, the one dish-meal has been a cornerstone of our culinary history. However, the history of one-dish meals in this country goes back even further, to the Indians cooking beans in clay pots. They filled these pots with beans, water, and possibly a piece of venison and then buried the pot in a hole in the ground that was filled with glowing embers. The pot was covered with a lid and then earth. It remained in the ground until the beans were done — usually for twelve to sixteen hours .

Until the advent of the cast iron stove in the mid-1800s, all cooking was down either in the open hearth or in the brick oven beside the fireplace. In pioneer days one-pot meals were the norm. They were cooked on the hearth in a large, three-legged iron kettle, a version of which we today call a Dutch oven. Meat and vegetables were cooked together in this pot. Often cornbread was added to the top to provide bread for the meal.

In pioneer days cooking was just another chore for the housewife, who had scores of other daily tasks to complete while dinner was cooking. Thus combination of meat and vegetables simmering in one pot unattended for several hours was the ideal solution for the harassed pioneer housewife preparing dinner. Many of the wild meats, which tended to be tough, needed this long period of cooking or stewing to make them edible.

Throughout the years one-dish meals have continued to be popular. Wrapped in gingham or a blanket, they were ideal to take to the church supper, the barn raising, or the quilting party. Today the one-dish meal has regained some of its popularity, because of limited time available to the two-wage earning family.

Cheese

An Ancient Food

Cheese is not a new food. It's history goes back in the distant past, but its origins are not entirely clear. The Greeks believed that cheese was a gift from the Olympian gods. They considered the miracle of milk being transformed into cheese to be a process beyond the understanding of mere mortals.

Cheese probably became part of meals when men learned to be herdsmen. Sheep were domesticated in Mesopotamia about twelve thousand years ago. In the Old Testament there are numerous references to ewes' and cows' milk cheese.

The discovery of cheese happened when the ancient herdsmen tried to store milk. They discovered a strange phenomenon. The milk quickly soured and turned from its fresh liquid state to a semi-solid mixture of curds and whey. This natural acid-curdling produced a very sour product.

In ancient times fresh milk was also often stored in pouches made from the stomachs of young goats or sheep. One legend has it that on one occasion the pouch had not been properly cured and the fresh milk inside was soon curdled but, on this occasion, without turning sour.

Thus it occurred to the herdsmen that solidified milk was also found in the stomachs of slaughtered unweaned animals. Although it was not until modern times that the natural chemical process of making cheese was understood, the awareness that an animal's stomach lining could solidify the protein in the milk without turning it sour was learned very early.

Classical Greek literature provides evidence that cheese-making had become quite advanced and that it was being made for both the domestic and foreign markets. Excavations in Jerusalem have provided evidence of a cheese market there and that there was a cheese factory in northern Israel.

The mysterious quality of milk's spontaneous fermentation gave rise to all types of beliefs about the curative and strengthening powers of cheese, long before it was realized that cheese is a nearly perfect food. It is rich in protein, fat, minerals, and vitamin A.

According to historians, Zoroaster, the Persian mystic, existed on nothing but cheese for twenty years. The Ancient Greeks fed their Olympic athletes cheese, believing it to be a divinely sustaining gift from Aristaeus, the son of Apollo.

The Romans doted on cheese. Wherever their empire reached, cheese-making was encouraged. Swiss Emmenthal, first made by the Helvetii tribe in the Alpine regions, is one of the cheeses that has survived since Roman times.

When the Roman Empire faded, cheese-making passed into the hands of equally dedicated food lovers — the monks of the Middle Ages. Until then, cheese had been of three types — soft and fresh, pressed and aged, and blue veined like Roquefort and Gorgonzola.

With patience and skill, the monks developed cheese with an entirely different character. One of the first cheeses developed by the French monks was a semi-hard, yet creamy cheese, which today is known as Port Salut. This cheese would keep for some time as opposed to the earlier soft and fresh types. Food historians say that the monks also developed France's most famous soft cheese — Brie.

Historically, the two most important centers of cheese-making have always been France and Italy. France leads with a staggering four hundred varieties, each subdivided according to the region or town where it is made. One of the most famous French cheeses is Roquefort, a blue cheese that is made from sheep's milk. The term "blue" refers to cheeses that are internally mold-ripened. From the eastern Alpine slopes of France come some of the best semi-hard and hard cheeses, such as Comté and Cantal, the French equivalents of Gruyère and Cheddar.

French goats'-milk cheeses are in a category all their own. These vary in size and shape, although they are usually small Their flavor ranges from mild and sweet to strong and pungent and their consistency runs the gamut from soft to very hard.

According to the great French cheese expert, Pierre Androuet, the best goat cheeses are covered with a thin bluish film. This indicates that these cheeses were made on farms and ripened in the traditional manner on wicker trays in cellars, enabling the cheeses to form a natural rind.

The Italians have created such familiar cheeses as Fontina, Gorgonzola, Mozzarella, Provolone, and Caciocayallo. The soft ricotta is the basis of many Italians dishes, including gnocchi and cheesecakes. The hard, grainy, grating cheeses — Parmesan, Pecorino Roman and Pecorino Sardo, and Asiago — are sprinkled on numerous Italian dishes.

England's greatest contribution to the cheese world is the blue-veined Stilton and an impressive range of the Cheddar family. These include Cheshire, Double and Single Gloucester, Derby, and Lancashire. Double Gloucester is denser, heavier, and longer-aged, but is mellow with a satin, creamy quality. Cheshire is believed to be England's oldest cheese, It has an unusual tangy flavor that comes from the salt in the soil of Cheshire.

Switzerland's unique contribution to the world of cheeses are those with "eyes" — Emmenthal, Gruyère, and Appenseller. Like Cheddar, Emmenthal is copied a great deal and usually sold under the generic name of Swiss cheese. However, the best Emmenthal cheese is made from milk of the cows that graze in the lush pastures of the green Emme Valley of Switzerland.

The characteristic large spherical eyes of Emmenthal cheese are formed by three species of bacteria. The cheese-maker must determine, by thumping and listening to the cheese, when the eyes are of the right size. Then the huge wheels of cheese are aged for six to ten months in curing cellars.

Gruyère, a smaller wheel of cheese than Emmenthal, has smaller eyes and a brownish rind. Appenseller, primarily available only in Switzerland, is similar to Gruyère but has a stronger, tangier flavor.

In the United States, cheese-makers have successfully produced most of the world's well-known cheeses. Although distantly related to Cheddar, Monterey Jack is an American innovation. A semi-hard cheese it was first made in Monterey, California in the 1840s. There are two kinds of Monterey Jack. The High Moisture Jack is made from whole milk and is ripened up to six weeks to produce a rather bland and buttery cheese. The Dry Jack is a hard tangy grating cheese made from skimmed and partly skimmed milk. It is aged for six months and usually has a black oiled skin.

"Apple pie without cheese is like a kiss without a squeeze," said the Reverend Henry Ward Beecher. Wisconsin took the Reverend Beecher literally and passed a law that is still on the books that requires eating establishments to have available Wisconsin Cheddar cheese for every piece of apple pie. The law does not state whether one is charged extra for the cheese, but the customer can demand it.

Chili

Many Varieties

Almost every cook has his or her favorite way of preparing chili — some like it very hot, others emphasize the beans, some use ground meat, and others say it is not authentic unless the meat is chopped. Men, particularly, seem to enjoy preparing chili, and it is usually men who win the numerous chili contests held annually throughout the country.

Chili Con Carne (chili with meat), the term by which the dish is officially known, sounds Spanish but it is not of Spanish origin. Although the Spanish found chili peppers growing in the New World, chili is probably an outgrowth of regional Indian, Mexican, and Texas cooking. There are numerous stories, claims, and non-claims about the origin of chili.

The Mexicans lay no claim to chili and one Mexican dictionary defines chili as "a detestable food with a false Mexican title which is sold in the United States from Texas to New York." There is a Mexican stew called Carne Con Chile (meat with chili), a specialty of northern Mexico. This stew, however, is neither sweet, tangy, nor full of tomatoes which are the characteristics of Chili Con Carne.

Chili Con Carne is purely a Southwestern creation. One story has it that it was created by nuns at the early Spanish missions in the Southwest. It was they, who first thought of extending the scarce, tough local meat by combining it with plentiful native beans to make a big warming stew. They flavored the stew with chili and the native herb comino (cumin).

Texans are adamant that chili was created in Texas and claim the dish as their own. They say that Chili Con Carne, which many call "a bowl of red," was invented somewhere in Texas, possibly San Antonio after the Civil War. Chili really got a boost in 1902 when a German in New Braunfels, Texas developed the concoction we know today as chili powder.

San Antonio was so enamored with chili that they had "Chili Queens." These ladies had little carts and tables and would appear late in the evening to sell chili and "whatever else." I suspect that they sold more of the latter as in 1943 the city health regulations forced them to close their operations.

An authentic "bowl of red," whose main ingredient is meat, is not very liquid and does not include beans. Beans, however, can be eaten on the side, not in the chili, although some Texans pour chili over the beans.

Traditionally, Chili Con Carne is made with beef, cut in cubes, and dried red chilies (about 12 pods to three pounds of meat). The chilies are precooked to soften them, then they are seeded and skinned, and added to the meat which has been browned. Oregano, cumin and a little garlic are added for flavoring. If a liquid is needed, some of the water used to cook the peppers is added. That's the traditional way, but there are many, many versions.

An unusual variation of chili is popular in Cincinnati, Ohio. The concoction was invented in the early 1900s by a young chef from Macedonia who had opened a chili stand in Cincinnati. He added additional spices — cinnamon, allspice, and nutmeg— as well as a little cocoa and Cincinnati chili was born.

Not only was the Cincinnati chili unusual but the method of serving it was, too. This chili is normally not made with beans. Thus, when you order Cincinnati chili you get a bowl of meat and spices. When you order it "two way" the sauce comes on a pile of spaghetti. In "three way" you get spaghetti topped with chili and grated Cheddar cheese. A "four way" chili adds chopped yellow onions and a "five way" adds the fifth ingredient — beans.

Chocolate

Fruit of the Cocoa Tree

An "original American," the cacao bean was one of the treasures Columbus brought back to Europe from the New World. But neither he nor his patrons, Ferdinand and Isabella of Spain, understood its potential pleasures. It took Cortez, while conquering Mexico for Spain several decades later, to realize that there must be something very special about this "chocoatl" if Emperor Montezuma and his Aztec court sipped it from goblets made of gold.

Golden goblets notwithstanding, the rich chocolate liquid was not to Spanish tastes until someone added a bit of sugar, a drop or so of vanilla, heated the mixture and topped it with a cinnamon stick. With that, chocolate became the "in" drink of the day in Spain.

For nearly a hundred years, the Spaniards kept the art of cocoa production a secret from the rest of Europe, but eventually the secret leaked out through Spanish monks. It did not take long before chocolate was being acclaimed throughout Europe as a delicious, health-giving food, primarily as a drink.

It was served at the fashionable court of Louis XIII in France. Then, in 1657, word of this drink spread across the English Channel to London. There its popularity was so great that soon there were Chocolate Houses, where meeting, greeting, and sipping were the order of the day.

At first only the very wealthy were able to afford chocolate. Its exclusiveness turned chocolate into such a fashionable drink that some of the shops became famous clubs, such as "The Cocoa Tree." By 1730 mass production had replaced the manual methods of chocolate- making in small shops and the price dropped to within reach of the less affluent.

The advent of the Industrial Revolution in the nineteenth century led to two major developments in the chocolate industry. The first was the perfection of the steam engine, which improved the cocoa-grinding process. The second, in 1828, was the invention of the cocoa press. The use of the cocoa press not only brought prices down, but also improved the quality of the beverage by squeezing out part of the cocoa butter. This process improved the flavor and produced the smooth consistency we are used to today.

Chocolate became an American pantry staple when James Hannon, an Irish immigrant, started milling chocolate in Dorchester, Massachusetts in the mid-1700s. (The Boston Tea Party caused many colonists to switch to chocolate, giving a further boost to its use.) Hannon was encouraged and helped financially by Dr. James Baker, a young Harvard graduate who had started a country store in Dorchester. In 1780, after Hannon was lost at sea, Dr. Baker took over the mill and made it a family enterprise, known as the Baker Chocolate Company.

It was the Swiss, however, who developed the first palatable solid, or "eating" chocolate. Around 1876, at Vevey, Switzerland near Geneva, M. Daniel Peter perfected a process of making milk chocolate by combining the cocoa nib with sugar, cocoa butter, and milk. Two decades later Milton Hershey further developed the process in Pennsylvania using local milk, which eventually resulted in the founding of the Hershey Company. Hershey developed the first milk chocolate bar in 1894 and made it affordable for every chocolate lover.

The end product of chocolate comes from a seed pod of the cocoa tree, which grows to a height of fifteen to twenty feet. Grown only in tropical climates, the cocoa tree is very sensitive to wind and excessive sunlight. Hence it is often planted among banana, coconut, or lemon trees, which are known as "cocoa mothers," since they provide shade and protection.

Cocoa beans are encased in a green spindle-shaped fruit, about four inches wide and ten inches long. The fruit, which is called a pod, hangs directly off the trunk of the tree or its larger branches. When the pods first form they are green or red, depending of the variety of cocoa tree, and as they ripen the outer shells become hard and turn golden or bright red.

Inside each pod are about thirty plump, almond-shaped white seeds encased in a whitish pulp. These seeds, which are white in color but turn purple as they are exposed to the air, are the cocoa beans.

The pods are harvested twice a-year, each harvest lasting about three months. The pods are cut from the trees by hand with a machete. They are then placed in baskets which are taken to the work area of the cocoa plantation. There the pods are split and the beans and pulp are scooped out. Then the beans and pulp are placed in large heaps on wooden platforms in a sunny area. These heaps are covered with leaves so that the pulp can start to ferment.

This fermentation also starts chemical reactions that remove the bitterness and develop the characteristic chocolate flavor. At the end of fermentation, which takes from two to six days, the beans have turned brown and have separated from the pulp. (The Aztecs, who introduced the Spanish conquistadors to chocolate, did not know about or use the fermentation process. Hence their chocolate drink was always bitter.)

While the beans are still wet, they are spread out on wooden platforms and dried in the sun. In larger commercial operations the beans are dried with hot air blowers. However, sun-drying gives the beans a deeper color and more aromatic flavor.

What happens to the little cocoa bean next depends on its end usage. Once the beans arrive at the chocolate factory, they are cleaned, sorted, and then roasted. During the roasting the beans become darker brown, the shell becomes brittle, and the beans take on their full chocolate aroma. Then the roasted beans are put into a machine that cracks them open and uses forced-air to blow away the shells. The remaining beans are known as "nibs."

Next the nibs are ground between rollers to produce a thick dark paste, which hardens upon cooling. At this stage some of the chocolate mass may be formed into bars and sold as unsweetened chocolate. The rest of the mass is further processed into a wide variety of cocoa products.

To make beverage cocoa, a large percentage of the cocoa butter (the fatty substance found in the bean) is pressed out, leaving a solid, dry mass. This is then ground, sieved, and sold as cocoa powder.

Whereas powdered cocoa is made by extracting the cocoa butter, eating chocolate is made by adding extra cocoa butter back to the chocolate mass. Various degrees of sweetness are obtained by adding sugar. The addition of sugar and milk produces milk chocolate. White chocolate is made from the cocoa butter (fat only) with the addition of sugar and milk.

To make the chocolate silky smooth to the tongue, it goes through another process known as "conching." This is a stirring process that takes place in a large drum or shell (hence the word conch from the Spanish meaning shell) and includes heating the chocolate and then kneading it with rollers. After conching, the liquid chocolate can be flowed into molds to harden.

Eggs

Hen's Eggs Are Best

Although there are many other choices of eggs, man has almost universally narrowed it down to one — the hen's egg. The second most important eggs are duck eggs, which, although hardly eaten in the United States, are quite popular in England, Holland, and Belgium. They are also common in the Orient where the famous Chinese "hundred-year eggs" (more like hundred day eggs) are usually duck eggs. Ducks bred for egg production lay as well as hens. However, our more timid American tastes are put off by the stronger and light oiliness of both duck and goose eggs, the latter being the third most important.

Although hens' eggs are almost a universal food today, they were slow to become a part of the human larder, particularly in the Western world. Food historians tell us that it is unlikely that the Egyptians knew of the chicken nor its eggs. The chicken is not mentioned in the Old Testament of the Bible. It is believed that hens' eggs were first eaten in India, with the domestication there of the wild jungle fowl, around 2000 B.C.

The first chickens in the West appeared in central Europe about 1500 B.C. They were also popular in the Mediterranean area. In 720 B.C. roosters were banished in several Greek cities so that their crowing would not wake late-sleeping citizens. The ancient Greeks and Romans were more interested in eggs than in the chickens that laid them, probably because poultry was too scrawny for eating. Later they learned to produce plumper birds, which also gave them better eggs.

After the collapse of the Roman Empire, it was not until the 1600 and 1700s that chickens were once again raised for their meat, and eggs grew even more popular. The renowned French chef, Pierre Francois de la Varenne wrote a cookbook containing sixty different recipes for eggs.

The New World acquired hen's eggs when Columbus brought chickens to the West Indies in 1493. However, there were no chickens on the mainland until the settlers at Jamestown and Plymouth brought the birds more than a century later.

Ever since then eggs have been an integral part of the American diet, providing animal proteins and essential vitamins. Nutritionists say that eating two eggs for breakfast gives you half of your total daily requirements of proteins and vitamins.

Historians tells us that the decorated egg predates Christianity. However it became popular as an Easter item after the Renaissance. Decorated eggs reached their zenith in Russia at the turn of the twentieth century. In 1884 Czar Alexander III had Karl Fabergé, his court jeweler, make a special Easter present for his wife, the Czarina. It was a white enamel egg that opened to disclose a "yolk" in the form of a golden hen with ruby eyes. The hen bore a replica of the imperial crown, which in turn held a ruby pendant.

The Czarina was delighted with her gift. From then on the Czar and his successor, Nicholas II, commissioned many more jeweled eggs for special occasions.

Gingerbread

Unique Flavor

Gingerbread and gingerbread cookies derive their unique flavor from the ginger root (for history of ginger, see page 195) which is grown in Asia, Australia, and also Hawaii.

Ginger was introduced into medieval Europe by traders and travelers from the Far East. The French palate did not take readily to this new spice, but the English immediately liked its "hot-in-the-mouth" taste. It also became popular in Germany.

The English and the Germans found that gingerbread dough could be easily molded into life-like shapes. Queen Elizabeth I is said to have created the gingerbread man when she ordered little cakes flavored with ginger to be baked in the shapes and likenesses of her favorite people.

When the English settlers arrived in America they brought with them their love of ginger and gingerbread. Ginger cookies were handed out in colonial days to the Virginia voters to encourage them to vote for the right candidates for the House of Burgesses.

The best known of all New England gingerbreads was the type sold on Muster Day, or General Training Day, held frequently prior to the Revolution. Companies of militia assembled on local parade grounds for training activities and people came from outlying farms and hamlets to watch. Peddlers set up booths and went through the crowd selling their wares, including the most popular of all — hard gingerbread squares.

Gingerbread keeps very well. During the War of 1812 housewives along the New England shore kept a store of gingerbread along with their clothing, and some personal belongings ready in case of immediate evacuation.

In Salem, Massachusetts, two centuries ago, children saved their pennies to buy Molly Saunder's gingerbread. The door of Molly's bake shop on Central Street was half wood and half glass and any young customer could peek in at the mouth-watering goodies. Usually when the door bell tinkled it announced a young customer who had made up his or her mind to buy either the ginger bread with butter for three cents or the gingerbread without butter for two cents. Molly's secret for making gingerbread was boiling butter with maple sugar and spreading it on the gingerbread after it was baked.

Today there are many versions of the dough used for gingerbread men — some very crisp, others puffy. In some countries ginger, molasses, and flour are mixed and then stored in a crock in a cool place to age for a year. In most countries the ingredients are mixed, the dough rests for a short time and then the cookies are baked.

Gingerbread cookies are not as popular today as they were years ago. Today gingerbread is usually thought of as a cake-like dessert topped with whipped cream or ice cream. Ginger is also one of the main ingredients in spice cakes.

For Gingerbread with Apricot-Sherry Glaze, see page 196. It makes a light and delicious dessert.

Hamburgers and Hot Dogs

American Innovations

Hamburgers and hot dogs are an American culinary innovation. The hamburger, one of the most popular hot sandwiches in America, was born in 1900 at Louis' Lunch, a small lunch wagon in New Haven, Connecticut. Until that time a hamburg denoted a chopped beef steak on a plate, named after the port city of Hamburg.

Louis' establishment was known for its steak sandwiches. The owner always took the steak trimmings home and ground them up for patties to be eaten by his family. As the business grew so did the trimmings. The logical solution was to sell the by-product at the lunch wagon. Louis broiled the hamburger patties and served them on a plate with a slice of onion and some home-fries, creating a hamburger plate. Unfortunately, this took more time to eat than his regular steak sandwiches. One of his customers solved the problem one day when he said, "Put that patty between two slices of bread, and let me get out of here."

The hamburger was born, but it took another fifty years for it to become firmly entrenched as America's favorite fast food. The automobile and a nation constantly on the move made the hamburger an institution and the cornerstone of fast food.

The German influence on American cuisine gave us our most popular sausage — the frankfurter, a Frankfurt-style sausage. More than twenty billion of them are eaten annually in this country. Frankfurters with buns first appeared in the United States in the German exhibit at the St. Louis World's Fair of 1904. That same year, Charles Feltman, a German immigrant introduced the frankfurter at his small eatery at Coney Island. There the frankfurter was often referred to as the "Coney Island chicken."

The frankfurter became a favorite food at baseball games. It was easy to hold when nestled in its specially tailored bun, and was just the item for outdoor munching.

It was at a ball park that the frankfurter made a lasting impression on Tad Dorgan, a sport's cartoonist. In one of his drawings he endowed a frankfurter with a tail, legs, and a head, so that it looked like a dachshund. The frankfurter has been called a "hot dog" ever since. It is even sold by that name in Europe, creating the false impression that it is an American invention.

Traditionally the hot dog was made of pure beef. It was usually brought from a street vendor, clasped in its hot dog bun, and daubed with lots of yellow mustard. The frills of piccalilli, cole slaw, or sauerkraut came later.

Ice Cream

Everybody's Favorite

One of the most delightful foods people of all ages savor is ice cream. Considering the long history of many foods ice cream is relatively one of the "new kids on the block."

Marco Polo learned about freezing sweet cream when he visited China late in the thirteenth century. At that time the Chinese emperors ate sweetened ground rice mixed with milk and frozen in porcelain bowls. In India there was also an iced dessert made by boiling milk until it was thickened and then freezing it in porous earthenware bowls.

Ice cream became popular in Europe around 1533 when fourteen-year-old Catherine de Medici came to Paris to marry the Duc d'Orleans (who later became King Henry II of France). Henry and his father were delighted when the young bride brought with her a retinue of cooks, whose culinary expertise astonished the French. One of the cooks showed off an Italian specialty -- an iced confection made with cream, called gelati. Today we know it as ice cream.

The French nobility ate ice creams on special occasions. At one dinner given by Louis XIV, an apparently fresh laid egg, colored like those at Easter, was served to each guest in a marble cup. To their surprise the guests discovered that this egg was cold and hard and consisted of a cream base with candied sweets. While French royalty and the well-to-do continued to enjoy ice cream, it took one hundred years for it to become a food of the common folk. By the late 1600s ice cream cafes abounded throughout Paris.

The history of ice cream in England began when Charles I (1600-1649) had it served at court. He had brought to England Gerard Tissain, a French chef who had been in charge of all ice cream making at the French court. Tissain was given an annual salary of twenty pounds to keep the ice cream formula secret. When Charles was beheaded in 1649, a group of noblemen bought the formula from the chef.

By the late 1600s English coffee houses were selling ice cream. The Viennese and Italians soon followed France's example of unique establishments selling only ice cream. Each country soon developed their own iced specialties — coupes, spumoni, cassata.

By the 1740s ice cream was becoming popular in America. George Washington was an early American ice cream aficionado. He often spent $200 on great quantities of ice for summer cooling. He owned a "cream machine for making ice."

Dolly Madison used ice cream to make her famous White House dinner parties special occasions. She often served pink ice cream in a large silver dome-shaped container.

In 1846 an American, Nancy Johnson, invented a machine for making ice cream. It not only simplified the process but increased control over the finished product. It was a portable, hand-cranked ice cream churn that beat the mixture of cream and flavoring with a paddle as it froze. The canister of cream sat in a wooden bucket full of ice and salt. In about twenty minutes it produced ice cream.

The invention of this machine made it possible for anyone to produce ice cream at home. Rock salt, commonly called "ice cream salt" had become a cheap commodity. The visits of the ice man, with his horse and cart and his iron claw to heave blocks of ice, kept the household supplied with ice. The new ice cream machine also made it possible to mass-produce ice cream and sell it commercially.

Ice cream vendors on the streets started in New York around 1828 when a group of boisterous fellows with kettles in their hands yelled "I scream, Ice Cream" to attract customers. At about the same time Italian ice cream vendors under the leadership of Carlo Gatti also became popular on the streets of London and other English cities. These vendors were Italian immigrants. Thus the dessert once the star of banquets became an everyday street commodity.

There are many claims as to the invention of the first ice cream cone. The French and Germans had metal and paper cones in the mid-1800s. Carlo Gatti invented an edible horn or cornet for holding ice cream by twisting pastry around his finger and baking the "cone." A Syrian immigrant to the United States, Ernest Harnwi, rolled up thin Persian waffles and topped them with a ball of ice cream at the St. Louis Fair in 1904.

At about the same time communal tin drinking cups at public water fountains began to be old-fashioned and were considered unsanitary. The individual drink Cup Company of New York started supplying paper cups, one for each person who wanted a drink of water. The operation became so successful that the company's name was changed to a more patriotic and snappy one — Dixie Cup. In 1923 the company's profits doubled after making a special version of their cup to hold a single portion of ice cream. The cup had a round lid with a tongue to help pull it off. The lid could be bent and used as a spoon.

In 1919 a means was found for making a chocolate coating adhere to ice cream. The result was marketed as the I-Scream Bar. Later the name was changed to Eskimo Pie with a disposable silver foil wrapper.

The idea of the Good Humor Bar, an ice-cream block on a stick like a lollipop, was conceived in 1920. It was developed by, Harry Burt, Sr. He made marketing history by selling Good Humor Bars from vans equipped with bells to announce their presence. Men in white uniforms manned these small trucks. The Good Humor Man became a fixture in many neighborhoods in large cities.

The ice cream sundae originated in Ed Berners ice cream parlor in Two Rivers, Wisconsin, around 1881. It seems that one summer evening one of Berners' customers, George Hallauer, dropped in and ordered a dish of ice cream. Hallauer saw a bottle of chocolate syrup, which Berners used to make sodas. "Why don't you put some of the chocolate on the ice cream?" Hallauer asked. Berners complained it would ruin the flavor of his ice cream, but Hallauer insisted he wanted to try it anyway. Chocolate-topped ice cream became the rage of the town, and Berners began experimenting with other flavors and toppings of nuts.

The name sundae, however, was born in the neighboring town of Manitowoc, Wisconsin. George Giffy, also the owner of an ice cream parlor, served the embellished ice cream dishes only on Sundays. One weekday, a little girl ordered a dish of ice cream "with stuff on it." When told that he only served it on Sundays, the child said, "This must be Sunday, for it's the kind of ice cream I want." Giffy gave it to her, and from then on the dish was called Sunday and eventually the spelling evolved into sundae.

The first large-scale commercial producer of ice cream was Jacob Fussell, a Baltimore milk dealer who had noticed the rising demand for ice cream and that there was a surplus of cream in the summer. He made much larger quantities than the local restaurants and hotels and provided them at a lower price. Fussell was the forerunner of today's ice cream manufacturers, including such boutique firms as Haagen-Dazs and Ben and Jerry's.

Maple Syrup

Exclusively American

Maple syrup and maple sugar are two of the few foods produced nowhere except in North America. Many native American foods such as corn, potatoes, tomatoes, beans, and turkey are now grown all over the world, but maple sugar is strictly a North American product.

Attempts have been made to grow the North American sugar maple (botanical name A. saccharum.) in Europe, but with no success. The Europeans have also tried to produce sugar with their own maple trees, primarily the Norwegian maple. It has been found that it is not the tree, but the climate that produces the sugar.

Only in the northeastern United States and adjacent areas of Canada is the weather just right to cause the maple sap to run in sufficient quantities to make tapping the trees worthwhile. The changes in the weather from winter cold to spring warmth act as a thermal pump which forces the sap to circulate in the maple trees and enables the trees to be tapped for this sap.

Today maple sugar and genuine maple syrup are luxuries and quite pricy. In Colonial times maple sugar and syrup were the commonest sweeteners. For the Indians they were the only sweeteners. Many of the northeastern Indians never learned to make salt from sea water and used maple sugar as their general seasoning. They also used cakes of maple sugar as a medium of exchange.

Early European explorers were enchanted with the Indian food and wrote about a liquor that runs from the trees at the end of winter. It was known as maple water. The colonists began to have a slightly larger choice of sweeteners after importing Italian honey bees in 1630.

Thus they had both "tree sweetenin" and "Bee sweetenin." Molasses also soon began to arrive from West Indian sugar cane plantations.

In the mid- and late 1600s imported molasses was still very expensive to settlers in the hinterland as it had to be brought inland from the ports by pack horse. Also molasses and cane sugar were disapproved of by many in the Northeast because they were produced with slave labor. "Make your own sugar," advised the Farmer's Almanac in 1803.

At that time anyone who lived not far from the sea in the Northeast had access to a number of maple sugar trees. Vermont became known primarily as the maple sugar state and it is still the number one producer of maple sugar. Maple sugar remained the main sweetener in the Northeast until the end of the nineteenth century.

Sugar making from maple trees is a tedious and laborious process. Only mature trees—at least forty years old, a "foot through," and some sixty feet tall—are selected for sugaring. In the spring the weather is variable, from warm days to freezing nights, all of which affect the sap run. Consequently, the sugar maker must check his trees several times a week.

Each tree produces, drip by drip, about forty quarts of sap. These forty quarts produce only one quart of maple syrup. The rest is water, which must be boiled away.

Long before the first settlers arrived from Europe, native Indians gathered the maple sap in the following manner. They cut a gouge in the tree to start the sap flowing and attached buckskin bags to catch the flow. After the bags were collected, they dropped hot coals into them to evaporate the water and reduce the sap to syrup.

The Indians also placed the sap in small dishes and let them stand overnight, then in the morning removed the ice that had formed on top. The early settlers improved on the Indian method of gathering sap by attaching wooden buckets to the trees. The full buckets were then dumped into large iron kettles and the sap was boiled to evaporate the water.

Until 1870 all sap boiling was done outdoors near the stand of maple trees. Gradually, small houses were built to enclose the boiling kettles in order to reduce the amount of fuel required. Today, during maple sugaring time one can see many small houses on the hillsides with immense clouds of steam pouring out of them.

Modern sugar makers, however, no longer need to transport buckets of sap from the individual trees to the sugaring house. Instead a network of tubing brings the sap from the trees directly to the kettles. One pipeline can handle thirty trees. A profitable commercial venture requires about five hundred trees, which is all one person can handle.

Traditionally, after the first night of the "boiling," the sugar maker's family sat at the kitchen table to sample the results. The hard work, the sap that had frozen, the new pipeline that had been chewed by deer —all problems were forgotten as they tasted the new syrup.

If there was still snow on the ground, there was a "sugaring-off" party. Hot maple syrup was poured onto platters of clean snow, which turned the mixture into a tasty candy. This tradition still occurs among many sugar-making families. Vermonters eat this candy with freshly baked doughnuts and tangy pickles that cut the sweetness.

Sugar production in Vermont reached its peak in the 1880s. Until the early 1900s, maple syrup was less expensive than white sugar, and Vermonters used it to sweeten and flavor almost everything. While annual production of maple sugar is only a fraction of that in the 1800s, Vermont still produces more maple sugar and syrup than any other state. Maple syrup and maple sugar has long since become a luxury food.

The following French toast has maple syrup in the batter and is alo served with additional maple syrup.

Maple French Toast

3 jumbo eggs
1/3 cup milk
1/3 cup light cream
1/3 cup maple syrup
1 tablespoon grated orange rind
8 slices white bread, 1-inch thick
4 tablespoons butter
Additional maple syrup

If using a non-stick griddle omit the butter. If not, use a skillet large enough to hold 3 slices of the bread.

In a shallow bowl whisk together the eggs, milk, cream, maple syrup, and orange rind.

If using griddle heat over medium heat, or heat 2 tablespoons of the butter in a skillet over medium heat.

Dip the bread, one slice at a time, into the egg mixture, coating each side well. Place the bread on the griddle or in the skillet and fry until browned on one side; turn and brown the other side. Keep cooked slices warm in a 200° F. oven, then fry the other slices.

Serve warm with maple syrup. Serves 4.

Olive Oil

Extra Virgin, Virgin, and Pure

Ninety-five percent of the world's olive oil production comes from the Mediterranean region, which has a history of olive tree cultivation that goes back over six thousand years.

Some olive oil producers determine the grades of their oil by the pressings while other determine the grade by the amount of acidity in the oil. Color varies from oil-to-oil depending on the type of olive, so it is difficult to use as a factor in determining quality.

In Italy the grades of olive oil are determined by the pressing. The very best olive oil is extra virgin, which is obtained from the first cold pressing of the finest, hand-picked olives. Green or green-gold in color, this oil is aromatic and tastes mellow and nutty, with no bitter after-taste.

The second best grade of olive oil is virgin. It is obtained through a second and third pressing of the olives This oil is also aromatic, but to a lesser degree.

Pure olive oil is the lowest grade and is produced from additional pressings of the olives Pure olive oil is produced in the largest quantity as it is used the most, in household and commercial cooking.

Extra Virgin olive oil has the finest flavor, color, and aroma and is the most expensive of the three grades. Within a given grade of olive oil, selection is a matter of taste. Like fine wines, colors and aromas of olive oils vary according to the type of olive and the soil and climatic conditions under which the fruit was grown. The extra virgin provides the widest range of flavors.

Extra virgin olive oil should be used with heartier, more robust dishes containing red meat and tomato-based sauces as well as dishes requiring uncooked oil such as salads. The sim-pler the dish, the greater the need to use extra virgin olive oil. Much of the flavors of extra virgin and virgin olive oils tend to be lost, however, at high temperature. Thus it is most economical to use pure olive oil for high-heat cooking.

Connoisseurs categorize olive oil by flavors and colors. In Italy, for example, the famous olive oil from the Chianti region of Italy is "fruity" and full bodied, with a slightly green color. The Liguria region produces pale golden oil which is more delicate and sweet. The olive oils from the Apulia and Calabria regions have a distinctive almond flavor.

Olive oil is still made today according to a process used centuries ago. As soon as the olives are harvested, they are taken to the factory called an olive mill, where the oil must be extracted within a week. The high quality oil, however, is extracted within the first day or so. The whole process takes place without any use of heat or chemicals

The production of olive oil is primarily the separation of the liquids contained in the olive from the solid components of the fruit. This is then followed by the separation of the oil from the olive's naturally-held water.

Beginning with whole, clean fruit which is harvested from November to March, depending on the region, a paste is made by crushing the whole fruit. This is done under granite (or metal) mill stones that still resemble those used a thousand years ago.

This paste is spread onto loosely-woven hemp mats which are stacked, interspersed with metal disks, in a hydraulic press. The mats undergo hundreds of tons of pressure to extract the liquid contained in the paste. The liquid also includes the fruit's own water. To separate out the water, the oil, being lighter than the water, is allowed to surface in a container and then removed. Some olive mills separate the oil in a centrifuge.

Olive oil is as old as civilization itself and there were other uses for this oil besides in food. In ancient Greece and Rome olive oil was used for health, healing, and illumination. The Greek and Roman nobility spent a great deal of time pouring olive oil over themselves. They oiled after the bath, before and sometimes during meals, before and after doing physical exercise, before long journeys on foot and again upon arrival and, in general, whenever they wished to relieve tension and fatigue.

The prescription for health of the Greek philosopher Democritus was "honey on the inside, olive on the outside." Later Greek and Roman versions of this rule was changed to wine on the inside and olive oil on the outside.

In ancient Rome there were a number of professional anointers who offered massages for a fee to anyone feeling in need of relaxation. This practice was usually associated with gymnasiums and public baths. Every athlete who took his sport seriously had two trainers — a gymnastic master for physical training and an "anointer." The latter gave the athlete medical check-ups, advised him about diet, and gave him olive oil massages.

Soap began to be imported into Italy in the early years after Christ. It eventually and drastically reduced the amount of olive oil that people used on their skins.

Olive oil, however, became the basis for making the highest quality soap, Castile. This industry was centered in Spain and the product became a world famous luxury item from the eighth century onward.

Olive oil is an excellent base for perfumes, and scented oils were used liberally on all social occasions in the ancient world.

The ancient Egyptians used to set large cones of perfumed ointment, which were made with olive oil, on top of their heads at dinner parties. As the atmosphere at these events warmed up the cones gradually melted and deliciously scented oil would drizzle through their hair and down their faces.

Olive oil covered the body of Roman dinner guests and crowns of olive or bay leaves were worn at banquets. Excavators at Pompeii discovered a shop that specialized in perfume and olive garlands. People invited to dinner could stop by on the way to the party and pick up headgear and the oils needed for the evening.

Today many people who live in the Mediterranean area drink small amounts of olive oil regularly — one or two teaspoons once a day, once a week or once a month. They claim that it is healthy. Olive oil is a gentle laxative.

Night-time lighting was commonly provided in the ancient Mediterranean world by lamps filled with olive oil. An oil-soaked wick takes a long time to burn. For sanctuary lamps and any light that burned continuously, olive oil was preferred as it was essentially smokeless and had very little odor. Until the early twentieth century it was customary in southern Europe to leave money in one's will for candles and lamp-oil for the funeral lights.

Olive oil has been used in the past for rust prevention, softening and lubricating leather, making ink, and diamond polishing. In the ancient world, statues in danger of cracking because of climate were kept constantly coated in olive oil.

Even with all of these other uses of olive oil, today most of us prefer to limit our use to cooking and as salad dressings, be it extra virgin, virgin, or pure.

Pancakes and Waffles

Favorite Breakfast Foods

Two of America's favorite breakfast foods are pancakes and waffles. They are easily prepared and provide a hearty meal. Their batter is similar, but that of waffles is slightly heavier in texture.

No one knows exactly when or where the first pancake was made. Many food historians say it was prehistoric man who created the first pancake when water and a fistful of pounded grain were combined and poured on a hot rock in the sun.

Historically pancakes have been a favorite food of both rich and poor alike. They have not been subjected to the snobbish division that was associated with bread for many centuries in Western civilizations.

Pancakes go back much further in history than does bread. Excavation of Egyptian tombs have yielded grinding stones used for grains and the tomb walls dating from 8000 B.C. have revealed pictorial proof that pancakes were important in the ancient Egyptian diet.

Many centuries later, at the time of Plato, a pancake recipe appeared in the writings of Apicius, a notorious Italian Epicurean of the first century A.D.. His recipe for pancakes has the same basic ingredients as are used today — eggs, flour, and milk. Apicius served his pancakes with a syrup of honey mixed with ground pepper.

Ancient cultures observed planting and harvesting with religious festival at which pancakes were featured. The early Slavonic tribes regarded these round flat cakes to be a symbol of their sun god. After the founding of Christianity these spring and harvest ceremonies became part of the church calendar and were celebrated with religious rites and food, including pancakes.

The observance of Lent furthered the enjoyment of pancakes. Meat was not the only food forbidden during this religious observance before Easter. All of meat's by-products such as eggs, milk, and animal fats were also forbidden. Thus before Ash Wednesday everyone made haste to eat up these perishables. One of the most logical ways to do this was to combine milk, eggs, butter, and flour and make pancakes.

In France, the second of February is Chandeleurs, Pancake Day. Many customs have grown up around this Lenten holiday, varying from province to province. In some, tossing a crepe (thin pancake) into the air with one hand and catching it in a pan using the same hand while holding a piece of money in the other hand assures a year of financial success. Other localities conceal yards of fine thread in one of the crepes, and the unsuspecting diner who bites into it is consoled with a prize.

In Holland pancakes are not just a Lenten tradition. Townships regularly compete in pancake contests which feature fanciful creations. Some of these are gigantic, puffy as soufflés, and decorated with an icing.

In England on Shrove Tuesday before Lent there are pancake races and pancake-eating contests. English eating contests are easily outdone by the Finns, who devour whole meals of "pannukakku" and pride themselves on outeating their neighbors. The quantity of pancakes consumed is also a contest in Russia during Maslyenitsa, or Butter Week. Everyone tries his or her hand at making a blini, the Russian crepe.

When done right pancake-making can be considered to be a gourmet craft and many people take it seriously. Serious pancake makers believe that the griddle used is an important element in the success of the final product. Some prefer a rectangular griddle that fits over two burners, others like a round one, although it holds fewer pancakes. Still others prefer a black-iron skillet or an electric table-top griddle.

The creation of the first waffle is lost in history. Holland and Germany have made them for centuries as has France. Waffles are mentioned in twelfth-century French ballads. The original French word for waffle iron, "fer à gaufres," first appeared in print in 1433. However, the gaufres were probably much closer to the thin waffled cookie we know today than to the thick waffles that are served for breakfast, and sometimes topped with fruit and whipped cream for dessert.

One theory as to the origin of the pancake dates back to the time of the Crusaders. Upon returning from one of the Holy Wars, a Crusader is supposed to have entered his house still wearing his cross-meshed foil and armor. He greeted his wife and family and being tired he sat down on the nearest stool. Unfortunately the stool contained a stack of freshly made pancakes. The waffled pattern of the gentlemen's armor supposedly gave the pancake the pattern of waffling.

Waffles were known in England and the Pilgrims learned of them either there or in Holland. In any event the Pilgrims brought the recipe and waffle irons used in the fireplace with them to the Massachusetts Colony. Shortly thereafter, the Dutch settled in the New Amsterdam Colony and they too had the recipe and equipment for waffles.

However, Thomas Jefferson is given credit for bringing the waffle iron back from Holland when he was Ambassador to France in the late 1700s. He was the first to serve waffles at a formal party. Waffle parties became popular in Virginia in the late 1700s due to Jefferson's enthusiasm for this pastry.

In America in the early 1800s, vendors on city streets sold waffles covered with butter and molasses or maple syrup. At about the same time waffles became a favorite breakfast item in the South. They were served topped with a fried piece of country ham and maple syrup or molasses.

The original recipe for waffles brought to New Amsterdam by the Dutch settlers were made with wheat flour . They used yeast made from stale beer for a leavening agent. The batter was very similar to plain pancakes, also thought to be a Dutch innovation. Pioneering colonists made waffles from sweet potatoes, buckwheat, and cornmeal as well as wheat flour. In the South a small amount of boiled white rice was frequently added to the waffle batter.

The early settlers heated their waffle irons in the fireplace. After the kitchen stove was invented housewives heated their waffle irons on top of the stove. When electric waffle irons were invented, early in the 1900s, waffles became very popular, not only for breakfast, but also as a Sunday night supper dish. In the summer fresh strawberries and whipped cream topped the waffles. In Baltimore kidney stew served on waffles was a traditional Sunday evening specialty.

Today we think of breakfast as a very simple meal often eaten on the run. Pancakes and waffles are frequently reserved as special treats for weekend breakfasts. During the week we save time by using the frozen version in the toaster.

Parmesan Cheese

Best Known Italian Cheese

How many times have you had one of the wait-staff at a restaurant ask you whether you would like some grated Parmesan cheese over your salad or pasta? Most of us either reply, "yes, or a little bit." That touch of cheese has become a norm, as have many Italian culinary innovations that we have adopted.

Italian food historians tell us that cheese has been made in the Parma region for at least two thousand years. Parmesan cheese originated in the province of Reggio Emilia in the Duchy of Parma. Hence the official name Parmigiano Reggiano for this cheese, although now commonly known merely as Parmesan. Today Parmesan is produced in government-approved areas in the provinces of Parma, Reggio Emilia, Modena, Bologna, and Mantova.

By the mid-1500s Italians were using Parmesan cheese in several dishes at elaborate banquets. The cheese was served with cooked truffles, cardoons(a type of celery), fresh grapes and pears, and other fruits that had been marinated in vinegar with fennel seeds, pine nuts, and pistachios. Today this Renaissance custom of serving Parmesan cheese with pears, grapes and other fruits as a dessert has been revived by many restaurants serving international cuisine.

Cheeses from these provinces are made the same way. The slight differences in the Parmesans comes from the forage on which the cows are fed, so that the milk differs from place to place.

Even today Parmesan is made in small cheese factories, called "caselli." Each caselli produces a maximum of sixteen cheeses a day. The method of making this cheese has remained unchanged through the centuries.

The milk used to make Parmesan comes from local cows fed entirely on fresh grasses. The best cheeses are made between April and November. Parmesan is shaped into large wheels, weighing between sixty and seventy pounds. The cheeses mature in vast storerooms for different periods of time.

There are three grades of Parmesan, named according to the length of time they have matured. The youngest Parmesan, the nuovo, which is good as a table cheese, has aged for one year. Parmigiano vecchio has aged for between one and a half to two years. Parmigiano stravecchio is Parmesan at its best. It has aged for at least two to two-and-a-half years. The latter two are used in cooking and when grated to sprinkle over cooked pasta dishes.

The ideal Parmesan is a straw color and has a crumbly texture. Its taste is mellow, rich, and slightly salty. Wrapped tightly in foil or plastic wrap Parmesan keeps for a long time in the refrigerator.

Although Parmesan is widely used in Italian cooking, it is used with discretion and only when considered to be a vital ingredient in the finished dish. For example, it is a common flavoring for pasta, but is not used in most traditional fish and seafood sauces. Few meat dishes call for Parmesan. It is never added to the traditional Tuscan bean soup but is always used with Minestrone alla Milanese.

Traditionally Parmesan is added to vegetables that have been sautéed in butter, but not to vegetables cooked in oil. Parmesan is used in risottos to make them thicker and creamier.

The true Parmesan aficionado never buys grated Parmesan. Also he or she never grates more than the amount needed, because once it is grated Parmesan loses some of its flavor.

Patés and Terrines

Luxury Foods

For years there has been confusion between the terms paté and terrine. Moreover, today the two terms are frequently used interchangeably. Both are molded in the cooking container.

Traditionally, patés and terrines were baked. However, in modern times a mixture of pureed livers, fat, and seasonings molded in a dish are also called patés. In preparing this type of paté, the livers are either sautéed or braised before pureeing.

The simpler of the two is the terrine. A terrine was originally designated an earthenware dish in which meat, fish, or vegetables were cooked. Sometimes terrines are composed of chopped-meat or pureed-fish, both known as forecemeat because they have been forced through a meat grinder. Cooks frequently add small pieces of meat, morsels of fish, chopped nuts or pieces of truffle for complexity and flavor. Many chefs describe terrines as "dressed-up" meat loaves.

Meat terrines are usually encased in a coating of fat, either bacon or sheets of pork fat, to keep the meat mixture moist. The terrine is generally baked in a hot water bath which ensures a gentle and even penetration of heat. Country terrines, composed of coarser pieces of meat, are baked without being encased in fat so that a brown crust will result and add to the flavor.

In recent years vegetable terrines have become popular. They include a variety of vegetables in a most colorful presentation. Part of the vegetables can be pureed, while another part might be chopped for texture and visual interest. Vegetable terrines are usually chilled and brought to room temperature before serving.

When a terrine mixture is wrapped and baked in pastry for a more formal presentation, it becomes a paté. Although this historical distinction between a terrine and a paté is straightforward, Americans have come to use the term paté to describe what is actually a terrine. Part of the confusion arises from the practice by many chefs of enclosing their terrine mixtures in strips or sheets of fat, baking it in an earthenware dish, and then unmolding it.

Terrines and patés originated in France and have a long history. Country terrines and pork pies have been made for centuries in farmhouse kitchens, particularly in Europe. Recipes for meat and fish patés have been found in medieval and Renaissance cooking manuals.

Pork pies were especially popular in American colonial days as they were a thrifty means of using the meat scraps after butchering the hog. In general pies are not molded and hence do not fit the paté or terrine definition.

The crust of early patés were designed for durability rather than delicacy. In eighteenth century England, patés (which the English called pies) containing concentric layers of small birds stuffed into larger ones were sent to friends and relatives at Christmas.

The custom of stuffing one bird inside another was also popular during colonial days in Williamsburg. The crust of this creation was inedible since it had a similar texture to that of a bread sculptures. This type of crust had the same effect as cooking something in a clay pot. The casing retained moisture for the birds inside it. The sturdy pastry also acted as a box in which to ship the parcel.

In France, the pastry for patés eventually became more delicate and the fillings increased in complexity. Many rich game patés consist of layers of light and dark meats enclosed in puff pastry.

For a delightful paté recipe, see Vineyard Paté on page 232.

Pies

Not an American Invention

Pie has traditionally been America's favorite dessert. Contrary to popular belief, pie was not invented in New England. Crust-enclosed fruit pastry can be traced back hundreds of years to the peasant cookery of almost every European country. English meat pies hve been famous for hundreds of years, for example.

The shallow, slope-sided pie pan, however, is truly American. It was designed to use less filling than the traditional European deep pie dishes.

The simple mixture of shortening, flour, and water, which are the ingredients of pie pastry, originated with the Greeks. The Romans carried home recipes for this pastry when they conquered Greece. Over the years as Roman influence spread throughout Europe so did the basic pie pastry which was used for both sweet and savory pies. The first settlers in America brought their traditional recipes for pies with them.

When one thinks of American pies, apple pie typically comes to mind, hence the expression "As American as Apple Pie."

For the Pennsylvania Dutch, pies have a special meaning. Poor man's pies known as "flitche" are made with any handy ingredients. Amish half-moon pies, called preaching pies, were given to children during long Sunday church services to keep them quiet. "Rosina Boi" or raisin pie, also called "funeral pie," is served to fortify mourners after a funeral.

In Arkansas traditional raisin funeral pie was enhanced with a touch of bourbon to console the mourners.

A meal without a pie seemed unthinkable to the early Shakers. When apple bins were empty in the spring they made sugar pies with butter, sugar, cream, and rosewater. Sugar pies were made in the South, too, except there they used vanilla for flavoring. In New England, sugar pies were made with maple sugar.

When pioneers traveled westward, their cherished pie recipes went with them. Pecan pies, cream pies, and a great variety of fruit pies were created. In the fall and during winter months, pumpkin and sweet potato pies enhanced with molasses or sugar and spices replaced summer fruit pies. Sweet potato pies with a little bourbon were popular in the South.

Abraham Lincoln had a great craving for molasses pie. According to the "White House Cookbook" the original recipe for Lincoln's Molasses Pie was: "Two tea cupfuls of molasses, one of sugar, three eggs, one tablespoonful of melted butter, one lemon, nutmeg; beat and bake in pastry."

In the Midwest "stack pies" became popular at barn raisings and at harvest time. These were simply six to eight different pies, stacked one on top of the other. Wedges were cut down through the whole stack and a wedge was one serving. This eliminated the dilemma of which pie to choose.

Deep-dish pies were developed by farm women to salvage fruit that might otherwise be wasted when the orchards had bumper crops.

Old favorites evolved into new creations, such as chiffon pie. They retained many of the characteristics of cream pies, but gelatin was added to transform the cream version into a spectacular refrigerated creation.

Pies were carried to potluck suppers, picnics, family reunions, and festivals. Pie-eating contests were organized at county fairs. Pie auctions were fund raising events. Pie-baking contests challenged homemakers. Today state fairs still have pie-baking contests.

Pie as an American dessert has stood the test of time and will likely go on forever.

Pizza

Thin or Thick Crust

Pizza became popular in this country in the mid-1940s when World War II servicemen, returning from Italy, brought back a liking for this traditional Italian pie. Americans started making pizzas at home and by the 1960s they were available in restaurants. Today pizza has expanded into a multi-billion dollar business.

Restaurant chains and carry-out facilities now specialize in serving only pizza. Supermarkets have entire sections devoted to frozen pizzas as well as multiple shelf space for pizza makings — from the special sauce to crust mixes and even ready-made pizza crusts.

Although pizza is a fairly recent culinary addition to the American diet, the origin of pizza can easily be traced back to Roman times. The Romans often enhanced rounds of dough by adding olive oil, herbs, and honey and then baking these rounds on stones. Previous to that, bread with toppings were popular throughout the Middle East, Greece, and Egypt.

Pizza as we know it today, however, was the creation of the citizens of Naples, Italy, who gave a new dimension to the traditional pizza when they added tomatoes. Tomatoes were first brought to Naples by Neapolitan sailors returning from the New World in the seventeenth century. These first Italian tomatoes were yellow in color and used as ornamental plants. To this day all tomatoes are referred to in Italian as pomodoro, meaning "golden apples."

It was not until a hundred years later, that large, red, sweet tomatoes were developed in Italy. They evolved from seeds brought to Italy from Peru by two Jesuits. The tomato soon gained popularity and found its place in the sauces of Southern Italy and as a favorite topping for pizza.

At first pizza was sold in stalls in Italy and eaten on the streets. Soon pizzerias appeared in Naples, and the popularity of pizza even spread to the nobility. When Italy's Queen Margherita arrived in Naples in 1889, with King Umberto I, she immediately wanted to sample the famous Neapolitan dish.

Since a woman of her rank could hardly go to a pizzeria, a famous pizza maker and his wife visited the queen. They prepared three kinds of pizza for her — one topped with pork fat, cheese, and garlic, another with tomatoes, garlic, and oil, and the third with tomatoes, mozzarella, and basil. The latter contained the colors of the Italian flag and became the queen's favorite. Ever since then it has been called Pizza Margherita.

Pizza first spread to America in the Italian neighborhoods of the major East coast cities. Italian immigrants opened small storefront restaurants and offered the traditional thin crust pizzas of their homeland.

The creation of deep-dish pizza occurred in Chicago in 1947. Restaurateurs Ike Sewell and Ric Riccardo opened a pizzaria called Pizzeria Uno.

They did not want to duplicate the thin-crusted pizza that had been common in the Italian neighborhoods throughout America, so the partners decided to invent their own style of pizza — something hearty, yet with gourmet ingredients. Chicago-style thick crust pizza was born.

By the late 1970s Sewell, the surviving partner, was operating two pizzarias. The two locations were baking two thousand deep dish pizzas daily.

Modern technology has contributed to pizza-making at home. The clay pizza stone, the round perforated pizza pans, and modern yeast have made pizza making easy for the home cook.

Pizza toppings, too, have become more varied. They now reflect trends toward lighter foods and they also feature ethnic flavors of different parts of the world. I am sure the Neapolitans never thought of using pineapple and ham as a pizza topping. Hawaiians, however, love it. Pizza dough, too, can be varied with the addition of whole wheat flour or herbs.

The dough for the following pizza is very simple to make and does not need to rise, simply to rest for a short while. If only one pizza is desired, cut the dough in half and freeze one half. Also cut the sauce and topping ingredients in half. I usually add additional toppings, such as chopped onions, sliced mushrooms, green pepper strips, fresh tomato slices, and some crumbled Italian sausage.

Easy Pizza

Dough

1 package dry yeast
1 cup warm water (105 to 115 degrees)
1 teaspoon sugar
1/2 teaspoon salt
2 tablespoons vegetable oil
2 1/2 cups all purpose flour

Dissolve the yeast in the warm water. Stir in the sugar, salt, oil, and flour. Beat vigorously, until a dough forms, about 20 strokes. Allow the dough to rest, 5 to 10 minutes, while preparing the sauce.

Sauce

1/2 cup chopped onion
1 (8 ounce) can tomato sauce
1/2 teaspoon chopped garlic
1/8 teaspoon pepper

Mix the sauce ingredients and set aside.

Divide the dough in half and pat each half of the dough into a 10-inch round pizza pan, which has been sprinkled with cornmeal. (May also be thrown into the air into a circle) Pinch the edges so that a rim is formed for the pizza. Spread half of the sauce onto each dough circle.

Topping

1/2 cup Parmesan cheese
2 teaspoons oregano
1 cup sliced pepperoni or dry salami
2 cups shredded mozzarella cheese

Sprinkle half of the Parmesan cheese and oregano over each dough circle. Arrange half of the pepperoni on each pizza and sprinkle each with half of the mozzarella cheese.

Bake on the bottom shelf of a preheated 425° F. oven for 20 to 25 minutes or until the crust is brown and the topping is bubbly and hot. (If a pizza stone is used for baking, follow manufacturer's directions.)

Salads

More than Lettuce

Because American dollar bills are green, "A wad of lettuce" is slang for a roll of dollar bills. The idea of lettuce and money is quite old.

The Italians used to call a gift of money "one of Sixtus V's salads," because the sixteenth-century pontiff is said to have helped old friends by sending them a head of lettuce. When opened the head of lettuce was full of paper money.

Salads are not new to the culinary scene. They have been around since almost the beginning of civilization. The earliest salads were probably mixtures of wild greens sprinkled with salt. The word "salad" is derived from the Latin "herba salata, " meaning salted greens.

The great Greek gastronome, Archestratos, recommended that lettuce (salad) be eaten "after dinner, the toasts, and the smearing of perfumes," in other words after the meal and before the serious after-dinner speeches and drinking began. The cool lettuce was supposed to create a solid basis in the body for the hot spots of alcohol.

The Romans began by following this Greek philosophy, but by the first century they decided to eat lettuce before dinner, since a good deal of drinking took place during the meal. This Roman decision became the lasting precedent. By Roman times, dressings of vinegar, oil, and dried herbs were used on greens, as well as on raw and cooked vegetables.

The structured, or more formal, salad came into being in the eighteenth century with the creation of Salamongundy. An early reference to this type of salad was given in an English cookbook, first published in 1747. The book, "The Art of Cookery, Made Plain and Easy" by Hannah Glasse was much used in the American colonies.

In succeeding generations the spelling changed to "salamongundi" and its meaning denoted a hodgepodge.

Several salads were either originated or perfected in America and are part of our cuisine. Coleslaw was brought to America by the Dutch who settled New York. Originally a salad of only cabbage with a dressing, it now includes carrots, celery, green and red peppers, and even crushed pineapple.

Waldorf Salad, an American creation of apples and mayonnaise now includes celery, grapes, nuts, and miniature marshmallows.

Caesar Salad, which originated in 1924 and is still popular, has also experienced variations since its creation.

The gelatin or molded salad gained popularity when a Pennsylvania housewife in the early 1900s won a national prize for her jellied salad. Molded salads were the rage in the 1940s and '50s. Almost every church supper featured an array of molded salads. They contained meat, vegetables, fruits, and nuts. Many of these salads consisted of multiple layers, each of a different color and flavor.

Cob Salad, which originated at the Brown Derby Restaurant in Hollywood, was created by its chef when he ran short of salad ingredients. He knew that food chopped in very small pieces always looked like more than was really there. He chopped meat, chicken and vegetables as fine as kernels on a corn cob and tossed them with a dressing.

A Chefs Salad has traditionally included julienned pieces of chicken, ham, and Swiss cheese with tomatoes and lettuce. Over time chefs have added other vegetables.

In recent years pasta salads have become the rage. No longer are they limited to cooked macaroni with mayonnaise; they now feature a great variety of ingredients and dressings.

Many restaurants include a Spinach Salad on their menus. Spinach salads include a variety of other ingredients such as pieces of orange or grapefruit with a citrus dressing. Others include sliced mushrooms and pieces of bacon with a mustard vinaigrette. Most restaurants feature a tossed green salad commonly known as the house salad, the ingredients of which are frequently left to the salad maker.

Warm salads of sautéed meats or seafoods on various lettuces are now featured as luncheon and dinner entrees by many restaurants and hostesses. Their popularity started in California when well-known chefs such as Bradley Ogden, Alice Waters, and Jeremiah Towers started preparing warm salads with slices of sautéed duck breast or with sautéed prawns.

Another contributing factor to today's wide variety of salads has been the availability of previously little known salad ingredients made available by rapid refrigerated transportation. No longer are radicchio, endive, yellow bell peppers, jicama, and fennel considered as exotic salad ingredients.

This molded salad combines a spinach layer with tomato aspic, a popular meat accompaniment. Each salad may also be prepared separately.

Spinach Salad with Tomato Aspic

Spinach Layer

1 package (3 ounces) lime gelatin
1 cup hot water
3/4 cup mayonnaise
1 cup small curd cottage cheese
1/3 cup minced red pepper
1/3 cup minced green pepper
2 cups finely chopped raw spinach

Dissolve the gelatin in hot water and cool to room temperature. Add the mayonnaise and cottage cheese and mix well. Fold in the peppers and spinach. Pour into an oiled 8-cup ring mold and refrigerate until set. After the spinach layer has set, prepare the tomato layer.

Tomato Aspic Layer

3 3/4 cups tomato juice
1 stalk celery, cut in pieces
1 small onion, quartered
1/8 teaspoon pepper
2 envelopes unflavored gelatin
1/4 cup vinegar
1/3 cup finely chopped green pepper
1/3 cup finely chopped celery

Combine 3 cups of the tomato juice, the celery pieces, onion, and pepper in a medium-size saucepan. Bring to a boil; then simmer for 10 minutes. Strain the mixture into a bowl.

While the tomato juice is simmering, soften the gelatin in the remaining 3/4 cup of tomato juice. Add softened gelatin to the strained tomato juice along with the vinegar. Stir until the gelatin is completely dissolved. Fold in the green pepper and celery and gently pour on top of the spinach layer. Refrigerate for 3 to 4 hours before serving. Unmold on lettuce leaves. Serve 8 to 10.

Soups

Great Variety

Soups have long been part of the world's cuisine. Historians say that prehistoric man filled an animal skin bag with meat, bones, green plants, and water and dropped hot stones into the bag to cook the mixture. Although the result was probably more like a stew, it provided the basis for modern soup cooking. The next stage of development in cooking soups and stews occurred with the invention of metal pots that could be placed directly over the fire.

In Roman times, soups became very complicated and were served in great variety at Roman banquets for the wealthy and the nobility. Soups were presented in gold dishes. For the common folk more hearty soups provided the sustenance needed for daily existence.

During the Dark and Middle Ages, soups consisted of anything and everything that could be foraged simply to sustain body and soul. It was also during this time that the first soup kitchens came into existence. The monasteries fed countless numbers of unfortunate people with soup during periods of famine.

Catherine de Medici, the young Italian princess who married the future French king Henry II, is reputed to have contributed much to French cooking. It is said that among her accomplishments was to popularize the modern version of soups in France. She drastically altered the dining habits of the French nobility by declaring that all meals should consist of only three courses. However, she defined the first course as including between four and six soups, in addition to patés and terrines.

Louis XIV later refined this tradition by decreeing that the soup courses be limited to two — one clear and one thick. The French chefs of the eighteenth century enhanced the flavors of soup by devising certain standards for stocks and seasonings. One French chef described a soup as "like an overture to a light opera. It sets the tone for the rest of the meal."

It was also during the rule of Louis XIV that cold soups came into vogue. As he was constantly afraid of some one doing him harm he had all of his food tasted before it was served. With this delay in service at least one of the soups might arrive at the table cold. Guests naturally thought these soups were meant to be served cold.

Cold soups, particularly fruit-based soups, are popular during the summer months in northern European countries and in the Pacific Northwest. Recipes for these cold soups were brought to America mainly by Scandinavian immigrants.

In America, the Indians prepared soup with local ingredients such as corn, beans, potatoes, squash, wild game, poultry, and fish.

The Indians taught the settlers how to make a concentrated essence of soup that could be used, not only at home, but also while traveling. This colonial version of the bouillon cube was made by boiling meat and local vegetables to a mush like stew. After the liquid had boiled off the mixture was allowed to sit until it became a dry-like cake.

Since then, Americans have created soups that are associated with particular regions — New England chowders, Louisiana gumbos, and San Francisco's cioppino, to name a few. The name chowder comes from the French "chaudiere," which means a caldron used for making fish stews.

The term chowder is not limited to seafood soups but refers to any thick soup containing chunks of meat or vegetables and cream. In the Midwest corn chowders are very popular. Ham and potato chowder is another popular American soup.

Sugar

The Sweetener of Choice

Ever since sugar became a reasonably-priced commodity Americans have had a love affair with sweetness. Sugar has become an essential ingredient in many culinary recipes.

The history of sugar production focuses on the countries within thirty-five parallels north and south of the equator where sugar cane flourishes. Throughout history the urge to satisfy the universal sweet tooth has led to the creation of seaports, the discovery of a continent, and the formation of rebellions.

The earliest written mention of sugar appears in the records of Alexander the Great's expedition down the Indies River in 325 B.C., where "honey bearing reeds" were found. Tai-taung, Emperor of China in the early fifth century B.C., sent envoys to India to learn how to extract syrup from these reeds. Diascribes, a Greek physician at the time of the Roman emperor, Nero, described "a sort of hard honey, called Saccharum, found upon canes in India, grainy like salt and brittle between the teeth, but sweet."

Arab traders in the Middle Ages took sugar cane to Sicily and the south of Spain. Dom Enrique, a prince of Portugal known as The Navigator, transported sugar cane to Madeira in 1420. Eighty years later sugar was taken to the Canaries, Brazil, Haiti, Mexico, and Cuba.

The Italian republics of Venice and Genoa grew rich and powerful with trade in spices and sugar between the Far East and Europe. In London in 1319, a shipment of 10,000 pounds of sugar from Thomasso Loredano, a Venetian merchant, was exchanged for wool.

Once sugar became obtainable it was widely used in France and Italy. Sugar went into all sauces except those with a piquant flavor. In the late 1300s the affluent French were in the habit of sprinkling sugar and cinnamon on toasted cheese.

In the 1400s sugar was used primarily for medical purposes. During the reign of Louis XIV it was sold only by apothecaries, who doled it out by the ounce. It was so important in the stock of an apothecary that someone who lacked all of his faculties was referred to as "He's like an apothecary without sugar."

When the Turks captured Constantinople in 1453 and levied a high tribute on passing caravans, Mediterranean merchants found their sugar and spice trade slipping away. They undoubtedly would have been much happier if Columbus had discovered a new route to India rather then finding a new continent to the west. However, Columbus did plant cuttings of sugar cane in the West Indies on his second voyage, which opened up new sources of sugar.

A hundred and fifty years later the West Indies engaged in a brisk trade in the products of sugar cane — rum, molasses, and sugar. The settlers of the Massachusetts colony first traded for sugar with the Dutch in New Amsterdam (later New York). Soon, however, the New Englanders were trading direct with the West Indies to the extent that molasses became the lifeblood of New England commerce. In 1728 the New England colonies imported more than 2 million gallons of rum from the West Indies. Later the colonies established their own rum industry from the West Indian sugar trade.

When the English Parliament passed the Sugar Act in 1733, levying a high duty on importations from the West Indies, irate New England colonists promptly turned to smuggling rum, sugar, and molasses. They also began to think about separating from England.

Sugarcane was cultivated on the banks of the Mississippi, where the first sugar mill was built in 1758. By 1770 locally-grown sugar was a common product in the area around New Orleans. Sixty years later a very successful sugar operation was established by John Hampden Randolph in Louisiana. He had bought several thousand acres to grow cotton but soon switched to sugar with great success. He owned 195 slaves to work the sugarcane fields.

Before the Civil War, sugar plantations of considerable size existed in Louisiana, Alabama, Florida, Georgia, and Mississippi. After the Civil War sugar production in these states declined because the sugar content of American-grown cane was low due to climatic conditions. Not until the United States acquired the Hawaiian Islands did American sugar become a significant item in the world market.

In the early days of America sugar was a luxury. The common sweeteners at the time were home-produced honey, maple sugar, and less-expensive molasses. As late as 1860, twenty-five million quarts of maple syrup were produced and sold annually, three times the amount consumed today. With the elimination of tariffs on sugar in the 1880s, white cane sugar became equal in price with maple sugar. Today, it is much cheaper and maple sugar is considered a luxury item.

Molasses was mainly imported, although farmers in warm climates as far north as Maryland, produced their own. Many of the farmers had a little patch of sugar cane, which was ground and processed locally. Sugar cane had been introduced into Louisiana in 1751 by Catholic missionaries from Santa Domingo.

Until the middle of the nineteenth century sugar was molded into cones, weighing up to fifty-five pounds each. The smaller cones, under twelve pounds, were fashioned with a rounded nose, and were commonly called loaves.

The method to refine sugar was to melt the raw sugar, then add milk of lime, egg albumen, or oxblood to the pot. This caused many of the impurities to coagulate and rise to the surface during cooking so that they could be skimmed off. The resulting light colored syrup was boiled to a heavy consistency, then poured into cone-shaped molds to cool and crystallize. The syrup which trickled through the aperture of the mold was collected and sold under the name Treacle.

Next the loaf or cone was gently knocked from the mold, and trimmed so that no colored part remained. It was then neatly wrapped, first in white, then in purple paper and dried at a temperature of 140 degrees in a drying oven for three to five days. Loaf sugar is still made in parts of Europe and Africa today in much this same fashion.

Many American colonists soaked the purple paper wrapper to obtain an extra fancy dye. Ladies of the house learned the art of breaking pieces from the sugar loaf with a sugar hammer and cutting them into lump sugar for table use. There were also special scissors to cut the cone sugar. In many households the sugar was kept under lock and key. According to recipe books of the mid-1800s, a lump of sugar weighed anywhere from a quarter of a pound to a full pound

Granulated sugar did not become popular until after the Civil War. Even then it was coarse and brown. This sugar was usually very hard when shipped in a barrel so that an augur was needed to loosen it. A sugar grinder, much like a coffee grinder, became a necessity for the grocer. Today we can buy granulated sugar in boxes, also the superfine granulated variety, powdered sugar, and light and dark brown sugar.

Yogurt

Staple for Many

With the current trend toward weight control, yogurt has come into its own. It used to be the "in" food product enjoyed mainly by the trend-setters. But now it has become a staple in many homes, either as a breakfast or lunch item.

This is the case throughout the world. In my travels abroad I frequently found selections of yogurt availabe on the breakfast table in many hotels throughout the world.

Although yogurt is thousands of years old, Americans did not begin to eat it in quantity until the late 1960s. Yogurt fit perfectly into our growing interest in health and body consciousness. At the time some believed that yogurt would provide the perfect balance of good health and well-being. Others touted yogurt's ability to help us live longer, well into a second century.

In the 1990s, we became more realistic about yogurt's health benefits. It is a tasty way to eat a dairy product. Yogurt is easy to eat and it is one of the few foods we can eat right from the carton.

According to a U.S. government survey two thirds of all yogurt eaters consume the product at lunch. The survey also stated that the average yogurt user is a woman between thirteen and forty-four who lives in a suburb on the Pacific Coast, in New England, or in the Mid-Atlantic states.

People in much of the world have been eating yogurt for thousands of years. Romantic folk tales have been told about the origins of yogurt, but it was probably discovered independently by accident in many different places.

One story is that in the preparation for a journey across the desert, a nomad packed his milk in a goatskin bag and slung it across the back of his camel. When he settled down around the campfire for his evening meal and attempted to drink his milk, he discovered that it had turned into a custard-like substance.

The nomad's milk had interacted with the bacteria in the goatskin bag, creating yogurt. The process was completed by the body warmth of the camel, the heat of the sun, and the rapid drop in the temperature at night.

Evidence of yogurt has been found in the writings of the ancient Egyptians, Greeks, and Romans. Genghis Khan not only fed yak's milk yogurt to his army to strengthen it for battle, but also used it as a marinade to preserve meat while traveling with his troops.

Despite the importance of yogurt throughout Asia and the Middle East, it was not introduced to Western Europe until the sixteenth century. When Francois I of France was laid low with an intestinal ailment, fearful court physicians sent for a healer from Constantinople. After a regimen of goat's-milk yogurt the king's health improved. The king dubbed yogurt " "the milk of eternal life." This may have marked the beginning of yogurt's reputation as a miracle food.

The earliest scientific study of yogurt dates to the turn of the last century. Ilya Metchnikoff, a Russian bacteriologist, Nobel Prize winner, and director of the prestigious Louis Pasteur Institute in France, traced the secret of longevity to yogurt.

After discovering that many Bulgarians who live past the age of 100 ate a large amount of yogurt, Metchnikoff isolated a bacterium in yogurt and called it "Bulgarian bacillus." He said that this supposedly miracle-working "good" bacterium chased the "bad" bacteria out of the large intestine of the Bulgarian centenarians and was the secret of their long life.

Ironically, Metchnikoff's followers were

somewhat disillusioned when he died at the age of 71 in 1916. His theories were later disproven when scientists discovered that Bulgarians did not keep good birth records and reports of advanced ages were exaggerated.

However, Metchnikoff's research had made it possible to produce yogurt commercially. A Spaniard named Isaac Carasso used some of Metchnikoff's bacteria and began making yogurt in Barcelona. His company was called Danone, after his son Daniel.

A few years later, in 1931, an Armenian family named Columbosian started the first commercial yogurt dairy in the Untied States, in Andover, Massachusetts. The name of their product was Americanized to Colombo. At the end of World War II the Spanish Danone company moved to New York where it changed its name to Dannon.

Although these two yogurt businesses flourished for the next two decades, practically the only Americans eating yogurt were those of Middle Eastern descent.

In 1946, Dannon made yogurt history by mass-producing a strawberry-flavored yogurt. This created the advertising slogan, "the ice cream without guilt." Today Dannon has captured about half of the American yogurt market, which is more than all local and regional brands put together.

But what exactly is yogurt and how is it made? Yogurt is a cultured milk product, as are buttermilk, cottage cheese, and sour cream. It is made by taking pasteurized milk — cow's milk, goat's milk, buffalo milk, or even soy milk — and adding *Streptcoccus thermophilus* or *Lactobacillus bulgarius*. These bacteria multiply and change the milk sugar, called lactose, into lactic acid. The milk curdles and the yogurt becomes, tart, thick, and creamy.

First the milk is homogenized and if the yogurt has a fruit flavoring it is added at that time. The milk is then pasteurized (heated to 145° F. to kill any bacteria), cooled to about 110° F., and the bacteria for making yogurt is mixed in. It takes only one ounce of yogurt bacteria to make 408,000 cups of yogurt.

There are various methods of producing the final product, including placing the yogurt mixture into large vats and holding it at 110° F. for three to six hours, or letting the yogurt ferment in the containers in which it will be purchased. The containers are kept at 110° F. until the bacteria have developed properly. Then the containers go into the refrigerator. Dannon, with its semi-firm, gelatinous texture, uses this latter technique

In both methods, if the yogurt has fruit, it is made sundae-style with the fruit on the bottom of the container. The fruit is pumped into the container before the flavored yogurt is poured on top. The French yogurt maker, Yoplait, stirs the fruit and flavoring into the yogurt before putting it into containers.

There are about as many types of yogurt on the market as there are ice creams — whole milk, low fat, nonfat. Then there is plain, containing no flavorings; flavored with such additions as lemon, coffee, chocolate, vanilla; and a myriad of fruit flavors.

More than ninety percent of the yogurt made in the United States is flavored. Of the fifty flavors of yogurt available in this country, the most popular five are strawberry, raspberry, blueberry, peach, and cherry.

Yogurt is different everywhere in the world. In the Middle East it is thick and strong, in Russia it is effervescent and can be alcoholic and in Scandinavia it is often thin and consumed as a drink.

As I finish writing this it's lunch time and I'm looking forward to my blueberry yogurt!

Bibliography

Bailey, Adrian. *Cook's Ingredients*. New York: William Morrow and Company, Inc., 1980

Conte, Anna Del. *Gastronomy of Italy*. New York: Prentice Hall Press, 1987.

Davidson, Alan. *Fruit*. New York: Simon & Schuster, 1991.

Dupree, Nathalie. *New Southern Cooking*. New York: Alfred A. Knopf, 1986.

Ferrary, Jeanette and Louise Fiszer. *Season to Taste*. New York: Simon & Schuster, 1988.

Frank, Dorothy C. *Cooking with Nuts*. New York: Clarkson N. Potter, Inc./ Publishers, 1979.

Fussell, Betty. The Story of Corn. New York: Farrar, Straus and Giroux, 1992.

Greene, Bert. *Greene on Greens*. New York: Workman Publishing, 1984.

Grogson, Jane, ed. *The World Atlas of Food*. London: Mitchell Beasley Publishers Limited, 1974.

Lee, Hilde Gabriel. *Taste of the States*. Charlottesville, VA: Howell Press, 1992.

London, Sherl and Mel. *The Versatile Grain and the Elegant Bean*. New York: Simon & Schuster, 1992.

McClane, A. J. The Encyclopedia of Fish. New York: Holt, Rinehart and Winston, 1977.

McGee, Harold. *On Food and Cooking*. New York: Charles Schribner's Sons, 1984.

Root, Waverley. *Food*. New York: Simon & Schuster, 1980.

Schneider, Elizabeth. *Uncommon Fruits and Vegetables*. New York: Harper & Row, 1986.

Stone, Sally and Martin. *The Essential Root Vegetable Cookbook*. New York: Clarkson Potter/ Publishers, 1991.

Visser, Margaret. *Much Depends on Dinner*. New York: Grove Press, 1986.

Recipe Index